Vehicle Accident Analysis
and
Reconstruction Methods

Other related resources from SAE International:

SAE Accident Reconstruction Technology Collection on CD-ROM
Order No. ARCD2004

Highway Vehicles Safety Database on the World Wide Web and CD-ROM
Order No. SAFEWEB and SAFE2004

Automotive Safety Handbook
By Ulrich Seiffert and Lothar Wech
Order No. R-325

Recent Developments in Automotive Safety Technology
Edited by Daniel J. Holt
Order No. PT-119

Neck Injury: The Use of X-Rays, CTs, and MRIs to Study Crash-Related Injury Mechanisms
By Jeffrey A. Pike
Order No. R-368

Role of the Seat in Rear Crash Safety
By David C. Viano
Order No. R-317

Automotive Vehicle Safety
By George A. Peters and Barbara J. Peters
Order No. R-341

Vehicle Crash Mechanics
By Matthew Huang
Order No. R-284

Vehicle Accident Analysis
and
Reconstruction Methods

Raymond M. Brach and **R. Matthew Brach**

Warrendale, Pennsylvania USA

For permission and licensing requests, contact
    SAE Permissions
    400 Commonwealth Drive
    Warrendale, PA 15096-0001 USA
    Email: permissions@sae.org
    Tel: 724-772-4028
    Fax: 724-772-4891

Library of Congress Cataloging-in-Publication Data

Brach, Raymond M.
    Vehicle accident analysis and reconstruction methods / Raymond M. and R. Matthew Brach.
      p. cm.
    Includes bibliographical references and index.
    ISBN 0-7680-0776-3
1. Traffic accident investigation. 2. Traffic accidents—Simulation methods. 3. Traffic accidents—Mathematical models. I. Brach, R. Matthew. II. Title.

HV8079.55.B723 2005
363.12′565—dc22   2004065363

SAE
400 Commonwealth Drive
Warrendale, PA 15096-0001 USA
Tel: 877-606-7323 (inside USA and Canada)
Tel: 724-776-4970 (outside USA)
Fax: 724-776-1615
Email: CustomerService@sae.org

Copyright © 2005 SAE International
ISBN 0-7680-0776-3
SAE Order No. R-311

Printed in USA

Dedication

A great deal of support was provided by our families during the preparation of this work. Our wives, Carol Brach and Paula Brach, encouraged this endeavor and shared in the effort required to complete the task. Matt's children, Elizabeth, Olivia, and Daniel, sacrificed family time to permit writing to be done. This book is dedicated to them.

Contents

Preface

More than 19,000 registered junkyards (junkyards.com) operate in the United States. Each can have hundreds, or even thousands, of wrecked vehicles. Each vehicle sent to a junkyard following an accident represents a tragedy of some degree, with accompanying financial loss, human injury, and perhaps loss of life. One of the objectives of the reconstruction of vehicle accidents is to tell a vital part of that story. Automotive accident reconstruction is the process of determining what happened to the vehicles and persons involved in an accident and how it happened, using the information available after the accident occurred. This task must produce results that are reasonably accurate. Reconstruction is a procedure carried out with the specific purpose of estimating in both a qualitative and quantitative manner how an accident occurred using engineering, scientific, and mathematical principles based on evidence obtained through an accident investigation.

The collection of facts associated with the circumstances of an accident is referred to as accident investigation. Determining what happened and how it happened is usually referred to as accident reconstruction.

A third facet of postaccident analysis attempts to answer the question of why the accident occurred (causation or fault). This is almost always of interest to the various parties involved. Since vehicles are, or should be, controlled by humans, answering the *why* question more often than not involves motivation and human psychology. Legal issues can also arise in these incidents. These issues include the violation of criminal and traffic laws where the question of fault is placed before a jury. In this book, the topics of accident investigation, human factors, causation, and fault are not explicitly addressed. Often the effects of these topics are interrelated, and this interrelationship must be addressed to some extent. Indeed, it would be rare to be able to carry out a good reconstruction with little or no physical evidence and data. This book concentrates on reconstruction—the determination of how an accident happened. That said, it is sometimes necessary to combine investigation and reconstruction. Often a reconstructionist may recognize a need for information not gathered initially and must obtain it later. An accurate reconstruction cannot be carried out without a good investigation.

A number of books already exist on the topic of accident reconstruction. With some notable exceptions, many of them are tomes devoted to how the authors and perhaps a few colleagues used intuition and insight to decide how they thought an accident happened. In a few cases, these books are collections of "war stories" or case histories, usually presentations of one view of the events. In contrast, this book is one of methods. The perspective taken here is that accident reconstruction is a field of applied science, namely an application of the principles of science, mathematics, and engineering; accident reconstruction is a quantitative endeavor. The same principles of mathematics, physics, and engineering that allow us to safely race vehicles more than 200 mph, build space stations, and navigate the depths of the oceans can be used to reconstruct vehicle accidents. This requires that reconstructions not only be based on the physical evidence and information gathered from an accident investigation but also be based on the laws of nature. A concerted goal of this book is to raise the analytical level of accident reconstruction practice such that commonly known scientific, engineering, and mathematical methods increasingly become a more common part of the field. During the preparation of this book, the authors have assumed that the readers and users of this book and accompanying software (available separately from the authors) have a proper educational background and experience to fully comprehend the material.

The United States is not the only country with junkyards (repositories of disadvantaged vehicles, to be politically correct). Vehicle accidents, of course, happen all over the world. Fortunately for engineers, and everyone else for that matter, the laws of mathematics and physics are the same everywhere. Consequently, applications of the material contained herein are not limited by geography. Applications using international units do arise. Therefore, dual units, customary U.S. units (based on the units of foot, pound force, and second) and the metric system (based on the meter, Newton, and second) are used throughout the book. Certain items are avoided, such as the confusion between mass and weight. In customary U.S. units, mass sometimes is given the unit of slug. Its use is avoided here. One slug is equivalent to 1 lb-s^2/ft; all appearances of the unit pound, abbreviated as lb, in this book refer to units of force. Similarly, in the metric system, a kilogram is considered to be a unit of mass and the corresponding unit of force is the Newton. The practice of stating weight (a force) in kilograms can cause confusion. This is avoided by always using units of Newtons for weight and kilograms for mass. The convention followed here is that weight is the measure of the force of gravity, and the metric unit of force is the Newton, abbreviated as N.

A summary of the topical coverage of the book is not given here. The reader can simply look at the table of contents to see the list of topics. Two features of this book are unique, however, and deserve some mention. One is the coverage of the topic of uncertainty, and the other is the use of many examples throughout the book. Many analysis and reconstruction methods can be implemented using spreadsheet technology. This has been done by the authors, and solutions to the examples are in the form of input information and results printed directly from computer output. Tools contained in popular spreadsheets often allow analysis techniques (time forward computations) to be used for reconstructions (time reverse computations).

A common omission made by all accident reconstructionists at one time or another is to measure something or make a calculation based on a measured or estimated parameter and come up with the answer, look at it, and if it seems to make sense, present it as a definite result or finding. For example, we say "that car was going 25 mph (36.7 ft/s, 11.2 m/s)." But could it have been 26.2 mph or 24.5 mph? How certain are we of the result? How certain can we be of the result? These questions refer to the uncertainty associated with a measurement or calculation based on a measurement, a group of measurements, or a group of calculations. A view is taken here that we actually are estimating values of dynamical variables. Some estimates have high accuracy and some not so high. The uncertainty associated with results based on these estimates of dynamic variables should always be considered. Determining uncertainty is not always easy to do—but difficulty is not a reason for omitting it. The topic of uncertainty is the first technical topic covered in this book. The uncertainty of a reconstruction may be difficult to calculate, but the authors hope that users of this book will appreciate that a reconstructed speed of a vehicle presented with five significant digits of precision has limited accuracy when the only available skid mark length used in the reconstruction calculation was measured by pacing off the distance.

As already mentioned, a distinction is drawn here between accident reconstruction and accident investigation. The latter is considered to be the process of gathering physical and testimonial evidence from an accident scene, vehicles, and eyewitnesses. It is considered as a field of its own. Investigation is most often executed by police officers and sometimes by insurance investigators. As any other human endeavor, it can be done well and can be done poorly. Several institutes exist across the country, such as the Northwestern University Traffic Institute, Texas Transportation Institute, Institute of Police Technology and Management (University of North Florida), and others, for training investigators to standardize and improve investigation practices. Although there is a need for each to know what the other does and there is an overlap in knowledge and tasks, a trained accident investigator is not the same as an accident reconstructionist, just as an accident reconstructionist is not a trained accident investigator.

Different aspects of an accident reconstruction frequently are segregated into the categories of human, vehicle, and environment. The study of human performance and behavior as it relates to vehicular accidents belongs to the study of human factors. This topic is not covered here. Another important aspect of accident reconstruction involving humans is that of occupant kinetics, kinematics, and biomechanics—the study of the motion of vehicle occupants and the physical interaction of a body with interior surfaces and restraints. These concepts are not covered. Environmental topics include such things as the design and performance of roadways, poles and barriers, signs, traffic signals, and their interaction with accidents and crashes. These topics are not covered. As in all professions, the work of accident reconstructionists involves communication and reporting of results. Though they can be extremely important, report writing and diagram preparation are not covered. Other topics omitted include those of finite element analysis of vehicle crash deformation and dynamical crush simulation, such as Simulation Model of Automobile Collisions (SMAC), Simulation Model Nonlinear (SIMON), and others.

Collectively, the authors of this book have over 45 years of experience in the practice of vehicle accident reconstruction as well as with the research associated with accident reconstruction methods. Based on this experience, the topics covered throughout the 11 chapters and appendices should provide the methods to quantitatively reconstruct the vast majority of vehicular accidents. Not all accidents involve a crash, or collision, of two vehicles, but most do. Planar impact mechanics (Chapters 6 and 7) is used extensively in the reconstruction of crashes, often combined with estimation of crush energy (Chapter 8). Evidence from the motion of vehicles before an impact or following an impact, or both, often supplies vital information to a reconstruction. Vehicle dynamics simulation (Chapter 11) is invaluable in modeling such motion. Simulation of vehicle dynamics requires the knowledge of how tire forces are generated (Chapter 2), a topic that all accident reconstructionists must thoroughly understand. Methods for the analysis of accidents involving a single vehicle, such as rollovers, pedestrians and bicycle riders hit by cars, or simply yaw marks made by a single vehicle during a sudden high-speed turn, are covered individually.

Each accident reconstruction is unique as no two accidents are the same. Moreover, the reconstruction of these accidents can also require the use of different methodologies because of variations in physical evidence and investigative information. This leaves plenty of room for ingenuity and insight for the application of the methods presented in this book. The authors hope this book is useful to those who want to find out how accidents occurred.

Acknowledgments

A book is never the work of its authors alone. This book is no exception. The impetus for undertaking the preparation of this book came from many years of involvement with the Accident Investigation and Reconstruction Practices Committee (AIRP) of the SAE and its many members. The text draws strongly and benefits directly from many of the papers presented at the annual SAE Congress and the countless conversations with the authors, presenters, and attendees too numerous to name individually.

The authors specifically wish to acknowledge the work of the many members, particularly Lynn Fricke, of the AIRP for their hard work in compiling the Glossary presented with this book. The authors have added some entries and made some changes but, by and large, the Glossary comes from them. The Table of Unit Conversions for Common Units (Appendix A.3) is abridged from the SP 811 of the National Institute of Science and Technology.

Special appreciation is extended to Kevin Manogue for his work organizing the book's manuscript, and for the many hours of preparing the spreadsheets used throughout the book to work examples and display the solutions. John McManus devoted a considerable amount of time reading over the original manuscript. He offered useful suggestions and the authors appreciate his work. Thanks are due to Bill Cliff of MacInnis Engineering and Stein Husher of KEVA Engineering, who each provided a set of data used for examples in the book. Thanks also are due to Alan Asay of Woolley Engineering Research, Jim Sprague of Packer Engineering, and Don Parker of Exponent Corporation, who read portions of the book and made many valuable suggestions to improve the manuscript. Special thanks goes to Alycia Kaczuwka for transforming many disparate documents into publisher-ready material.

RAYMOND M. BRACH
R. MATTHEW BRACH
South Bend, Indiana

Uncertainty in Measurements and Calculations

1.1 Introduction

Although there may be some cases when and/or where an accident can be reconstructed effectively without the use of calculations and without the use of experimental data, such cases are rare. And they are becoming more rare as the professional level of the field advances and as the demand for more professional and accurate reconstructions increases. Whenever measurements are made and whenever calculations are based on experimental data, a level of uncertainty exists. It is the purpose of this chapter to provide ways of quantifying uncertainty. Consider an example involving a measurement. Suppose a car with a conventional braking system is brought up to a speed, v, and the brakes are applied suddenly to a level at which the wheels are locked. The tires leave visible tire marks on the road as the car skids to a stop. Suppose further that the speed of the car at the beginning of the skid marks is measured using a radar gun and the length, d, of the skid marks is measured using a tape measure. A well-known equation from mechanics used to estimate the speed of a car leaving skid marks from an emergency stop[1] is

$$v = \sqrt{2fgd}. \tag{1.1}$$

Because the speed and distance were measured, this equation can be used to compute the corresponding frictional drag coefficient, f. Although this is a common way of measuring f, it is just one way (for example, Goudie et al.[2]). Solving Eq. 1.1 for f gives

$$f = \frac{v^2}{2gd}. \tag{1.2}$$

It is easy to see that if an error exists in the measurement of either v or d, there will be a corresponding error in f. As used here, the term error does not mean a "mistake" (for example, using the metric value of g instead of U.S. units). Rather, error is a difference from the "true" value of f because of measurement inaccuracy (for example, because the radar gun was held a few degrees off to the side or not directly behind the vehicle, or perhaps both), or even something else. The "something else" could be that the test conditions differed from a straight-line skid—such as if only three wheels locked and the car yawed before it stopped.

Uncertainty can arise in other ways. Suppose each of two independent observers of the same friction experiment report the result as $f_1 = 0.45$ and $f_2 = 0.454$. One of the differences between f_1 and f_2 is that the latter has one more significant digit that the first; can they be the same?* Is one more correct than the other? Is one more accurate than the other? Sometimes these questions are difficult to answer. Another source of uncertainty when making reconstruction calculations has to do with the inadequacy of the model. For example, Eq. 1.1 can be used to calculate velocity from distance and frictional drag. But suppose the road is not exactly level. To reduce uncertainty, Eq. 1.1 should be replaced by an equation that takes varying grade into account.

Suppose the above example is changed so that Eq. 1.1 is to be used to reconstruct the speed of a vehicle from the length, d, of a measured skidding distance and a value, f, of the frictional drag coefficient. Suppose further that the values of f and d are not known exactly but are known to lie in given ranges about nominal values. For example, suppose the length, d, was measured several hours or more after an accident and the skid mark may have been changed due to the effects of weather and/or traffic. Suppose further that a value of f was measured at the accident site using a vehicle different from the stopping vehicle. Any variations in f and d are "propagated" through Eq. 1.1 and result in uncertainty in the speed. In the first example, variations due to measurements of v and d are propagated through Eq. 1.2 and result in uncertainty in the measured value of f. The above experimental and reconstruction examples have the common characteristic that variations in input values in an equation lead to uncertainty in the result. This is the subject of this chapter.

The terminology and notation used in this book are similar to these used in other references, but there are some specific differences. Although the word "error" is commonly used, particularly with respect to measurements,[3-5] its use is avoided here. This is to prevent any connotation that nonexact results are the result of some sort of mistake or blunder, and because error is defined differently by different authors. In general, the quantity to be calculated, such as v and f on the left-hand sides of Eqs. 1.1 and 1.2, is given the symbol y. The quantity, y, is expressed as a sum of a *reference value*, Y, and a *variation*, δy. So the result of an operation (measurement or calculation of a quantity, y) results in $y = Y \pm \delta y$. The closeness of the reference value to some "true" value often is

---

* Readers not familiar with the concepts of significant digits and rounding are encouraged to turn to Appendix A.2, Numbers, Significant Figures, Rounding, and Unit Conversions.

referred to as the *accuracy* of y. In some circumstances, the difference $y - Y$ is called a *bias*. The variation, δy, about the reference value often is referred to as the *precision* of y, or as Mandel[6] points out, the *imprecision* of y. After Mandel, the reference value, Y, can be placed into any of three categories based on how it is defined:

A. A "true" value, which generally is unknown. Any value used for Y is an estimate, and values are chosen using a method appropriate for the application.
B. An "assigned" value that is agreed upon among experts in a field. An example of this is the value of the acceleration of gravity, g, at sea level, which is assigned the value $g = 9.806650$ m/s/s.[7]
C. The mean of a randomly distributed population. With such a statistical definition, Y never is truly known but is estimated by the sample mean of a set of experiments.

To generalize the above examples, the problem approached in this chapter is to determine Y and δy when they depend on variations of other variables, say $x_1, x_2, \ldots, x_n$. That is, suppose that

$$y = f(x_1, x_2, \ldots, x_n). \tag{1.3}$$

Note that Eq. 1.3 can represent a complex sequence of more than one calculation carried out by a computer. In such cases, the variables $x_1, x_2, \ldots, x_n$ could be functions of other variables, that is, $x_1 = x_1(u_1, u_2, \ldots, u_n)$, $x_2 = x_2(u_1, u_2, \ldots, u_n)$, $x_n = x_n(u_1, u_2, \ldots, u_n)$, etc., where $u_1, u_2, \ldots, u_n$ are different independent variables.

Three different approaches are covered. The first is to determine upper and lower bounds on y. Another is to use the analytical form of Eq. 1.3 and calculus to relate variations in the independent variables $x_1, x_2, \ldots, x_n$ to Y and δy. Finally, a statistical approach is taken in which the independent variables have known statistical properties. The meaning and interpretation of each of the components, Y and δy, differ in the three approaches and will be discussed in more detail.

1.2 Upper and Lower Bounds

One of the simplest ways of quantifying uncertainty is to establish upper and lower bounds on the dependent variable, y, caused by variations in all independent variables that possess significant variations. First, those quantities in the equation that possess a significant degree of variation are identified as variables of interest. Then a maximum range of each variable's variation is determined. Finally, the lowest and highest values of the dependent variable are calculated for all possible combinations of the values of the independent variables. Values of all specific combinations of the independent variables are used in Eq. 1.3 in such a way as to produce the maximum and minimum values of y. From this, δy and Y are assigned the values

$$\delta y = \frac{1}{2}(y_{max} - y_{min}) \quad \text{and} \quad Y = \frac{1}{2}(y_{max} + y_{min}). \tag{1.4}$$

Consider again the example given by Eq. 1.1. In this example, y is the speed v, so $Y = V$ and $\delta y = \delta v$ are sought. Under typical circumstances, f and d are known with less than perfect certainty. These are the independent variables. It is assumed that the acceleration of gravity, g, is known with sufficient accuracy and with negligible uncertainty and is a known constant. Suppose that d and f are unknown but can be bounded such that $d_{min} \leq d \leq d_{max}$ and that $f_{min} \leq f \leq f_{max}$. Corresponding upper and lower bounds on the estimate of the initial speed, v, is

$$\sqrt{2f_{min}gd_{min}} \leq v \leq \sqrt{2f_{max}gd_{max}}. \tag{1.5}$$

The uncertainty, δv, is taken to be half of the difference between the upper and lower bounds,

$$\delta v = \frac{1}{2}(\sqrt{2f_{max}gd_{max}} - \sqrt{2f_{min}gd_{min}}), \tag{1.6}$$

and the reference value, V, is the average of the upper and lower values of v, that is,

$$V = \frac{1}{2}(\sqrt{2f_{max}gd_{max}} + \sqrt{2f_{min}gd_{min}}). \tag{1.7}$$

The result is that $v = V \pm \delta v$. For example, if $f_{min} = 0.6$, $f_{max} = 0.8$, $d_{min} = 32.0$ m, and $d_{max} = 34.0$ m, then 19.4 m/s $\leq v \leq$ 23.1 m/s. Then $\delta f = 0.1$, $\delta d = 1$ m, and $v = 21.3 \pm 1.8$ m/s.

This example illustrates what is probably the simplest and most versatile method for determining uncertainty. It applies to any formula, no matter how complex, and is easy to execute. It even is possible to use this approach with computer simulations using multiple runs with different input. Care must be used when the formula for Y involves differences and division. For example, the lower limit of $y = (x_1 - x_2)/x_3$ is obtained by using the lower limit of x_1 and the upper limits of x_2 and x_3. Negative numbers also can be tricky.

A drawback of this (and the next) method is that any likelihood of y to tend to be near the center of, or near either limit of, the range of $Y \pm \delta y$ cannot be assessed. Attributing the upper and lower bounds to a specific percentage of a population should not be done; statistical conclusions should follow the use of statistical methods and always be based on statistical data.

Example 1.1   Suppose a vehicle leaves skid marks of length, d, from an emergency stop with locked wheels over a road surface with a frictional drag coefficient, f. The distance d is not known exactly, but is known to be greater than 32 m and less than 34 m. The frictional drag coefficient is known to be somewhere between 0.6 and 0.8. Determine the initial speed of the vehicle and associated bounds on the uncertainty.

Solution   The maximum speed is when $d = d_{max} = 34$ m and $f = f_{max} = 0.8$. From Eq. 1.1, $v_{max} = 23.1$ m/s (51.7 mph). For $d = d_{min} = 32$ m and $f = f_{min} = 0.6$, Eq. 1.1 gives $v_{min} = 19.4$ m/s (43.4 mph). Equations 1.6 and 1.7 give $V = 21.3$ m/s (47.6 mph) and $\delta v = 1.8$ m/s (4.1 mph). The end result is that the speed of the vehicle at the beginning of the skid marks is $v = 21.3 \pm 1.8$ m/s (47.6 $\pm$ 4.1 mph).   ◯

1.3   Differential Variations

Another common method of estimating uncertainty, often referred to as *propagation of error,* is covered in many laboratory courses in science and engineering (for example, see texts such as Taylor[3] and Beers[4]). As above, an equation or formula is being used in a reconstruction to calculate a physical quantity, y, representing a speed, time distance, speed change, etc. The method uses differential calculus to relate y to the dependent variables $x_1, x_2, \ldots, x_n$. As before, the variables $x_1, x_2, \ldots, x_n$ could be functions of other variables, that is, $x_1 = x_1(u_1, u_2, \ldots, u_n)$, $x_2 = x_2(u_1, u_2, \ldots, u_n)$, $x_n = x_n(u_1, u_2, \ldots, u_n)$, and so on.

Using calculus, $y = y(x)$ can be expressed in a Taylor series near $x = a$, as:

$$y(x) = y(a) + \left.\frac{\partial y}{\partial x}\right|_a (x - a) + \frac{1}{2!}\left.\frac{\partial^2 y}{\partial x^2}\right|_a (x - a)^2 + \ldots \tag{1.8}$$

If $(x - a)$ is small, where a is a reference value of x, then $\delta x = (x - a)$ is small and $(x - a)^2$ and like terms of higher powers can be neglected. Let $\delta y = y(x) - y(a)$, where $y(a) = Y$ is the reference value of y. For a function of several independent variables, the nominal or reference values of $x_1, x_2, \ldots, x_n$ are given by $X_1, X_2, \ldots, X_n$. Under these conditions, a general formula for uncertainty can be found by replacing the variable differentials by variations, such that

$$\delta y = \frac{\partial y}{\partial x_1}\delta x_1 + \frac{\partial y}{\partial x_2}\delta x_2 + \ldots + \frac{\partial y}{\partial x_n}\delta x_n. \tag{1.9}$$

The derivatives in each of the terms in Eq. 1.9 often are referred to as *sensitivity coefficients* because their signs and magnitudes indicate how each of the variations, δx_i, influences the uncertainty, δy. In applications, the absolute values of the sensitivity coefficients sometimes are used to prevent cancellation of the terms when using Eq. 1.9 to estimate uncertainty. Equation 1.9 is an approximation that amounts to a linearization of the function $y(x_1, x_2, \ldots, x_n)$ around its reference value $Y(X_1, X_2, \ldots, X_n)$. Note that the derivatives are evaluated at the reference or nominal values. The relative uncertainty often is used and found by dividing Eq. 1.9 by Y, giving

$$\frac{\delta}{Y} = \frac{X_1}{Y}\frac{\partial y}{\partial x_1}\frac{\delta x_1}{X_1} + \frac{X_2}{Y}\frac{\partial y}{\partial x_2}\frac{\delta x_2}{X_2} + \ldots + \frac{X_n}{Y}\frac{\partial y}{\partial x_n}\frac{\delta x_n}{X_n}. \tag{1.10}$$

Note that $y = Y \pm \delta y$, and for relative uncertainty,

$$\frac{y}{Y} = 1 + \frac{\delta y}{Y}. \tag{1.11}$$

The independent variables in the function $y(x_1, x_2, \ldots, x_n)$ given by Eq. 1.3 often are thought to be representable in an n-dimensional vector space. In such circumstances it is common to define a *norm** of δy, where

$$\delta y = \sqrt{\left(\frac{\partial y}{\partial x_1}\right)^2 \delta x_1^2 + \left(\frac{\partial y}{\partial x_2}\right)^2 \delta x_2^2 + \ldots + \left(\frac{\partial y}{\partial x_n}\right)^2 \delta x_n^2}. \tag{1.12}$$

Equations 1.9 and 1.12 are different expressions for the same quantity, and it is natural to ask which is correct, or at least, which is better? If the variations, $\delta x_1, \delta x_2, \ldots, \delta x_n$ are viewed as orthogonal components of an n-dimensional vector, then it can be shown that the value from Eq. 1.12 will always be less than or equal to the value from Eq. 1.9, and so Eq. 1.9 gives a larger, or more conservative, value. However, the value from Eq. 1.12 generally provides a realistic estimate of uncertainty, and so it is commonly used. Another important difference is that each of the terms in Eq. 1.9 can have signs that depend on the form of the function y and its derivatives $\partial y/\partial x_i$. This means that positive and negative variations can cancel each other. Although cancellations can occur, even to the extent where δy could be zero, this is not something that can be expected. Consequently, absolute value signs sometimes are used with each term of Eq. 1.9. This is not done here, but caution must be used when applying Eq. 1.9. The use of Eq. 1.12 avoids such problems and is recommended.

In Example 1.1, $y = v$, and there are two variables, $x_1 = f$ and $x_2 = d$. After using Eq. 1.10, the relative uncertainty of v is given by

$$\frac{\delta v}{V} = \frac{1}{2}\left(\frac{\delta f}{F} + \frac{\delta d}{D}\right), \tag{1.13}$$

where the quantities D and F are the reference values of the independent variables. Using the values from the example, it is clear that the variation in friction often has a considerably greater effect than the variation in the distance measurements. This is because, for values typically encountered in practice, $\delta f/F$ is larger than $\delta d/D$. This is particularly true when the friction coefficient is small, such as under icy conditions.

Recall that the derivation of Eq. 1.9 involves replacement of infinitesimal differentials by finite variations. Consequently there is some degree of approximation involved when using differential variations. As an approximation, higher order terms were dropped after expansion of y in a Taylor series about the reference values $X_1, X_2, \ldots, X_n$. It is difficult to assess the error of the approximation because it depends on the functional form of the expression for y, and it depends on the size of the variations in the dependent variables. The following example demonstrates that the agreement can be reasonably close.

Example 1.2   A vehicle skids to rest over a distance $d = 33$ m (108.3 ft) in a straight line with its wheels locked. The measured value of the frictional drag coefficient is $f = 0.70$. Variations of the measured values of d and f are established as

---

*In mathematics, a norm is a measure of the size or length of a vector.

$\delta d = \pm 1$ m and $\delta f = \pm 0.10$. Determine the initial speed and its uncertainty by (a) computing upper and lower bounds and (b) using differential variations.

Solution   The reference, or nominal, value of the reconstructed speed can be obtained from Eq. 1.1 using $D = 33$ m and $F = 0.70$. This gives $V = 21.3$ m/s (69.8 ft/s). Using the same equation, computation of lower and upper bounds for $(d_{min}, f_{min}) = (33, 0.60)$ and $(d_{max}, f_{max}) = (34, 0.80)$ gives lower and upper bounds $(v_{min}, v_{max}) = (19.41, 23.1)$ m/s (63.7, 75.8) ft/s, respectively. Therefore, bounding gives the initial speed as $v = 21.3 \pm 1.8$ m/s (69.7 $\pm$ 6.1 ft/s).

Using the method of differential variations, the uncertainty in the speed, δv, can be found using Eq. 1.13 after multiplying by the reference value of the speed. This gives $\delta v = 1.8$ m/s (6.0 ft/s). The reference value, V, is the same as before, so the reconstructed speed using differential variations is $v = 21.3 \pm 1.8$ m/s (69.7 $\pm$ 6.0 ft/s). If Eq. 1.12 is used instead of Eq. 1.13, the uncertainty is $\delta v = 1.6$ m/s (5.1 ft/s) and the reconstructed speed is $v = 21.3 \pm 1.6$ m/s (69.7 $\pm$ 5.1 ft/s). As mentioned above, the use of Eq. 1.13 gives more conservative results than Eq. 1.12. To summarize, bounding gives the broadest uncertainty, $\delta v = \pm 1.8$ m/s; the differential variations method gives $\delta v = \pm 1.6$ m/s (or $\delta v = \pm 1.8$ m/s from Eq. 1.13). ⬡

1.4 Statistics of Related Variables

Sometimes the statistical distribution of a quantity or variable is known. For example, it is known that the height, h, of males in the United States is normally distributed with a certain mean, μ_h, and variance, σ_h^2; or that the distribution of skid numbers (see Appendix B, Glossary) measured at intervals along roads is, at least approximately, normally distributed (see Fig. 1.1). Furthermore, it often happens that the variable, say x, whose statistical properties are known is related through a mathematical equation to another variable, say y. Let

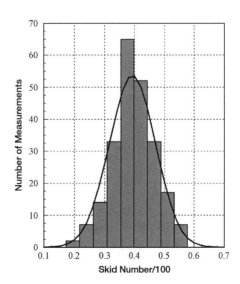

Figure 1.1
Distribution of skid numbers from 230 test sections of a two-lane country road with a wide range of average daily traffic. The average is 0.392 and the standard deviation is 0.077 (data from Rizenbergs et al.[7]).

$$y = f(x) \tag{1.14}$$

be the mathematical equation where the function $f(x)$ is given and the statistical distribution of x is known. In this context, x and y are referred to as random variables. The question often arises: what is the distribution of y? This is not an easy question to answer with mathematical rigor for an arbitrary function $f(x)$, but there are some important cases in which useful results can be found. In one case, the function is linear; in another, an approximate method of answering the question is satisfactory, or it is the only means available.

Each of the variables x and y has a certain statistical distribution (such as a normal distribution, a uniform distribution, a chi-square distribution, etc.). Each distribution has parameters (mean, median, variance, etc.). When random variables are related, such as by Eq. 1.14, it is common to find that knowing the statistical distribution of x does not mean the distribution of y is known or can be found. In fact, relating distributions is a very difficult problem. The following section concentrates on finding the parameters μ_y and σ_y from the parameters μ_x and σ_x.

1.4.1   Linear Functions

When the function in Eq. 1.14 is linear, that is,

$$y = f(x) = ax + b, \tag{1.15}$$

where a and b are constants, the statistical properties of y are well known (for example, see Guttman et al.[8] and Montgomery and Runger[9]) and relatively simple. If x has any statistical distribution with mean, μ_x, and variance, σ_x^2, then the mean of y is

$$\mu_y = a\mu_x + b \tag{1.16}$$

and the variance of y is

$$\sigma_y^2 = a^2 \sigma_x^2. \tag{1.17}$$

For linear functions (Eq. 1.15), if x is normally distributed, then y will be normally distributed. Knowing this is helpful in relating uncertainty to variations through equations using statistics.

Example 1.3   Suppose that under certain circumstances, the perception–decision–reaction time, t_{pdr}, for drivers is known to be normally distributed with a mean, μ_t, of 1.75 s and a standard deviation of $\sigma_t = 0.2$ s. What are the mean and standard deviation of the distance, d, traveled by a vehicle with a uniform speed of 20 m/s (65.6 mph) under such circumstances?

Solution   From mechanics, it is known that distance is the product of speed, v, and time, τ, so,

$$d = v\tau.$$

Here, v is a constant and the relationship between d and τ is linear. If the time $\tau = \tau_{pdr}$, then d has a normal distribution where the mean, μ_d, is

$$\mu_d = v\mu_t = 20.0\ (1.75) = 35.0\ \text{m}\ (98.4\ \text{ft})$$

and the variance of d is

$$\sigma_d^2 = v^2\sigma_t^2 = 20^2\ (0.2^2) = 16.0\ \text{m}^2\ (172.2\ \text{ft}^2).$$

The standard deviation of d is $\sigma_d = 4.0$ m (13.1 ft). With this information and based on the properties of the normal distribution, it can be stated that under the given conditions, drivers will fully react in a distance of $35.0 \pm 2\ (4.0) =$ (27.0, 43.0) m, (88.6, 141.1) ft, 95% of the time. Because of the bell shape of the normal probability curve, values near the center are more likely than those near the tails. ⬡

1.4.2 Arbitrary Functions (Approximate Method)

For an arbitrary function, $f(x)$, a way of relating the statistical parameters of x and y is to expand the function in a Taylor series about the mean of x, neglect higher order terms (that is, linearize the expansion), and then use Eq. 1.16 and 1.17. The Taylor series of y about the point $x = \mu_x$ is

$$y(x) = f(\mu_x) + \frac{\partial f}{\partial x}\bigg|_{\mu_x}(x - \mu_x) + \frac{1}{2!}\frac{\partial^2 f}{\partial x^2}\bigg|_{\mu_x}(x - \mu_x)^2 + \ldots \tag{1.18}$$

If terms of power 2 and higher are neglected, then this reduces to

$$y(x) = f(\mu_x) + \frac{\partial f}{\partial x}\bigg|_{\mu_x}(x - \mu_x). \tag{1.19}$$

Evaluating this at the mean of x, μ_x gives the mean of y,

$$y(\mu_x) = f(\mu_x) = \mu_y. \tag{1.20}$$

Substituting this into Eq. 1.19 and rearranging gives

$$y(x) - \mu_y = \frac{\partial f}{\partial x}\bigg|_{\mu_x}(x - \mu_x). \tag{1.21}$$

Viewing Eq. 1.21 as a linear relationship, such as Eq. 1.15, and using Eq. 1.17 give the variance of y as

$$\sigma_y^2 = \left[\left(\frac{\partial f}{\partial x}\right)\bigg|_{\mu_x}\right]^2 \sigma_x^2. \tag{1.22}$$

This process can be generalized to a function of many variables, $y = f(x_1, x_2, \ldots, x_n)$, which gives

$$\sigma_y^2 = \sum_{i=1}^{n}\left(\frac{\partial f}{\partial x_i}\bigg|_{\mu_{xi}}\right)^2\sigma_{xi}^2 + 2\sum_{i=1}^{n}\sum_{j=1}^{n}\left(\frac{\partial f}{\partial x_i}\bigg|_{\mu_{xi}}\right)\left(\frac{\partial f}{\partial x_j}\bigg|_{\mu_{xj}}\right)\sigma_{x_ix_j}, \tag{1.23}$$

where the variables in all of the terms in Eq. 1.23 are evaluated at their mean values. The quantity $\sigma_{x_ix_j}$ is the covariance of x_i and x_j, and is zero if variables x_i and x_j are statistically independent. When all of the variables x_i and x_j are statistically independent, then

$$\sigma_y = \sqrt{\sigma_{x_1}^2 + \sigma_{x_2}^2 + \ldots + \sigma_{x_n}^2}. \qquad (1.24)$$

This shows that the standard deviation, σ_y, of the result of a calculation involving many variables ($n \geq 2$) grows as the root-mean-square of the variance of the input quantities, x_i.

Some words of caution: These expressions are approximate because the Taylor series expansion was linearized. In addition, although expressions for the mean and variance of y have been found, the *statistical distribution* of y generally is unknown, even when the distribution of x is known. Whereas the distribution of y is the same as the distribution of x when x is normally distributed and when x and y are related linearly, the same is not true when the function $f(x)$ is nonlinear.

Example 1.4   The well-known formula from mechanics, Eq. 1.1,

$$v = \sqrt{2fgd},$$

gives the initial velocity, v, for a vehicle that slows to rest uniformly with deceleration, fg, over a distance, d, where f is a constant frictional drag coefficient. Suppose that f is normally distributed with a mean, $\mu_f = 0.4$, and a standard deviation, $\sigma_f = 0.08$. What are the mean and standard deviation of the initial speed if the stopping distance is known to be exactly $d = 20$ m?

Solution   From Eq. 1.20, the mean of the distribution of the initial speed is

$$\mu_v = \sqrt{2\mu_f g \mu_d} = \sqrt{2(0.4)9.81(20)} = 12.53 \ \text{m/s} \ (41.1 \ \text{ft/s}),$$

and from Eq. 1.22 the standard deviation of v is:

$$\sigma_v = \left(\frac{gd}{\sqrt{2fgd}}\right)\bigg|_{f=\mu_f} \sigma_f = 15.66 \ (0.08) = 1.25 \ \text{m/s} \ (4.1 \ \text{ft/s}). \qquad \lozenge$$

1.5   Application Issues

Three methods were covered in this chapter for determining the uncertainty. Whenever more than one method is available for the solution of a problem, questions arise as to which is best and which should be used. An answer is dependent on the information available for the solution of the problem. But another response could be to use as many approaches as are available to solve the problem. If the answers agree, multiple results from independent approaches reinforce their validity and reduce the uncertainty in a subjective manner. If the answers differ significantly, this is an indication of a need to question the formulation of the problem or, at least, one of the solutions.

Statisticians are careful to distinguish between a population and a sample. For example, the mean and standard deviation of a sample are designated as $\bar{x}$ and s, whereas the mean and standard deviation of a population are designated as μ and σ. When we make measurements, we are "sampling" from a population and the statistics ($\bar{x}$, s) are *estimates* of (μ, σ). How close the estimates are to the population parameters depends on many factors, such as how well the experiments are controlled and the number of times, n, we repeat the measurements (the sample size). In fact, most statistics books devote chapters, usually under the titles of *point estimation, interval estimation,* and/or *confidence intervals,* to how close samples estimate populations and how much confidence can be placed on the sample values. So, can $(\bar{x}, s)$ be used for (μ, σ)? The answer is found by using a statistical test. When sample sizes are large (see, for example, Fig. 1.1, where $n = 230$), transference of $(\bar{x}, s)$ to (μ, σ) has little risk of error; but if the sample size is small, then this should be done with caution and awareness. When dealing with a normal distribution, a rule of thumb is that for $n \geq 30$, $\bar{x} \approx \mu$ and $s \approx \sigma$. For small samples sizes, other methods can be used, such as in the following example.

Table 4.1 shows measurements that were made of the radius of a tire's yaw mark from seven critical speed tests. The radii are 130, 137, 128, 126, 126, 115, and 132 ft. **Example 1.5**

  A. Develop a normal probability plot of the radius data to examine if it follows a straight-line trend and thus indicates normality of the sample.
  B. Assuming the measurements are from a normal population, using formulas from a statistics book or statistical software, determine a 95% confidence interval for the mean of the population.

Solution A A normal probability plot[8] of the data is shown in Fig. 1.2. The points follow a straight-line trend reasonably well (a criterion for normality), so the data can be considered to be from a normal population.

Solution B The descriptive statistics of the radius data are given in Table 1.1. The statistics were found using a spreadsheet function that includes a

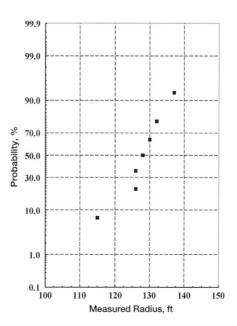

Figure 1.2
Normal probability plot of the measured radii from yaw marks showing points that approximately form a straight line.

Table 1.1
Descriptive statistics
of seven yaw radius
measurements,
used in Example 1.2.

Mean	127.7143
Standard error	2.5701
Median	128.0000
Mode	126.0000
Standard deviation	6.7999
Sample variance	46.2381
Kurtosis	2.0101
Skewness	−0.8713
Range	22.0000
Minimum	115.0000
Maximum	137.0000
Sum	894.0000
Count	7.0000
Confidence interval ±(95%)	6.2888

95% confidence interval for the population mean of the radius. It is $127.7143 \pm 6.2888 = (121, 134)$ ft and $(37.0, 40.8)$ m. Interpretation of the remaining descriptive statistics in the table is left to the reader. ⬡

Finally, a method of evaluating uncertainty associated with evaluation of formulas or functions that is gaining popularity is the use of Monte Carlo methods. Examples of this method are presented in later sections of this book. Applications of Monte Carlo methods are presented in a book on uncertainty.[10] This and other books on the subject should be consulted.

Tire Forces

2.1   Introduction

In addition to gravitational forces, aerodynamic forces, and inter-vehicular forces developed during collisions, the forces and moments generated by the interaction between the tires of a vehicle and the road surface control the motion of a vehicle. Hence, vehicle dynamicists and vehicle accident reconstructionists require an understanding of these tire forces to effectively perform many of their tasks. Developing a means by which these forces can be accurately modeled is very important. This chapter presents the concepts underlying tire–ground forces and moments. Various concepts regarding a single rolling tire are presented, followed by the quantification of the individual lateral and longitudinal tire forces that lie in the plane of the road. These are of particular interest to accident reconstructionists. The chapter ends with the presentation of two different models available for use in predicting the combined lateral and longitudinal force that results from a wheel subjected to simultaneous braking and steering.

To describe the forces and moments acting on a tire, it is important to establish a coordinate system that will serve as a reference with which system parameters, component characteristics, forces, and moments can be described. One widely used coordinate system is the one adopted by the Society of Automotive Engineers,[1] shown in Fig. 2.1. This figure shows all the forces F_x, F_y, F_z and moments M_x, M_y, and M_z associated with a rolling wheel as well as two angular parameters: α, the sideslip angle, and γ, the camber angle.

The force F_x is commonly referred to as the longitudinal force or the forward force. It will be referred to here as the longitudinal force. It can be developed by engine torque as a driving or traction force, or it can be developed by brake application as a braking force. F_y is referred to as the transverse, side, cornering, steering, or lateral force. It will be referred to here as the lateral force. It arises primarily as a result of a steering (sideslip) input. It is perpendicular to the heading of the wheel. The vector resultant, F, of these lateral and longitudinal force components is in the plane of the contact patch where $F^2 = F_x^2 + F_y^2$, and it is a type of friction force generated at the tire and road interface. The force, F_z, is the normal force at the tire patch. The moment about the z-axis is called the aligning moment. The moment about the x-axis is referred to as the over-turning moment and the moment about the y-axis is due to rolling resistance, brake torque, or drive torque. These three moments are not discussed in detail here, as the topic of interest for accident reconstructionists typically concerns only F_x and F_y individually and for combined braking and steering conditions. These moments are discussed elsewhere.[2] An analytical approach has been developed that includes all tire forces and moments.[3-5]

Figure 2.1
SAE tire axis coordinate system (from SAE J670e[1]).

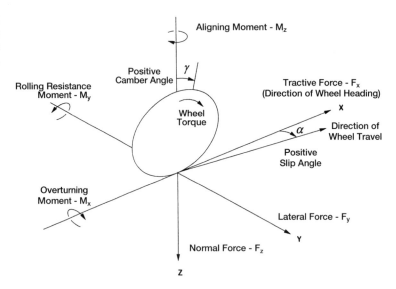

Two parameters are shown in Fig. 2.1, the camber angle, γ, and the sideslip angle, α. The sideslip angle is the angle formed between the direction of the wheel heading and the velocity of the wheel, or direction of wheel travel. The direction of the wheel heading is defined for convenience as the x-axis. The camber angle is defined as the angle between the wheel plane and the z-axis.

The area of mutual contact between the tire and the stationary surface over which it is rolling is commonly referred to as the contact patch. Various factors influence the nature of the static and dynamic contact patches between the tire and ground. These factors include the static vehicle weight supported by the tire, the inflation pressure of the tire, the tire construction (bias ply versus radial) and profile, the velocity of the tire, the suspension system characteristics and the presence of other substances in the tire patch (water), road irregularities (potholes, etc.), and the motion of the tire with respect to road contour. These dependencies are covered in detail elsewhere.[6]

2.2 Rolling Resistance

The rolling resistance of the tire is primarily a function of the hysteresis of the tire materials due to the deflection of the tire carcass that occurs as a portion of a tire passes through the contact patch while the wheel is rolling. Experimental data show that these deformations of the rolling tire account for approximately 87–94% of the rolling resistance losses. Friction at the patch accounts for an additional 5–10%, and 1–3% is attributed to drag due to friction of the wheel with the surrounding air.[6] It has further been shown that for a radial truck tire, the energy losses can be further broken down to the various parts of the tire carcass as follows: tread region, 73%; sidewall, 13%; shoulder, 12%; and the beads, 2%.[7] At high vehicle speeds, tires develop standing waves that introduce additional carcass deflections. This topic and the dependence of the deflections on the vehicle speed is presented elsewhere.[6]

Numerous factors affect the value of the rolling resistance of a tire. These include the construction of the tire, the tire material, surface roughness of the road, inflation pressure, and velocity. Discussion of these factors is presented elsewhere.[7] The dependence of the rolling resistance on the velocity of the tire is shown in Fig. 2.2. In general for passenger tires, this value ranges from 1.3–1.6% of the normal force at 100 km/h to 1.9–2.4% of the normal force at 180 km/h.[6] Recent work has investigated the dependence of the rolling resistance of a tire as a function of the temperature of the tire carcass.[8]

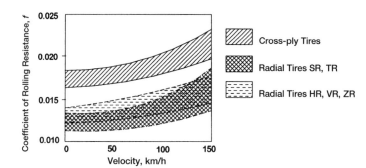

Figure 2.2
Rolling resistance of radial and cross-ply tires on smooth, level road surfaces under normal load and at a prescribed pressure (derived from Adler.[9] Used with permission).

2.3 Slip, Longitudinal Force, and Lateral Force

In free-rolling, straight-line motion, tread elements of a tire undergo small deformations in the plane of tire–road contact as they enter the contact patch, travel through it and interact with the roadway surface, and exit out the rear of the patch. These deformations cause slippage of a given point on the surface of the tire relative to the surface of the road on the order of a few thousandths of an inch, and this is referred to as secondary slip. This slippage may be in the longitudinal direction or the lateral direction, or both, and the specific displacement will be a function of the roadway surface as well as the construction of the tire.

In contrast to secondary slip, there is a more appreciable slip that occurs at the tire patch, and this is referred to as primary slip. Primary slip at the tire road interface is more a function of steering input to the tire, or an applied wheel torque through braking or accelerating, as opposed to the tire carcass merely traversing the tire patch. Qualitative observations of the primary slip that occurs during a steering input have been reported.[6] An area of the contact patch consisting of predominantly secondary slip is called an adhesive area.

Figure 2.3
Slip as a function of sideslip angle (from Clark[6]).

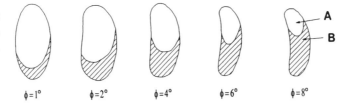

A – adhesive area (secondary slip area)
B – partial skidding area (primary slip area)

An area of the contact patch consisting predominantly of primary slip is called the partial skidding area. Figure 2.3 illustrates the qualitative change in the patch shape for sideslip angles of various magnitudes, and shows the changes in the relative size of the adhesive area (stationary portion) of the contact patch and that part of the contact patch undergoing primary slip. The secondary slip occurring in the adhesive area is often considered negligible in terms of generating tire forces.

Slip at the tire patch during straight-line braking and acceleration can be assessed conceptually by assessing the extreme conditions. The portion of the patch undergoing primary slip increases from none for a free-rolling tire with zero steering input to 100% for a tire undergoing a locked wheel skid. Figure 2.4 (C and D) illustrates another means to visualize the primary slip of a tire at the patch area due to straight line-braking under various conditions.

2.3.1　Longitudinal Slip

In a broad sense, longitudinal forces, F_x, are responsible for the acceleration and deceleration of a vehicle, and lateral forces, F_y, are responsible for steering and lateral control of the vehicle. The longitudinal force is described in terms of a parameter called the longitudinal slip, s, whereas the lateral force is described in terms of a parameter called the sideslip angle, α. Understanding the longitudinal and lateral forces developed at the tire patch requires an understanding of the longitudinal slip and sideslip.

Acceleration and deceleration forces on a vehicle are typically developed at each tire patch through the application of wheel torque. As the tire reacts in an elastic manner to the application of torque, it is expected that the tire carcass will deform. It is instructional to look at the deformation of the tire for each of the cases of a braking force and a driving force.

Consider the case of the tire with zero sideslip angle under the application of a braking force. In this instance, the rotational motion of the tire is accompanied

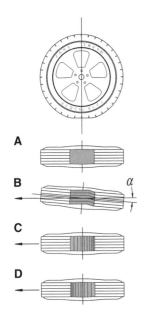

Figure 2.4
Illustrations of tire patch slip conditions. Typical passenger car tire undergoing (A) straight-line free-rolling motion, (B) sideslip of angle α, (C) straight-line braking, and (D) straight-line acceleration. (Arrow indicates the direction of tire velocity.)

by a rearward displacement of the tire relative to its axle. The longitudinal tire force, F_x, tends to stretch the tread elements just forward of the patch and compress the tread elements just aft of the patch, as shown in Fig. 2.4C and Fig. 2.5, where $F_x = F_B$. The distribution of the longitudinal shear forces for a free-rolling tire is represented by line 1 in Fig. 2.5. Line 2 represents the additional shear force created by the braking torque. Line 3 shows the resultant shear force distribution along the length of the contact patch. Note that the resultant of the vertical force, F_N, distribution for the braking tire is forward of the contact patch center.

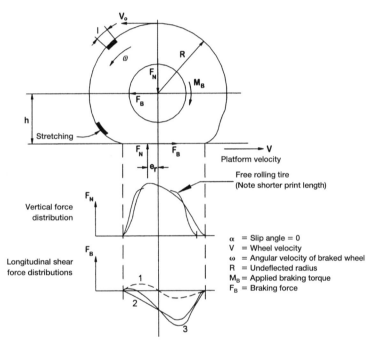

Figure 2.5
Distribution of longitudinal force and vertical force distribution over the contact patch for braking (from Clark[6]).

The net longitudinal force distribution at the tire patch shown in Fig. 2.5 has been found to be a nonlinear function of longitudinal wheel slip, s. To understand the characteristics of this force, consider the depiction in Fig. 2.6 of the kinematic quantities and forces in a side profile of a wheel rotating about its axle with an angular velocity, ω. The longitudinal force, F_x, is a traction force acting in the direction of the velocity of the wheel at the tire-ground interface, V_F. The force, F_z, is the normal reaction force of the ground on the wheel, R is the rolling radius of the tire, and V_w is the velocity of the hub, or axle, of the wheel. The longitudinal force, F_x, is known to be a nonlinear function of the primary wheel slip at the tire patch. The slip at the tire patch is called wheel slip, and is given the designation s.

In the literature, wheel slip has been defined in various ways.[2] In this book, wheel slip is defined separately for a wheel under the application of a braking torque and a wheel under traction torque. The advantage of using two separate definitions for the two different conditions is that the range of the

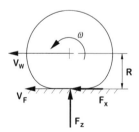

Figure 2.6
Side profile of a wheel with forward traction.

longitudinal slip is defined in both cases (which are mutually exclusive) to be between 0 and 1, as will be illustrated.

For a braking wheel, the slip, s, can be defined as

$$s = \frac{V_F}{V_W} = \frac{V_W - R\omega}{V_W} = 1 - \frac{R\omega}{V_W}, \qquad (2.1)$$

where V_W is the velocity of the wheel hub, V_F is the velocity of the tire at the tire patch, and ω is the angular velocity of the wheel. For a freely rolling wheel under straight-line motion, $V_W = R\omega$ and $s = 0$; that is, no slipping takes place between the wheel and the ground. If the wheel is locked from rotation by braking ($\omega = 0$), then by Eq. 2.1, $s = 1$. This corresponds to a locked wheel skid. As a consequence of this definition of (longitudinal) wheel slip, all levels of braking can be described by $0 < s \leq 1$.

For a wheel with positive traction such as F_x in Fig. 2.6, wheel slip can be defined as

$$s = -\frac{V_F}{R\omega} = \frac{R\omega - V_W}{R\omega} = 1 - \frac{V_W}{R\omega}. \qquad (2.2)$$

When $V_W = R\omega$, then $s = 0$. If the forward velocity of the wheel is restrained to zero but the wheel is rotating, or spinning, then Eq. 2.2 gives $s = 1$. For all other cases, axle torque causes wheel slip to be in the range of $0 < s \leq 1$.

The reason for the two different definitions is as follows. The limiting case of the traction force applied with a constrained wheel for which $R\omega \neq 0$ and $V_W = 0$ will produce a slip of ∞ from Eq. 2.1. Correspondingly, the case of the limiting condition of a locked wheel skid, $\omega = 0$ and $V_W \neq 0$, will produce a slip of ∞ from Eq. 2.2. By using the two different definitions, slip is always bounded between 0 and 1, thereby establishing an intuitive range for the values of wheel slip independent of whether the applied torque is traction or braking. Before considering the longitudinal and lateral forces generated at the tire, a short section on the characteristics and quantification of the frictional force at the tire is presented. This section also discusses the notation used in this book to represent friction.

2.3.2   Comments about Friction, the Coefficient of Friction, and the Frictional Drag Coefficient

Friction is ubiquitous. We continually try to overcome it, for example, through the use of lubricants, yet we cannot even walk or drive without it. Engineers and scientists spend much time measuring it and even more time trying to devise effective mathematical models to simulate it. In some ways friction is very simple (it brings moving things to a stop); yet in other ways we cannot explain it (pulling a tire segment over a pavement by hand may not provide the same drag behavior as a tire on a vehicle sliding over the same pavement). Yet, friction must be discussed and modeled. Based on his observations and measurements, Charles Augustin de Coulomb (1736–1806) devised laws governing friction of solids that still are used today. Coulomb observed that if the normal force over the contact surface between two flat rigid bodies is N, then the force, F, to produce sliding is equal to a constant times the normal force, that is, $F = fN$. The constant, f, is referred to as the *coefficient of friction*. He further observed that the force necessary to cause sliding to begin, F_S, is greater than the force, F_D, necessary to sustain sliding. This leads to the concepts of the static coefficient of friction, f_S, and the dynamic coefficient of friction, f_D, where, typically, $f_S > f_D$. In addition, Coulomb observed that the friction force, F, is independent of the contact area and that the coefficient of friction differs for different materials.

Most engineering books use μ as the symbol representing the friction coefficient. In this book, the symbol f is used. The use of f is not uncommon in vehicle dynamic applications. Here, the symbol μ is reserved to represent the mean of a statistical distribution or a ratio of impulses later when discussing vehicle collisions.

Experiments have shown that when the wheels of a forward-moving vehicle are locked by sudden brake application and as it skids to a stop over a typical roadway surface, the retarding force is not a constant. As depicted in Fig. 2.7, the acceleration (and force) peaks, drops somewhat, continues to vary, and eventually goes to zero when the vehicle comes to a stop. This is not exactly the type of behavior associated with Coulomb's model. At any instant of time, the ratio of the braking force to the normal force (the weight of the vehicle) can be thought of as an instantaneous value of the coefficient of friction. This means that the friction coefficient developed by sliding tires is not a constant. Though this may be true, the situation is much more complicated. As discussed earlier in this chapter, the longitudinal force depends upon wheel slip (which can vary over the contact patch), and the force is not constant, at least not until it reaches a value of $s = 1$. But other conditions differ from Coulomb's. Unlike a block of metal or wood, a tire is not a rigid solid. It has been observed that friction coefficients are not truly constants and can vary with speed. Therefore, when applied to vehicles, Coulomb's law is an approximation. On the other hand, such an approximation can be reasonably accurate, particularly when an appropriate value of f is used. In Fig. 2.7, note that an average value of acceleration is shown.

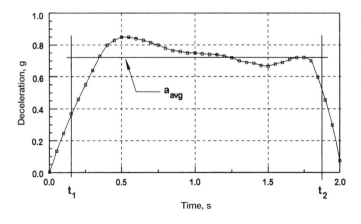

Figure 2.7
Typical deceleration versus time of a braking vehicle measured at the center of mass of the vehicle.

The average frictional coefficient corresponding to this average acceleration is $f = a_{\text{avg}}$, where a_{avg} is expressed in units of g, that is, a fraction of the acceleration due to gravity. In the figure, this value is $f = 0.72$. The use of the average value will lead to a reasonably accurate value of stopping distance when used in calculations.

To distinguish between a true, Coulomb coefficient of friction and a constant value, f, appropriate to a vehicle analysis or reconstruction (such as the average value in Fig. 2.7), this book uses the term *frictional drag coefficient*. This implies a constant value suited to an application. Other equivalent terms, such as friction factor, are in common use but are not used here. So, the term *coefficient of friction* implies an ideal value corresponding to frictional theory, whereas *frictional drag coefficient* refers to an averaged value used in reconstruction applications.

2.3.3 Longitudinal Force

Longitudinal forces, both traction and braking, are found experimentally to be functions of the wheel slip, s; that is, $F_x = F_x(s)$. Consider a braked wheel that is locked ($s = 1$). This wheel produces a longitudinal force, F_x, such that $F_x = f_x F_z$, where f_x is the coefficient of sliding friction between the tire and the ground in the longitudinal direction. It is convenient to look at the longitudinal force in a normalized form, represented here by $Q_x(s)$, where

$$Q_x(s) \;=\; \frac{F_x(s)}{f_x F_z}. \tag{2.3}$$

This normalized form of the force, $Q_x(s)$ has the benefit of producing a force that has all the features and characteristics of an actual longitudinal tire force, but where $Q_x(s = 1) = 1$. This scales the force curve by the constant $f_x F_z$, and a force distribution can be obtained simply by multiplying the curve by the appropriate value of $f_x F_z$.

Figure 2.8 shows a typical distribution of a normalized longitudinal force $Q_x(s)$. Initially, the braking force grows rapidly with s and is approximately linear with slope C_s. The slope of this linear portion of the curve is often referred to as the slip stiffness. $F_x(s)$ increases in a nonlinear fashion as s increases

Figure 2.8
Typical normalized
longitudinal force $Q_x(s)$.

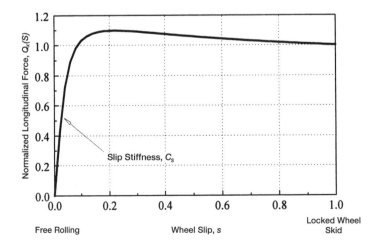

beyond a value of $s \approx 0.1$, and reaches a maximum typically in the range $0.15 < s < 0.30$. The braking force decreases as the wheel slip s increases beyond this range. The shape of this curve and its associated maximum are one of the reasons for the development of antilock braking systems. In straight-line braking the antilock brake system will attempt to maintain the longitudinal force, F_x, near the maximum. This maximizes the stopping force and decreases the braking distance and time as compared to a locked wheel skid (the antilock braking system does even more by maintaining steering control, as seen later). As before, the normalization process in Eq. 2.3 creates the condition that the actual longitudinal force is equal to $f_x F_z Q_x(s)$.

2.3.4 Lateral Force

The lateral tire force lies in the plane of the tire patch, is parallel to the axis of rotation, and is perpendicular to the heading of the wheel in the direction opposing the transverse velocity, V_T, as shown in Fig. 2.9. This lateral force, developed through a steering input, provides directional control of a vehicle. When a lateral velocity exists at any wheel, whether at a steered wheel or a

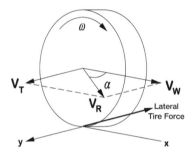

Figure 2.9
Lateral force and velocity components of a freely rolling wheel under steering input.

fixed wheel, a lateral tire force develops. During a steering maneuver, the heading angle of the wheel and the resultant velocity, V_R, differ by an angle, α, which is called the sideslip angle (or the slip angle), as shown in Fig. 2.9. The sideslip angle is defined as

$$\alpha = \tan^{-1}\left(\frac{V_T}{V_W}\right). \tag{2.4}$$

V_T and V_W are shown in Fig. 2.9.

For a freely rolling wheel ($s = 0$), the lateral force, $F_y = F_y(\alpha)$, is a nonlinear function of slip angle, α. The lateral force is also a function of other parameters, such as velocity, camber angle, temperature, and normal force, but these effects are considered second order and not studied here. For no lateral velocity ($\alpha = 0$), the lateral force is 0 and corresponds to a wheel velocity aligned with its heading. At another extreme, when the slip angle $\alpha = \pi/2$, the lateral force is normal to the heading of the wheel and is equal to the coefficient of sliding friction in the lateral direction multiplied by the normal force at the wheel, $F_y = f_y F_z$. A normalized version of the lateral force can be defined as

$$Q_y(\alpha) = \frac{F_y(\alpha)}{f_y F_z}. \tag{2.5}$$

A representative plot of a normalized lateral force, $Q_y(\alpha)$ (Fig. 2.10), shows that $Q_y(\alpha)$ is approximately linear for small values of the sideslip angle, α. As α increases, $Q_y(\alpha)$ becomes nonlinear, the slope decreases, and the normalized force approaches 1 as α approaches $\pi/2$. The slope of the actual force $F_y(\alpha)$ at $\alpha = 0$ is called the sideslip stiffness, C_α, also referred to as the cornering stiffness. $F_y(\alpha)$ also approaches the road friction limit, $f_y F_z$ at, $\alpha = \pi/2$. The lateral tire force is obtained from the normalized force such that $F_y(\alpha) = f F_z Q(\alpha)$.

Figure 2.10
Typical normalized lateral force $Q_y(\alpha)$.

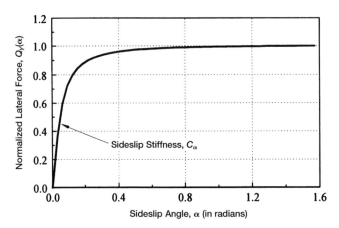

According to Coulomb's theory of rigid body friction, the coefficient of sliding friction is independent of direction and load; that is, $f_y = f_x = f$. However, experimental data has shown that for tires, differences between these values do occur.[10] Hence, the lateral and longitudinal coefficients are considered distinct. This particular characteristic of friction at the tire patch is explored in the next section.

2.4   Friction Circle and Friction Ellipse

In the previous two sections, the two force components developed by a tire in the plane of the road, the longitudinal force F_x and the lateral force F_y, were investigated independently. The situation in which both forces act simultaneously at the tire patch is quite common, for example, during braking while steering. In this section an illustration is presented in which both lateral and longitudinal forces are plotted on the same diagram. Here the longitudinal force, F_x, is plotted along the vertical axis and the lateral force, F_y, is plotted along the horizontal axis, and the wheel slip, s, and the sideslip angle, α, are implicit parameters. (This is commonly referred to as a parametric plot.) This selection of axes is atypical from much of the previous literature, but it is used here because it has the added benefit of having the forces appear on the plot in the direction of their application (as viewed from the perspective of a driver) and is thus associated with looking at the tire along the z-axis. This selection of axes has been used elsewhere.[2] In Fig. 2.11, the braking force acts toward the bottom of the page and would have the net effect of slowing the vehicle down, and the lateral force acting to the right causes the vehicle to turn right. The actual data were taken for braking only and for a symmetric fixed slip angle, but is presented here and in other figures with symmetry for the traction data for completeness.

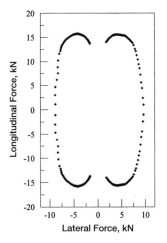
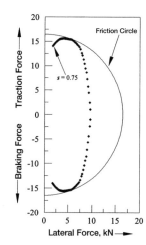

Figure 2.11 (*left*) Experimental data showing the trend of the combined steering and braking forces for $\alpha = \pm 4°, 0 \leq s \leq 0.75$ for traction and braking and $F_z = 20.6$ kN (data from [11]).

Figure 2.12 (*right*) Friction circle and a data set for $\alpha = +4°, 0 \leq s \leq 0.75$ for traction and braking and $F_z = 20.6$ kN (data from [11]).

Suppose temporarily that the coefficients of friction in the lateral and the longitudinal directions are the same. In Fig. 2.12, the origin represents the condition under which the tire is experiencing free-rolling with no steering, $s = 0$ and $\alpha = 0$. For $s = 0$ and $\alpha = 0$, the only force acting on the tire at the tire patch in the plane of the road under these conditions is a small rolling resistance force which is neglected here. The positive vertical axis represents the traction force in kN acting during positive acceleration of the vehicle. The magnitude of the maximum force that can be developed is fF_z. The negative vertical axis represents the braking force. The magnitude of the maximum force that can be developed in this direction is fF_z. The positive horizontal axis represents the lateral force in kN developed at the tire patch acting perpendicular to the wheel heading for positive sideslip angle, α. The maximum force that can be developed in this direction is fF_z. Because it was assumed that the coefficient of friction is independent of direction, $f_x = f_y$, then the three points of maximum force taken together permit the use of a circle as an indicator of the maximum force that can be developed at the tire patch for any combination of s and α. This construction has acquired the moniker of the "friction circle." The most interesting and useful part of the friction circle is that it permits the conceptual consideration of combined lateral and longitudinal tire force components and the limit of their combination.

This representation of tire force components states that for any combination of s and α, as long as the resultant of the lateral and longitudinal forces is less than the total available frictional force, fF_z, the tire continues to track, permitting directional control of the vehicle. If the resultant of the two forces is equal to the total available frictional force, fF_z, and hence is on the perimeter of the friction circle, then the tire skids and directional control of the tire is lost. The condition of the combined force at the tire patch equaling fF_z is sometimes referred to as "saturation." The direction of the resultant force under these conditions is opposite V_R (see Fig. 2.9). In accordance with intuition and physics, the magnitude of the resultant force is limited to the magnitude of the frictional force, fF_z.

Further consideration of the transition of a tire from tracking to skidding will help develop insight into the characteristics of the combined force. Consider, hypothetically, a tire under the action of free-rolling ($s = 0$) cornering (to the right) with a large sideslip angle, α. The only force acting at the tire patch is the lateral force as shown in Fig. 2.13A. In this case, the lateral force developed is acting to the right, along the positive y-axis, and is slightly less than the total available frictional force. Suppose a braking force is added incrementally, increasing wheel slip, s, from zero, while keeping α constant. At a certain point, the combined braking and steering is of sufficient magnitude that force almost reaches the friction circle and saturation. The resultant of the combined steering and braking force, F_{res}, is shown in Fig. 2.13B. If the braking force reaches a magnitude such that the combined force reaches the friction limit of the tire and the road, fF_z, the direction of the force generated at the tire–road interface changes rapidly to oppose the velocity vector of the tire. The motion of the tire is no longer kinematically constrained to rolling and is now skidding. At this point the tire has reached saturation.

Figure 2.13
Depiction of the friction circle.

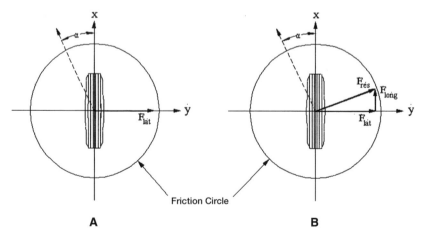

A   **B**

Up to this point, it has been assumed that the total available frictional force for a tire in the longitudinal direction equals that in the lateral direction; that is, $f_x = f = f_y$. It has been demonstrated by testing that the limiting friction forces in the lateral and longitudinal directions can differ. Unequal lateral and longitudinal coefficients of friction, $f_x \neq f_y$, have the net effect of transforming the concept of the friction circle as described in the previous paragraph into a friction ellipse. Conceptually, there is little difference between the two theories, but the friction ellipse can more closely represent actual tire behavior.

One additional point should be made regarding the general shape of the combined force data for a varying longitudinal slip with a constant nonzero sideslip angle as shown in Fig. 2.11. The force curves actually "hook back" as the independent variable, the wheel slip (which is a parameter in the plot and not shown explicitly), increases for a given value of the slip angle, α. The source of this trend in the combined force plot is easiest to see by looking at the individual plots of $F_x(\alpha,s)$ and $F_y(\alpha,s)$ as a function of s for a fixed value of α and s ranging from 0 to 1. Typical plots of these two forces are shown in Fig. 2.14. The hooking back is due to the fact that while the lateral force decreases monotonically from its maximum value at $s = 0$ to its minimum value at $s = 1$, the longitudinal force takes on the typical shape with the characteristic peak for relatively low values of wheel slip, s, and decreases monotonically at that point.

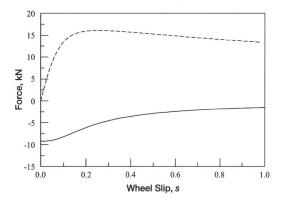

Figure 2.14
Plot of $F_x(\alpha,s)$ - - - - , and $F_y(\alpha,s)$ ———, for $\alpha = +4°, 0 \leq s \leq 1$.

It is important to point out that the experimental data presented in Fig. 2.11, while somewhat in the shape of an ellipse, does not represent the friction ellipse. The friction ellipse is determined by the locus of points that represent the maximum magnitude of the combined force for a given sideslip angle and range of longitudinal slip. This situation is shown in Fig. 2.15, where two sets of data for $\alpha = 4°$ and $\alpha = 6°$ for $0 \leq s \leq 0.75$ are shown for both traction and braking. It can be seen that the circle superimposed over the data intersects each curve where the data are farthest from the origin. This distance is nearly the same for a given set of conditions and differing sideslip angles. The friction ellipse is defined by the locus of the maximum points from a set of curves for a range of α and s.

Following the qualitative discussion of the interaction of the forces at the tire patch, it is useful to look quantitatively at the concept of the friction ellipse. An expression for the equation of the friction ellipse can be developed based on the tire forces at the patch $F_x(\alpha,s)$, $F_y(\alpha,s)$, F_z, and the coefficients of

Figure 2.15
Longitudinal force versus
the lateral force for α =
$4°$ and $6°$, $0 \leq s \leq 0.75$,
for both traction and
braking (data from [11]).

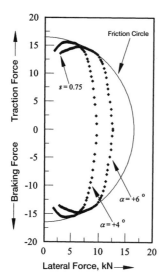

friction f_x, and f_y. Similar concepts have been developed elsewhere.[7] The development here uses the quantities previously presented in order to further build on the conceptual approach to the friction ellipse.

Using the fundamental equation of an ellipse with the major axis equal to $2f_xF_z$, the minor axis equal to $2f_yF_z$, the abscissa variable equal to $F_y(\alpha,s)$, and the ordinate variable equal to $F_x(\alpha,s)$, which is in keeping with the convention used in this book of the lateral force acting along the abscissa and the longitudinal force acting along the ordinate, yields

$$\frac{F_y^2(\alpha,s)}{f_y^2 F_z^2} + \frac{F_x^2(\alpha,s)}{f_x^2 F_z^2} \leq 1. \tag{2.6}$$

The inequality in Eq. 2.6 indicates that as long as the resultant force remains inside the friction ellipse, sliding (skidding) does not occur and steering control is maintained. Equality in Eq. 2.6 corresponds to sliding, for instance, when the wheel slip $s = 1$ for any α or $\alpha = \pi/2$ for any s. Under these conditions, the direction of the resultant force, F, opposes the velocity; $\beta_F = \alpha$, $F_x = -F\cos\alpha$, $F_y = -F\sin\alpha$ (see Fig. 2.16), and

$$\frac{F^2\cos^2\alpha}{f_x^2 F_z^2} + \frac{F^2\sin^2\alpha}{f_y^2 F_z^2} = 1. \tag{2.7}$$

During sliding, $F = fF_z$; then Eq. 2.7 can be written as

$$\frac{\cos^2\alpha}{f_x^2} + \frac{\sin^2\alpha}{f_y^2} = \frac{1}{f^2}. \tag{2.8}$$

Further simplification yields

$$f^2 = \frac{f_x^2 f_y^2}{f_y^2\cos^2\alpha + f_x^2\sin^2\alpha}, \tag{2.9}$$

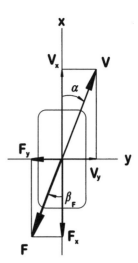

Figure 2.16
Force/velocity diagram of
a tire patch for a sliding
tire. β_F is the angle
between the heading and
the resultant force.

and taking the square root of both sides gives

$$f = \frac{f_x f_y}{\sqrt{f_x^2 \sin^2 \alpha + f_y^2 \cos^2 \alpha}}. \tag{2.10}$$

Equation 2.10 permits the coefficient of sliding friction to be determined for any combination of f_x, f_y, and α. The sliding friction force, fF_z, can then be determined for a given value of F_z; Eq. 2.9 reduces to an identity for $f_x = f_y$.

2.5 Modeling Combined Steering and Braking Forces

The discussion up to this point has focused predominantly on the qualitative description of the individual lateral and longitudinal forces developed at the tire road contact patch. Vehicle engineers and accident reconstructionists frequently need to model these forces. The reasons for this need could range from a simple order of magnitude check of a tire force to the input to a vehicle dynamics simulation package. In the latter situation, it is important to understand the kinematics and dynamics of a vehicle prior to or following a vehicle collision.

Various models exist for the purpose of predicting the combined lateral and longitudinal force.[12–14] Prior to presenting the specific models that represent the combined force, a means to model the lateral and longitudinal forces individually is discussed. The Bakker–Nyborg–Pacejka model, better known as the BNP model and frequently referred to as the "Magic Formula," has emerged as the most commonly used approach to modeling the longitudinal and lateral forces generated by a tire. After a treatment of that topic, two different combined force tire models are presented. The first of the two models has found widespread usage and is commonly referred to as the "Fiala" model after the author who presented the concept.[15] The second model is a modified form of the Nicolas–Comstock model.[16] Coverage of all the combined-force tire models that exist is beyond the scope of this book, and coverage here is kept to these two models. This restricted coverage is not meant to imply that the other models are inadequate. Interested readers are encouraged to investigate other models that satisfy the requirements of a given problem or application.

2.5.1 The Bakker–Nyborg–Pacejka Model for Lateral and Longitudinal Tire Forces

In the past, various mathematical equations have been used, depending on the application, to represent tire forces, including piece-wise linear approximations and exponential functions (for details, see Nguyen and Case[12]). Work by Bakker, Nyborg, and Pacejka[17] produced a convenient tire force formula based on a combination of trigonometric and algebraic functions. This is referred to in this book as the BNP model or the BNP equations. The BNP model applies equally well to both the longitudinal and lateral forces (as well as to contact patch moments). Due to its convenient form and its ability to fit experimental data reasonably well, the BNP model has supplanted previous methods and has been adopted by various authors, including Schuring et al.[18] and d'Entremont.[19] Because of the versatility of the BNP model, it is used here. The equations that follow are presented in a normalized form.

The BNP tire force equation expresses a tire force, P, as a function of a parameter, u, where $0 \leq u \leq 1$ and can represent either longitudinal wheel slip, s, or sideslip angle, α, where α has been normalized to the range of 0 to 1. The variable Q, the normalized force, is used here where $Q(u) = P(u)/P(1)$, where $P(1) = P(u)|_{u=1}$. The BNP equations in two-part, normalized form, can be written as

$$Q(u) = \frac{P(u)}{P(1)} = \frac{D \sin [C \tan^{-1} (B\phi)]}{P(1)}, \qquad (2.11)$$

where

$$\phi = (1 - E)Ku + \left(\frac{E}{B}\right) \tan^{-1} (BKu). \qquad (2.12)$$

The parameters B, C, D, and E are constants chosen to model specific wheel and tire systems and/or to give forces that correspond to specific experimental data. (The original BNP equations contain additional constants S_v and S_h that permit a vertical and horizontal offset of the origin to allow a more accurate match to experimental data; for simplicity, these are set to zero here.) For the longitudinal force model, the constant, K, is given a value of 100 so that $0 \leq Ku \leq 100$ corresponds to a percentage wheel slip, a common interpretation of the slip used by some authors. For the lateral force, the constant, K, is given a value of 90 so that $0 \leq Ku \leq 90$ corresponds to degrees of sideslip. Furthermore, because the forces are normalized to their value at $u = 1$, the constant D is given the value of 1. When modeling a longitudinal force, u represents longitudinal wheel slip s. When modeling a lateral force, the sideslip angle is such that $0 \leq \alpha \leq \pi/2$ and so $u = 2\alpha/\pi$. The initial slope of $Q(u)$ is $BCK/P(1)$, which is the first derivative of $Q(u)$ evaluated at $u = 0$ with $D = 1$ (see the appendix in Brach and Brach[14]). Equations 2.11 and 2.12 are used with different values for the constants B, C, and E to model longitudinal and lateral tire force components.

The force magnitudes are found simply by multiplying each $Q(u)$ by its appropriate limiting frictional force. That is, $F_x(s) = Q(s) \cdot f_x F_z$ and $F_y(\alpha) = Q(\alpha) \cdot f_y F_z$. The initial slopes of $F_x(s)$ and $F_y(\alpha)$ are the stiffness coefficients, so

$$C_s = \frac{BCK}{P(1)} f_x F_z \qquad (2.13)$$

and

$$C_a = \frac{BCK}{P(1)} f_y F_z, \qquad (2.14)$$

respectively. When modeling wheel and tire systems with specific, known stiffness coefficients, Eqs. 2.13 and 2.14 can be used to solve for the corresponding values of B. Figures 2.8 and 2.10 were created using the BNP formula with an appropriate set of parameters and then normalized as described above.

With the appropriate coefficients B, C, D, E, and K, the BNP equations provide expressions for the longitudinal force component $F_x(s)$ for no sideslip angle ($\alpha = 0$), and for the lateral force component $F_y(\alpha)$ when there is no wheel slip ($s = 0$), frequently referred to as free-rolling cornering. During combined steering and braking, however, each of these components will simultaneously be a function of both the longitudinal wheel slip, s, and the sideslip angle, α. Hence, the force components $F_x(s)$ and $F_y(\alpha)$ must be described as $F_x(\alpha,s)$ and $F_y(\alpha,s)$, respectively. Conceptually, the individual longitudinal and lateral force components can be determined such that a single force, F, tangent to the roadway surface can be computed with

$$F(a,s) = \sqrt{F_x^2(a,s) + F_y^2(a,s)}, \qquad (2.15)$$

where $F(\alpha,s)$ lies in the plane of the road. All models of the combined tire force, regardless of the formulation, must provide realistic results. This consideration, in combination of other performance criteria related to the limiting cases of the combined force, are presented elsewhere.[14]

2.5.2 Fiala Lateral Tire Force Model

The Fiala model[15] is expressed explicitly in terms of the lateral force $F_y(\alpha)$. To determine the combined forces $F_x(\alpha,s)$ and $F_y(\alpha,s)$, an initial value of $F_x(s)$ is first tried and the friction circle is used to calculate $F_y(\alpha,s)$. Both components are then checked against the friction circle.

Consider an attempted force as F_x, where the direction of the force is monitored by assessing the sign of the force relative to a convention. Next the parameter $\bar{\alpha}$ is determined:

$$\bar{\alpha} = \frac{C_a \sin \alpha}{f_p F_z}, \qquad (2.16)$$

where C_α (lb/radian) is the tire cornering stiffness, F_z (lb) is the normal force at the tire patch, f_p is the peak coefficient of friction (dimensionless), and α is the slip angle (radians). Note that $\bar{\alpha}$ has the units of 1/radian. The magnitude of $\bar{\alpha}$ is checked. For $\bar{\alpha} > 3$ the tire is considered saturated, and the lateral force, F_y, equals the following:

$$F_y = -f_p F_z \, \text{sgn}\,(\bar{\alpha}), \quad \bar{\alpha} > 3. \tag{2.17}$$

Note that with this approach, the maximum lateral force is equal to the maximum longitudinal force, thereby indicating that the model follows the concept of the friction circle as opposed to the friction ellipse. When the lateral force has not reached the saturation condition, its magnitude is given by

$$-F_y = -f_p F_z \left[\bar{\alpha} - \left(\frac{\bar{\alpha}|\bar{\alpha}|}{3} \right) + \frac{\bar{\alpha}^3}{27} \right], \quad \bar{\alpha} > 3. \tag{2.18}$$

Using the definition of $\bar{\alpha}$ given by Eq. 2.16, Eq. 2.18 becomes

$$F_y = -f_p F_z \left[\frac{C_a \sin \alpha}{f_p F_z} - \frac{C_a \sin \alpha}{3 f_p F_z} \left| \frac{C_a \sin \alpha}{f_p F_z} \right| + \left(\frac{C_a \sin \alpha}{3 f_p F_z} \right)^3 \right]. \tag{2.19}$$

In either of the two cases, the direction of the lateral force is given by the sign of $\bar{\alpha}$. A potential reduction of the tire forces F_x and F_y due to the amount of lateral tire slip is determined. The peak friction coefficient, f_p, is modified by the slip angle, α:

$$f_{\text{mod}} = f_p (1 - 1.72 \, |\sin \alpha|). \tag{2.20}$$

If $f_{\text{mod}} < |f_s \cos \alpha|$, then $f_{\text{mod}} = |f_s \cos \alpha|$. The attempted longitudinal wheel force, F_x, is compared to the available wheel force at the wheel slip angle, α. The available wheel force is

$$f_{\text{max}} = f_{\text{mod}} F_z. \tag{2.21}$$

If the attempted longitudinal force, F_x, is less than F_{max}, the amount of longitudinal tire slip is computed using the following two equations:

$$f_x = \left| \frac{F_x}{F_z} \right| \tag{2.22}$$

$$s = \frac{f_x}{f_p} f_{\text{slip}}, \tag{2.23}$$

where f_{slip} is the percent slip at f_p. The longitudinal tire slip, s, is used with the slip versus rolloff table to determine the reduction in the lateral tire force, F_y. The computed lateral force, F_y, is adjusted by the rolloff: $F_y = F_y \times$ rolloff. If the attempted longitudinal wheel force, F_x, is greater then F_{max}, the tire is either locked (braking) or spinning (accelerating). The magnitudes of the longitudinal and lateral forces are then given by:

$$F_x = f_s \cos \alpha F_z, \tag{2.24}$$

$$F_y = f_s \sin \alpha F_z. \tag{2.25}$$

Using these equations, a plot of the lateral force, F_y, as a function of the sideslip angle, α, can be examined. Nominal values for the parameters are used: C_α = 55,158 N/rad (12,400 lb/rad), f_p = 0.75, F_z = 4448.2 N (1000 lb). Note that $F_y(\alpha,s) \le f_p F_z$ = 3336.2 N (750 lb). The value of the sideslip angle, α, for which $\bar{\alpha}$ = 3 is found to be 10.5° (0.182 radians). Beyond this value of α the Fiala model gives a lateral tire force of magnitude $F_y = f_p F_z$ = 3336.2 N (750 lb). Figure 2.17 depicts the tire force given by the Fiala model for the values presented above for $0 \le \alpha \le \pi/2$.

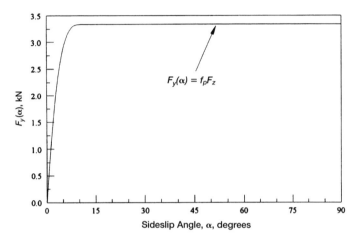

Figure 2.17
Lateral tire force $F_y(\alpha)$ from the Fiala tire model for $0 \le \alpha \le \pi/2$, C_α = 55,158 N/rad (12,400 lb/rad), f_p = 0.75, F_z = 4448.2 N (1000 lb). The value of α for which $\bar{\alpha}$ = 3 is found to be 10.5° (0.182 radians).

It is interesting to note that the Fiala model, as shown in Eq. 2.19, can be simplified using the small angle assumption. This results in

$$F_y = -f_p F_z \left[\frac{C_\alpha \alpha}{f_p F_z} \right] = -C_\alpha \alpha, \quad \alpha << \frac{\pi}{2}. \qquad (2.26)$$

The trend for this simplified equation can be seen by looking at the left part of the plot in Fig. 2.17. As expected from Eq. 2.26, the trend of the tire force is nearly linear over the small range of α.

2.5.3 Modified Nicolas–Comstock Combined Tire Force Model

While the friction ellipse, Eq. 2.6, is useful for an intuitive understanding of the physical conditions at the tire–road interface under combined loading, it provides a bound on the resultant force. For quantitative use of the combined force, an equation for $F(\alpha,s)$ is needed, not an inequality. Various models have been proposed over the years; see, for example, Nicolas and Comstock,[16] Bakker et al.,[17] Wong,[7] and Schuring et al.[13]

The model proposed by Nicolas and Comstock is based on two conditions. The first is that the resultant force, $F(\alpha,s)$ for $s = 1$, is collinear with and opposite to the resultant velocity, V_R. The second condition is that as α is varied from 0 to $\pi/2$, the resultant force, F, can be described by an ellipse of semiaxes, F_x and F_y. Semiaxis F_x is the longitudinal friction force when the sideslip is zero, and semiaxis F_y is the lateral friction force when the longitudinal force is zero. The following expressions, proposed by Nicolas and Comstock, meet these criteria.

$$F_x(\alpha, s) = \frac{F_x(s)F_y(\alpha)s}{\sqrt{s^2 F_y^2(\alpha) + F_x^2(s)\tan^2\alpha}} \qquad (2.27)$$

$$F_y(\alpha, s) = \frac{F_x(s)F_y(\alpha)\tan\alpha}{\sqrt{s^2 F_y^2(\alpha) + F_x^2(s)\tan^2\alpha}} \qquad (2.28)$$

Note that from these two equations the ratio of $F_y(\alpha,s)$ to $F_x(\alpha,s)$ is always $(\tan\alpha)/s$.

Each of Eqs. 2.27 and 2.28 is easily evaluated for a given s and α by first evaluating $F_x(s)$ and $F_y(\alpha)$. For either $\alpha = 0$ or $s = 0$, however, the expressions as written above are undefined. In particular, when $\alpha = 0$, there is no lateral force on the tire; that is, $F_y|_{\alpha=0} = 0$ by definition. With both α and $F_y(\alpha)$ equal to zero, both the numerator and the denominator of the two equations goes to zero. This is inconvenient, as one would expect that $F_x(0,s)$ should reduce to $F_x(s)$. Similarly, with s and $F_x(s)$ equal to zero, both the numerator and the denominator of the two equations go to zero. For combined steering and braking, it is expected as $\alpha \to 0$ that $F_x(s,\alpha) \to F_x(s)$ and as $s \to 0$ that $F_y(s,\alpha) \to F_y(\alpha)$. The Nicolas–Comstock model does not behave in this manner, as is shown below.

For small values of α and s, the tire is operating in the linear region of the force curves (see Figs. 2.8 and 2.10). Therefore, linear approximations can be used for the longitudinal and lateral forces. Hence, $F_x(s) \approx C_s s$ and $F_y(\alpha) \approx C_\alpha \alpha$ and $\tan\alpha \approx \alpha$. Introducing these approximations into Eqs. 2.27 and 2.28 yields

$$F_x(\alpha,s) = F_x(s)\frac{C_a}{\sqrt{C_\alpha^2 + C_s^2}} \quad \text{where } 0 < \alpha << \frac{\pi}{2} \text{ and } 0 < s << 1, \quad (2.29)$$

$$F_y(\alpha,s) = F_y(\alpha)\frac{C_s}{\sqrt{C_\alpha^2 + C_s^2}} \quad \text{where } 0 < \alpha << \frac{\pi}{2} \text{ and } 0 < s << 1. \quad (2.30)$$

This shows that the Nicolas–Comstock equations have biased slopes in the combined linear regions of the tire force curves.

Moreover, the Nicolas–Comstock equations are considered relative to two limiting performance criteria, that of straight-ahead braking ($s = 1$ and $\alpha = 0$) and lateral sliding ($s = 0$ and $\alpha = \pi/2$). Using these values in Eqs. 2.27 and 2.28 yields the conditions of 0/0 and ∞/∞, respectively.

The bias factors and inconsistent limiting performance of Eqs. 2.29 and 2.30 can be mitigated by appropriate modification of the equations. Such modifications are presented and investigated in the next section, and the results are referred to as the Modified Nicolas–Comstock (MNC) equations. Typical plots of the force predicted by the MNC tire friction force model are presented. The capability of the model to match actual tire behavior is presented using data recorded by the SAE. A new way of graphically presenting the force plots is also presented.

The following Modified Nicolas–Comstock equations are proposed to correct the deficiencies discussed above:

$$F_x(\alpha,s) = \frac{F_x(s)F_y(\alpha)}{\sqrt{s^2 F_y^2(\alpha) + F_x^2(s)\tan^2\alpha}} \frac{\sqrt{s^2 C_\alpha^2 + (1-s)^2 \cos^2\alpha F_x^2(s)}}{C_\alpha} \qquad (2.31)$$

$$F_y(\alpha,s) = \frac{F_x(s)F_y(\alpha)}{\sqrt{s^2 F_y^2(\alpha) + F_x^2(s)\tan^2\alpha}} \frac{\sqrt{(1-s)^2 \cos^2\alpha F_y^2(\alpha) + \sin^2\alpha C}}{C_s \cos\alpha} \qquad (2.32)$$

Equations 2.31 and 2.32 provide the tire force components for any combination of the parameters α and s such that $0 \le \alpha \le \pi/2$ and $0 \le s \le 1$ for any pair of functions $F_x(s)$ and $F_y(\alpha)$ (such as the BNP equations). The equations have a relatively simple form for use in vehicle dynamic simulations. They easily can be evaluated for the range of sideslip angle such that $0 \le \alpha \le 2\pi$. It can be seen that $F_x(\alpha,s)$ and $F_y(\alpha,s)$ as given by Eqs. 2.31 and 2.32 approach $F_x(s)$ and $F_y(\alpha)$, respectively, for $0 < \alpha << \pi/2$ and $0 < s << 1$, when $F_x(s) \approx C_S s$ and $F_y(\alpha) \approx C_\alpha \alpha$.

A typical means of viewing models of the combined forces is to plot the combined forces for given values of α over the full range of s as shown in Fig. 2.18, or for given values of s over the full range of α. These and all following model curves use the BNP equations for $F_x(s)$ and $F_y(\alpha)$.

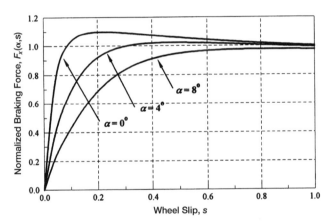

Figure 2.18
Modified Nicolas–Comstock longitudinal force for different sideslip angles.

To be an effective model, the combined tire force, $F(\alpha,s)$, predicted by the model must agree at least approximately with experimental results. The combined force data, free-rolling cornering, and straight-line braking data collected as part of an SAE project[11] was used to evaluate the effectiveness of the modified Nicolas–Comstock combined force tire model. This individual force data has been used here with an optimization algorithm to determine the appropriate coefficients for the BNP formula, B, C, D, and E, for longitudinal forces versus s (straight-line braking) and lateral forces versus α (free-rolling cornering). Figures 2.19 and 2.20 show the data with the accompanying BNP curve generated by the fitting process for one normal force, $F_z = 20.6$ kN.

The BNP coefficients and formulas then were used with the modified Nicolas–Comstock equations to compute the combined force for braking and steering, $F(\alpha,s)$. A set of data was selected to compare the experimental to the

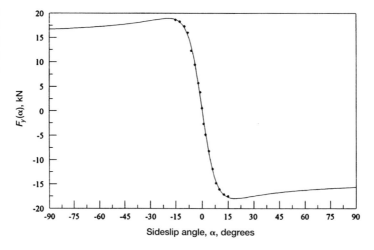

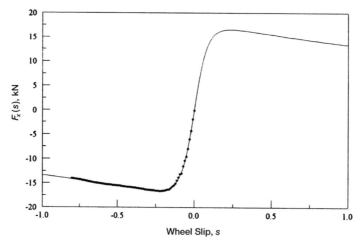

analytical. The data chosen show the combined force for a 295/75R22.5 truck tire for a slip angle of ±4°.[11] The resulting plot comparing the experimental and analytical data are shown in Fig. 2.21. This comparison indicates that a good fit for the combined force can be obtained from MNC equations using just free-rolling cornering and straight-line braking data.

2.6   Application Issues

The treatment of tire forces presented above is based on behavior and data of real tires traveling on actual road surfaces under good friction conditions. Unfortunately, tires on vehicles involved in many accidents are not always operating in the same or similar environment. In particular, the tire–road interface may have a surface contaminant, be wet, or be icy, reducing the ability of a force to be generated. In a general sense, such influences can be accounted for in the above models by using an appropriate value for the limiting sliding force, $f_x F_z$ and $f_y F_z$.

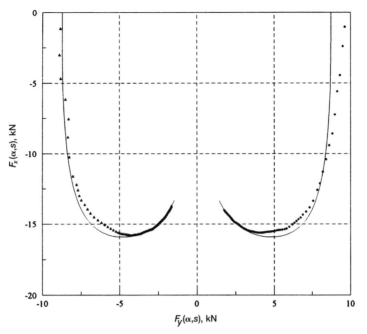

Figure 2.21
Solid lines are MNC forces for $0 \leq s \leq 1$; the left curve is for $\alpha = +4°$ and the right curve is for $\alpha = -4°$, $F_z = 20.6$ kN. Experimental data for same conditions is shown by ◆ and ▲ (data from [11]).

This situation can be further complicated by a combination of factors. In particular, vehicle speed and the combination of a wet road surface and the wear condition of the tires can have a significant influence on the ability of the tire to develop forces at the tire–road interface. This topic has been studied in the past,[6] and more recently new data has been collected.[20] In the more recent reference, the variation in tire–road friction as a function of tread depth, water depth, and vehicle speed is quantified and presented. The term hydroplaning is defined as the complete separation of the tire from the road surface by a fluid film.[21] This condition results in the loss of the ability to develop longitudinal or lateral forces at that wheel, that is, no braking or directional control of the wheel is possible.

As an example of this effect, consider Figs. 2.22 and 2.23.[20] These figures show the peak longitudinal force and sliding force normalized by the vertical load, respectively. The normal force was kept constant through the tests. In all tests shown in the figures, the same model passenger tire, a P215/75R15, was used. The inflation pressure was kept constant at 206.4 kPa (30 psi) between the tests. The only difference between the tires was the depth of the tread, created by shaving new tires to the desired depth.

These data show that there is a pronounced reduction in the peak longitudinal and sliding forces as the speed of the vehicle increases. Significant reductions in the ability of the tire to develop force at the contact patch with the presence of water occurs for worn tires (2/32 in.) at 50 mph and above. Also notable is the scatter of the data for the sliding force for speeds below 50 mph, as shown in Fig. 2.23.

Similar results are seen for the effect of water on the peak lateral force.

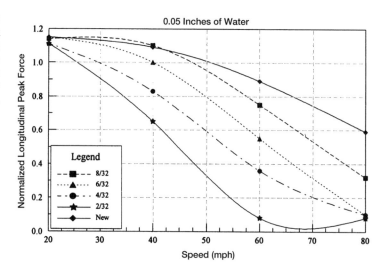

Figure 2.22
Normalized peak longitudinal force with 0.05 inches of water as tread depth changes (data from Blythe and Day[20]).

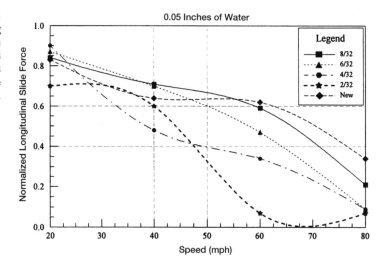

Figure 2.23
Normalized sliding longitudinal force with 0.05 inches of water as tread depth changes (data from Blythe and Day[20]).

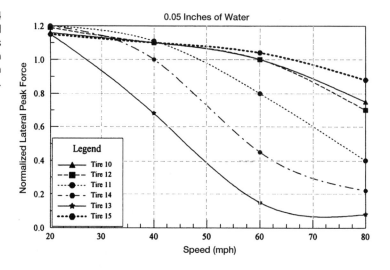

Figure 2.24
Normalized peak lateral force with 0.05 inches of water as tread depth changes (data from Blythe and Day[20]).

Figure 2.24[20] shows the lateral peak force normalized by the normal force for five tires. The tires again are all the same model, P215/75R15, tested at the same pressure, 206.4 kPa (30 psi). Table 2.1 lists the tire number used in the figure with the associated tread depth.

Tire number	Nominal tread depth (inches)
10	10/32
11	6/32
12	8/32
13	2/32
14	4/32
15	New–10/32

Table 2.1
Tire tread depths.

The data shown in Fig. 2.24 are similar to those shown in Fig. 2.22, as might be expected. It is quite apparent from the figure that as with the longitudinal force, a significant reduction in the lateral force at the tire–road interface is seen with water at the interface for highway speeds of the vehicle.

It has been considered that hydroplaning occurs if the normalized force generated by the tire falls below 0.1.[20] Therefore, it can be seen that a tire with 2/32-in. tread remaining, traveling over a road with a 0.05-in. thick layer of water, at a speed greater than 55 mph, is hydroplaning, as shown in Fig. 2.22.

Additional factors that influence the ability of the tire to develop force at the tire–road interface in the presence of water, such as inflation pressure, thickness of the water film, and tread design, are covered elsewhere.[20] Interested readers are encouraged to consult that reference.

Straight-Line Motion

3.1   Uniform Acceleration and Braking Motion

According to Newton's laws of motion, a vehicle heading and moving in the x direction with velocity $\dot{x}$ and acceleration $\ddot{x}$ (each dot over a variable represents a derivative with respect to time, τ), has an equation of motion,

$$m\ddot{x} = F_{\Sigma}, \tag{3.1}$$

where m is the vehicle mass (mass is defined as weight, W, divided by the acceleration, g, due to gravity, that is, $m = W/g$) and F_{Σ} is the resultant of all forces acting on the vehicle in the x direction. Motion in the x direction only implies a vehicle with no sideslip or yaw. Some of the more common forces that are included in the resultant are traction between the tires and the ground (such as from engine torque or braking), rolling resistance, aerodynamic forces and crash forces. Typically these forces vary with time so that $F_{\Sigma} = F_{\Sigma}(\tau)$, and Eq. 3.1 must be integrated to obtain velocity and displacement. Initially, this chapter examines cases in which F_{Σ} is a constant. Although it is rare for the resultant force to be exactly a constant, forces created by traction (acceleration and braking), such as locked-wheel skidding, can be estimated as constant for many practical applications.

3.1.1   Equations of Constant Acceleration

Let $F_{\Sigma}/m = a$, where a is a constant. Integration of Eq. 3.1 gives the velocity as a function of time,

$$\dot{x}(\tau) = v_0 + a\tau. \tag{3.2}$$

Integration of Eq. 3.2 gives the displacement

$$x(\tau) = x_0 + v_0\tau + \frac{a\tau^2}{2}, \tag{3.3}$$

where v_0 and x_0 are the initial velocity and initial displacement, respectively.

Another relationship among the displacement, velocity, and acceleration follows from the change in kinetic energy of a moving vehicle. The change in kinetic energy must equal the work done by the resultant external force (here a constant). When the vehicle moves over a distance $x - x_0$ with a velocity change $\dot{x} - v_0$ and with constant acceleration, a, the work–energy principle gives

$$\frac{1}{2}m\dot{x}^2 - \frac{1}{2}mv_0^2 = ma(x - x_0). \tag{3.4}$$

Placing this in a more common form allows calculation of the velocity in terms of position:

$$\dot{x}(x) = \sqrt{v_0^2 + 2a(x - x_0)}. \tag{3.5}$$

If a vehicle makes a full stop with a uniform acceleration of $a = -fg$ from an initial velocity of v_0 over a distance of $x - x_0 = d$, then after solving for d, Eq. 3.4 gives

$$d = -\frac{v_0^2}{2a} = -\frac{v_0^2}{2fg}. \tag{3.6}$$

This is probably the most frequently used equation in accident reconstruction for estimating the braking distance of a vehicle with a frictional drag coefficient, f.

Sometimes the time for a given velocity change is needed. From Eq. 3.2, the time, τ, to reach a velocity, $\dot{x}$, is

$$\tau = \frac{\dot{x} - v_0}{a}. \tag{3.7}$$

Another expression for time can be obtained from Eq. 3.3:

$$\tau = -\frac{v_0}{a} \pm \sqrt{\left(\frac{v_0}{a}\right)^2 + \frac{2(x - x_0)}{a}}. \tag{3.8}$$

These equations are very useful in accident reconstruction for estimating vehicle dynamics under constant acceleration conditions.

Example 3.1   A vehicle travels on a road with a uniform grade of $\theta = 3°$ at a speed of 40 km/h (11.11 m/s, 36.45 ft/s, 24.9 mph). Its brakes are fully applied, locking all wheels. The frictional drag between the pavement and the tires is $f = 0.7$. Estimate the distance and time to come to a complete stop.

Solution   Using Fig. 3.1, the resultant force, F_Σ, in the x direction is

$$F_\Sigma = -W\sin\theta - F_B = -mg\sin\theta - fmg\cos\theta,$$

where g is the acceleration due to gravity, and F_B is the sum of the tire drag forces due to sliding. The acceleration is $a = F_\Sigma/m = -g(f\cos\theta + \sin\theta)$. Equation 3.6 gives the distance to skid to a stop,

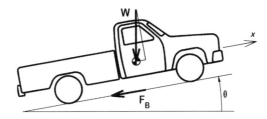

Figure 3.1
Gravity and braking forces
on a vehicle braking on a
grade with angle θ.

$$d = -\frac{v_0^2}{2a} = \frac{v_0^2}{2g(f \cos \theta + \sin \theta)} = \frac{11.11^2}{14.74} = 8.4 \text{ m (27 ft)}.$$

The time to stop is computed using Eq. 3.7:

$$\tau = \frac{-11.11}{-8.46} = 1.3 \text{ s}.$$

The vehicle skids to a stop in 1.3 s over a distance of 8.4 m (27 ft). ⬡

3.1.2   Grade and Equivalent Drag Coefficients

It is seen from the previous example that when a vehicle is braked on a grade, gravity influences the acceleration. A road grade is measured by the angle the road makes with the local horizontal and can be stated in units of degrees or percent. Percent grade is 100 × rise ÷ run. For example, if a road rises 2 ft in 80 ft, the grade is 2.5% or 1.43°. When on a positive grade (uphill), gravity enhances braking and when on a negative grade (downhill), gravity counteracts braking. Following the above example, it is possible to establish an equivalent frictional drag coefficient, f_{eq}, to represent this effect. That is, the acceleration due to braking on a uniform grade is $a = -f_{eq} g$ where (from Example 3.1)

$$f_{eq} = f \cos \theta + \sin \theta \tag{3.9}$$

and where θ is the grade in degrees and f is the frictional drag coefficient for zero grade. The angle θ is positive for an upgrade and negative for a downgrade. The equivalent frictional drag coefficient, f_{eq}, from Eq. 3.9 can be used in place of f in equations such as Eq. 3.6.

3.2   Vehicle Forward-Motion Performance Equations

Some vehicles transmit engine power through the front wheels (front-wheel drive, FWD), some through the rear wheels (rear-wheel drive, RWD) and some through all four wheels (four-wheel drive, 4WD; or all-wheel drive, AWD). Consequently, engine torque can be transmitted from the wheels to the road in different ways. The vertical force at the front and rear wheels differs with the weight distribution of a vehicle, and its acceleration. It is sometimes necessary to take these variations into account. Front-to-rear weight distribution can also be important when malfunctions occur, such as when either rear or front brakes fail or when drag coefficients differ from front to rear. In such cases, the constant-acceleration equations presented earlier cannot be used, and more detailed equations are necessary. A summary of such vehicle performance equations follows. More complete analyses can be found in Gillespie[1] and Wong,[2] including some forces not included here.

Figure 3.2 shows the forces acting on a vehicle under reasonably general conditions and includes free body diagrams of the vehicle and front and rear wheels. Notation is given in Table 3.1.

Figure 3.2
Free body diagram of a vehicle and drive components.

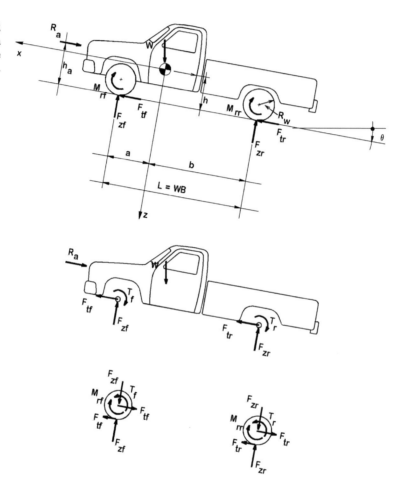

Three equations can be derived from Newton's laws for accelerations in the x, z, and θ directions

$$m\ddot{x} = F_{tf} + F_{tr} - R_a - W \sin \theta, \tag{3.10}$$

$$m\ddot{z} = 0 = F_{zf} + F_{zr} - W \cos \theta, \tag{3.11}$$

and

$$I\ddot{\theta} = 0 = (h_a - h)R_a + T_f + T_r + aF_{zf} - bF_{zr} + (h - R_w)F_{tf} + (h - R_w)F_{tr}. \tag{3.12}$$

		Table 3.1
A_f	Frontal area of vehicle	Notation for
c_R	Coefficient of vehicle tire rolling resistance	performance equations.
c_D	Aerodynamic drag coefficient	
F_t	Traction force	
F_y	Normal force at tire–pavement contact	
h	Height of vehicle center of gravity from pavement	
h_a	Height of the aerodynamic drag force	
I	Vehicle pitch moment of inertia	
I_w	Moment of inertia of wheels and axle system	
m	Mass of vehicle = W/g	
m_w	Mass of wheels and axle system	
M_r	Rolling resistance moment	
R_a	Aerodynamic drag force	
R_w	Rolling radius of tire and wheel	
T	Wheel torque	
V_r	Relative velocity of vehicle and air	
W	Vehicle weight	
α	Angular displacement of wheel	
ρ	Air density	

Note: Subscript f indicates front; subscript R indicates rolling; subscript r indicates rear.

Equation 3.12 follows from the summation of moments about the center of gravity. Equations of rotational acceleration, $\ddot{\alpha}$, of the individual wheels are

$$I_{wf}\ddot{\alpha}_f = M_{rf} - T_f + R_w F_{tf}, \tag{3.13}$$

$$I_{wr}\ddot{\alpha}_r = M_{rr} - T_r + R_w F_{tr}. \tag{3.14}$$

The quantities I_{wf} and I_{wr} are moments of inertia of the rotating parts, front and rear. The symbols T_f and T_r represent the total torque applied to the front wheel and axle system (left and right wheels) and the rear wheel and axle system (left and right wheels), respectively. These include engine torques, powertrain drag, braking torques, etc. M_{rf} and M_{rr} represent rotational drag due to rolling of the front (left and right) and rear (left and right) wheels, respectively, over a roadway surface. Except perhaps when spinning on ice, the angular accelerations, $\ddot{\alpha}_f$ and $\ddot{\alpha}_r$, of the wheels are small and can be neglected. This means that

$$T_f = M_{rf} + R_w F_{tf}, \quad \ddot{\alpha}_f = 0, \tag{3.15}$$

$$T_r = M_{rr} + R_w F_{tr}, \quad \ddot{\alpha}_r = 0. \tag{3.16}$$

It follows from Eqs. 3.11, 3.12, 3.15, and 3.16 that the vertical forces at the front and rear wheels are

$$F_{zf} = \frac{1}{a+b}\left[bW\cos\theta - (h_a - h)R_a + (h - R_w)c_R W - \frac{h}{R_w}(T_f + T_r)\right], \tag{3.17}$$

$$F_{zr} = \frac{1}{a+b}\left[aW\cos\theta + (h_a - h)R_a - (h - R_w)c_R W + \frac{h}{R_w}(T_f + T_r)\right], \tag{3.18}$$

where the rolling resistance of all of the vehicle wheels have been combined into a single force of the form, F_R, where

$$F_R = c_R W = \frac{M_{rf} + M_{rr}}{R_w} \tag{3.19}$$

and where c_R is the rolling resistance coefficient.[2] If the front or rear or the front and rear wheels lock, then the angular velocities, $\dot{\alpha}_f$ and $\dot{\alpha}_r$, of the locked wheels are zero and the rolling drag reduces to zero. Equations 3.13 and 3.14 then give

$$T_f = R_w F_{tf}, \quad \dot{\alpha}_f = 0, \tag{3.20}$$

$$T_r = R_w F_{tr}, \quad \dot{\alpha}_r = 0. \tag{3.21}$$

For locked wheels, the frictional drag forces can be represented by

$$F_{tf} = -f_f F_{zf}, \tag{3.22}$$

$$F_{tr} = -f_r F_{zr}, \tag{3.23}$$

and the vertical forces at the front and rear are

$$F_{zf} = \frac{(b + hf_r)W \cos\theta - (h_a - h)R_a}{a + b - h(f_f - f_r)}, \tag{3.24}$$

$$F_{zr} = \frac{(a - hf_r)W \cos\theta + (h_a - h)R_a}{a + b - h(f_f - f_r)}. \tag{3.25}$$

Example 3.2   A vehicle with a wheelbase of 102 in. (2.59 m) is traveling on level pavement with a frictional drag coefficient, $f = 0.8$. Its center of gravity is located a distance forward of the rear axle equal to 65% of the wheelbase and has a height, $h = 13$ in. (0.33 m) above the pavement. The vehicle has an initial speed of 32 mph (46.9 ft/s, 14.3 m/s). Due to a malfunction, its rear brakes are inoperable and the vehicle is brought to a stop with its front wheels locked. Neglect aerodynamic drag on the vehicle and rolling resistance of the rear wheels. What is the deceleration of the vehicle while braking with its front wheels locked? Compare the distance to stop to the braking distance when all wheels are locked.

   Solution   For the conditions stated, $f_f = 0.8$, $f_r = 0$, $\theta = 0$, and $R_a = 0$. The wheelbase is $a + b = 8.50$ ft and $b = 0.65 \times 8.50 = 5.53$ ft. Equation 3.22 gives $F_{tf} = -f F_{zf}$. Using this with Eq. 3.10 gives

$$m\ddot{x} = F_{tf} = -f F_{zf}.$$

Equation 3.24 gives

$$\ddot{x} = f\frac{bg}{a + b - hf} = 0.8 \times \frac{5.53 \times 32.17}{8.50 - 1.08 \times 0.8} = 18.6 \text{ ft/s}^2 = 0.579 \text{ g.}$$

The braking distance can be found using this acceleration in Eq. 3.6, which gives $d = 59.1$ ft (18.0 m). With braking from all four wheels, the corresponding braking distance is $d = 42.8$ ft (13.0 m).   ⬡

Example 3.3   A heavily loaded pickup truck with rear-wheel drive is traveling up a 17.7% grade at a speed of 60 km/h (16.67 m/s, 54.68 ft/s, 37.3 mph) against a 20 km/h

(5.56 m/s, 18.23 ft/s, 12.4 mph) headwind. The truck has a gross weight of 22.5 kN (5058 lb) with 60% of the weight at the rear wheels when at rest. The aerodynamic drag coefficient is $c_D = 0.55$, the frontal area of the vehicle is $A_f = 2.5$ m^2 (26.9 ft^2) and the rolling resistance is negligible. The engine and power-train deliver a total torque of $T_r = 1.935$ kN·m (1427 lb-ft) to the rear wheels. The height of the center of gravity is $h = 0.37$ m (1.21 ft), the height of the frontal aerodynamic center is $h_a = 0.46$ m (1.51 ft), the wheelbase is $L = 3.3$ m (10.83 ft), and the wheel rolling radius is $R_w = 0.34$ m (1.12 ft). Determine the vertical force on the rear wheels, F_{zr}, the acceleration, $\ddot{x}$, and the minimum tire–roadway frictional drag coefficient necessary to prevent the rear wheels from losing traction under these conditions.

Solution According to Wong[2] and other books on vehicle aerodynamics, aerodynamic drag can be calculated from the equation

$$R_a = \frac{1}{2}\rho c_D A_f V_r^2 = \frac{1}{2}(1.23)0.55(2.5)(16.67 + 5.57)^2 = 417.6 \text{ N},$$

where V_r is the relative velocity of the vehicle and air, and $\rho = 1.23$ kg/m^3 is the density of air under standard conditions. Equation 3.10 can be solved for the acceleration, giving

$$\ddot{x} = \frac{F_{tr} - R_a}{m} - g \sin \theta = \frac{1935 / 0.34 - 417.6}{22500 / 9.807} - 9.807 \times 0.174$$
$$= 0.592 \text{ m/s}^2 = 0.060 \text{ g}.$$

The total vertical force at the rear wheels is found from Eq. 3.18:

$$F_{zr} = \frac{1}{3.3}\left[1.98 \times 22500 \times 0.985 + (0.46 - 0.37) \times 417.6 + \frac{0.37}{0.34}1935\right]$$
$$= 13.9 \text{ kN}.$$

The condition for sliding of the rear wheels is $F_{tr} = f_r F_{zr}$. solving for f_r gives

$$f_r = \frac{F_{tr}}{F_{zr}} = \frac{1935}{13947} = 0.139.$$

A tire–pavement frictional drag coefficient equal to or higher than about 0.14 will allow the rear wheel torque to be transmitted without spinning the rear wheels. Note that the engine torque (which causes forward acceleration) and the moment of the aerodynamic drag force increase the normal force at the rear wheels to 62% from its static value of 60% of the vehicle weight. ⬡

3.3 Stopping Distance

In the field of accident reconstruction, *braking distance* and *stopping distance* are usually considered to be different. Stopping distance is the distance required by a driver to bring a vehicle to rest in straight forward motion by braking, and includes the distance traveled during a perception–decision–reaction time prior to the actual braking. Braking distance is the distance traveled while the brakes are applied. So braking distance is a part, or component, of stopping distance. Drivers always bring a vehicle to a stop as a consequence of some event or stimulus. The stimulus can be routine, such as the sight of a stop sign, or unexpected, such as a child darting onto the road from behind a parked car. As a result of a stimulus, a series of events on the part of the driver takes place before the vehicle is brought to a stop.[3–5] These events include distinct perception, decision, and reaction phases of mental and physical activity. The culmination of these phases is a response or action such as brake application or a steering input to change the heading of the vehicle. In the context here, emergency braking (maximum braking) to a stop is being considered. Perception, decision, and reaction frequently are lumped together and referred to as *reaction time* or *perception–reaction time*. The full term is used here through the acronym PDR. PDR always takes a measurable amount of time, which varies with conditions and circumstances. In addition to person-to-person differences, factors that affect PDR time include expectation, weather environment, traffic and traffic control environment, roadside conditions, daytime/nighttime, type of vehicle, familiarity with the vehicle, driving experience, age, gender, sleep deprivation, drugs, medication, alcohol, and other factors. PDR times can range widely and vary with the task that forms the reaction.[3,4] Typically, the PDR time corresponding to emergency braking of a light vehicle can range from 0.5 to 2.5 s. It is almost impossible to accurately reconstruct the exact mental and physical conditions of a driver in a specific accident, and so a value of 1.5 s is often used for comparative purposes in accident reconstruction. It is more prudent, however, to use a range of values to represent uncertainty. A value of 2.5 s often is used for highway and railroad crossing design.[6]

Suppose a vehicle is traveling at a speed of v_0 and the driver initially becomes aware of an event at time $\tau = 0$, takes a time of τ_{PDR} to rapidly and fully apply the vehicle brakes, and the vehicle comes to a stop with uniform acceleration over a braking time to stop of τ_b. The braking takes place with a uniform drag coefficient of f. The drag can represent locked-wheel skidding, drag due to antilock braking system actuation, or any reasonably uniform level of braking. Then the stopping time is $\tau_s = \tau_{PDR} + \tau_b$. After $\tau = 0$ and before the brakes are applied, it is assumed that the vehicle is not accelerating and maintains the speed of v_0. The action of brake application for vehicles is not instantaneous and can take a fraction of a second. The amount varies with the type of vehicle (longer for heavy trucks), the type of brakes, and the quickness of brake application by the driver. During this time some kinetic energy is removed and a reduction in speed takes place.[7] This additional braking drag is not taken into account here, and full brake application is assumed to be instantaneous. Two scenarios are typically encountered in accident reconstruction. In one the initial speed, frictional drag, and PDR time are known, and the stopping distance is to be calculated. In the other, stopping distance, frictional drag, and PDR time are known and the initial speed is to be calculated. The constant acceleration equations derived above can be used to provide the unknown quantities as listed below.

3.3.1   Distance from Speed

$$d_s = v_0\tau_{PDR} + \frac{v_0^2}{2fg} \qquad (3.26)$$

The corresponding stopping time is

$$\tau_s = \tau_{PDR} + \frac{v_0}{fg}. \qquad (3.27)$$

3.3.2   Speed from Distance

In this case, the stopping distance is found from Eq. 3.26. Using the quadratic formula, Eq. 3.26 can be solved for the speed.

$$v_0 = fg\left[-\tau_{PDR} + \sqrt{\tau_{PDR}^2 + \frac{2d_s}{fg}}\,\right] \qquad (3.28)$$

Equations such as these can easily be placed into a spreadsheet.

An automobile with an ABS braking system is traveling up a 5% grade over a road with a tire–roadway sliding frictional drag coefficient of $f = 0.50$. The driver perceives a need for an emergency stop, applies the brakes quickly, actuates the ABS system, and comes to a stop 128 ft from the point of initial perception. Using $\tau_{PDR} = 1.25$ s, estimate the initial speed of the vehicle. **Example 3.4**

Solution   Because an ABS system can develop an effective braking drag higher than the locked-wheel sliding value (see Chapter 2), and to represent a range of uncertainty of how much higher, the calculations will be carried out for values of f ranging from 0.50 to $1.2 \times 0.50 = 0.60$. In addition, braking is on an upgrade so equivalent values of f from Eq. 3.9 must be used. For a positive grade of 5%, the corresponding effective values are $f_{eq} = 0.585$ (as shown in Fig. 3.3) and $f_{eq} = 0.685$ (as shown in Fig. 3.4). Results from a spreadsheet solution are shown for both values of f in Figs. 3.3 and 3.4. They indicate that the initial speed of the sedan was between 33.4 mph (53.8 km/h) and 35.2 mph (56.6 km/h). Corresponding times to stop are 3.85 s and 3.59 s, respectively. Although the initial speed is higher for the higher effective drag coefficient, the time to stop is shorter. $\bigcirc$

3.4   Application Issues

3.4.1   Stopping Distance

In some cases a reconstructionist may wish to take a statistical approach to a problem, assuming that statistical data are available. Such an approach for a straight line motion problem is illustrated with the following example. The solution uses some of the material from Chapter 1.

While traveling at a speed of 30 mph (13.41 m/s, 44 ft/s) over a pavement with a frictional drag coefficient of $f = 0.7$, a driver encounters an event requiring **Example 3.5**

Figure 3.3
Spreadsheet results for
$f = 0.50$.

Initial Speed, v_0, and Stopping Distance, d_s							
• uniform acceleration with drag coefficient, f							
• including perception-decision-reaction time, t_{pdr}							

g, ft/s²	frictional drag coefficient			perception-decision-reaction time			
32.17	coeff, f	0.585		t_{pdr}, s	1.25		

A	distance from speed, v_0, mph		0.0				
	time, t_{pdr}, and drag, f	v_0, ft/s	0.00				
		v_0, kph	0.0				
	d_s, ft	0.0	d_{pdr}, ft	0.0	d_b, ft	0.0	t_{brake}, s	0.00
	d_s, m	0.0	d_{pdr}, m	0.0	d_b, m	0.0	t_{stop}, s	1.25

B	speed from distance, d_s, ft		125.00				
	time, t_{pdr}, and drag, f	d_s, m	38.10				
	v_0, mph	33.4					
	v_0, ft/s	48.99	d_{pdr}, ft	61.2	d_b, ft	63.8	t_{brake}, s	2.60
	v_0, kph	53.8	d_{pdr}, m	18.7	d_b, m	19.4	t_{stop}, s	3.85

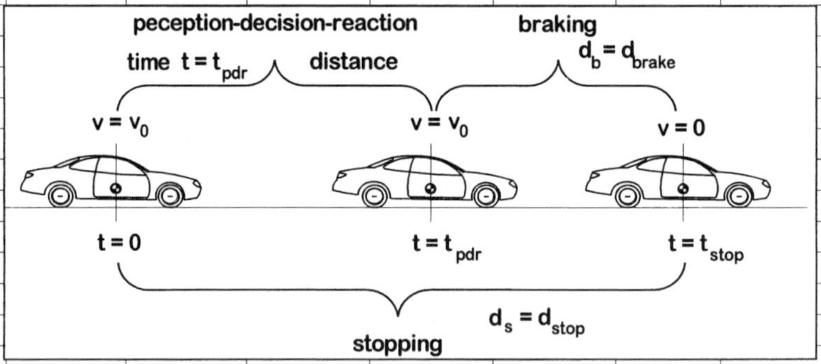

perception-decision-reaction time $t = t_{pdr}$ distance   braking $d_b = d_{brake}$

$v = v_0$ $v = v_0$ $v = 0$

$t = 0$ $t = t_{pdr}$ $t = t_{stop}$

$d_s = d_{stop}$

stopping

an emergency stop. Assume that under the conditions at the time and place of this event the driver's PDR time has a normal statistical distribution with a mean value of $\mu_{PDR} = 1.25$ s and a standard deviation of $\sigma_{PDR} = 0.083$ s. What is the mean and standard deviation of the stopping time and distance?

Solution   Equations 3.26 and 3.27 give the stopping distance and stopping time, respectively. From a statistical point of view, each of these equations is linear (such as Eq. 1.15) in the PDR time. The use of Eq. 3.26 and Eq. 1.16 provide the mean (average) stopping distance, which is

$$\mu_s = v_0 \mu_{dPDR} + \frac{v_0^2}{2fg} = 44(1.25) + \frac{44^2}{2(0.7)32.17} = 98.0 \text{ ft/s,}$$

and Eq. 3.27 and Eq. 1.16 provide the mean (average) stopping time, which is

$$\tau_s = \mu_{tPDR} + \frac{v_0}{fg} = 1.25 + \frac{44}{(0.7)32.17} = 3.2 \text{ s.}$$

Initial Speed, v_0, and Stopping Distance, d_s
- uniform acceleration with drag coefficient, f
- including perception-decision-reaction time, t_{pdr}

g, ft/s²	frictional drag coefficient			perception-decision-reaction time	
32.17	coeff, f	0.685		t_{pdr}, s	1.25

A	distance from speed, v_0, mph		0.0						
	time, t_{pdr}, and drag, f	v_0, ft/s	0.00						
		v_0, kph	0.0						
	d_s, ft	0.0	d_{pdr}, ft	0.0	d_b, ft	0.0	t_{brake}, s	0.00
	d_s, m	0.0	d_{pdr}, m	0.0	d_b, m	0.0	t_{stop}, s	1.25

B	speed from distance, d_s, ft		125.00						
	time, t_{pdr}, and drag, f	d_s, m	38.10						
	v_0, mph	35.2							
	v_0, ft/s	51.63	d_{pdr}, ft	64.5	d_b, ft	60.5	t_{brake}, s	2.34
	v_0, kph	56.6	d_{pdr}, m	19.7	d_b, m	18.4	t_{stop}, s	3.59

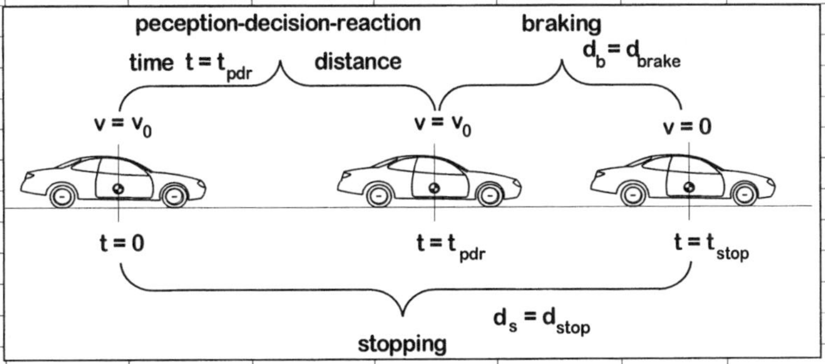

Figure 3.4
Spreadsheet results for $f = 0.60$.

The corresponding standard deviations are found using Eq. 1.17, which gives

$$\sigma_d = v_0 \sigma_{PDR} = 44 \times 0.833 = 3.65 \text{ ft}$$

and

$$\sigma_t = \sigma_{PDR} = 0.83 \text{ s}$$

This means that the stopping distance is normally distributed with a mean of 98.0 ft (29.9 m) and a standard deviation of 3.65 ft (1.11 m) and the stopping time is normally distributed with a mean of 3.20 s and a standard deviation of 0.83 s. Because $\mu \pm 3\sigma$ of a normal distribution contains approximately 99% of a normal population, it can be concluded that 99% of such emergency stops would have a stopping distance in the range of about 87 to 109 ft (27 to 33 m) and stop in a range of times from about 3.0 to 3.5 s.

If, in the above example, the frictional drag coefficient, f, also was given a statistical distribution, Eqs. 3.26 and 3.27 would no longer be statistically linear (since f appears in the denominator) and other methods (such as those presented in Chapter 1) would have to be used to obtain comparable results.

3.4.2 Motion Around Curves

Although this chapter is titled "Straight-Line Motion," some equations can be used to cover cases in which a vehicle is traveling on a curve. Suppose, for example, a vehicle makes a stop at an intersection and makes a turn from one street to the other with uniform acceleration. If the path is known, such as a circular one, then Eqs. 3.2 through 3.8 still apply where the distance, x, is replaced by the arc length, s. If the path is not known and must be determined by input to the steering wheels, then a vehicle dynamic simulation is needed to study the motion (see Chapter 11). Also, note that the vehicle forward-motion performance equations presented in Section 3.2 cannot be applied to motion around a curve. In straight-line motion, it can be assumed that the forces on the wheels are the same from one side of the vehicle to the other, which is not true for motion around a curve. The normal forces in the performance equations also vary from side to side due to centrifugal forces.

Critical Speed
from
Tire Yaw Marks

4.1   Estimation of Speed from Yaw Marks

Yaw marks are curved marks from one or more tires on a road surface caused by a vehicle making a sudden turn at a relatively high speed. Front and rear wheels do not follow each other over the same path. Often, yaw marks are the result of an avoidance maneuver, where a driver perceives an object or potential hazard (such as a child running into the road) in front of the vehicle and swerves suddenly to the left or right. Yaw marks can also result from a sudden yaw velocity, such as emergence from a pavement edge drop.[1] A turn leading to yaw marks generally is severe enough to lead to loss of driver steering control and can also precede a rollover. The speed at the beginning of the maneuver can often be calculated from yaw marks and is often referred to as a *critical speed*. For the purpose of reconstruction, a portion of a yaw mark is treated as a circular arc; the radius of the arc and the roadway surface friction coefficient are used to estimate the speed.

Various methods exist for calculating critical speed. Most have the form of an equation, but some require the use of vehicle dynamic simulations; examples of the latter are Fittanto and Puig-Suari[2] and Brach.[1] The simplest form is an equation called the critical speed formula which is derived below. A paper by Sledge and Marshek[3] reviews many of the methods for the calculation using equations, most of which in some way are extensions of the simple critical speed formula. An article by Semon[4] does an excellent job of reviewing many aspects of the use of the critical speed calculation process. Semon's article includes some auxiliary topics such as the choice and measurement of appropriate values of the friction coefficient and the measurement and uncertainty of the radius of yaw marks. In more advanced methods, tire and vehicle properties are used in addition to the road friction and yaw mark properties.

The formula for the critical speed, $V_{cr} = \sqrt{gfR}$, is simple, and is presented in many references (see above). The quantity, f, is the frictional drag coefficient, g is the gravitational constant, and R is the radius of the circular path. The use of the critical speed formula for estimating speed of a yawing vehicle has been controversial from both theoretical and experimental perspectives. A theoretical argument is that the critical speed formula is derived for vehicle dynamic conditions different from those where it is applied. As will be seen shortly, the equation is derived under the assumptions that a vehicle is a point mass, that it is traversing a circular path at constant velocity, and that the wheels of the vehicle undergo a threshold change from a condition of no sliding to a full slip condition. The argument continues that a vehicle is not a point mass (it possesses significant rotational inertia), the maneuver leading to yaw marks is not steady but a transient one, and, as seen in the earlier chapter on tire forces, the sideslip on tires changes continuously and that sideslip is not a threshold phenomenon.

Authors such as Dickerson et al.[5] have published experimental results showing that the speed of a vehicle driven at increasing speeds over a near-circular curve and leaving tire marks can differ significantly from that calculated by the critical speed formula. On the other hand, their results indicate that the speed following a single, significantly large step change in the steer angle of a vehicle does correspond to the value from the critical speed formula. So the findings of a great majority of experimentalists and researchers over the years seem to indicate that even though there are theoretical differences, the critical speed formula, if used properly, can produce reasonably accurate results. This is a conclusion reached by Semon[4] from examination of numerous experimental results. Lambourn[6] also found experimentally that the critical speed formula can provide accurate ($\pm 10\%$) estimates of the speed of a variety of vehicles at the beginning of yaw marks. The validity and accuracy of the critical speed formula is further verified in this chapter, using computerized vehicle dynamic simulations (see Chapter 11) and experimental data.

Curved tire marks can be made in ways other than from a sudden steer maneuver. These other ways include a moving vehicle that has developed a significant yaw spin as the result of a collision with another vehicle, a vehicle under severe braking on a road with a cross slope or under a high cross wind, or a vehicle undergoing hard braking with right and left wheels developing different frictional drag coefficients. The method of speed determination in this chapter does not apply to these other situations.

Although the more sophisticated formulas[3] attempt to achieve greater accuracy, some drawbacks can arise with their practical application. One drawback is that they can require tire and/or vehicle properties such as tire sideslip coefficients that may be unknown and are difficult to determine. It is not always clear that the added properties significantly affect the accuracy of the critical speed calculation. Furthermore, it is not always clear that the more sophisticated methods have been verified experimentally to establish their accuracy and limitations. To some extent, the latter is also true of methods that use dynamic simulation computer models. Although these models are usually validated in some general way, verification may not have been specifically for the generation of yaw marks. Nevertheless, it is generally agreed that simulations can provide reasonably good results, and are considered to be more accurate than individual equations.

A characteristic of all critical speed methods, including the use of simulation models, is that there appear to have been no studies done to determine under what conditions a sideslipping tire leaves *visible* marks, data that would be useful and informative. Different tire models used in vehicle dynamic simulations may also affect model performance. Simulations have a significant advantage when yaw marks exist over a surface with more than a single friction coefficient, such as a mark that begins on a paved surface but extends onto a gravel shoulder. Under these conditions only simulation methods can be used.

The material in this chapter does not apply to articulated vehicles and heavy trucks. Other than simulation techniques, formulas for the calculation of the critical speed of vehicles with more than two axles, particularly articulated vehicles and heavy trucks, do not exist.

4.2   Yaw Marks

When a vehicle is traveling at a relatively high speed, over about 13 m/s (30 mph), and is given a sudden steer angle in one direction by a driver (frequently as an emergency avoidance maneuver), the front of the vehicle changes its heading toward the direction of the steer, the rear of the vehicle swings out in the opposite direction, and the vehicle develops a significant yaw angle and yaw rate. Based on tire mechanics, for any such steer maneuver each tire of the vehicle develops an individual, varying sideslip angle. If the maneuver is severe, the pavement is rough, and the normal force of each tire is large enough, a tire will leave a visible curved mark on the roadway or travel surface. Because the yaw angle of the vehicle is changing, each tire traces out a different path, an example of which is shown in Fig. 4.1.

Note that contrary to discussions of the critical speed formula by some

Figure 4.1
Experimentally generated yaw marks from a 1992 Ford Taurus SHO braked and steered from an initial speed of 83.7 km/h (52 mph).

authors, tire sideslip does not take place only when a friction limit is exceeded. As discussed in Chapter 2, sideslip occurs for any turn, even for small steer angles, with or without forward traction or braking. The process of generating *visible* yaw marks under high tire sideslip is a complex tire–road interaction that depends on the forward speed, magnitude of the steer angle, level of sideslip, vehicle physical characteristics, tire rubber properties, tire inflation pressure, abrasion level of the surface, and so on. Each of these characteristics influences the generation of visible tire marks on the surface. Furthermore, because tire sideslip is a continuous process, the suggestion of some authors that a static coefficient of friction applies here is not correct. That static friction plays no role for a moving vehicle is further supported by the fact that some tire slip always exists over the contact patch of a rolling tire as the curved circumferential surface of the tire conforms to the flat road surface. Even while driving under steady conditions, some longitudinal slip always occurs as well, due to transmission of engine power to overcome aerodynamic drag. As such, sliding friction coefficients always apply.

Curved tire marks such as those discussed here are referred to as *yaw marks* in distinction to *skid marks* (see, for example, Fricke[7]). Skid marks usually are straight and show a consistent striped pattern corresponding to the tread, parallel to the heading of the tire mark. The intensity of yaw marks depends on the speed of the vehicle, the material and condition of the roadway surface, the tire material, roadway moisture, contamination, and so forth. Yaw marks usually differ in intensity from one side of the vehicle to the other and from front to rear due to inertial load transfer, driver traction control (braking, coasting, or forward acceleration), and suspension system design and condition. Due to weight transfer, the *leading front tire* (right front for a left turn and left front for a right turn) usually leaves the darkest mark. In a yaw maneuver the tires simultaneously are rotating about their axles (spindles) and sideslipping, so the marks usually display a cross-striping, called striations, due to a tire's geometry and its dynamic deformation as it sweeps over the road surface. Not all yaw marks display striations (such as yaw marks made over gravel), but they are common. The striations can be affected by a tire's construction and may be related to dynamic buckling of the tire.[6]

When yaw marks are encountered in an accident setting, they provide evidence that can be used to estimate vehicle forward speed. The theory is that if the yaw marks are visible, the tires must have had a high sideslip and reached, or were near, their frictional limit. In most cases, point mass mechanics is used to determine a relationship between speed, friction, and the radius of a path. Three modes of driver–vehicle traction control (hereafter called *driver control mode*) play a role during the generation of yaw marks: braking, coasting, and acceleration.

4.2.1 Radius from Yaw Marks

The radius, R, of a tire yaw mark can be determined using at least two methods. One is to measure the coordinates of three points along the arc relative to a fixed reference. The equation of a circle can be written in terms of the coordinates x_i and y_i of point i,

$$(x_i - a)^2 + (y_i - b)^2 = R^2, \quad i = 1,2,3, \tag{4.1}$$

where a and b are the coordinates of the center of the circle, x_i and y_i are measured coordinates, and R is the radius. Eliminating R^2 from the equations for $i = 1$ and $i = 2$ gives one equation; doing the same for $i = 2$ and $i = 3$ gives another. These two algebraic equations are linear in a and b:

$$\begin{bmatrix} x_1 - x_2 & y_1 - y_2 \\ x_2 - x_3 & y_2 - y_3 \end{bmatrix} \begin{Bmatrix} a \\ b \end{Bmatrix} = \begin{bmatrix} (x_1^2 - x_2^2)/2 + y_1^2 - y_2^2/2 \\ (x_2^2 - x_3^2)/2 + y_2^2 - y_3^2/2 \end{bmatrix}. \tag{4.2}$$

Equation 4.2 can be solved for a and b. These values can be placed into Eq. 4.1 for $i = 1$, 2, or 3 and R is obtained. Another way of determining the radius of an arc is to measure the length of a chord, c, between two points on the arc

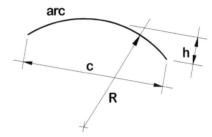

Figure 4.2
Circular arc with radius, R, chord length, c, and middle ordinate, h.

and its middle ordinate, h. These quantities are illustrated in Fig. 4.2. R can be computed using

$$R = \frac{c^2}{8h} + \frac{h}{2}. \tag{4.3}$$

Equations 4.1, 4.2, and 4.3 and their solutions for R can be placed into a spreadsheet for convenient solution. The radius can also be found using computer aided design (CAD) software.

4.3 Critical Speed

Two forms of the critical speed formula are derived here. One is the *simple critical speed formula* applicable to flat level surfaces. The other is for roads that have a significant cross slope, or superelevation.

4.3.1 Critical Speed Formula

If a point mass travels at a forward speed, V, tangent to and on a circular path of radius R, it has a centripetal acceleration of V^2/R and requires a corresponding radial force, $F_r = mV^2/R$, to maintain the circular path. For a four-wheeled vehicle traveling in a circular path (such as a freeway entrance ramp), F_r is supplied by friction, with a coefficient, f, between the tires and the road surface.

If the vehicle speed is increased and becomes high enough, significant radial (outward) sliding begins and F_r is near the sliding value; so $mV^2/R = f\,mg$. This occurs at the velocity

$$V_{cr} = \sqrt{gfR},\qquad(4.4)$$

called the critical velocity, or critical speed. If the tire–roadway frictional coefficient, f, and the radius of the path of the sliding tires are known, the speed of the vehicle can be estimated using Eq. 4.4. Typically the radii swept out by the tires of a yawing vehicle are different and are measured directly from the pavement markings or, if the yaw marks no longer exist, can sometimes be determined from a photograph using the technique of photogrammetry (see Chapter 10).

If a vehicle traveling at moderate to high speed is not initially traveling on a circular path but undergoes a sudden steer maneuver resulting in a near-circular path and the production of yaw marks, Eq. 4.4 can be used to estimate vehicle speed at the beginning of the marks.

4.3.2 Roadway with Superelevation

Consider now a vehicle in a steady turn as above, but where the road has a significant side slope, or superelevation. Equation 4.4 no longer applies. Figure 4.3 shows a vehicle traveling on a curve with a bank angle, γ (superelevation),

Figure 4.3
Frontal view of a vehicle traveling on a roadway with a superelevation angle, γ.

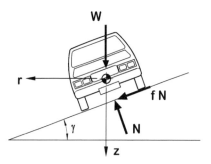

and with (r,z) coordinates. Using point mass theory again for motion on a circular path, Newton's second law in the radial direction in this case is

$$m\frac{V^2}{R} = fN\cos\gamma + N\sin\gamma.\qquad(4.5)$$

Due to equilibrium in the z direction,

$$N = \frac{mg}{\cos\gamma - f\sin\gamma}.\qquad(4.6)$$

Combining these equations by elimination of N gives

$$V_{cr} = \sqrt{gR\frac{f + \tan\gamma}{1 - f\tan\gamma}} = \sqrt{gR\frac{f + e}{1 - fe}},\qquad(4.7)$$

where the symbol e is commonly used to represent $\tan\gamma$.[8] This is the greatest speed that a vehicle can have on a curved path of radius R without significant lateral sliding and without a loss in directional control. If e and $\tan \gamma$ are zero, Eq. 4.7 reduces to Eq. 4.4. Note that γ can be positive or negative.

It is evident that the equation for the speed of a sudden yaw steer maneuver and the equation for the highest speed for a steady turn are the same.

The measured values of chord and middle ordinate are 12.8 m (42 ft) and **Example 4.1** 0.354 m (1.16 ft), from a single controlled test[9] of a sudden steer maneuver in a Ford SHO (see Fig. 4.1). The site was a shopping center parking lot with zero grade and zero superelevation. An average frictional drag coefficient value of 0.86 was measured at the site using stopping distance tests of the SHO. Determine:

A. the speed over the measured arc of the yaw marks, and
B. the frictional drag coefficient that gives the speed of 83.69 km/h (52 mph) as was measured by radar.

Solution A   Using Eq. 4.3, the radius of the circular arc is

$$R = \frac{c^2}{8h} + \frac{h}{2} = \frac{12.8^2}{8(0.354)} + \frac{0.354}{2} = 58.03 \text{ m } (190.4 \text{ ft}).$$

The corresponding estimate of the initial speed is

$$V_{cr} = \sqrt{gfR} = \sqrt{9.81(0.86)58.03} = 22.13 \text{ m/s } (49.5 \text{ mph})$$

Solution B   Based on a measured speed of 23.25 m/s (83.69 km/h), Eq. 4.4 solved for the frictional drag coefficient gives

$$f_c = \frac{V_{cr}^2}{gR} = \frac{23.25^2}{9.81(58.03)} = 0.95.$$

The difference between this value and the measured value, $f = 0.86$, is an inconsistency that is not unusual and often cannot be resolved, even for well controlled experiments. This points out the need to consider the level of uncertainty and the need for repeated measurements when running tests.   ◯

What is the highest speed a car can travel with a circular path on a level, **Example 4.2** unbanked road with a 1000 ft radius under icy conditions, with $f = 0.10$?

Solution   Equation 4.4 (or Eq. 4.7 with $e = \tan \gamma = 0$) applies, so

$$V_{cr} = \sqrt{9.81(0.10)304.8} = 17.3 \text{ m/s } (38.7 \text{ mph}).$$ ◯

4.4   Application Issues

4.4.1   Tire Marks in Practice

Lambourn[6] prescribes a useful set of guidelines for the use of determining and measuring yaw marks in practice. In part, these guidelines are as follows:

1. There should be at least two tire marks visible, they should be from the outside wheels, and they should show lateral striations or scratches.

There should be clear evidence that the rear wheels were tracking outside the front wheels.

2. The measurement of the radius should be made from the front outside mark (leading front tire).

3. The measurement of the chord should be made at the earliest point corresponding to Guideline 1.

4. A chord length of about 15 m (about 50 ft) is suitable but a longer chord should be taken when the middle ordinate is less than 0.3 m (1 ft) to minimize measurement errors.

5. The separation of the front and rear tire marks over the length of the measured chord should be no more than about one half of the track width (although they may diverge more along the marks).

4.4.2   Other Curved Tire Marks

As mentioned earlier, curved tire marks can be made on a roadway in ways other than described above. For example, at low speeds, a rear-wheel drive vehicle with its front wheels turned can create a single, curved tire mark with engine power and acceleration high enough to spin one of the rear wheels. In such a maneuver, in which the rear wheel is spinning at a high rate relative to the vehicle yaw rate, an acceleration mark usually shows a tread pattern that remains parallel to the tire heading. Such acceleration marks (see Fig. 4.4)

Figure 4.4
Illustration of different tire marks on an asphalt road.

frequently are from a single wheel and show no striations. Another way curved tire marks can be generated is by a vehicle that has a mass center velocity in a straight line and a high yaw rate. These conditions are developed from an off-center high-speed collision. Such events occur frequently as postimpact motion. The critical speed formula does not apply to these cases.

4.4.3   Coefficient of Friction, *f*

As noted in Chapter 2, the friction limit (sliding coefficient) corresponding to side- or lateral slip of a rubber tire and the friction limit corresponding to forward or longitudinal slip can differ.[10,11] This asymmetry is the reason that the curve often used to model tire limit forces is referred to as a friction *ellipse* rather than a friction *circle*. In most asymmetric cases, side or lateral friction limit is somewhat higher. Because of this, and because the tire motion leading to critical speeds produces predominantly lateral slip, it is sometimes suggested (for example, see Sledge and Marshek[12]) that a lateral friction coefficient be used for *f* in the critical speed equations. This is not ordinarily done; longitudinal friction values should be used. Lateral friction values are difficult to find in published references and they rarely are measured experimentally. Another reason that longitudinal values are used is because the friction coefficient values used with critical speed studies typically are from experimental stopping distance tests conducted in the direction of heading of vehicles, namely longitudinal values. Most testing leading to experimental verification of the critical speed formula uses values of *f* from longitudinal tests such as stopping distance tests.

4.4.4   Driver Control Modes

The issue of driver traction control modes (braking or acceleration during a sudden steer maneuver) was raised earlier. A question arises as to whether there is any relationship between the driver control mode and critical speed formula and if there is, how is speed reconstruction accuracy affected? A corollary issue is the question of where along the extent of the yaw marks should curvature be measured? Brach[1] used simulation techniques (see Chapter 11) to compare the accuracy of critical speed calculation using Eq. 4.4 with the radius, R_{CG}, measured at the center of gravity of the vehicle and the radius, R_{LFT}, made by the leading front tire. The study also included a comparison of the radii computed from three coordinates taken from the initial 1-s duration of the yaw trajectory, with the radius computed from three points over the third 1-s duration of the same yaw maneuver. Figure 4.5 summarizes the results. It shows that in all three driver control modes (braking, acceleration, and coasting),

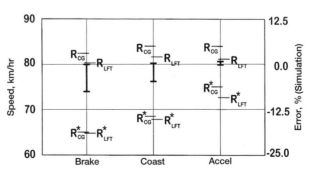

Driver Forward Control Mode

Figure 4.5
For each mode of driver control, the vertical bars indicate the speed range over the first 1 s of each simulation from an initial speed of 80.5 km/h (50 mph). R_{CG} indicates a critical speed calculated using the radius of the center of gravity of the vehicle. R_{LFT} is the critical speed using the radius of the leading front tire. Values of *R* without an asterisk are from the first third of the 3-s trajectory; *R* with an asterisk uses the last third (from Brach[1]).

using the radius from the first 1 s of yaw (about 73 ft for 50 mph, 22.4 m/s) gave significantly more accurate results. In addition, Fig. 4.5 shows that using the radius measured from the leading front tire mark gave more accurate results than using the radius of the trajectory of the vehicle's mass center. In all cases, using the leading front tire radius gave a value of vehicle speed at or slightly above the beginning forward speed of the vehicle. These results apply to all three driver control modes.

4.4.5   Tire Forces in a Severe Yaw

The derivation of the critical speed formula is based upon a point mass moving at a constant speed. Yet applications are to a rigid body (light vehicles) with potential braking or acceleration (see Section 4.4.4, Driver Control Modes, above). This has led to claims that the critical speed formula is grossly inaccurate and should never be used. A main criticism is that speed change due to energy loss from yaw tire slip and additionally, due to the effects of braking or acceleration, violates the constant-speed assumption and causes significant errors. To shed some light on this issue, the longitudinal and transverse tire force components on a yawing tire are examined using the Modified Nicolas–Comstock equations (MNC, see Chapter 2). Analytically, it is shown in the following paragraphs that the action of braking or acceleration during a severe yaw has little effect on a tire's side force, which controls the yaw.

For a tire with neither braking nor acceleration, $F_x(s) = 0$. Consider a steer maneuver where the front wheels of a vehicle are given a sudden, significant steer angle, δ. This places the vehicle into a yaw and each of its tires has a relatively high sideslip angle, α. Figure 2.10 shows that for $2\alpha/\pi$ greater than about 0.8, the side force $F_y(s) \approx \mu_y F_z$. If any traction force (braking or acceleration), $F_x(s)$, is applied, the MNC equations can be used to estimate the combined force components, $F_x(\alpha,s)$ and $F_y(\alpha,s)$. Using the conditions that $\alpha \approx \pi/2$, $\cos\alpha \approx 0$, and $\sin\alpha \approx 1$, or that braking is in the linear range, $F_x(\alpha,s) = C_s s$, Eqs. 2.30 and 2.29 give

$$F_y(a_i,s) \approx \mu f_z \tag{4.8}$$

and

$$F_x(a_i,s) \approx 0. \tag{4.9}$$

Equations 4.8 and 4.9 imply that if a tire is already near saturation due to a sudden increase in steer angle, δ, it remains near saturation even during an application of a longitudinal traction force. In other words, if the lateral tire force component, F_y, already is near the condition of sliding, addition of longitudinal traction (acceleration or braking) does not significantly alter the resultant tire–road force. It remains essentially a side force. However, an addition of longitudinal traction (braking or acceleration) does affect how quickly the radius of the tire yaw mark changes and influences the satisfaction of the constant-speed and constant-radius assumptions.

4.4.6 The Critical Speed Formula and Edge Drop-Off (Road Edge Reentry)

A situation frequently arises in accident reconstructions in which the wheels of one side of a car drop off from the paved portion of a roadway into a road-edge rut and the inside of the wheels ride against the edge of the pavement. Then, a steering reentry is attempted to overcome the rise of the roadway edge. Forced steering of the front wheels to initiate reentry can cause an interaction of tire flexibility and causes the steer wheels to develop different steer angles with the road edge. This introduces a significant yaw rate as the tire suddenly lifts over the edge onto the pavement. A significant steer angle, δ, is needed to cause the wheels to ride up over the edge. As the car reenters the roadway, the steering angle causes a yaw behavior similar to a sudden steer maneuver as analyzed above. Simulations show[1] that as long as the initial yaw rate is not high enough to cause the vehicle to spin more than about 90° as it crosses one or two lanes, the critical speed formula, Eq. 4.4, gives an estimate with an accuracy similar to that seen above for a sudden steer maneuver. This is the case even when the steer angle is given a sudden reversal after reentry to the roadway to simulate a correctional response of the driver. This steer reversal has little effect, because by the time it is introduced, steering control already has been lost.

4.5 Uncertainty of Critical Speed Calculations

4.5.1 Estimation of Uncertainty by Differential Variations

Uncertainties can occur independently in calculating the radius of a yaw mark from measurements and from using the critical speed formula. These are investigated here. Equation 4.7 can be written as

$$V_{cr}^2(1 - ef) = gR(f + e).\qquad(4.10)$$

The differential uncertainty formula (see Chapter 1) can be developed using calculus from Eq. 4.10 and written as

$$\frac{\delta V_{cr}}{V_{cr}} = \frac{1}{2}\left(\frac{\delta R}{R} + \frac{\delta f}{f + e} + \frac{\delta e}{f + e}\right).\qquad(4.11)$$

The quotient form, $\delta V_{cr}/V_{cr}$, of the uncertainty in Eq. 4.11 is sometimes referred to as the relative uncertainty. In the derivation of Eq. 4.11, second-order quantities (products of small numbers) such as ef and e^2 have been neglected because e ($e = \tan \gamma$) and f typically are much less than one. Equation 4.11 can be used to estimate the uncertainty associated with critical speed calculations. The values of the variations of the independent variables such as R, f, and e must be established for the conditions applicable to each particular reconstruction. (As mentioned in Chapter 1, care must be used in selecting the signs of the variations δR, δf, and δe.) In addition to Eq. 4.11, the uncertainty, δV_{cr}, can be computed by using Eq. 1.12. This gives

$$\delta V_{cr} = \frac{gR}{2V_{cr}}\sqrt{(f + e)^2 \frac{\delta R^2}{R^2} + \delta e^2 + \delta f^2}.\qquad(4.12)$$

Equation 4.12 often is preferred because it is less conservative than Eq. 4.11.

If Eq. 4.3 is used to determine the radius, R, then it can have its own uncertainty due to variations in the determination of the chord, c, and the middle ordinate, h. The method of differential variations can be applied to Eq. 4.3. It produces an expression for the relative uncertainty,

$$\frac{\delta R}{R} = 2\frac{\delta c}{c} - \frac{\delta h}{h}. \tag{4.13}$$

Equation 4.13 can be used independently or it can be used to eliminate $\delta R/R$ from Eqs. 4.11 and 4.12. In either case, the results provide the uncertainty in the estimate of the critical speed including the effects of measurement variations.

4.5.2   Accuracy of the Critical Speed Method

Using a value of R from Eq. 4.1 or Eq. 4.3 with a frictional drag coefficient, f, placed into Eq. 4.4 (or Eq. 4.7) to estimate forward vehicle speed is sometimes referred to as the *critical speed method* (CSM). The accuracy of this method was investigated by Brach[1] using an analysis of considerable experimental data gathered by Shelton.[13] The analysis shows that statistically significant differences exist in the accuracy of speed estimation between each of the driver control modes. Results were summarized as the difference between the measured speed of a vehicle beginning a yaw maneuver and the speed reconstructed using the CSM. The average differences between the calculated and measured speeds are:

1. Braking, -13.5%,
2. Coasting, -4.6%
3. Accelerating, -1.2%

As indicated by the negative signs, speed values of the vehicle computed by the CSM were, on average, lower than the measured speeds. Note that the trend from these data and Fig. 4.5 are identical; comparison with the results of the simulation implies that the radius measurements reported by Shelton[13] were made somewhere between the early, 1 s, and later, 3 s, portions of the trajectories. An analysis of the Shelton data showed that the accuracy of the CSM did not vary significantly with the experimental speeds over an experimental range of approximately 15 to 40 m/s (roughly 30 to 95 mph).

4.5.3   Statistical Variations

When investigating uncertainty, it is useful to know the statistical variations that arise due to measurements in a method such as the CSM. Shelton's data again provide some insight. Figure 4.6 shows the sample distribution of the uncertainty associated with the CSM for vehicles in coast mode (this mode is illustrated because it has the largest sample size and is most often encountered in practice). The shape of the histogram in Fig. 4.6 is reasonably close to that of a normal (Gaussian) distribution; transferring the properties of normal distributions to the CSM implies that the errors have a 95% confidence interval of about $\pm 11.5\%$ about the mean.

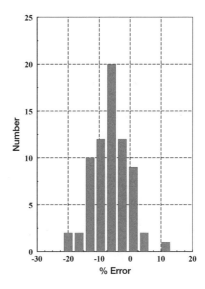

Figure 4.6
Distribution of a sample
of 70 values[13] of the
difference, in percent,
between calculated and
measured speeds for
coast driver control
mode. The mean value is
−4.6% and the standard
deviation is 5.76%.

Results by Heusser et al.[14] from four tests for each mode and using the radius computed from the outside rear tire gave these results: braking, −6.9 to 3.5%; coast, −3.1 to 0.2%; acceleration, −3.3 to 19.8%. These results for the coast mode fall within the results shown in Fig. 4.6, but the trend over the three modes is not the same as in Fig. 4.5.

Following Example 4.1, if two frictional coefficients were measured with val-   **Example 4.3**
ues of 0.85 and 0.87, and R is measured to within ±2%, estimate the uncertainty in the critical speed from the Taurus test.

Solution   Because the surface was reasonably level, e and δe are 0. Equation 4.11 gives

$$\frac{\delta V_{cr}}{V_{cr}} = \frac{1}{2}\left(\frac{\delta R}{R} + \frac{\delta f}{f}\right) = \frac{1}{2}\left(\frac{0.02R}{R} + \frac{0.87 - 0.85}{0.86}\right) = 0.022.$$

This implies that for these measurements, $\delta V_{cr} = 0.022\,(22.13) = 0.48$ m/s (1.57 ft/s); that is, $V_{cr} = 22.13 \pm 0.48$ m/s (49.5 ± 1.07 mph).

Equation 4.12 can also be used to estimate the uncertainty of V_{cr}. This gives

$$\frac{\delta V_{cr}}{V_{cr}} = \frac{9.81(58.20)}{2(22.13)^2}\sqrt{0.86^2(0.02)^2 + 0.02^2} = 0.015. \qquad \bigcirc$$

Martinez[15] reports tests where vehicles generated seven yaw marks. Each speed   **Example 4.4**
was measured using radar, each yaw mark radius was measured, and critical speeds were calculated. The road friction coefficient was measured independently to be $f = 0.85$. Results are as listed in Table 4.1.

  A. Let $\delta V_{cr}/V_{cr} = (V_m - V_r)/V_r$ from the table. Calculate the relative uncertainty, $\delta V_{cr}/V_r$, for each of the tests; find their mean and standard deviation.
  B. Compare these values to those from the measurements of Shelton (see Fig. 4.6).

Table 4.1
Results from
seven tests of
yawing vehicles
(data from Martinez[15]).

R, ft	V_r, mph (speed by radar)	V_m, mph (speed by calculation)
130	41	40
137	40	42
128	41	40
126	41	39
126	39	39
115	44	38
132	45	41

C. Assuming no uncertainty in radar measurements and that the variations in measurements of R are negligible, estimate the corresponding variations of the friction values.

Solution A Computed values of $\delta V_{cr}/V_{cr}$ are -0.0244, 0.0500, -0.0244, -0.0488, 0.0000, -0.1364, and -0.889. The mean and standard deviation of the measurements are, respectively

$$\bar{x} = -0.0390, \ s = 0.0605.$$

Solution B The corresponding values from Fig. 4.6 are $\bar{x} = -0.046$ and $s = 0.0575$. These indicate similar results from the different experiments.

Solution C Using Eq. 4.11 with $e = 0$ and $\delta R = 0$, and solving for δf, gives

$$\delta f = 2\frac{\delta V_{cr}}{V_{cr}}f = 2(0.0605)0.85 = 0.10,$$

where $\delta f = 0.10$ is an estimate of the variation of f from the Martinez tests. ◇

Reconstruction of Vehicular Rollover Accidents

5.1 Introduction

Rollover accidents typically occur at high speeds and have serious consequences for the vehicle occupants. The reconstructionist of a rollover accident is generally called on to determine the vehicle speed at the onset of loss of control. Reconstructions of these accidents include tasks such as the determination of the number of rolls of the vehicle, the position and orientation of the vehicle during the impacts with the ground during the roll, and the roll rate of the vehicle. These latter tasks are necessary for detailed analysis of the specific vehicle deformations, occupant motions, and injury causation.

The rollover of a vehicle can be broken down into three sequential phases: the pretrip phase, the trip phase, and the roll-out phase. This chapter presents techniques for the reconstruction of an entire rollover accident of a single vehicle through the analysis of each of these three phases. The conditions and characteristics of these phases can vary widely from accident to accident. Application of the methods presented here requires evaluation and possible modification on a case-by-case basis depending on specific circumstances. The beginning and end of each phase are defined, and techniques for the reconstruction of the speed change of a vehicle during these three phases are described.

The techniques presented in this chapter are applicable to the reconstruction of rollover accidents involving standard four-wheeled light vehicles. Light vehicles include cars, pickup trucks, vans, and sport utility vehicles. A subset of the methods sometimes can be applied to the reconstruction of the rollover of other vehicles, such as articulated vehicles and some large straight trucks. However, heavy trucks, commercial vehicles, tractor semitrailers, and military vehicles frequently have special characteristics that are not considered within the scope of this chapter. Some of these characteristics are: shifting and sloshing loads, articulation, and torsional compliance of the trailer(s). These topics and others are investigated elsewhere.[1] That reference has a large bibliography pertaining to the many facets and characteristics of the rollover of commercial vehicles.

The topics of roof crush, occupant kinematics, and occupant kinetics are frequently of interest following a vehicle rollover accident. These topics also are not covered here. More than 100 papers have been written since the 1960s regarding the analysis of roof crush and occupant injury as it pertains to rollover. See, for example, Orlowski et al.,[2] Bahling et al.,[3] Moffatt and Padmanaban,[4] and Rains and Kanianthra.[5]

5.2   Rollover Test Methods

Vehicle rollover testing has been under investigation and development for decades with no consensus on a methodology. One of the principal motivations of the research on this topic stems from the goal of establishing a repeatable and realistic rollover testing methodology. Additional motivation comes from the desire to conduct rollover testing to establish the conditions under which a vehicle will or will not roll. Determining such conditions is currently something that Federal Motor Vehicle Safety Standard (FMVSS) 208, does not address.[6] Most of the testing methods described in the literature, although frequently discussing the FMVSS 208 rollover test, differ significantly from the FMVSS 208 dolly rollover test procedure.

In the FMVSS 208 rollover test, the test vehicle is loaded onto a movable platform, as shown in Fig. 5.1. The vehicle and platform are accelerated to

Figure 5.1
FMVSS 208 dolly
rollover test.

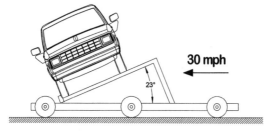

30 mph and then decelerated to 0 mph in not more than 3 ft. The vehicle is predisposed to roll over because the platform on which it rests supports the vehicle at 23°. Some alternative test methods have examined dolly systems that facilitate the assessment of characteristics of a specific rollover accident.[7]

At the time of the publication of this book, the National Highway Traffic Safety Administration (NHTSA) was in the process of incorporating a dynamic rollover testing into their New Car Assessment Program (NCAP).[8] This test is based on a "fishhook" steering maneuver that consists of a number of abrupt turns at varying speeds performed with a given vehicle. A computerized steering system is used to maintain objectivity with respect to the input to the vehicle.

Vehicles manufactured for the 2004 model year will be the first vehicles evaluated by the new system.

Other rollover test research has focused primarily on three different methodologies. In the first, the vehicle is accelerated laterally via a cable system. The tires of the vehicle slide laterally on a road surface coated with a lubricant, such as a soap solution, to reduce the frictional drag. The vehicle is released from the tow system just prior to impact with a curb or soil. The interaction with the curb or soil precipitates a rollover of the vehicle.[9,10] In a second methodology, the rollover propensity of vehicles has been investigated through steering maneuvers such as J-turns, obstacle avoidance courses, and similar situations. Some of these tests use human drivers in a vehicle equipped with outriggers.[11] Others have used remote steering equipment rather than drivers.[7] The dynamic effects of outrigger design on the response of a vehicle tested under various handling maneuvers have been investigated.[12] A third method of rollover testing is aimed primarily at establishing a testing procedure that gives more control over the conditions of initial contact between the vehicle and the ground during a rollover accident. In this scenario, the vehicle is suspended through its roll axis on a platform traveling at a prescribed velocity. The vehicle is suspended at a prescribed height from the ground and is spun about its roll axis at a known rate. After it is released from the platform it falls and strikes the roadway at a predetermined orientation.[13] All of these tests contribute to the body of rollover test data from which reconstructionists can obtain data and insight into the behavior of vehicles involved in rollover accidents.

Although the reconstruction of most accidents, rollover accidents included, typically proceeds in a reverse chronological fashion, the three phases of a rollover accident will be presented here in the order of occurrence. Section 5.7 demonstrates the application of some of the analysis techniques developed in this chapter. The reverse chronological approach is used in that example. Prior to looking at the three phases, a section on the general documentation of the site and scene (see Glossary) information and evidence is covered. Additional information about some specific aspects of the documentation of the accident site and the accident vehicle is also covered in more detail.

5.3 Documentation of the Accident Site

An important step in the reconstruction of a vehicular rollover accident is acquisition of the evidence that can be used to determine the path of the vehicle prior to and during the roll phase. This information should be incorporated into a scale diagram. The importance of this scale diagram for the reconstruction of a rollover accident cannot be overstated. Accurate information about the physical characteristics of the site and the location and orientation of the vehicle as it moves through each of the rollover phases must be based on physical evidence. Care should be taken to ensure that the information measured at the scene by the police, measured by the reconstructionist during site inspections, and obtained by photogrammetric or other methods is accurate. Significant roadway features with which the vehicle interacted, such as inclines, trees, utility poles, fences, culvert headers, and driveway surfaces, should be located accurately on the accident diagram. Features and evidence created by the vehicle, such as rim strikes, scrapes, scuffs, gouges, and tire marks, should also be accurately located on the accident diagram. In addition to these marks and the generic site information such as road width, utility poles, and police reference points, information on the accident diagram should include the rest position and orientation of the vehicle. Information can also include paint transfers and the location of any parts that separated from the vehicle during the roll phase. Items frequently separated from the vehicle include side mirrors, lenses from exterior lights and/or complete light assemblies, glass from broken windows and mirrors, hood ornaments, and possibly some vehicle contents. Such items typically are located on or near the path of the vehicle downstream of the trip location. The rest position of any occupants ejected from the vehicle should be included on the accident diagram.

5.4   Pretrip Phase

The pretrip trajectory of the vehicle typically involves the yawing of the vehicle. This yaw orientation of the vehicle is defined by the vehicle sideslip angle, α, which is the angle between the mass center velocity and the vehicle heading axis. This motion, coupled with translational motion, develops lateral forces at the contact patches of the tires. The development of these forces is usually accompanied by the creation of tire marks on the roadway or furrowing or surface disruption in the case of this motion of the vehicle off-road. The resulting tire marks, typically from the leading side tires, are diverging as the vehicle translates and rotates. The vehicle sideslip angle of a yawing vehicle and a set of diverging tire marks is shown in Fig. 5.2.

Figure 5.2
Diverging tire marks associated with the pretrip phase of a rollover accident. (α, vehicle sideslip angle.)

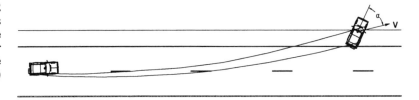

A traditional method for the reconstruction of the speed of the vehicle at the start of the pretrip phase of a rollover accident is to divide the vehicle trajectory into segments and compute the change in vehicle speed due to the energy loss of sliding for each of the segments. This process is performed in reverse chronological order starting with the speed of the vehicle at the beginning of the trip phase.[14,15] This approach requires knowledge of the conditions of the vehicle and roadway during the pretrip trajectory. Neglecting aerodynamic forces and the possible interaction with off-road items, the speed of the vehicle changes due only to frictional forces developed between the tires and the surface over which the vehicle is traveling. The work done by the frictional forces acting at the four wheels over a given distance is equal to the change in kinetic energy of the vehicle over the same distance. The presence of a grade or an appreciable bank or crown of the road may also influence the deceleration of the vehicle.

Previous applications of this approach take into account the drag associated only with vehicle sideslip angle with the assumption that the steer angle, if any, of the front wheels does not greatly affect the overall deceleration of the vehicle. This method also assumes that the wheels are free to rotate about the axle while the vehicle traverses the pretrip path. The effects of combined braking (if any) and tire sideslip forces (see Chapter 2) are ignored. Also, the effects of the vehicle's yaw velocity on the tire forces are ignored. The method proposes an effective vehicle drag factor, f_E, to characterize the deceleration of the center of mass of the vehicle. The effective drag factor is based on the average vehicle sideslip angle over the selected segment and the nominal drag factor for the tires and the roadway for the conditions over that segment of the path. The effective drag factor is given by Orlowski et al.[2] as

$$f_E = f_t \sin \alpha, \tag{5.1}$$

where f_t is the nominal drag factor between the tires and the road surface, and α is the average sideslip angle of the vehicle over the segment of interest.

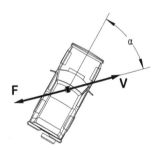

Figure 5.3
Vehicle with vehicle sideslip angle, α, with velocity and force vectors shown.

Figure 5.3 shows the vehicle sideslip angle, α, the vehicle velocity vector, **V**, of the center of mass, and the vector force, **F**, that acts at the center of mass of the vehicle to reduce the velocity of the vehicle. This equation can be augmented to include the effects of engine drag, wheel rolling resistance, and the presence of a grade, resulting in the equation

$$f_E = f_t \sin \alpha + f_f \cos \alpha + \sin \theta. \tag{5.2}$$

In this equation, f_p is the drag associated with the powertrain and rolling resistance, and θ is the angle associated with the average grade of the road in the direction of vehicle travel. A positive θ is associated with uphill vehicle motion, and negative θ is associated with downhill vehicle motion.

Braking has been incorporated into the development of this technique[15] such that striation patterns in tire marks can be interpreted as the application of braking in the presence of a yaw angle. Few publications exist that consider the interpretation of the angular characteristics of striation patterns in tire marks.*

The model presented—in which a single effective drag factor acts at the center of mass of the yawing and translating vehicle—is, in effect, an approximate combined-force tire model. The sine and cosine of the vehicle sideslip angle are used to apportion the lateral and longitudinal forces generated at the tires into components acting along the direction of motion of the vehicle at its center of mass. This technique neglects the moments about the vehicle mass center associated with these forces. Although this method of analysis for a yawing and translating vehicle has been in use for many years, no literature exists demonstrating its accuracy. Comparison of this method to the use of a vehicle dynamics approach for predicting the motion of the vehicle is included in Example 5.1.

The use of a vehicle dynamics simulation that includes a valid tire model (see Chapter 11) is the most accurate means available to model the complex pretrip motion of a translating and rotating vehicle. Such a simulation method can be applied provided the necessary vehicle parameters for the model, such as the tire, vehicle, and environmental characteristics, are available or can be reasonably estimated. An example is presented below that demonstrates the use of a vehicle dynamics program to a translating and rotating vehicle. An example in Section 5.7 extends the use of the program to the reconstruction of the pretrip phase of a rollover accident. The use of a vehicle dynamics simulation for this purpose has appeared in other publications.[17,18]

The tire marks at the start of the pretrip phase frequently meet the guidelines for the use of the critical speed formula (Chapter 4). Under these circumstances, the critical speed formula can be applied to establish the initial velocity of the vehicle for input into the vehicle dynamics program. The use of this method is demonstrated in the following example.

Example 5.1 This example presents the results of two different methods to model the pretrip motion of a rollover. The first is the use of a vehicle dynamics simulation (see Chapter 11). The second is to divide the trajectory into segments and use different equivalent frictional drag coefficients for each segment based on the sideslip angle of the vehicle. Both methods match the computed yawing motions to a set of tire marks produced experimentally. The experimental data used in this example is not from a rollover accident. There was no trip; the vehicle came to a stop on all four wheels. In an actual rollover accident, the distance over which the tire marks appear will likely be shorter than the marks produced in this test for the same initial speed.

Figure 5.4 shows diverging tire marks produced during a vehicle test. A vehicle is superimposed at the start and the finish of the tire marks to illustrate its positions and orientations. Matching the paths of the tire marks provides a basis of comparison of the analyses and experimental results. The

---

*One publication that considers the characteristics of tire marks made by skidding, scrubbing, and sliding tires is available from the Northwestern University Traffic Institute.[16]

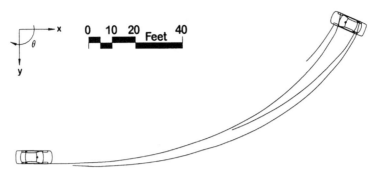

Figure 5.4
Experimentally measured
tire marks from a
simultaneously translating
and rotating vehicle (data
acquired from Cliff et al.[19]
Used with permission).

translational displacements of the center of mass and the final angular orientation of the vehicle predicted in successive calculations are compared to the motion of the vehicle from the test until an acceptable match is found.

The vehicle used in the test was a 1991 Honda Accord EX four-door sedan. Vehicle parameters needed in the analysis such as weight, inertia, and geometric properties were selected from available industry information unless more accurate information was specifically reported in the reference.[19] The speed of the vehicle prior to the input of the steering maneuver, 45.4 mph (73.1 km/h), was measured with a fifth wheel during the testing.

Solution A   Vehicle Dynamics Simulation. Physical vehicle and tire parameters are needed in order to use a vehicle dynamics simulation program. The tire model in the vehicle dynamics simulation used in this example (see Chapter 11) requires that the longitudinal slip coefficient, C_s, and the lateral sideslip coefficient, C_α, values for each of the four tires (see Chapter 2) be known. Values for specific vehicles and tires are usually not easily found in the open literature. However, typical values can sometimes be obtained through analysis of experimental data available in the literature. For this example, the longitudinal stiffness coefficient, C_s, has a value in the range of 44.5 kN (10,000 lb) to 53.4 kN (12,000 lb) determined from experimental data.[20] Values of C_α for a passenger tire depend on the normal force at the tire. Values of C_α of 33.8 kN/rad (F_z = 2000 N) to 55.6 kN/rad (F_z = 4500 N) are determined from experimentally available data.[21]

Because the initial speed of the vehicle in this case is known, parameters were varied in the simulation to obtain an acceptable solution using an iterative approach. The main parameters varied within appropriate ranges were the steering angle, the rate at which the steering angle was applied, the ratio between the lateral coefficient for the front tires, $C_{\alpha 1}$ and $C_{\alpha 2}$, and the lateral coefficient for the rear tires, $C_{\alpha 3}$ and $C_{\alpha 4}$. The ratio $C_{\alpha 1}$:$C_{\alpha 3}$ ($C_{\alpha 2}$:$C_{\alpha 4}$ is identical) used in the final analysis was 1.82:1. The tire-to-road frictional drag coefficient was increased from the nominal value of 0.75, measured at the testing site, to 0.9, in part to account for aerodynamic drag of a moving vehicle. The steering angle at the front wheels used through the entire maneuver was −10°. The 1991 Honda Accord has a steering ratio of 17.55:1. This gives a steering wheel rotation of 176° for the input at the start of the maneuver and is consistent with the description given in the reference for a sudden steering input of about 180°.

The tire marks were measured at the test site using a total station. A computer-aided design program was used to fit a circular arc to the first 48 ft (14.6 m) of the tire mark for the right front tire. The radius of the resulting circle was 194.5 ft (59.3 m). Using the critical speed formula (see Chapter 4) and a frictional drag coefficient for a dry road surface of 0.75, the speed of the vehicle at the start of the tire marks is determined to be about 46.7 mph (75.2 km/h). This compares closely with the speed of the vehicle measured using a fifth wheel of 45.4 mph (73.1 km/h). The initial angular velocity of the vehicle for the simulation was set to zero because the maneuver was a sudden steering wheel input of about 180°. An iterative approach was used with the vehicle dynamics simulation to obtain an acceptable match between the location and orientation of the vehicle at the point of rest.

The motion of the vehicle predicted by the vehicle dynamics simulation was close to the motion of the test data within several iterations. Using the coordinate system shown in Fig. 5.4, the final position of the center of mass and the angular orientation of the vehicle, (Δx, Δy, $\Delta\theta$), after testing were (132.7 ft, −56.6 ft, −156.6° [40.4 m, −17.3 m, −156.6°]). The values predicted by the vehicle dynamics simulation were (130.7 ft, −56.3 ft, −174.6° [39.8 m, −17.2 m, −174.6°]). Figure 5.5 shows the input data to the simulation. Figure 5.6 shows

Figure 5.5 Input data to the vehicle dynamics simulation, Example 5.1.

VEHICLE DYNAMICAL SIMULATION

1991 Accord EX

	single vehicle (or tow vehicle)				semitrailer	
	weight, W_C	inertia, J_C			weight, W_T	inertia, J_T
	3185.7	1870.6			0.0	0.0
	L_1	L_2	L_3	L_4	L_5	L_6
lengths, ft	3.48	3.48	5.44	5.44	0.00	0.00
	W_1	W_2	W_3	W_4	W_5	W_6
widths, ft	2.42	2.42	2.42	2.42	0.00	0.00
trailer/pin			L_{CP}	W_{CP}	L_{TP}	W_{TP}
dimensions, ft			0.00	0.00	0.00	0.00
center of gravity	h_C				h_T	
heights, ft	1.77				0.00	
tire lateral (steering)	$C_{\alpha 1}$	$C_{\alpha 2}$	$C_{\alpha 3}$	$C_{\alpha 4}$	$C_{\alpha 5}$	$C_{\alpha 6}$
coefficients, lb/rad	12460.0	12460.0	6834.6	6834.6	0.0	0.0
tire forward (braking)	C_{s1}	C_{s2}	C_{s3}	C_{s4}	C_{s5}	C_{s6}
coefficients, lb/rad	10000.0	10000.0	10000.0	10000.0	0.0	0.0
wheel brake slip	s_1	s_2	s_3	s_4	s_5	s_6
values, 0 < s < 1	0.008	0.008	0.000	0.000	0.000	0.000
wheel acceleration		vehicle uniform accel, g's		0.000		
traction coefficients	0.00	0.00	0.00	0.00	0.00	0.00
	X_C	X_C - dot	Y_C	Y_C - dot		
initial conditions	0.00	66.20	0.00	0.00		
	θ_C	θ_C - dot			θ_T	θ_T - dot
initial conditions	0.00	0.00			0.00	0.00
steer angle, δ, deg	-10.000					

Sheet 1:	data input
Sheet 2:	motion output
Sheet 3:	tire ground forces
Sheet 4:	graphs

			friction coefficients		
	R_W, road		road	shoulder	
roadway	width, ft		f_R	f_B	
parameters	24.0		0.90	0.90	
	integration	print	steering	number of	
program	interval, s	interval	mode, KM	wheels	
run	0.0050	4	-1	4	no trailer
parameters	final time, s				
	4.00		KM	mode	
			-1	tabular steer (S5:T25)	
			0	all wheels locked	
			1	lane change	

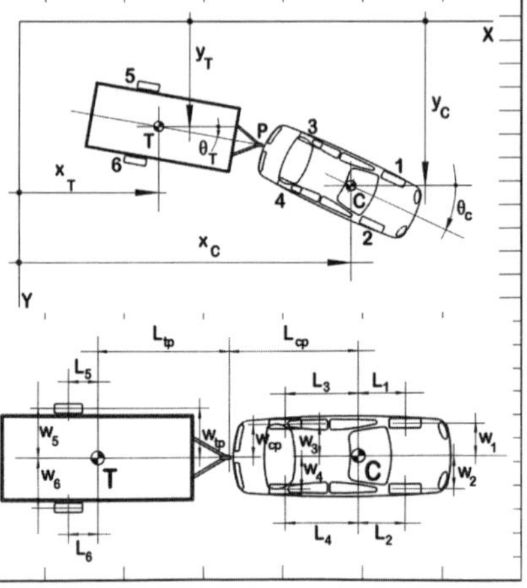

the results of the simulation for the start and the finish of the simulation in tabular form. While the results of the analysis capture the motion of the vehicle, additional iterations could have been performed to give a closer match, particularly for the final angular orientation.

time, t	X	X - Vel	Y	Y - Vel	θ	θ - Vel	δ
s	ft	ft/s	ft	ft/s	deg	deg/s	deg
0.00	0.00	66.20	0.00	0.00	0.00	0.00	0.000
0.02	1.32	66.13	0.00	-0.29	-0.03	-3.01	-10.000
0.04	2.65	66.06	-0.01	-0.59	-0.12	-5.95	-10.000
0.06	3.97	65.99	-0.03	-0.88	-0.27	-8.80	-10.000
0.08	5.29	65.93	-0.05	-1.17	-0.47	-11.56	-10.000
0.10	6.60	65.86	-0.07	-1.47	-0.73	-14.19	-10.000
0.12	7.92	65.78	-0.11	-1.77	-1.04	-16.68	-10.000
0.14	9.23	65.71	-0.14	-2.08	-1.40	-19.04	-10.000
0.16	10.55	65.63	-0.19	-2.39	-1.80	-21.24	-10.000
0.18	11.86	65.56	-0.24	-2.72	-2.24	-23.31	-10.000
0.20	13.17	65.48	-0.30	-3.05	-2.73	-25.23	-10.000
0.22	14.48	65.39	-0.36	-3.39	-3.25	-27.01	-10.000
0.24	15.79	65.30	-0.43	-3.74	-3.81	-28.68	-10.000
3.24	128.57	8.44	-55.87	-2.92	-167.85	-53.36	-10.000
3.26	128.73	8.37	-55.93	-2.67	-168.89	-49.68	-10.000
3.28	128.90	8.31	-55.98	-2.48	-169.84	-45.49	-10.000
3.30	129.07	8.24	-56.03	-2.31	-170.70	-41.03	-10.000
3.32	129.23	8.18	-56.07	-2.15	-171.48	-36.48	-10.000
3.34	129.39	8.12	-56.11	-1.99	-172.16	-31.92	-10.000
3.36	129.55	8.06	-56.15	-1.83	-172.76	-27.42	-10.000
3.38	129.72	8.01	-56.19	-1.66	-173.26	-23.01	-10.000
3.40	129.88	7.95	-56.22	-1.49	-173.68	-18.70	-10.000
3.42	130.03	7.90	-56.25	-1.31	-174.01	-14.53	-10.000
3.44	130.19	7.85	-56.27	-1.13	-174.26	-10.51	-10.000
3.46	130.35	7.80	-56.29	-0.94	-174.43	-6.68	-10.000
3.48	130.50	7.76	-56.31	-0.75	-174.53	-3.09	-10.000
3.50	130.66	7.71	-56.32	-0.58	-174.56	0.17	-10.000

Figure 5.6
Output data from the vehicle dynamics simulation for the first ¼ second and the last ¼ second.

Solution B Segmented Sliding. The speed of the vehicle at the start of the marks was also determined using the method of dividing the path of the vehicle into segments and assessing the speed change of the vehicle during each segment using formulas for constant deceleration.[2,15] The path of the vehicle was divided into six segments as shown in Fig. 5.7. The first four segments

Figure 5.7
The six segments of the vehicle path used for the analysis and the associated vehicle sideslip angles. Continuous lines indicate tire paths.

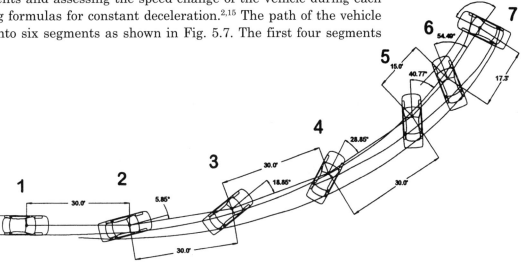

were each 30 ft (9.1 m) long and the last two segments were 15 (4.6) and 17.3 ft (5.3 m) long, respectively. The location of the vehicle at the end of each segment is indicated in the figure.

The method was applied using a locked-wheel-skid frictional drag coefficient of $f = 0.9$ and a powertrain drag coefficient of $f_p = 0.1$. The method was used to predict the decrease in the speed of the translating and yawing vehicle. Results are shown in Table 5.1. The calculations yield zero vehicle speed after travel-

Table 5.1
Predicted vehicle velocity at the seven vehicle locations using the segmentation method.

Path segment	Initial speed (mph)	Average vehicle sideslip angle (deg)	Equivalent frictional drag
1–2	46.2	3.0	$f_{eq} = 0.15$
2–3	44.7	12.4	$f_{eq} = 0.29$
3–4	41.7	23.9	$f_{eq} = 0.46$
4–5	36.5	34.9	$f_{eq} = 0.60$
5–6	28.2	47.7	$f_{eq} = 0.73$
6–7	21.6	78.4	$f_{eq} = 0.90$
7	0.0	—	—

ing the necessary distance with an initial vehicle speed of 46.2 mph (74.4 km/h) compared to the speed measured experimentally of 45.4 mph (73.1 km/h).

While the use of this segmentation method has produced reasonably accurate results when applied to the motion of the vehicle in this example, the accuracy of the segmentation method over a range of vehicle motion and conditions remains unverified.

5.5   Trip Phase

A vehicle that is translating and rotating, as in the pretrip phase of a rollover accident, generates lateral forces at the tire–road interface. These lateral forces acting over time create impulses at the leading side tires that impose a moment about the center of mass of the vehicle. These impulses can cause the center of mass of the vehicle to rise. If the impulses are large enough and occur over a short time duration, the moment of the impulse will cause the vehicle to roll over. The process whereby the short-duration, large tire forces cause the center of mass of the vehicle to rise and the vehicle to roll is referred to as the trip phase of a rollover accident.

An impulse is defined as the integral of a force with respect to time. Therefore, the magnitude of an impulse is a function of the duration of the applied force as well as the magnitude of the force. An impulse of a certain magnitude is required to elevate the center of mass of the vehicle and cause the vehicle to roll. The impulse acting at the leading side tires of a vehicle undergoing yaw can be such that it is a large force applied over a short time, such as when a vehicle with appreciable yaw encounters a significant terrain feature such as a curb or a transition from ice to pavement. For a vehicle with sufficiently high speed, the impulse can also be a result of a force applied over a longer time duration. This is seen, for example, in a rollover that occurs after significant yaw and translation of a vehicle on a road surface. The only difference between the two scenarios is the magnitude of the force and the duration of application.

Before presenting the reconstruction of the trip phase of a rollover accident, several models are presented that consider the tripping of a rigid body.

5.5.1   Analysis of Vehicle Trip

An understanding of the trip phase of a rollover accident begins with a review of the various mathematical approaches to quantify the trip of a vehicle. These approaches start by looking at the roll of a vehicle as a static or quasi-static event. More involved approaches look at the trip of a vehicle in a dynamic fashion. Several of these analytical treatments are presented here starting with a quasi-static approach and then looking at some of the dynamic analyses. This topic is presented as a means to understand the complex nature of the tripping of a vehicle. These methods have limited application as tools for reconstructing rollover accidents.

Consider the vehicle shown in Fig. 5.8 with weight $W = mg$. Assume that the vehicle is moving at a constant forward velocity on a curve of constant

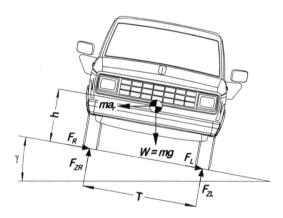

Figure 5.8
Force diagram of a vehicle.

radius on a road with superelevation, γ, as shown. The constant velocity of the vehicle creates a steady-state condition such that no roll acceleration of the vehicle results. The radial acceleration acting on the vehicle is indicated by a_r. The force F_R represents the total lateral force acting at the right front and right rear wheels, and the force F_L represents the total lateral force acting at the left front and left rear wheels. F_{ZR} and F_{ZL} are the total normal forces at the right and left wheels, respectively. Taking moments about the center of contact for the passenger-side tires of the vehicle gives the following equation:

$$\Sigma M_R = 0$$
$$= \frac{-MgT}{2} \cos \theta - Mgh \sin \theta + F_{ZL}T + Ma_rh \cos \theta + \frac{Ma_rT}{2} \sin \theta. \quad (5.3)$$

For small angle approximations, suitable for a typical superelevation, $\cos\theta \approx 1$ and $\sin\theta \approx \theta$. Using these approximations and solving for the radial acceleration, a_r/g (yielding the resulting quantity in units of gravity or g),

$$\frac{a_r}{g} = \frac{h\theta + \dfrac{T}{2} - \dfrac{F_{ZL}T}{Mg}}{h + \dfrac{T}{2}\theta}.$$

(5.4)

Setting the superelevation to zero, $\theta = 0$, and letting the normal force at the inside tire, F_{ZL}, go to zero (considered in the present analysis as the start of the trip of the vehicle), reduces the equation to

$$\frac{a_r}{g} = \frac{T}{2h}.$$

(5.5)

This result yields an acceleration higher than is actually required to initiate roll of an actual vehicle under these circumstances. The suspension on an actual vehicle and the compliance of the tires can reduce the acceleration (and hence the velocity) at which F_{ZL} will go to zero. This is due to the fact that with a typical suspension system, the body of the vehicle will lean toward the outside of the curve, thereby shortening the moment arm of the force, F_{ZR}. This leaning also has the potential effect of reducing the height of the center of mass as the suspension on the outer side of the vehicle compresses, an effect potentially offset by the fact that the suspension on the inboard side of the vehicle will be relaxing. The details of the effects of a vehicle suspension under these conditions have been previously considered.[22–24] Methods to experimentally determine parameters of suspension systems that affect vehicle roll characteristics have been presented elsewhere.[25]

The simple formula in Eq. 5.5 is known as the static stability factor (SSF). It is the basis for the rollover resistance rating system put in place by the NHTSA in January 2001. Under this system, a star ranking is assigned to a vehicle based on its SSF and is used to indicate the propensity of the vehicle to roll over in a single-vehicle crash. The rationale used in developing the rollover resistance rating system is that the smaller the ratio of T/2h, the more likely it is that the vehicle will roll over. The data for each vehicle is presented to the general public as a star rating system in which five stars is the highest rating (less likely to roll) and a single star is the lowest rating. Details of the five-star system, ratings for the vehicles tested, and additional information can be found at the NHTSA website (www.nhtsa.dot.gov). A description of the technique used by NHTSA to measure the height of the center of mass of vehicles, a critical parameter in the rating but one not easily measured, is not included at that website but is presented elsewhere.[26]

In addition to the quasi-static model presented above, there have been other models developed in an attempt to quantify the dynamics of a vehicle moving laterally and tripped as a result of encountering a rigid stop. A typical criterion for rollover is the minimum velocity required for the center of mass of the vehicle to reach the position above the line defined by the points of contact at tire patches. This position of the center of mass is frequently referred to as the *neutral stability position*. These models use the principles of the conservation of energy and impulse/momentum.

Consider the block shown in Fig. 5.9 with initial velocity, V, encountering a rigid stop at point O and rotating to the position of neutral stability as shown.

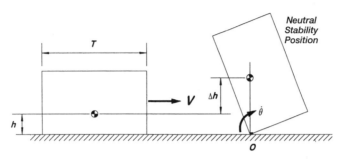

Figure 5.9
Sliding block with velocity, V, encountering a rigid stop.

Assuming that no energy is lost at the point of impact ($e = 1$), the kinetic energy immediately before contact can be equated with the increase in potential energy at neutral stability due to Δh. Solving for V yields the following equation for the minimum velocity for the block to reach the position of neutral stability:

$$V = \sqrt{2gh\left(\sqrt{\left(\frac{T}{2h}\right)^2 - 1} - 1\right)}. \qquad (5.6)$$

Another approach uses the conservation of angular momentum in conjunction with the conservation of energy after impact. The linear momentum of the vehicle prior to trip is equated to the angular momentum of the vehicle after impact. The condition of rotation of the vehicle to the neutral stability point, as shown in Fig. 5.9, is again used for the condition of vehicle roll. The conservation of angular momentum of the block about the contact point, O, gives

$$I_o\dot{\theta} = mVh. \qquad (5.7)$$

For the block to rotate such that it reaches the angle for neutral stability, the kinetic energy of the block just after contact is equated with the change in potential energy due to Δh. When the center of mass of the block is above point O, the following condition must be met:

$$\frac{1}{2}I_o\dot{\theta} = mg\left(\sqrt{\left(\frac{T}{2}\right)^2 + h^2} - h\right). \qquad (5.8)$$

Solving Eq. 5.7 for $\dot{\theta}_o$, substituting into Eq. 5.8, and solving for the velocity, V, gives

$$V = \sqrt{\frac{2I_og}{mh}\left(\sqrt{\left(\frac{T}{2h}\right)^2 + 1} - 1\right)}. \qquad (5.9)$$

In contrast to the results for the conservation of energy approach, Eq. 5.9 depends on knowledge of the rotational inertia of the vehicle, not just the height of the center of mass and the track width. Consideration of this issue and the sensitivity of the equation to T and h are given elsewhere.[27,28]

The two models presented above predict the velocity required for the vehicle to reach the neutral stability point after encountering a rigid stop. The time duration of the tripping force was not considered. A model has been developed called the constant force trip model[9] that includes time explicitly. Although derived in a fashion similar to the previous models, this model is different in that it considers the impulse applied at the leading side tires by providing a relationship between the magnitude of a force, which is independent of time, and the duration of application of that force necessary for the vehicle to achieve the neutral stability position. Three equations of motion of the yawing vehicle are written, two translational and one for the rotational degree of freedom. The equation of motion for the rotational degree of freedom is integrated with respect to time and is substituted into the expression that equates the kinetic energy of the rolling and translating vehicle to the increase in potential energy in reaching the neutral stability point, producing the equation

$$\left(\frac{F_T}{mg} - \frac{T}{2h}\right)\Delta\tau^2 + \frac{T}{2h}\left(\frac{F_T}{mg} - \frac{T}{2h}\right)\Delta\tau^2 = \frac{2}{mgh}\left(I_R + \frac{mT^2}{4}\right)\left[\sqrt{\left(\frac{T}{2h}\right)^2 + 1} - 1\right].$$

$$(5.10)$$

F_T is the total lateral force applied to the vehicle at the leading tires, I_R is the roll mass moment of inertia of the vehicle about the center of mass, h is the height of the center of mass, T is the track width of the vehicle, $\Delta\tau$ is the trip force duration, and m is the mass of the vehicle. Equation 5.10 can be solved for F_T. After some simplification, and using $I_R = mk_R^2$, the solution is

$$\frac{F_T}{mg} = \frac{1}{2\Delta\tau}\left[\Delta\tau\left(\frac{T}{2h}\right) + \sqrt{\Delta\tau^2\left(\frac{T}{2h}\right)^2 + \frac{8h}{g}\left(\frac{k_R^2}{h^2} + \left(\frac{T}{2h}\right)^2\right)\left(\sqrt{\left(\frac{T}{2h}\right)^2 + 1} - 1\right)}\right]. \quad (5.11)$$

The relationship in Eq. 5.11 is not contained in the paper describing the model. It was obtained through a symbolic solution of Eq. 5.10. A slightly different, but equivalent, form of this solution appears elsewhere.[28] In contrast to the previous models that predict the speed of the vehicle required for trip, this model predicts the constant level of force required for trip of the vehicle for a given set of vehicle characteristics and time duration of application, $\Delta\tau$. It can be useful for the assessment of the effect that the change of a parameter will have on the level of force and the required time of application to roll a vehicle.

Equation 5.11 is useful for an assessment of the nature of the impulse required to achieve rollover of a vehicle as the vehicle parameters change. Figure 5.9 shows a plot of the normalized lateral force, F_T/mg, as given in Eq. 5.11, as a function of time duration. The three curves depict the normalized

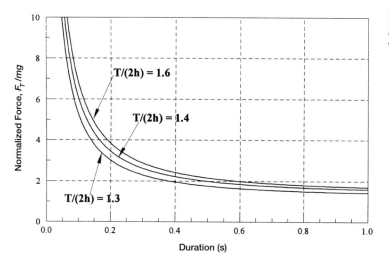

Figure 5.10
F_T/mg versus duration for differing $T/2h$.

force, F_T/mg, as a function of time duration for three different track widths, T, of 4.5 ft (1.4 m), 5.0 ft (1.5 m) and 5.5 ft (1.7 m). Other vehicle parameters were held fixed: $h = 1.8$ ft (0.5 m), m = 93.2 lb-s^2/ft (68.7 N-s^2/m), and $I_R = 400$ ft-lb-s^2 (27.4 m-N-s^2) held constant. The trend shown by the curves predicts that the vehicle with the wider track width (with constant height of the mass center) will require a larger impulse to cause the vehicle to roll. Favorable comparison of this model to data collected from testing is presented in the reference.[9]

The progression of these models leads to the conclusion that the rollover of a yawing vehicle is the result of a lateral impulse applied to the vehicle at the leading side wheels. The application of such an impulse leads to an increase in the angular momentum sufficient to cause the center of mass of the vehicle to rotate past the position above the line defined by the contact locations of leading side tires.

Models of vehicle trip of increasing complexity have also been investigated. Several of the models are similar in development to the models presented above, but include suspension characteristics for the vehicle.[22,23]

5.5.2   Complex Vehicle Trip Models

Various authors have derived the differential equations of motion of a sliding vehicle such that the solution (the position and velocity of the center of gravity) is obtained through numerical integration.[27,29–31] Moreover, analysis of rollover sequences of vehicles using dynamic modeling packages such as ADAMS[6] has been performed.[32]

A review of the issues involved in the application of full-vehicle models for the reconstruction of rollover accidents, and in particular the roll phase of the accident, has been presented.[30] There are two principal difficulties with the application of these models for reconstruction of rollover accidents listed in that reference. These two principal difficulties are as follows:

1. It is difficult to obtain accurate input for the analysis. This input includes vehicle parameters such as values for all three mass moments of inertia,

tire characteristics, and the mass of the vehicle at the time of the accident. In these modeling situations an accurate combined (lateral and longitudinal) tire force model is needed. Moreover, accurate terrain information is needed.

2. The task of reconstructing a rollover accident to obtain a satisfactory match between the physical evidence and the vehicle response predicted by the computer program can be time-consuming. The ability to obtain a reasonable match between the physical evidence and the vehicle response from the model decreases with the number of rolls involved in the reconstruction. The difficulty of this method of reconstruction increases if there are impacts with roadside objects such as trees, utility poles, culvert headers, fences, and so forth, as each impact must be modeled.

Typically a reconstructionist is not interested in the ability to predict the detailed rollover motion of a vehicle or may have limited time to devote to the reconstruction of any given rollover accident. Therefore, the models provided above and those in the references are presented for those who wish to gain insight into the nature and characteristics of a rollover accident.

While useful in gaining insight into the mechanics of a tripping vehicle, these models have limited utility in the reconstruction of the trip phase of a rollover accident. Reconstructing the trip phase of a rollover accident requires that the position and orientation of the vehicle at the start and end of the phase be known. The location of the vehicle at the end of the trip phase can often be determined from physical evidence during a site inspection or from photographs. The location of the vehicle at the start of the trip phase is often much more difficult to establish from physical evidence. Therefore, it is established using the vehicle position at the end of the trip phase and an appropriate deceleration of a certain duration. This approach is presented in the next section.

5.5.3   Reconstruction of the Trip Phase

The location of the leading side tires at the termination of the trip phase is typically easy to establish. In the case of a rollover that takes place on a road surface, the end of sliding and start of the rolling of the vehicle is often accompanied by the end of the tire marks and sometimes rim gouges on the roadway. In the case of a rollover that occurs off the road surface, the location of the end of trip phase is often associated with the end of furrowing of the leading side wheels in dirt or turf. The tire marks may also end at an object or structure, such as a curb or ditch, that applies a short-duration impulse to the leading side wheels.

The end of the trip phase described as the transition of the vehicle to a certain (roll) angular velocity has been studied experimentally.[10] In results from soil-trip rollover tests that included furrowing, the angular rate of 100°/s was proposed as a possible threshold for an end of trip condition. Direct comparison was made between the time duration, average acceleration, and mass center velocity change from two different tests for two end-of-trip conditions:

reaching an angular velocity of 100°/s and the position of the center of mass over the leading side wheels (approximately 52° for the vehicle tested). The beginning of the trip phase was defined to be the first contact of the tires with the soil after acceleration laterally via a cable drive system on a lubricated road surface. The data from two of these tests using the same vehicle at different initial speeds is presented in Table 5.2.

	Oldsmobile at 23.0 mph	Oldsmobile at 42.9 mph
Δt to 100°/s	624 ms	664 ms
ΔV at 100°/s	−16.8 mph	−17.9 mph
Avgerage acceleration to 100°/s	1.23 g	1.23 g
Δt to 52°	784 ms	792 ms
ΔV at 52°	−18.1 mph	−24.2 mph
Average acceleration to 52°	1.05 g	1.39 g

Table 5.2
Comparison of trip data for 1984 Oldsmobile Cutlass Ciera.

Source: Data from Cooperider et al.[10]

The data show general agreement between the two conditions. Unfortunately, the data do not establish the relationship between the position of the center of mass of the vehicle at the time at which the furrowing ended. This would permit the correlation of these end-of-trip conditions with the end of the furrow or end-of-tire marks. The latter condition is based on physical evidence that can be measured at the scene or site after an accident has occurred. This aspect of the metric makes it directly applicable in the reconstruction of rollover accidents. Therefore it is assumed that the end of the trip phase occurs when the vehicle exceeds the point of neutral stability. For practical purposes, the vehicle is positioned with the leading side tires at the end of their marks or at the end of the furrowing when the neutral stability point is exceeded.

While determining the end of the trip phase is reasonably well-defined, there does not appear to be consensus on establishing the physical location of the vehicle at the start of the trip phase. Some analysts have defined the start of the trip phase as the location of the vehicle when the lateral forces overwhelm the ability of the vehicle to maintain four-wheel contact on the ground.[15] This agrees philosophically with other descriptions in which the authors prefer the definition of "wheel lift"[33] or "roll threshold."[23] Another author refers to the periods of "lift-off" and "launch," in which lift-off is associated with a zero normal force at the trailing wheels and launch is the subsequent condition of zero normal force at the leading wheels.[31]

Test data from vehicles undergoing the pretrip phase in soil indicate just that, prior to trip, the lateral deceleration of the vehicle increases for approximately 0.5 s.[9] The increase in the lateral deceleration indicates that the force at the leading side tires is increasing and therefore the lateral impulse is increasing. These experimental data can be used with the formulas for uniform deceleration (see Chapter 3) to determine the distance over which the increase in the lateral force took place. This period during which the lateral force increases has been used to define the duration and distance of the trip phase.

The understanding of vehicle trip conveyed by the experimental information about the range of time and acceleration associated with the various trip mechanisms supports the use of a separate trip phase in the reconstruction of rollover accidents. The time, τ, and an equivalent drag factor, f, can be used to determine the distance of vehicle travel associated with the trip phase. A short example (Example 5.2) presents an application of the approach to the trip phase alone. An example in Section 5.7 uses this approach in a complete reconstruction of a rollover accident.

In general, experimental data show that the duration for a curb trip is about 0.1 s and for a soil trip is about 0.5 s.[9,10] Table 5.3 is a summary of the experimental data available in the literature attributable to the trip phase of a rollover accident.

Table 5.3
Experimentally determined frictional drag coefficients for the trip phase.

Paper, author/Trip mechanism	Frictional drag coefficient	Trip time (ms)	Speed at start of trip (mph)	ΔV (mph)	Furrow length (ft)	Vehicle
SAE 980022, Cooperrider et al.[10]						
Soil	1.23/1.05[a]	624/784[a]	23.0	16.8/18.1[a]	12.3	1984 Olds Cutlass Ciera
Soil	1.23/1.39[a]	664/792[a]	42.9	17.9/24.2[a]	37.3	1984 Olds Cutlass Ciera
SAE 900366, Cooperrider et al.[9]						
Curb	12.4	60	29.6	14	—	1981 Dodge Challenger
Soil	1.62	513	33.7	18	19	1981 Dodge Challenger
Dolly	1.3	430	30.2	12	—	1981 Dodge Challenger
Curb	13.2	40	29.3	12	—	1979 Datsun B210
Soil	1.71	460	27	17	10	1979 Datsun B210

[a]The first number corresponds with the end of trip at $\omega = 100°/s$ and the second number corresponds with the end of trip for the center of mass positioned over the leading tires.

Example 5.2 Assume that the speed of a vehicle at the beginning of the roll phase of the accident (the end of the trip phase) is determined to be 30 mph (48.3 km/h). The location of the beginning of the roll has been identified by the end of the furrows created by the leading tires of the vehicle. Since this is a soil trip situation, experimental data indicate that a typical deceleration associated with a soil trip is about 1.5 g over a time of about 0.5 s. The speed of the vehicle at the start of the trip phase can be computed using the constant acceleration equations from Chapter 3. A variation of Eq. 3.2 gives

$$v_{\text{start}} = v_{\text{end}} + fg\tau. \tag{5.12}$$

For $v_{\text{end}} = 44.0$ ft/s (13.4 m/s) and $f = 1.5$, the velocity at the start of the trip phase is 46.5 mph (74.8 km/h). The distance over which the trip phase took place can now be determined using a variation of Eq. 3.6:

$$d_{\text{trip}} = \frac{v_{\text{start}}^2 - v_{\text{end}}^2}{2fg}. \tag{5.13}$$

The trip distance, d_{trip}, is 28.1 ft (8.6 m). This distance is subtracted from the end of the furrowing to estimate the beginning of trip phase (the end of the pretrip phase). This location should be assessed relative to the physical evidence obtained from the accident scene/site. If a location of the end of tire marks from the trailing tires has been measured, the distance computed in this part of the reconstruction should not put the beginning of trip before the location of the end of these marks. ◯

5.5.4 Rim Contact

In some rollover accidents, the weight transfer to the leading wheels and the change in roll orientation of the vehicle are enough that one or both of the leading tires deflects, permitting the wheel rim to contact the roadway or the ground. When this contact occurs, scraping of the roadway surface will typically occur. A gouge can also appear when the forces due to sliding and weight shift deflect and debead the tire(s) allowing the rim(s) to come into contact with the pavement. These two events leave different evidence. The debeaded tire typically leaves a narrow tire mark adjacent to the rim gouge compared to a wider tire mark, possibly with striations, left by the wheel with an inflated, but deformed, tire.

Data on the effects of the deceleration of a vehicle as a result of rim contact with pavement have been published.[34] A number of fishhook maneuver tests with instrumented vehicles were conducted to evaluate vehicle rollover performance. Several of the tests resulted in rim contact with the pavement. The results of this testing are the first data to be presented in the open literature on the deceleration developed as a result of rim contact. There were two main conclusions:

1. There was no evidence that wheel rim-to-pavement contact promoted the vehicle to trip, and in some cases this contact actually inhibited vehicle trip.
2. No unusually high deceleration was generated during rim contact.

Of the 14 occurrences of rim contact studied in the paper, only one produced furrowing in the asphalt. That occurrence did produce lateral decelerations higher than the other occurrences and the furrowing did act as a tripping mechanism. The other 13 tests produced decelerations generally equal to or lower than tests with vehicles whose rims did not contact the pavement. These data imply that the presence of rim contact preceding the roll phase does not necessarily indicate an increase in the lateral deceleration of the vehicle. Care should be taken when assessing the level of rim contact and assigning the vehicle deceleration value in the pretrip and trip phases of the analysis.

5.6 Roll Phase

There are two principal aspects to the reconstruction of the roll phase of a rollover accident. The first aspect is the determination of the total distance traveled while rolling and the reconstruction of the speed of the vehicle at the start of the roll phase (the end of the trip phase). The second aspect of the reconstruction is the determination of the number of times that the vehicle rolled and the position and orientation of the vehicle during the roll phase. The first aspect uses an effective drag coefficient over the appropriate roll distance to obtain the speed. In general, the estimate of the speed at the beginning of the roll phase can be computed without detailed knowledge of the number of times that the vehicle rolled before coming to rest. Determination of the number of rolls of the vehicle is a time-consuming process that requires a systematic approach to matching the deformation and evidence on the vehicle with the evidence at the scene and site. The tasks of determining the orientation of the vehicle during impacts with the ground and estimating the roll rate of the vehicle through the roll phase are performed to acquire information for the assessment of the kinematics and kinetics of the occupants of the vehicle during the rollover phase.

5.6.1   Speed Analysis

The rollover of a vehicle is a complex, three-dimensional dynamic event. Uneven terrain can add to the complexity. Sophisticated dynamic simulations that can be used for detailed reconstruction of the rolling motion of a specific vehicle do not exist. Consequently, simplified methods must be used. These methods use the concept of an average deceleration as the vehicle moves from trip to rest. The principles for constant acceleration presented in Chapter 3 are applied to reconstruct the vehicle speed at the start of the roll phase. The final velocity at rest is zero and the total rollover distance is determined from evidence from the accident investigation. Equation 3.5 can be applied. Solving Eq. 3.5 for the initial velocity, v_0, and using slightly different notation gives

$$v_0 = \sqrt{v_f^2 - 2ad}\,. \tag{5.14}$$

In Eq. 5.15, it is known that $v_f = 0$ (vehicle at rest) and d is the total roll distance. Letting $a = -fg$ (negative because the vehicle is decelerating), the equation can be written as

$$v_0 = \sqrt{2fgd}\,. \tag{5.15}$$

The velocity at the start of the roll phase can be calculated using Eq. 5.15 if estimates of the roll distance and the drag factor of the rolling vehicle over that distance are known. An estimate of the roll distance is usually easy to determine from the evidence. Values for the deceleration of the vehicle during the roll have been the reported in the literature.[2,7,9,10,13,14]

The deceleration data from the studies has been presented in the literature in two forms. The first considers the posttrip rollover deceleration of the vehicle from initial contact with the roadway surface until rest. This approach combines the trip and roll phases into a single deceleration value. Test data reported in this manner in the literature is presented in Table 5.4. The second form considers the trip phase separate from the roll phase and reports the decelerations from each phase. Some testing includes only a roll phase (dolly

Paper, author/Roll surface	Frictional drag coefficient for combined trip and roll	Speed at start of trip (mph)	Vehicle
SAE 980022, Cooperrider et al.[10]			
Soil	0.8	23.0	1984 Olds Cutlass Ciera
Soil	0.8	42.9	1984 Olds Cutlass Ciera
Soil	0.9	33.7	1981 Dodge Challenger
Soil	0.9	27	1979 Datsun B210
SAE 2000-01-1641, Larson et al.[7]			
Soil	0.8	40.7	1991 Jeep Wrangler
Soil	0.8	41.1	1986 Chevrolet S10 Blazer
Pavement	0.7	~70	1979 Datsun B210

Table 5.4
Frictional drag coefficients reported in the literature for combined trip phase and roll phase.

Paper, author/Roll surface	Frictional drag coefficient over the roll distance	Speed at start of trip (mph)	Vehicle
SAE 2002-01-0694, Carter et al.[13]			
Asphalt	0.44	51.0	1999 Ford Econoline E-350
Asphalt	0.46	55.3	1999 Ford Econoline E-350
SAE 980022, Cooperrider et al.[10]			
Soil	0.49/0.30[a]	42.9	1984 Olds Cutlass Ciera
SAE 900366, Cooperrider et al.[9]			
Soil	0.48	~30	1981 Dodge Challenger
Soil	0.47	~30	1979 Datsun B210
SAE 851734, Orlowski et al.[2]			
Pavement	0.43	32	1983 Chevrolet Malibu
SAE 890857, Orlowski et al.[14]			
Unknown	Min: 0.36 Avg: 0.42 Max: 0.61	Unknown	41 separate tests based on various sources

Table 5.5
Frictional drag coefficients reported in the literature for roll phase.

[a]The first number corresponds with the end of trip at ω = 100°/s and the second number corresponds with the end of trip for the center of mass positioned over the leading tires.

testing) and the deceleration data is inherently posttrip. Known data for the trip phase were presented in Table 5.3. Table 5.5 is a compilation of the deceleration values for the roll phase of vehicles available in the literature.

Figure 5.11 shows the plan view of a vehicle positioned at the start and the end (on its roof) of the roll phase of a rollover accident. The total distance measured between the centers of mass of the vehicle at these two positions is indicated on the drawing as 84.1 ft (25.6 m). The speed of the vehicle at the start of the roll phase can be calculated using Eq. 5.16. Using a range of the effective drag coefficient of $0.4 \leq f \leq 0.5$ and the distance $d = 84.1$ ft (25.6 m), the speed at the start of the roll phase is calculated to be in the range of 31.7 mph to 35.5 mph (51.0 km/h to 57.1 km/h). ⬡

Example 5.3

Figure 5.11
Roll phase of a
rollover accident.

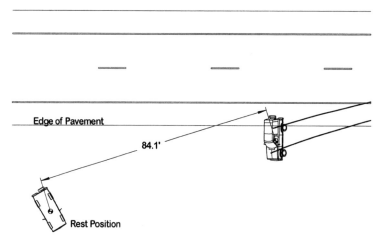

5.6.2   Analysis of the Rolling Vehicle

After the speed of the vehicle at the start of the roll phase has been determined using the roll distance and an appropriate drag factor, the attention of the reconstructionist frequently turns to establishing the number of times the vehicle rolled over. Such an analysis includes determination of the location and orientation of the vehicle during significant impacts with the ground. Knowledge of the number of rolls of the vehicle, the effective drag factor, and the roll distance can be used to calculate the average roll rate of the vehicle.

The process of analyzing the roll phase of the vehicle consists of three steps. The first step is the gathering of the specific information related to the accident that will be required to perform the reconstruction. Some of this information has been used previously in the calculation of the vehicle speed prior to roll. The second step is the assimilation of the information whereby the information is processed in preparation for the analysis of the roll phase. The roll analysis requires organization and understanding of the deformation to the vehicle, scrape marks on the surfaces of the vehicle, and the corresponding evidence at the accident scene. Much of the information at the scene is transient in nature, although most of the information related to the vehicle is relatively permanent (as long as the vehicle is not disposed of or seriously mishandled). The third step is the use of the information to reconstruct the positions and orientations of the vehicle during the roll phase.

5.6.3   Information about the Accident Scene and Site

Investigating officers typically return the accident location to normal traffic well before any opportunity for a reconstructionist to inspect it. Therefore, the two primary sources of information regarding the accident scene, the police report and the police photographs, are extremely important in reconstructing a rollover accident. Such evidence contains essential information about the state of the accident scene and are typically the first pieces of information available to the accident reconstructionist. The quality and quantity of the police photographs can affect the ability of the reconstructionist to accurately perform the task of reconstructing the accident beyond the calculation of the speed of the vehicle prior to the roll phase.

The police report for a rollover accident may contain a detailed survey conducted by the investigating officer. This survey typically contains important evidence such as the rest position of the vehicle and the location of tire marks and significant pieces of debris. The reference points used in the survey should be noted and identified during the reconstructionist's site inspection.

If available, the police report and the scene photographs should be studied prior to the reconstructionist's inspection of the site. The site inspection should be conducted to confirm the dimensions listed on the police survey and also to make measurements not typically made by the police. The slope of the ground over the path of the vehicle should be measured, and marks made by the vehicle, such as rim strikes, gouge marks, paint transfer, and furrows, should be located and measured. Any items with which the vehicle interacted, such as culvert headers, poles, trees, mailboxes, and rocks, should be noted. The interaction of these items with the vehicle usually leaves a distinct mark or deformation on the vehicle, and this information can be used to great advantage in reconstructing the position of the vehicle during the roll phase.

While the inspection of the accident site for a rollover accident can be conducted with the use of traditional measurement devices such as tape measures and measuring wheels, the preferred method is with the use of professional surveying equipment, such as a theodolite or a total station. In addition to greater accuracy than typical inspection methods, the theodolite gives three-dimensional data for all points measured at the site. This permits the incorporation of any changes in slope in the analysis of the deceleration of the rolling vehicle.

Information that is present in the police photographs that cannot be located at the site can usually be located using photogrammetric analysis. Chapter 10 discusses such techniques.

The information obtained from the accident scene photographs, the police report, and the site inspection(s) can be used to create a scale diagram of the accident site. This diagram should contain all the relevant evidence and site information related to the accident. The diagram will look similar in content to the one shown in Fig. 5.12.

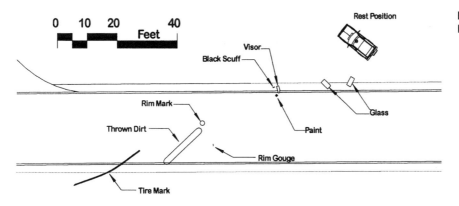

Figure 5.12
Rollover accident diagram.

5.6.4   Information about the Accident Vehicle

The physical evidence on the vehicle itself contains valuable information about the dynamics and kinematics experienced by the vehicle during the roll phase. An inspection of the vehicle is a mandatory prerequisite for performing a reconstruction and for understanding the roll motion. It is implicit at any vehicle inspection that photographs will be taken. This section presents some additional inspection techniques to supplement photography. The inspection should not be limited to these techniques; inspectors may improve upon the techniques presented here or may develop other methods.

The inspection is the best opportunity for the reconstructionist to examine the vehicle and acquire the information necessary to perform the reconstruction of the roll sequence. During the inspection, the reconstructionist should first note the general nature of the deformation of the vehicle and the general directions and characteristics of the scrapes and scratches at the contact points of the vehicle with the ground and possibly other objects (trees, etc.), then draw sketches of this information. These sketches can be field sketches or can be drawn using prepared templates of the various profiles of the vehicle. Figure 5.13 shows both a blank template of a vehicle and the same profile with

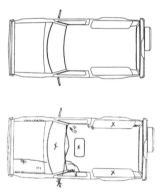

Figure 5.13
Profiles for documenting deformation, scratch, and scrape patterns.

deformation and scratch information marked on it by hand from direct observation during an inspection. A profile for the front, rear, top, and both side views should be completed at the time of the inspection. Variations of this technique may employ colors to distinguish sets of scratches or damage that occurred during different contacts between the vehicle and the ground. Although sometimes more difficult to obtain, information from deformation to the bottom of the vehicle should also be documented. This information is typically easier to document with photographs than drawings.

These profiles should be used to document the scratch patterns, the deformation to the body, an indication as to which windows were broken (such as indicated in Fig. 5.13 by an "X" on the window), and which parts of the exterior of the vehicle were damaged or removed during the rolling. The tires and rims should be examined and photographed carefully. Damage to these should be noted in the side views. Care should be taken to distinguish between damage to the vehicle that is a result of the rolling during the accident and damage that occurred after the accident, such as during extrication and winching. The police photographs can be used for comparison to identify postaccident vehicle damage.

The tires and rims should also be carefully evaluated for deformation. The leading tires in the trip phase may show scuffing on the sidewall. They may also show evidence of rim contact. Attention should be paid to distinguish between damage to the tire from the trip phase and damage to a tire that came from a strike during the roll phase. Frequently, debris is caught between the bead of the tire and the rim from the trip phase. Debris can also become lodged in the bead of a tire from other contacts during the roll sequence. Wheel/tire contact during the roll phase often will be accompanied by rim damage. Inspection of the underside of the wheel wells and the jounce bumpers may show significant contact that can indicate whether the vehicle landed on one or more wheels during the roll sequence causing the suspension to be completely compressed. Complete compression of the suspension is a very unlikely event during normal vehicle operation.

Vehicles involved in a rollover accident frequently accumulate debris during contact with the ground, ranging from asphalt from a rim gouge to dirt or turf collected between the body panels. The type of debris (asphalt, mud, etc.) and its location on the vehicle should be carefully noted on the field sketch and photographed. The direction of motion of the vehicle during the contact can often be ascertained from the position of the debris collected.

The characteristics of the scratches on the surfaces of the vehicle are one of the means through which the orientation during contact with the ground can be ascertained. Scratch patterns created by different surfaces can usually be distinguished from one another by assessing direction and texture. Scratches made by contact with asphalt are usually different from those made by contact with sand, gravel, dirt, or grass. Moreover, the direction associated with the scratches or the presence of characteristics such as curvature or a hook at the beginning or end of a group (or family) of scratch marks can assist in the grouping of the marks. The direction of a family of scratch marks can also help establish the orientation and motion of the vehicle when the scratch was created. An investigation was made into establishing a systematic method of analyzing the direction of scratch marks.[35] In addition to the notation on the field sketch indicating the direction of a scratch mark or a group of scratch marks, placement of arrows or tape on the vehicle adjacent to the scratch marks can be used within a photograph to more readily depict this characteristic. This technique is illustrated in Fig. 5.14.

Characteristics of the scratches on the vehicle sheet metal and the deformation of the sheet metal can be used to establish the order in which the scratches were created. In certain situations, contact with the ground will create a concave surface. If that same part of the vehicle comes into contact with the ground again during a later roll, the scratching on the second contact will not be present in the concave portion of the sheet metal. This can be used during the reconstruction to determine the order of the two contact events.

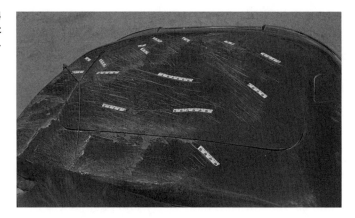

Figure 5.14
Use of tape to document groups of scratch marks.

The direction of a group of scratches on a vehicle does not uniquely determine the direction of motion of the vehicle relative to the ground. In fact, two alternatives exist: the motion of the vehicle relative to the ground in one position and the motion of the vehicle relative to the ground with the vehicle rotated 180° from the previous position. Distinguishing between these two possibilities is sometimes possible through consideration of the rigid body motion of the vehicle. However, when this is not possible, the vehicle motion can frequently be determined by close analysis of the flow of the surface material removed during contact. For example, in the case of a plastic component such as a bumper, roof rack, window molding, or side-view mirror housing, the flow of material may be quite obvious. In addition to flow of surface material, a molding strip may have been pulled away from the vehicle, thus indicating the direction of motion of the vehicle during contact in that area. This type of scratch analysis is difficult to apply to painted sheet metal that has been scraped on contact with the ground. In certain cases, close examination of applied pin stripes can be useful. The material of the pin stripe is often pushed opposite the direction of motion where a scratch crosses the pin stripe.

Parts that have been knocked off during contact with the ground can also yield insight into the orientation of the vehicle at the time of contact. This information can come from the nature of the failure of the fastener (screws, bolts, plastic boss, etc.) that was holding the part and the deformation of the surrounding material as the fastener was put in tension or compression prior to failure. For parts that protrude from the vehicle prior to being knocked off during ground contact, the location of the scratches or evidence of force application on a particular side of the piece can indicate the orientation and direction of motion of the vehicle as contact was made. For example, a driver-side side-view mirror that was knocked off as the vehicle rolled passenger-side leading might show scratches on the outside (front-facing side) of the housing that are upward and outward. This would indicate that the vehicle had a lateral and longitudinal velocity component as the mirror contacted the ground. This conclusion should be validated using other information, such as the deformation of the fasteners holding the mirror on the vehicle and possibly other aspects of the roll phase.

Once all the information about the accident scene, the accident site, and the accident vehicle has been obtained and assimilated, the reconstruction of the details of the roll phase can begin. The reconstruction of the position and orientation of the vehicle during the rolling of the vehicle is a process whereby the scene evidence and the vehicle evidence are matched feature by feature. This is a tedious, detail-oriented process. Several tools that have proven quite useful in prior rollover accident reconstruction projects can be used to facilitate this process.

5.6.5 Rollover Reconstruction Tools

Unlike the accident geometries considered in this book, such as an intersection collision, the roll phase of a rollover accident cannot be assumed to be planar in nature. On the contrary, the very nature of the accident dictates that the three-dimensional motion of the vehicle be considered in the reconstruction. The three-dimensional rigid body motion of the vehicle can be quite complicated because the vehicle is both translating (both in the horizontal plane and vertically) and rotating during the roll phase. In considering and evaluating this motion relative to the physical evidence, a physical model of the vehicle is of immeasurable utility. If the reconstructionist is fortunate, a commercially manufactured scale model of the vehicle is suitable for this purpose. A 1:18 to 1:25 scale model is an appropriate size for the purpose of accident reconstruction. If a commercial model is not available, a substitute can be used if critical dimensions such as the wheelbase and vehicle length, width, and height are the same as or very close to the accident vehicle. If this is not the case, then a custom model can be created for this purpose from polystyrene or wood.

A second useful tool is the capability to plot the accident diagram with all the accident information onto paper at the same scale as the physical vehicle model described above. This combination of scale model vehicle and scale site diagram allows the reconstructionist to physically move the model from location to location on the accident diagram while evaluating the match between the evidence located on the diagram and the position of the vehicle. As distinct positions of the vehicle are reconstructed, the accident diagram can be updated to show the vehicle orientation at that position of the roll. The vehicle position at the start of the roll and intermediate positions up to the rest position are linked together to define the positions and path of the vehicle.

This evaluation process is further facilitated by marking the scale model of the accident vehicle, preferably light in color, with the scratch marks, deformation lines, and other damage information. A custom model marked in this fashion is shown in Fig. 5.15. Deformation is shown on the model vehicle with a continuous line, and the position and orientation of scrapes are also drawn on the model vehicle. Scrapes that belong to different groups on the same part of the vehicle can be marked on the model using different colors. The colors make the marks easier to distinguish during the reconstruction process. The windows of the vehicle broken in the accident are indicated on the model as "out."

In addition to the light-colored model in combination with a scale drawing for reconstructing the ground contacts of the rollover—particularly the contacts

Figure 5.15
A custom scale model
with damage and scratch
deformation information
marked on the vehicle.

involving the roof or hood when the vehicle is inverted—a clear plastic cover that fits over the model vehicle can be used to great advantage. The clear cover can be marked with the scrape patterns similar to the marks put on the light-colored model. In assessing the match in direction and location between the marks on the roof and marks on the road surface, for example, the reconstructionist can physically see the marks on both surfaces at the same time by looking through the clear cover when the model has been removed.

The details of the process of matching the evidence located on the vehicle to the evidence located on the accident diagram will be presented in the section below. Once the reader understands these concepts, the process is best learned by reconstructing an actual vehicle rollover accident using the reconstruction techniques described here.

5.7 Example Rollover Reconstruction

This section demonstrates the reconstruction of vehicle speed, position, and orientation of a rollover accident using a number of techniques. Because each rollover accident is unique, the reconstruction of other rollover accidents may require the application of other reconstruction techniques.

The vehicle involved in the rollover accident used in this example is a 1998 Chevrolet Astro eight-passenger minivan equipped with ABS. The van was traveling southbound in the left lane of a four-lane divided highway when the right rear tire suddenly deflated. Figure 5.16 shows the southbound lanes of the highway, the shoulders on either side of the roadway, and the vehicle in various positions along its path. The highway and shoulder surfaces were asphalt. The driver of the van attempted to control the vehicle by steering and braking, leaving visible tire marks, but the vehicle ultimately traveled off the roadway to the east onto the grassy median. The median slopes slightly downward away from the shoulder. While the vehicle was traveling across the shoulder onto the median, the driver attempted to steer the vehicle to the right and back onto the road. As a result of the steering input, the vehicle began a clockwise yaw. The yawing of the vehicle led to the furrowing of the left side wheels into the grass. The road conditions were dry and the accident occurred during

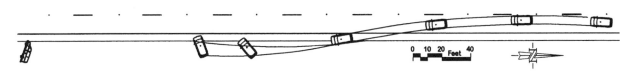

Figure 5.16
Accident diagram.

daylight hours. The van was carrying ten passengers including the driver at the time of the accident.

The speed of the van at the start of the visible tire marks can be reconstructed, as well as the number of times that the vehicle rolled. The reconstruction determines the speed of the vehicle by using the approach that sequentially separates the deceleration of the vehicle into rollover, trip, and pretrip phases. The number of times the vehicle rolled is determined through a detailed analysis of the physical evidence.

5.7.1   Speed Analysis

The rollover phase of the accident occurred over a distance of 116.3 ft (35.4 m). Figure 5.17 shows the accident diagram with the roll distance indicated. This distance is measured from the center of mass of the vehicle at rest to the center

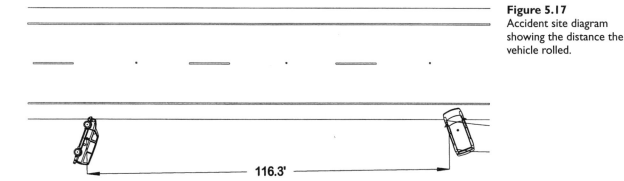

Figure 5.17
Accident site diagram showing the distance the vehicle rolled.

116.3'

of mass of the vehicle at trip. The position of the center of mass of the vehicle at the start of the roll phase is taken when the leading side wheels are at the end of the furrows and the vehicle is in the neutral stability position rather than with all four wheels of the vehicle on the ground. This amounts to re-apportioning a distance of roughly half the vehicle width from the roll phase to the trip phase. Since the frictional drag coefficient for the trip phase is larger than the frictional drag coefficient for the roll phase, the net effect of this reapportionment is a small increase in the speed of the vehicle. Using a range of the effective drag coefficient of $f = 0.4$ to $f = 0.5$ for the rollover phase, the speed of the center of mass of the vehicle at the neutral stability position can be calculated using Eq. 5.16. The range of speed of the vehicle at the end of the trip phase is 37.3 to 41.7 mph (60.0 to 67.1 km/h).

The speed of the vehicle at the start of the trip phase can be calculated using Eq. 5.13. The tripping of the vehicle occurred with both of the leading side tires in the grassy median. Equation 5.13 is used with a trip duration of $\tau = 0.5$ s and a single empirical drag coefficient of $f = 1.5$ (see Table 5.3) consistent with a soil trip. The corresponding speed range of the vehicle at the start of the trip was 53.8 to 58.2 mph (86.5 to 93.6 km/h). The distance the center of mass traveled during the trip phase (Eq. 5.14) is approximately 33.4 to 36.6 ft (10.2 to 11.2 m). A vehicle is positioned in Fig. 5.18 at the average of these two distances, 35.0 ft (10.7 m).

Figure 5.18
The trip phase of
the accident.

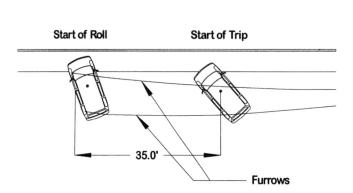

Analysis of the pretrip phase of the rollover accident using vehicle dynamics software requires information about the physical characteristics of the vehicle, the conditions under which it was driven (braking, steering), and its path. The circumstances of this accident gleaned from the police report and the physical evidence indicate that after the sudden loss of pressure in the right rear tire, the vehicle was steered or drifted to the right side of the left-hand lane. The driver then began to steer the vehicle to the left due to the presence of another vehicle in the adjacent lane. The steering back to the left created tire marks on the roadway and led the vehicle off the roadway as shown in Fig. 5.19. The police report indicates that the driver stated that he applied the brakes hard in an attempt to slow the vehicle and steer it left onto the median.

The mark made by the right front tire was a yaw mark and can be used with the critical speed formula (see Chapter 4) to determine the speed of the vehicle near the start of the yaw mark. Before presenting the balance of the analysis of the pretrip motion of the vehicle, it is worthwhile noting that although the right rear tire of the van had deflated, the driver maintained steering control of the front wheels. The evidence supporting this is the fact that the vehicle reacted to the steering input by moving to the left. Tire marks from both front tires were made on the roadway surface. This indicates that although the deflated right rear tire creates the possibility of the vehicle rocking about the right front

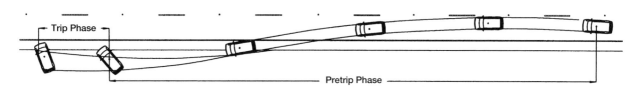

Figure 5.19
Pretrip and trip phases.

and left rear tires, this did not occur because the normal force at the left front tire was sufficient to produce a tire mark. Maintaining contact with the road at both front tires may also be due to the braking of the vehicle. According to the report prepared by the police, the driver of the vehicle stated that he applied the brakes after the sudden loss of pressure in the right rear tire and prior to the vehicle beginning to roll. Details about the duration and level of braking are unknown. Braking would tend to increase the normal force at the front wheels. This vehicle was equipped with antilock brakes at all four wheels and therefore could be steered and braked at the same time without locking the wheels.

A circle of 710.2 ft (216.5 m) was fitted to the mark made by the right front tire using the first 77 ft of the mark. Using a frictional drag coefficient of $f =$ 0.7 for dry asphalt pavement, the critical speed formula predicts the speed of the vehicle at the start of the visible tire marks to be 86.3 mph (138.8 km/h). The critical speed formula tends to underestimate the speed of the vehicle in the presence of braking (see Chapter 4). Therefore, depending on the specific braking conditions over the arc used in the calculation, the actual speed of the vehicle may have been higher than 86.3 mph (138.8 km/h).

The remaining task is to determine whether the speed of the vehicle predicted at the start of the tire marks (using the critical speed formula) is consistent with the motion and the speed of the vehicle at the start of the trip. This could be done by trial and error with a vehicle dynamics program using different combinations of braking and steering. However, it is much simpler to compute an effective drag coefficient for this motion. The speed at the start of the tire marks was about 86.3 mph (138.8 km/h) and the speed of the vehicle at the start of the trip ranged from 53.8 mph to 58.2 mph (86.5 to 93.6 km/h). The distance traveled was about 244.8 ft (74.6 m). Using these values, the effective frictional drag coefficient for the vehicle over the distance ranges from $f_{eff} =$ 0.55 to $f_{eff} = 0.62$. The magnitude of this frictional drag coefficient is within the capabilities of the vehicle braking system and indicates that it is likely that the brakes of the vehicle were applied during most if not all of the distance over which the tire marks were made.

In summary, these calculations indicate that the speed of the vehicle at the start of the tire marks was at, or somewhat above, 86 mph (138 km/h) and its speed at the start of the roll phase was about 39 mph (63 km/h).

5.7.2 Detailed Roll Analysis

This analysis demonstrates a process to determine the number of times that a vehicle has rolled during the roll phase of a rollover accident, information that may be needed to support an occupant kinematic analysis. The method matches the evidence on the vehicle to the evidence found at the accident scene and site. This process is tedious and requires considerable time to execute. Only a portion of the process is presented here through the analysis of several pieces of evidence from the vehicle and the accident scene. The goal of a complete analysis is to attribute each piece of evidence on the vehicle, such as a scratch pattern, particular body deformation, or glass breakage, to a specific position, and orientation of the vehicle during the roll. Matching evidence on the vehicle with evidence at the scene, such as a broken window on the vehicle with a patch of glass found at the site, should be used in the process whenever possible. The process is completed when an explanation of the positions of the vehicle during the entire rollover phase can be made that accounts for all or most of the evidence.

Figure 5.20
Accident diagram showing the vehicle positions for the start of the trip position, the rest position, and the location of several artifacts of the rollover accident.

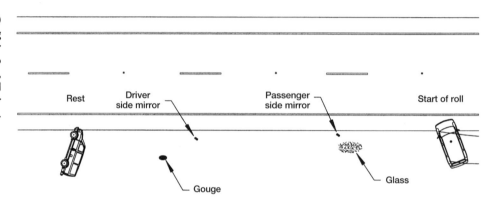

One of the first steps in reconstructing the positions and orientations of the vehicle during the roll phase is to place the location of the artifacts from the accident scene on a scale drawing. Figure 5.20 shows the accident diagram with the location of four pieces of evidence found at the scene: the passenger and driver side mirrors, a patch of broken glass, and a gouge in the grass. For convenience, Fig. 5.21 shows the results of the analysis with vehicles depicted at every quarter turn. The vehicle started a driver-side leading rollover at the vehicle location labeled in Fig. 5.21 as Start of Roll, rolled 2¾ times, and came to rest on the passenger side.

Figure 5.21
Accident diagram showing the vehicle positions and orientations during the roll phase.

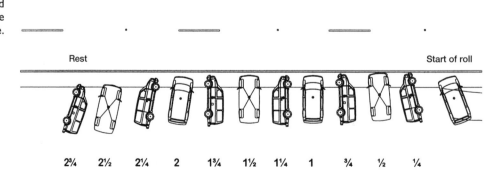

After the trip, the first contact between the vehicle and the ground occurred at the passenger side roof rail near the A-pillar. This caused the roof to be pushed in and toward the driver side of the vehicle. The deformation to the vehicle is shown in Fig. 5.22. This type of vehicle motion, an initial rotation of about 180–200° prior to the first contact, is observed frequently. It is likely that this vehicle motion is due partially to vaulting of the vehicle as a result of the restoration of the leading side suspension. This suspension is compressed as a result of weight transfer during the trip phase. See Stevens[36] for further discussion of this type of vehicle motion.

Figure 5.22
Deformation of the passenger-side A-pillar from first contact.

Figure 5.23
Damage to the passenger side of the vehicle.

The first contact resulted in the deforming of the sliding door on the passenger side of the vehicle and the breaking of the window in that door. The door is shown in the side view in Fig. 5.23. The position and orientation of the vehicle during that contact can be estimated using the corresponding patch of glass (from the broken window) observed at the accident scene. At the inspection, it was determined that the front driver and passenger windows were rolled down at the time of the accident. Hence, no glass was found at the site corresponding to these windows.

As shown in Fig. 5.20, the passenger side rearview mirror was found adjacent to the patch of glass. This is consistent with the nature of the impact between the passenger side and the ground. Figure 5.24 shows the front side of the mirror housing, and a set of scratch marks on the left side that correspond to the first contact between the housing and the shoulder. This contact would have folded the mirror in toward the vehicle. These scratches angle toward the

Figure 5.24
Passenger side rearview mirror housing.

front of the mirror and are likely caused by the mirror rotating in toward the vehicle as the mirror was moving along the shoulder. Another set of scratches on the housing is located at the hinge area. These scratches, essentially in the same direction as the first set, correspond to the contact between that portion of the mirror housing and the shoulder slightly later in the roll sequence after the mirror had been folded in.

The lateral position of the vehicle relative to the roadway and the shoulder during the first contact can be ascertained from the location of the scratch patterns on the side of the vehicle. Figure 5.25 shows a portion of the right front fender and door of the vehicle after the accident. The scratching ends just aft of the front edge of the door, indicating that this portion of the vehicle was positioned along the edge of the shoulder.

Figure 5.25
Rear of right front fender and right front door of vehicle showing the demarcation between the portions of the sheet metal scratched by the shoulder and the portion not scratched.

The driver side rearview mirror was found farther downstream from the location of the passenger side mirror. This indicates that it likely separated from the vehicle later in the roll sequence. This is supported by the two different scratch patterns on the mirror housing shown in Fig. 5.26. The mirror would have been in position to contact the ground at 1¼ rolls and 2¼ rolls, because the vehicle did not touch the ground at ¼ roll. The marks on the outside of the housing run fore–aft of the vehicle perpendicular to the direction expected for the motion of the vehicle during the roll. The unusual direction of these scratches came from the motion of the housing while it was breaking. (Note the crack in the housing shown in the photograph.) The scratches nearer the hinge area occurred slightly later in the roll after the mirror had folded inward.

Figure 5.26
Driver side rearview
mirror housing.

Two contacts between the left front part of the vehicle and the shoulder at
1¼ rolls and 2¼ rolls are also supported by two different scratch patterns. Figure 5.27 shows the left front fender of the vehicle. Two groups of scratch patterns in slightly different directions can be discerned in the photograph.

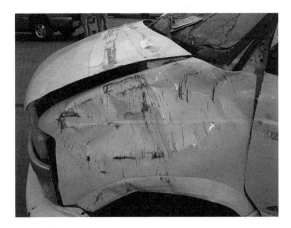

Figure 5.27
Left front fender
of the vehicle.

A gouge in the median, indicated in Fig. 5.20, was created by contact of the
left rear wheel when the vehicle rotated to 2 rolls. During this type of wheel-to-
ground contact, the suspension at the contacting wheel is typically completely
compressed. The suspension also frequently deforms laterally, permitting wheel/
suspension to body contact. This typically leaves
marks in the wheel well and at the contact point
between the jounce bumper and the frame of
the vehicle. Figure 5.28 shows the location where
the jounce bumper of the left rear suspension
came into contact with the left frame rail.
Although the mark on the frame rail from the
jounce bumper cannot be attributed exclusively
to the rollover accident, contact between a jounce
bumper and its stop is an uncommon occurrence
in the normal use of a passenger vehicle. Figure
5.29 shows the left rear wheel-well area of the
vehicle. This photograph shows the damage that
occurred when the leaf spring assembly moved

Figure 5.28
Left rear jounce
bumper contact.

Figure 5.29
Damage in the left rear
wheel well due to contact
between the leaf spring
and the frame rail and the
tire and the wheel well.

Figure 5.29
Damage in the left rear wheel well due to contact between the leaf spring and the frame rail and the tire and the wheel well.

laterally and contacted the left frame rail during the compression and deformation of the suspension. During the compression, the tire came into contact with the wheel well shown by the blackened area on the face of the wheel well. Similar damage and deformation occurred on the right rear suspension system. The compression of the right rear suspension occurred at the ¾ or 1¾ roll positions. Figure 5.30 shows a final diagram of the roll phase that includes the sequence of vehicle positions and the evidence.

Figure 5.30
Accident diagram showing the physical evidence at the accident scene and the vehicle positions corresponding to that evidence.

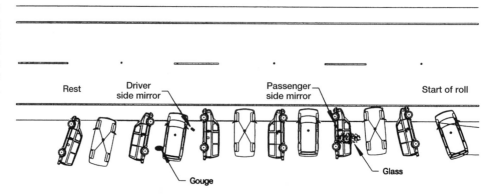

5.8   Vehicle Roll Rate during Rollover

In addition to the location and orientation of the vehicle during the roll phase, the roll rate of the vehicle during the roll phase is also of interest. One reference was found that specifically considers the roll rate of the vehicle during the rollover phase.[37] In that analysis, the roll rate of the vehicle is assigned the triangular profile shown in Fig. 5.31. The general shape of the angular acceleration shown in Fig. 5.31 was based on the experimental data from a dolly rollover test.[2] Roll rate data from other dolly style rollover tests show a similar trend.[9,13] Roll rate data for rollovers resulting from interaction with soil also exhibit a similar ramping up to a maximum rotational velocity after the start of furrowing and then a ramping down to zero.[9] Roll rate data from a test

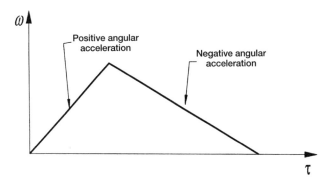

Figure 5.31
Profile of the roll rate for vehicles involved in dolly rollover tests and soil trip rollover testing.

using a curb as the trip mechanism exhibit a much sharper rise in the roll rate.[9] Not all of the data follows this trend. In addition to some high-frequency content in most of the data, the roll velocity of some vehicles reached a plateau rather than a peak before decreasing to zero.[10] None of the data provides the specific information necessary to discern the transition from the trip phase to the roll phase of the vehicle relative to the roll rate data. Therefore, it is not possible to generalize the relationship between the end of the trip phase and the location of the peak roll rate. The relationship between the roll rate and the transition from the trip phase to the roll phase is a topic that requires additional investigation.

The peak angular roll rate for vehicles depends on the speed of the vehicle at the start of the rollover and the type of mechanism used to trip the vehicle. Table 5.6 lists the peak roll rate data available in the literature. Where appli-

Paper, author/Initial peak roll rate (°/s)	Time at peak (s)	Vehicle speed at roll (mph)	Trip mechanism	Vehicle
SAE 900366, Cooperider et al.[9]				
470	0.6	30.2	Dolly	1981 Dodge Challenger
250	0.75	29.6	Curb	1981 Dodge Challenger
390	1.05	33.7	Soil	1981 Dodge Challenger
210	0.2	29.3	Curb	1979 Datsun B210
240	0.9	27	Soil	1979 Datsun B210
SAE 980022, Cooperider et al.[10]				
140	1	23.0	Soil	1984 Olds Cutlass
340	1	42.9	Soil	1984 Olds Cutlass
SAE 851734, Orlowski et al.[2]				
550	1.5	30 mph	Dolly	1983 Chevy Malibu
SAE 2002-01-0694, Carter et al.[13]				
>620[a]	1.1	51 mph w/ roll rate of 149°/s in the direction of the roll	Controlled rollover impact system	2000 Ford E350

Table 5.6
Roll rate data available in the literature.

[a]Data appears to be clipped at 620°/s.

cable, the peak roll rate associated with the initial rise in the roll rate data are provided rather than the global maximum for the data.

5.9   Further Considerations

The reconstructions of many rollover accidents are related to litigation. The task of presenting the analysis and results to a judge and jury still remains after the technical work of reconstructing the accident has been completed. Various means for communicating the details of the reconstruction are available, from computer renderings and animations to three-dimensional scale models of the vehicle and the local terrain. The latter incorporates vehicles displayed in successive positions to show observers the path and positions of the vehicle during the accident. Various aspects of this task have been presented in the literature.[15,33,37]

CHAPTER

6

Analysis of Collisions, Impulse–Momentum Theory

6.1 Introduction

To draw reliable and valid conclusions about an accident, quantitative methods should always be used for reconstructions as long as reliable and valid information is available. This statement does not mean that intuition and judgment should not be used. They should, but with care. Intuition and judgment are not inborn; they are learned and can be developed. An understanding of the basic concepts of mechanics is necessary to understand vehicle crashes. A common phrase that often is tossed about when discussing crashes is that of *conservation of momentum*. Momentum is the product of mass and velocity. Mass, m, is an inherent property of an object. It is a measure of the effort needed to push something and make it move faster—or the effort to tug on an object to make it move slower. It remains constant, independent of the acceleration of gravity. Weight, W, is a force, a measure of the effect of gravity pulling an object toward the earth. Weight is the product of mass and the local acceleration of gravity, g; that is, $W = mg$. So the mass of an object is the same everywhere; its weight depends on the value of g. For accidents that occur near sea level, g has the values of 9.81 m/s² or 32.2 ft/s². So, in this sense, mass and weight are equivalent. The other part of momentum is velocity, speed with an associated direction. So a vehicle with a lot of momentum could be a light vehicle with a high speed or a heavy vehicle with a low speed. If no external forces act on an object (and an object could be two objects in contact), the laws of mechanics say that the momentum of the system (combined momentum of the two objects) does not change. So from the time two objects (vehicles) come together in a crash until they separate, their momentum doesn't change, provided that any forces—such as tire forces—during the contact duration are negligible. Actually, it is the *impulse* of the tire frictional forces that must be small relative to the impulse of the intervehicular forces, where the impulse of the forces is the accumulation of the force over time. So as long as the contact duration is small, momentum in a crash is approximately conserved.

How is this connected to intuition and judgment? Figure 6.1 shows a right-angled intersection collision. Consider the concept of a *momentum clock*. If Vehicle 1 has a high initial (at the instant contact begins) momentum and Vehicle 2

Figure 6.1
An intersection collision (left-hand drive motorway).

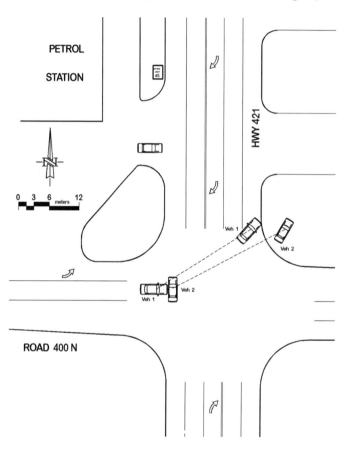

has a very small initial momentum, then for unspectacular postimpact motion (no rollovers, collisions with fixed objects, etc.), the rest positions of both vehicles would be expected to be near 3 o'clock. If the distribution of initial momentum was reversed—that is, Vehicle 1 had little momentum and Vehicle 2 had a lot—then the rest positions would be near 12 o'clock. Other cases are proportionately between 12 and 3 o'clock. If the amount of total initial momentum is small, the vehicles will stay inside the clock. If the total initial momentum is large, the vehicles will go outside of the clock. Remember that Vehicle 1 could be light and have high momentum due to high speed, or it could be a heavy vehicle with a low speed. If both vehicles weigh about the same and it is a 2 o'clock crash (as in Fig. 6.1), then intuition indicates that Vehicle 1 was going faster than Vehicle 2. But without mathematical models and calculations, that's about as much as intuition can provide.

6.2 Quantitative Concepts

To analyze collisions quantitatively, more rigorous concepts from mechanics must be considered. Some concepts are reviewed here. Newton's second law for a constant mass moving in a given direction, say x, can be written as

$$m\frac{dv(\tau)}{d\tau} = F(\tau), \tag{6.1}$$

where m is a constant mass, τ is time, $v(\tau)$ is velocity, and $v(\tau) = dx/d\tau$. The force, $F(\tau)$, represents the resultant or sum of all forces in the x direction acting on the mass. Equation 6.1 can be integrated over the time interval τ_1 to τ_2, which gives

$$m\int_{\tau_1}^{\tau_2} dv = mv(\tau_2) - mv(\tau_1) = mV - mv = \int_{\tau_1}^{\tau_2} F(\tau)d\tau. \tag{6.2}$$

Velocities are written as $v(\tau_2) \equiv V$ and $v(\tau_1) \equiv v$; this notation is used whenever possible throughout the following chapters. That is, capital or uppercase symbols are used for final velocities and small or lowercase symbols are used for initial velocities. The product of mass and velocity is given the special name of *momentum*; that is, mv is the momentum of a body of mass m moving with a velocity $v(\tau)$, mV is final momentum, and mv is the initial momentum. The indefinite integral of a force, $F(\tau)$, over an interval of time from τ_1 to τ, is defined as the *impulse*, $p(\tau)$, of the force and is written as

$$p(\tau) = \int_{\tau_1}^{\tau} F(\tau)d\tau. \tag{6.3}$$

Substituting Eq. 6.3 into Eq. 6.2 gives

$$mV - mv = P, \tag{6.4}$$

where (uppercase) P is the impulse at τ_2. These relationships follow directly from Newton's second law and show that the change in momentum (final minus initial) of a body is equal to the impulse of the resultant force.

Consider a rigid block of weight $W = 25$ lb (111 N) that slides over a flat surface to rest from an initial velocity $v_0 = 24$ ft/s (7.32 m/s). It travels along a straight line on the surface over a distance, d. The friction between the block and the surface has a constant friction coefficient, $f = 0.65$. Determine the distance, d, the total (final) impulse, P, and the change in momentum of the block. **Example 6.1**

Solution Because friction is constant, constant-acceleration equations can be used in this problem. The acceleration is due to friction and supplies a retarding force equal to the product of the weight and the friction coefficient. This retarding force is $F_f = -fW = -0.65(25) = -16.25$ lb (-72.3 N). From Newton's second law, the acceleration is the force divided by the mass, or simply $a = -fg$. The velocity as a function of time, τ, is given by (see Eq. 3.2)

$$v(\tau) = v_0 + a\tau.$$

The block comes to rest when $v(\tau) = V = 0$. Solving for the time to rest gives $\tau = -v_0/a$ and has the value $\tau = 1.15$ s. The impulse supplied by the friction force is computed from Eq. 6.3:

$$P = \int_{\tau_1}^{\tau_2} F(\tau)d\tau = \int_0^{1.15} -16.25\,d\tau = -18.63 \text{ lb-s } (-82.87 \text{ N-s}).$$

The sign of the impulse is negative because the force is a retarding force. The change in momentum is $m(V - v)$, so the change in momentum is $-(25/32.2)24 = -18.63$ lb-s (-82.87 N-s). These results verify Eq. 6.4, that is, that the change in momentum is equal to the impulse of the resultant force.

Note that this example uses concepts of impulse and momentum, yet has nothing to do with impact or collisions. Equation 6.4 is true in general, not just for studying collisions. It does have special significance for the study of impact, as will be seen shortly.

6.3 Point-Mass Impulse–Momentum Collision Theory

When two moving bodies collide and are in contact for a relatively short time, the contact force tends to be significantly higher than other forces acting on the bodies. The resulting high acceleration of the contact force and its large impulse dominate impulses of much smaller forces. In these circumstances, Newton's laws of impulse and momentum can be applied to each of the bodies without considering other forces during the contact duration. Consider bodies m_1 and m_2 as shown in Fig. 6.2. The x–y axes are fixed reference coordinates. Because the collision depends on the geometry of the contact, the normal (or perpendicular), at the contact area has its own normal and tangential axes, n–t. Applying Eq. 6.4 to body m_1 in the n, or normal, direction gives

$$m_1 V_{1n} - m_1 v_{1n} = P_n. \tag{6.5}$$

Doing the same in the t direction gives

$$m_1 V_{1t} - m_1 v_{1t} = P_t. \tag{6.6}$$

Figure 6.2
Free body diagram of two colliding point masses with contact impulse components, P_n and P_t.

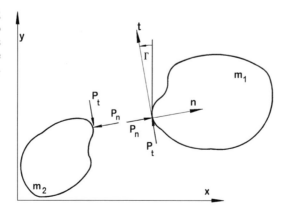

Likewise, Eq. 6.4 applied to body m_2 gives two more equations:

$$m_2 V_{2n} - m_2 v_{2n} = -P_n, \qquad (6.7)$$

$$m_2 V_{2t} - m_2 v_{2t} = -P_t. \qquad (6.8)$$

Because the contact duration is relatively short, the positions of the bodies do not change significantly, so it is assumed that the velocities change instantaneously without any changes in position. Equations 6.5 through 6.8 are known as the planar point-mass impulse–momentum equations. If Eqs. 6.5 and 6.7 are added and Eqs. 6.6 and 6.8 are added, two new equations result:

$$(m_1 V_{1n} - m_1 v_{1n}) + (m_2 V_{2n} - m_2 v_{2n}) = 0, \qquad (6.9)$$

$$(m_1 V_{1t} - m_1 v_{1t}) + (m_2 V_{2t} - m_2 v_{2t}) = 0. \qquad (6.10)$$

Equation 6.9 is the change in the momentum of the system (the combination of both point masses) in the n direction. Because the sum is zero, the system momentum does not change and Eq. 6.9 is an expression of the conservation of momentum in the n direction. Likewise, Eq. 6.10 expresses the conservation of system momentum in the t direction.

Suppose the masses and initial velocities are known. Can the above equations be solved for the final velocities? To answer this question, it is necessary to count equations and unknowns. When two point masses such as in Fig. 6.2 collide, there are six unknowns: V_{1n}, V_{1t}, V_{2n}, V_{2t}, P_n, and P_t. But so far there are only four independent equations (Eqs. 6.9 and 6.10 cannot be counted because they came from Eqs. 6.5 through 6.8 and add nothing new). To get a solution, two more equations are needed. The first comes from the definition of a *coefficient of restitution, e*. The coefficient of restitution relates the final relative normal rebound velocity to the initial relative normal velocity:

$$V_{2n} - V_{1n} = -e(v_{2n} - v_{1n}). \qquad (6.11)$$

Other definitions of the coefficient of restitution exist that relate the rebound normal impulse and the approach normal impulse, but they are not discussed here. The coefficient of restitution, e, defined by Eq. 6.11 is known as Newton's coefficient of restitution and is also known as the kinematic coefficient of restitution. A sixth equation is found by relating the tangential impulse component to the normal impulse component:

$$P_t = \mu P_n, \qquad (6.12)$$

where the quantity μ is called the *impulse ratio*. The impulse ratio is *not* a coefficient of friction, although it can be related to it. At this point, the quantity μ should be viewed simply as $\mu = P_t / P_n$. It is also important to note that μ can be positive or negative, depending on the initial conditions. More on the relationship between friction and the impulse ratio is presented later.

The impulse ratio given by Eq. 6.12 is not the only valid sixth equation that can be used for modeling the tangential contact process and formulating the planar point-mass impact problem. Another possibility is to use a tangential coefficient of restitution, and there are even other possibilities; see Brach[1] for a more in-depth discussion of this topic. Equation 6.12 has been found to be the best way of characterizing the tangential contact process for the solution of planar impact problems.

At this point there are six equations (6.5, 6.6, 6.7, 6.8, 6.11, and 6.12) and the six unknowns listed earlier. These are called the *system equations*. Because they are linear, the system equations can be solved for the unknowns; the solutions comprise six *solution equations*. The solution equations for the final velocities can be placed into a convenient form as

$$V_{1n} = v_{1n} + \overline{m}(1 + e)(v_{2n} - v_{1n})/m_1, \tag{6.13}$$

$$V_{2n} = v_{2n} - \overline{m}(1 + e)(v_{2n} - v_{1n})/m_2, \tag{6.14}$$

$$V_{1t} = v_{1t} + \mu\overline{m}(1 + e)(v_{2n} - v_{1n})/m_1, \tag{6.15}$$

$$V_{2t} = v_{2t} - \mu\overline{m}(1 + e)(v_{2n} - v_{1n})/m_2, \tag{6.16}$$

where

$$\overline{m} = \frac{m_1 m_2}{m_1 + m_2}. \tag{6.17}$$

If the impulse components are needed, they can be obtained by substituting the final velocities from these equations into two of Eqs. 6.5 through 6.8 and solving for P_n and P_t.

For the study of vehicle collisions, some additional information is always important. Two such quantities are the velocity changes and the kinetic energy loss in the collision. The velocity change, ΔV_1, of m_1 is the vector magnitude of the components $(V_{1n} - v_{1n})$ and $(V_{1t} - v_{1t})$. The velocity change, Δv_2, of m_2 is the same with subscripts $2n$ and $2t$. A convenient expression can be shown to be

$$\Delta V_i = \frac{\overline{m}(v_{2n} - v_{1n})}{m_i}(1 + e)\sqrt{1 + \mu^2}, \quad i = 1, 2. \tag{6.18}$$

The kinetic energy loss of the collision, T_L, can be found by subtracting the final kinetic energy from the initial:

$$T_L = \frac{1}{2}m_1(v_{1n}^2 + v_{1t}^2) + \frac{1}{2}m_2(v_{2n}^2 + v_{2t}^2) - \frac{1}{2}m_1(V_{1n}^2 + V_{1t}^2) \tag{6.19}$$

$$- \frac{1}{2}m_2(V_{2n}^2 + V_{2t}^2).$$

The final velocity components from the solution equations can be substituted into Eq. 6.19 to get

$$T_L = \frac{1}{2}\overline{m}(v_{2n} - v_{1n})^2(1 + e)[(1 - e) + 2\mu r - (1 + e)\mu^2], \tag{6.20}$$

where r depends on the initial velocity components,

$$r = \frac{v_{2t} - v_{1t}}{v_{2n} - v_{1n}}. \tag{6.21}$$

Note that the energy loss in a collision is proportional to $(v_{2n} - v_{1n})^2$, where $(v_{2n} - v_{1n})$ is the initial relative normal velocity of the masses, sometimes referred to as the *closing speed*.

6.3.1   Coefficient of Restitution, Frictionless Point-Mass Collisions

To better understand the meaning of some of these results, consider some special cases. Suppose that the tangential impulse, P_t, is zero; that is, the collision is "frictionless." To achieve this, μ is set to zero in all of the equations. Note that this also corresponds to a normal, or head-on, collision. For $\mu = 0$, the kinetic energy loss is

$$T_L = \frac{1}{2}\overline{m}(1 - e^2)(v_{2n} - v_{1n})^2. \tag{6.22}$$

This shows that the value of the coefficient of restitution, e, determines the energy loss in a way such that when $e = 1$, the kinetic energy loss is zero (a perfectly elastic collision). When $e = 0$, the collision is perfectly plastic, the bodies remain together after the collision, and the kinetic energy loss is a maximum. Because energy *loss* cannot be negative, $e^2 \leqslant 1$. By definition, e^2 cannot be negative, so it can be concluded that $0 \leqslant e^2 \leqslant 1$. If $e > 0$, then this implies that $0 \leqslant e \leqslant 1$ as well. Note that $e = 0$ does not mean that all of the system's initial kinetic energy is lost.

What about $e < 0$? According to Eq. 6.22, negative values of $-1 \leqslant e \leqslant 0$ do not violate energy conservation. Examination of Eq. 6.11 indicates that negative values of e imply that the bodies pass through each other. For ordinary collisions, this is impossible. There are some exceptions, but these are rare and are not discussed here.

6.3.2   Collisions Where Sliding Ends; the Critical Impulse Ratio, μ_0

Consider the special case where rough contact conditions develop a tangential impulse, P_t, large enough to cause sliding (relative tangential velocity between m_1 and m_2) to end at or prior to separation of the two bodies. This corresponds to the final condition where $V_{2t} - V_{1t} = 0$. Using this condition with Eqs. 6.15 and 6.16 gives an interesting and very useful result; that is, $V_{2t} - V_{1t} = 0$ when

$$\mu = \mu_0 = \frac{r}{1 + e}, \tag{6.23}$$

where r is given by Eq. 6.21. This impulse ratio, μ_0, is called the *critical impulse ratio*. Note that μ_0 takes on the sign of r, which, in turn, is determined by the initial conditions. So this means that when $\mu = \mu_0$ the bodies have the same velocity components in the t, or tangential, direction at separation. There is another way of looking at this. By definition, $P_t = \mu P_n$, so sliding does not exist at separation when $P_t = \mu_0 P_n$. It is reasonable to conclude that when

$|P_t| < |\mu_0 P_n|$, sliding exists at separation, which implies that sliding exists at separation when $|\mu| < |\mu_0|$. The absolute value signs are necessary because the sign of μ determines the direction of the tangential impulse, P_t. If now it is assumed that the tangential impulse is generated by a frictional type force with an average frictional drag coefficient, f and $f < |\mu_0|$, then sliding continues through separation, whereas if the average frictional drag coefficient is such that $f = |\mu_0|$, then sliding will end at separation, and if $f > |\mu_0|$, sliding will end before separation. Further investigation shows that, in general, as μ is increased from 0 to μ_0, a maximum kinetic energy loss occurs when μ reaches μ_0.[1]

To summarize, in a collision of two point masses with a frictional drag coefficient, f, over the contact surface where $f < |\mu_0|$, then $\mu = f \, \text{sgn}\,(\mu)$. If $f \geq |\mu_0|$, then $\mu = \mu_0$, and sliding ends at or before separation.

6.3.3 Sideswipe Collisions and Common-Velocity Conditions

In the context of vehicle collisions, a value of the impulse ratio $\mu < \mu_0$ implies a sideswipe collision, because the vehicles continue to slide over the intervehicular contact surface throughout the contact duration. In fact, this is used as a definition of a sideswipe collision in this book, that is, a *sideswipe* collision is a collision where $\mu < \mu_0$.

When $\mu = \mu_0$, relative tangential motion (sliding) ends at or before separation. Furthermore, when the coefficient of restitution $e = 0$, the bodies (automobiles) do not rebound or separate in the normal direction either. Consequently, at the end of the collision, the bodies have identical velocity components—that is, a condition frequently referred to as a common velocity. So, in this book, the *common-velocity conditions* are when $e = 0$ and $\mu = \mu_0$. For point-mass theory, this means the bodies remain attached after impact.

At this point it can be said that the common-velocity conditions are satisfied for most direct, high-speed collisions. This will be discussed later.

Example 6.2

Two vehicles collide at right angles, as shown in Fig. 6.3. Vehicle 2 initially is at rest; Vehicle 1 moves in the direction of its heading at a speed of 13.41 m/s (44 ft/s) into Vehicle 2. Following the impact, both move with the same speed in the original direction of Vehicle 1. The solid curve in the graph in Fig. 6.4 is typical of an experimental acceleration record of the mass center of Vehicle 1 from this type of collision. Use the shape of this curve and the dashed triangular pulse to estimate the peak (maximum) deceleration of Vehicle 1 and the peak intervehicular force during the impact. Vehicle weights are $W_1 = 2223$ kg (4900 lb); $W_2 = 1023$ kg (2255 lb). Assume that the impulse of the tire–roadway forces are negligible.

Solution Because both vehicles have the same final speed, $e = 0$. Equations 6.13 and 6.14 give

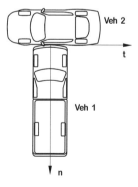

Figure 6.3
Collision configuration of two vehicles, Vehicle 2 initially at rest.

$$V_{2n} = V_{1n} = v_{1n} + \frac{m_2}{m_1 + m_2}(v_{2n} - v_{1n}) = -13.41 + (0.315)13.41$$
$$= 9.18 \text{ m/s} (-30.1 \text{ ft/s}).$$

The velocity change of Vehicle 1 is $\Delta v_1 = -4.23$ m/s (-13.9 ft/s). The area of the dashed, idealized, triangular peak force is equal to the impulse, P_n. Equation 6.5 gives

$$P_n = m_1(V_{1n} - v_{1n}) = 2223(-9.18 + 13.41) = 9403 \text{ N-s (2114 lb-s)}$$

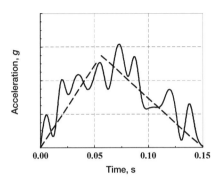

Figure 6.4
Normal acceleration component, g, of Vehicle 1, Example 6.2.

From Fig. 6.4, the impulse duration is 0.15 s. The average force is $P_n/(\tau_2 - \tau_1) =$ 62,689 N (14,094 lb); based on a triangular shape, the peak force is 125,377 N (28,186 lb). The corresponding peak deceleration for Vehicle 1 is 5.75 g. The actual peak from the solid curve is about 15% higher than the peak of the triangle, or 6.61 g. A rule of thumb for vehicle impacts is that the maximum acceleration and force are about two to three times the average values. Shapes other than triangles can be used to approximate vehicle crash pulses; for more information, see Varat and Husher.[2] ⬡

For a pair of bodies with known properties and with known coefficient values, the above equations (Eqs. 13 through 16) permit calculation of the final velocities from known initial velocities. For accident reconstruction purposes, it is often convenient to solve the inverse problem, that is, to determine the initial velocities given final velocities. Despite the fact that Eqs. 13 through 16 are linear and an inverse mathematical solution is possible, this approach is not practical, because most vehicle collision applications use the common-velocity conditions. The inverse solution contains terms involving $1/e$, which becomes unbounded when $e = 0$. Consequently, in typical applications the equations are solved in an iterative fashion to find a solution.

6.4 Controlled Collisions

Barrier collisions are used to collect a wide variety of data, including monitoring performance of safety components such as sensors and restraints, measurements of anthropometric accelerations, leakage of flammable liquids, structural crashworthiness of vehicles and vehicle component designs, and so on. Barrier collisions are used to test for conformance to FMVSS regulations. Certain configurations of crash tests are more common than others. Full frontal impacts into rigid fixed barriers, rear impacts by moving rigid barriers, side impacts with moving rigid and deformable barriers, and frontal offset impacts into rigid and deformable barriers are used the most. Vehicle-to-vehicle collisions also are used for testing, although this type of test is less frequent and finds application in reproducing collisions between specific vehicles in technical work for litigation. The New Car Assessment Program (NCAP) conducted by the National Highway Traffic Safety Administration (NHTSA) uses full frontal fixed rigid barrier tests at 35 mph (56.33 km/h) and is said to represent the effect of a vehicle directly colliding at 70 mph (112.65 km/h) with another identical, but stationary, vehicle. It also can be said that the NCAP tests are equivalent to a direct collision with an identical vehicle where both vehicles move toward each other at 35 mph. A point here is that barrier crash tests in some way are viewed as being equivalent to accidental crashes. By and large, such concepts of equivalency are useful in reconstructions in a subjective sense and permit comparisons of actual crashes to hypothetical and/or controlled ones.

Before questions of equivalency can be established, the conditions of equivalency must be determined. If the same ΔV is desired from the barrier test, the barrier speed may be different than if the same structural energy absorption from crash to test is desired. In most cases, the equations for the collinear point-mass collisions can be used to establish equivalency.

Example 6.3   An experimental frontal collision of a vehicle with mass, m_1, into a fixed rigid barrier is intended to reproduce approximately a direct frontal collision into another vehicle with mass, m_2. The initial vehicle-to-vehicle speeds are $-v$ and v, respectively. Determine the equivalent barrier speed, v_b, of m_1

    A. to have the same ΔV and momentum change for m_1 as in the vehicle-to-vehicle collision, and

    B. to dissipate the same kinetic energy of m_1 as the vehicle-to-vehicle collision.

Assume perfectly plastic collisions (common velocity condition) for all collisions.

Solution A   For a direct collinear collision, no transverse force or impulse can develop, so $\mu = 0$. Equation 6.18 gives ΔV_1 as

$$\Delta V_1 = \overline{m}(1 + e)(v_{2n} - v_{1n}) / m_1 = 2m_2 v_1 / (m_1 + m_2).$$

From the same equation, ΔV_1 for a fixed barrier collision, for $m_2 \to \infty$ and $v_{2n} = 0$, simply is v_b. Equating these gives

$$v_b = v_1 \frac{2m_2}{m_1 + m_2},$$

where v_b is the equivalent barrier speed.

Solution B   In the case of energy dissipation, the kinetic energy loss, T_{L1}, of m_1 must first be determined. For $e = 0$ and using Eq. 6.13 this is

$$T_{L1} = \frac{1}{2}m_1 v_{1n}^2 - \frac{1}{2}m_1 V_{1n}^2 = 2\overline{m}\left(1 - \frac{\overline{m}}{m_1}\right)v^2.$$

The energy loss to m_1 from a barrier collision for $e = 0$ is $\frac{1}{2}m_1 v_b^2$. Equating these gives

$$v_b = 2v\sqrt{\frac{\overline{m}}{m_1 + m_2}}. \qquad\qquad \bigcirc$$

The two equivalent barrier speeds in Example 6.3 are different; however, both are useful and practical quantities. If the main interest is injury potential, equivalency based on ΔV makes sense. On the other hand, if structural crashworthiness is important, then ΔV based on energy loss can be more pertinent. The example clearly shows that different equivalent barrier speeds can exist for a given collision, and they should be fully defined and explained.

An interesting question can be raised in the interpretation of the results of B of Example 6.3. Is the crush energy, E_c, for m_1 from the barrier test the same as for the collision between m_1 and m_2? Without additional information, this question cannot be answered. In the barrier collision, all of the energy loss goes into crushing m_1. In the vehicle-to-vehicle crash, the amount of crush depends on the relative stiffness (resistance to deformation) of the two vehicles. The stiffer vehicle will deform less and absorb less energy. In an extreme where m_2 is a rigid movable barrier, m_1 will absorb all of the energy loss of the collision, not just its own energy loss as posed in the problem. This is covered more thoroughly in Chapter 7.

Energy equivalent barrier speed (EEBS), equivalent barrier speed (EBS), and barrier equivalent velocity (BEV) are terms commonly used to analogize the severity of an accident reconstruction. These terms typically refer to the forward speed and corresponding kinetic energy with which a vehicle must contact a flat fixed rigid barrier at 90° for equivalence to conditions of another collision. For example, the energy may be equal to a specified amount of residual crush. It is usually assumed that in the equivalent barrier collision, all energy is absorbed and there is no rebound. The nature of the equivalency should always be spelled out.

6.4.1 Coefficients of Restitution

When full frontal rigid barrier crash tests are conducted, it is rare that there is absolutely no rebound of the vehicle. This means that the coefficient of restitution is not actually zero. For most high-speed collisions, contact rebound is small and often can be ignored, but there always are cases where it should be taken into account. Table 6.1 shows the results of tests carried out for the NHTSA from barrier crashes of 26 vehicles manufactured in 1989 and 1990. The average and standard deviation are $e_{bavg} = 0.112$ and $s_b = 0.028$, respectively. Individual collision speeds for these test values were not listed, but typically were 30 or 35 mph (48.3 or 56.3 km/h). Use of this data for reconstructions of collisions requires care. First, application should be restricted to full frontal collisions to maintain similar damage patterns. Second, values of the coefficients of restitution from frontal barrier tests are associated with an individual vehicle, to the specific crush pattern, and, to a small extent, to the physical properties of the barrier. On the other hand, the coefficient of restitution defined and used in the theory of point-mass impact mechanics covered above (and the planar mechanics to be covered later), corresponds to a single collision of two different

Table 6.1
Coefficients of
restitution from
rigid barrier tests.

Table 6.1 Coefficients of restitution from rigid barrier tests.

Year	Make	Model	e
89	Toyota	Cressida	0.115
89	Ford	Bronco	0.036
89	Hyundai	Sonata	0.116
89	Audi	80	0.124
89	Volkswagen	Fox	0.070
89	Peugeot	505	0.118
89	Geo	Metro	0.100
89	Geo	Metro	0.104
89	Nissan/Datsun	Maxima	0.074
89	Nissan/Datsun	Pickup	0.096
90	Lexus	ES250	0.131
90	Hyundai	Excel GLS	0.120
90	Ford	Taurus	0.143
90	Geo	Prizm	0.141
90	Nissan/Datsun	Axxess	0.136
90	Toyota	Celica	0.138
90	Chevrolet	Blazer MPV	0.109
90	Chevrolet	S10 Pickup	0.102
90	Ford	Ranger	0.054
90	Nissan/Datsun	Infinity M30	0.131
90	Lincoln	Town Car	0.166
90	Ford	Mustang	0.106
90	BMW	325 I	0.110
90	Honda	Prelude	0.128
90	Mercedes	190	0.121
90	Buick	LeSabre	0.111

Source: Data from Prasad.[3]

vehicles. In fact, it is an impact parameter, a collision parameter, that characterizes the energy loss *of the collision*, not the individual vehicles. As will be shown shortly, it is possible to relate individual, vehicle/barrier values, e_1 and e_2, and determine a single, combined value for a collision of those specific vehicles. In fact, it can be done in more than one way. Other reconstruction techniques, such as SMAC[4] and CRASH,[5] have been extended to use individual vehicle coefficients of restitution; see McHenry and McHenry.[6]

6.4.1.1 Stiffness Equivalent Collision Coefficient of Restitution

The two coefficients, e_1 and e_2, from barrier tests of Vehicle 1 and Vehicle 2, respectively, can be related for direct central impacts through their energy losses and their crush stiffnesses. The approach presented here has been used by others; for example, see Prasad.[3] Collisions can be viewed as having two phases or stages: approach and rebound. The point of demarcation is the point of maximum compression. The kinetic energy given back (through "restitution") is e^2 times what is stored and the amount lost is $(1 - e^2)$ times what is stored. From Eq. 6.22, for direct central collisions at the time of maximum approach, the energy stored in the combined vehicles at maximum deformation is $E_T = \frac{1}{2}\overline{m} \, (v_{2n} - v_{1n})^2$. The amount of energy returned as kinetic energy during rebound is $e^2 \times \frac{1}{2}\overline{m}(v_{2n} - v_{1n})^2$ and the amount lost is $(1 - e^2)E_T$. The total energy lost during the collision can be written as

$$T_L = (1 - e_1^2)E_1 + (1 - e_2^2)E_2 = (1 - e^2)E_T, \qquad (6.24)$$

where E_1 and E_2 are the energy losses of each vehicle corresponding to the respective, individual barrier-test coefficients of restitution, e_1 and e_2. If it is assumed that the crushing deformation during the approach phase for each vehicle can be modeled as linear elastic springs with stiffness k, then each must have equal and opposite force levels at all times and $k_1C_1 = k_2C_2$, where C_i represents crush deformation. Squaring this relationship and recognizing that for a linear spring, $E = \frac{1}{2}kC^2$, the crush energies in the vehicles are related by

$$E_1 k_1 = E_2 k_2 = E_T \bar{k}, \qquad (6.25)$$

where

$$\bar{k} = \frac{k_1 k_2}{k_1 + k_2}. \qquad (6.26)$$

Using these in Eq. 6.24 and solving for e gives a single stiffness equivalent coefficient or restitution,

$$e_k = \frac{e_1^2 k_2 + e_2^2 k_1}{k_1 + k_2}. \qquad (6.27)$$

6.4.1.2 Mass Equivalent Collision Coefficient of Restitution

Another approach can be used to determine a single, equivalent coefficient of restitution from two barrier-test values. During a direct, central vehicle-to-vehicle collision, at the time of maximum compression (at the end of approach), both vehicles have the same velocity, v_c. This velocity can be found by letting $V_{1n} = V_{2n} = v_c$ in Eq. 6.9. Omitting subscripts, n, gives

$$v_c = \frac{m_1 v_1 + m_2 v_2}{m_1 + m_2}. \qquad (6.28)$$

A view can be taken that during a direct central vehicle-to-vehicle collision, approach and rebound is equivalent to each vehicle hitting (or being hit by) a rigid barrier moving with closing speed v_c. This means that the closing speed for Vehicle 1 is $v_c - v_1$ and is $v_2 - v_c$ for Vehicle 2. Equating the sum of the individual energy losses to the collision energy loss using Eq. 6.22 gives

$$\frac{1}{2}(1 - e_1^2)m_1(v_c - v_1)^2 + \frac{1}{2}(1 - e_2^2)m_2(v_2 - v_c)^2 = \frac{1}{2}(1 - e^2)\bar{m}(v_2 - v_1)^2, \qquad (6.29)$$

where

$$\bar{m} = \frac{m_1 m_2}{m_1 + m_2}. \qquad (6.30)$$

Solving for e from Eq. 6.29 and using Eq. 6.30 gives a single, mass equivalent coefficient of restitution,

$$e_m = \sqrt{\frac{e_1^2 m_2 + e_2^2 m_1}{m_1 + m_2}}. \qquad (6.31)$$

It is clear that, in general, e_k and e_m will give different results. A question immediately arises concerning which gives better results or under what circumstances one is more accurate than the other. There appears to be no comparison made on the basis of experiments. Because stiffness modeling is a common procedure in accident reconstruction based on residual crush (see Chapter 8), it might be inferred that e_k might be more realistic. However, it must be kept in mind that the derivation of Eq. 6.27 is based on an assumption that crush deformation behavior during approach is similar to a pair of linear elastic springs. This assumption certainly is not true. On the other hand, Eq. 6.31 is based on an assumption that the energy loss of each vehicle during the vehicle-to-vehicle collision is identical to the individual vehicle-to-barrier collisions. This is not likely to be true because crush patterns can differ significantly. So which should be used? Absent specific knowledge in an individual application that favors e_k or e_m, a prudent approach would be to calculate and use both quantities for a reconstruction and use the two results as a measure of uncertainty.

6.5   Planar Impact Mechanics

In the earlier equations and applications of this chapter, angular velocities, rotational inertia, and angular rotational momentum were ignored. In some applications, this is acceptable. Fortunately, rotational effects can be treated rigorously without difficulty. In this section, the system equations and solution equations of planar impact mechanics are derived and presented following the approach developed by Brach.[1] Sometimes the theory that follows is referred to as *rigid-body impact theory*. Rigid-body theory does not mean that the colliding bodies are not deformable but rather that rotational inertia is taken into account and each body's preimpact dimensions are used. Before deriving equations, however, consider some concepts that were learned in the section on point-mass equations:

- Application of Newton's second law in the form of impulse and momentum provided a algebraic approach to the modeling of impacts; no integration is necessary.
- The impact problem was formulated where the final velocities and impulses were calculated from known initial velocities.
- Newton's laws alone produced too few equations to formulate the problem and get solution equations; equations defining, or characterizing, the normal and tangential processes had to be defined.

The definitions of the coefficient of restitution and impulse ratio coefficient, respectively, earlier filled the need for additional equations. These concepts carry over into the planar impact problem. The derivation here is a completely general formulation of the planar problem. However, keep in mind that all applications herein are to vehicle collisions that almost always have low values of the coefficient of restitution; that is, they are highly inelastic.

Figure 6.5 shows two bodies, separated in the form of free body diagrams, representing vehicles with masses m_1 and m_2, rotational inertias I_1, and I_2, and with a common contact point, C. A local, fixed (x,y) reference coordinate system

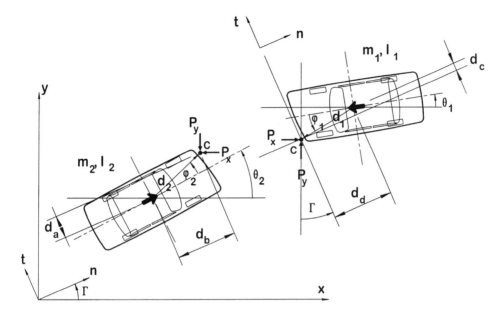

Figure 6.5
Free body diagram of the planar impact of two vehicles showing coordinates and dimensions.

is attached to the ground. The orientations of the bodies at the time of impact are indicated by heading angles, θ_1 and θ_2, relative to the (x,y) system. The common point, C, is located relative to the centers of gravity by distances d_1 and d_2 and angles φ_1 and φ_2. A normal and tangential coordinate system, (n,t), is referenced to a common contact or crush surface and is oriented with respect to the (x,y) system by the angle, Γ. Other distances are

$$d_a = d_2 \sin (\theta_2 + \varphi_2 - \Gamma), \tag{6.32}$$

$$d_b = d_2 \cos (\theta_2 + \varphi_2 - \Gamma), \tag{6.33}$$

$$d_c = d_1 \sin (\theta_1 + \varphi_1 - \Gamma), \tag{6.34}$$

$$d_d = d_1 \cos (\theta_1 + \varphi_1 - \Gamma). \tag{6.35}$$

These are the moment arms of the normal and tangential impulse components, P_n and P_t, and are needed shortly. Impulse components and initial and final velocity components can be transformed from the (x,y) to the (n,t) systems using trigonometry. For example, the relationship between impulse components is given by

$$P_n = P_x \cos \Gamma + P_y \sin \Gamma \tag{6.36}$$

and

$$P_t = P_x \sin \Gamma + P_y \cos \Gamma. \tag{6.37}$$

An assumption now is made that the level of force acting over the common contact surface is significantly higher than other forces. (In accident reconstructions, these other forces would be aerodynamic force, tire–roadway friction, etc.) So impulses of all forces other than contact forces are neglected. In addition, the contact duration, or more accurately the duration of the contact force impulse, is assumed to be very short. This implies that during contact, accelerations are high, so that velocities change suddenly and displacements (changes in position and orientation) are negligible. With these assumptions, Newton's laws in the form of impulse and momentum can be applied directly to the bodies as shown in Fig. 6.5. The equations of impulse and momentum for m_1 and m_2 in the x and y direction are

$$m_1 V_{1x} - m_1 v_{1x} = P_x, \tag{6.38}$$

$$m_2 V_{2x} - m_2 v_{2x} = -P_x, \tag{6.39}$$

$$m_1 V_{1y} - m_1 v_{1y} = P_y, \tag{6.40}$$

$$m_2 V_{2y} - m_2 v_{2y} = -P_y. \tag{6.41}$$

According to Newton's second law, the change in angular momentum is equal to the moments of the impulses on each body. Applying to each mass gives

$$m_1 k_1^2 \, (\Omega_1 - \omega_1) = P_n d_c - P_t d_d, \tag{6.42}$$

$$m_2 k_2^2 \, (\Omega_2 - \omega_2) = P_n d_a - P_t d_b. \tag{6.43}$$

The variables k_1 and k_2 are the radii of gyration of the bodies about their mass centers. In other words, the corresponding moments of inertia are given by $I_1 = m_1 k_1^2$ and $I_2 = m_2 k_2^2$. Recall that uppercase symbols represent values of variables at the end of the contact duration and lowercase symbols represent the beginning of contact. This is true for the linear velocities, angular velocities, and impulses (the initial impulses, at the beginning of contact, are zero). Counting equations and unknowns at this point gives six equations, Eqs. 6.38 through 6.43, and eight unknowns, V_{1x}, V_{1y}, V_{2x}, V_{2y}, Ω_1, Ω_2, P_x, and P_y. Two more equations are needed and so two coefficients are defined.

The coefficient of restitution is defined as the ratio of the relative normal velocity at point C at the end of contact to the relative normal velocity at the beginning of contact. That is,

$$e = -V_{Crn} / v_{crn}, \tag{6.44}$$

where the subscript C indicates the location, r indicates relative velocity, and n indicates the normal velocity components. These relative velocities at point C are

$$V_{Crn} = V_{1n} + d_c \Omega_1 - V_{2n} + d_a \Omega_2 \tag{6.45}$$

and

$$v_{Crn} = v_{1n} + d_c \omega_1 - v_{2n} + d_a \omega_2. \tag{6.46}$$

The impulse ratio coefficient, μ, defined earlier as the ratio of the tangential to normal impulse components, is used as well:

$$P_t = \mu P_n. \tag{6.47}$$

There now are eight equations and eight unknowns. The equations are linear and can be solved; in fact, the solution equations can be written explicitly as follows:[1]

$$V_{1n} = v_{1n} + \overline{m}\,(1 + e)\,v_{rn}\mathrm{q}\,/\,m_1\,, \tag{6.48}$$

$$V_{1t} = v_{1t} + \mu\overline{m}\,(1 + e)v_{rn}\mathrm{q}\,/\,m_1\,, \tag{6.49}$$

$$V_{2n} = v_{2n} - \overline{m}\,(1 + e)\,v_{rn}\mathrm{q}\,/\,m_2\,, \tag{6.50}$$

$$V_{2t} = v_{2t} - \mu\overline{m}\,(1 + e)v_{rn}\mathrm{q}\,/\,m_2\,, \tag{6.51}$$

$$\Omega_1 = \omega_1 + \overline{m}\,(1 + e)v_{rn}\,(d_c - \mu d_d)\mathrm{q}\,/\,(m_1 k_1^2), \tag{6.52}$$

$$\Omega_2 = \omega_2 + \overline{m}\,(1 + e)v_{rn}\,(d_a - \mu d_b)\mathrm{q}\,/\,(m_2 k_2^2), \tag{6.53}$$

where $\overline{m}$ is given by Eq. 6.17,

$$v_{rn} = (v_{2n} - d_a\omega_2) - (v_{1n} + d_c\omega_1), \tag{6.54}$$

and q is found from

$$\frac{1}{q} = 1 + \frac{\overline{m}d_a^2}{m_2 k_2^2} + \frac{\overline{m}d_c^2}{m_1 k_1^2} - \mu\left(\frac{\overline{m}d_c d_d}{m_1 k_1^2} + \frac{\overline{m}d_a d_b}{m_2 k_2^2}\right). \tag{6.55}$$

Note that the velocities in the above equations, $V_{1n}, V_{2n}, V_{1t}, V_{2t}, v_{1n}, v_{2n}, v_{1t},$ and v_{2t} all are mass center velocities. With the solution equations available, some important quantities can be determined. The combined kinetic energy lost by both bodies in the collision, T_L, can be expressed as

$$T_L = \frac{1}{2}\overline{m}qv_{rn}^2(1 + e)\left[2 + 2\mu r - (1 + e)q\left(1 + \mu^2 + \frac{\overline{m}d_e^2}{m_1 k_1^2} + \frac{\overline{m}d_f^2}{m_2 k_2^2}\right)\right], \tag{6.56}$$

where

$$d_e = d_c - \mu d_d, \tag{6.57}$$

$$d_f = d_a - \mu d_b, \tag{6.58}$$

and

$$r = \frac{(v_{2t} - d_b\omega_2) - (v_{1t} + d_d\omega_1)}{(v_{2n} - d_a\omega_2) - (v_{1n} + d_c\omega_1)}. \tag{6.59}$$

An important quantity is the impulse ratio that gives the tangential common-velocity condition—that is, where $V_{1Ct} - V_{2Ct} = 0$. Note that this condition and the corresponding velocity components are at the contact point, C, not at the mass center. This gives the critical impulse ratio,

$$\mu_0 = \frac{rA + (1 + e)B}{(1 + e)(1 + C) + rB}, \tag{6.60}$$

where

$$A = 1 + \frac{\overline{m}d_c^2}{m_1 k_1^2} + \frac{\overline{m}d_a^2}{m_2 k_2^2}, \tag{6.61}$$

$$B = \frac{\overline{m}d_c d_d}{m_1 k_1^2} + \frac{\overline{m}d_a d_b}{m_2 k_2^2}, \tag{6.62}$$

$$C = \frac{\overline{m}d_d^2}{m_1 k_1^2} + \frac{\overline{m}d_b^2}{m_2 k_2^2}. \tag{6.63}$$

Recall that a final relative tangential velocity of zero is one of the common velocity conditions. Together, the common velocity conditions are $e = 0$ and $\mu = \mu_0$. Impulse components, P_x and P_y, can be calculated from Eqs. 6.38 and 6.40 once the final velocity components are determined from the solution equations.

6.5.1 Overview of Planar Impact Mechanics Model

Given certain information, the planar impact mechanics model provides a way of calculating the final velocity components and impulse components of two colliding vehicles. The input information can be grouped into four physical categories: the initial velocity components, the physical properties of the vehicles, the orientation angles (headings), and the collision-damage characteristics. In symbols these are:

- Initial velocity components: v_{1x}, v_{1y}, ω_1, v_{2x}, v_{2y}, ω_2
- Vehicle physical properties: m_1, I_1, m_2, I_2
- Orientation angles (headings): θ_1, θ_2
- Collision-damage characteristics: d_1, φ_1, d_2, φ_2, Γ, e, μ

In the last group of parameters, d_1, φ_1, d_2, φ_2, and Γ relate the damage and intervehicular contact surface of the combined vehicles to the collision, and e and μ relate to the level of energy loss. That e and μ characterize the energy loss is seen by the fact that when $e = 1$ and $\mu = 0$ the collision is a perfectly elastic and frictionless collision with no energy lost, and when $e = 0$ and $\mu = \mu_0$ the energy loss is a maximum.[1]

Example 6.4 Vehicle 1, a pickup truck with a weight of $W_1 = 4720$ lb (21.0 kN) is westbound at a speed of $v_1 = 30$ mph (48.3 km/h). It collides at a right angle with a northbound sedan, $W_2 = 2450$ lb (10.9 kN) with a speed of $v_2 = 30$ mph (48.3 km/h). The moments of inertia about the centers of gravity for the vehicles are $I_1 = 3655.6$ ft-lb-s² (4956.3 kg-m²) and $I_2 = 1317.5$ ft-lb-s² (1786.3 kg-m²). The vehicles are shown in Fig. 6.6 with the amount of penetration indicated. Neither vehicle has an initial yaw velocity. Use both point-mass theory and planar impact mechanics to calculate the final velocity components of both vehicles using common-velocity conditions. Compare the solutions including the kinetic energy loss, T_L.

Solution Taking the normal axis positive to the right and the tangential axis positive upward, the initial velocity components are $v_{1n} = -44.00$ ft/s $(-13.41$ m/s), $v_{1t} = 0.00$, $v_{2n} = 0.00$, and $v_{2t} = 44.00$ ft/s (13.41 m/s). The common-velocity conditions are $e = 0$ and $\mu = \mu_0$.

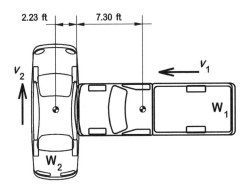

Figure 6.6
Collision configuration.

Point-mass equations: For $e = 0$, Eq. 6.23 for the critical impulse ratio gives $\mu_0 = r/(1 + e) = (v_{2t} - v_{1t})/(v_{2n} - v_{1n}) = 44/44 = 1$. Using Eqs. 6.13 through 6.16, the final velocity components are $V_{1n} = -28.97$ ft/s (8.83 m/s), $V_{1t} = 15.04$ ft/s 4.58 m/s), $V_{2n} = -28.97$ ft/s (8.83 m/s), and $V_{2t} = 15.04$ ft/s (4.58 m/s). According to point-mass impact theory, both vehicles have identical post-impact velocities. From Eq. 6.20, the kinetic energy loss is $T_L = 97,047$ ft-lb (131.6 kJ), which is 45% of the original system kinetic energy.

Planar impact mechanics: To evaluate the planar impact mechanics solution equations the input must be determined. The common-velocity conditions give that $e = 0$ and that $\mu = 100\% \ \mu_0$. Both the (x,y) and (n,t) axes coincide, and the crush surface angle $\Gamma = 0$. Vehicle 1 is oriented with a heading to the left (negative n direction) and so, from Fig. 6.5, $\theta_1 = 0°$; whereas Vehicle 2 is headed in the positive t direction, so $\theta_2 = 90°$. The angles φ_1 and φ_2 give the angles of the position of the distance vectors with lengths, d_1 and d_2, to the common point on the crush surface. From Fig. 6.6, $d_1 = 7.30$ ft (2.23 m) and $d_2 = 2.23$ ft (0.68 m). Furthermore, the vectors from the centers of gravity to point C make angles $\varphi_1 = 0°$ and $\varphi_2 = -90°$ (see Fig. 6.5). These form the input data to the solution of the planar impact mechanics equations. Figure 6.7 shows the results for this input from a spreadsheet solution. The final velocity components are $V_{1n} = -28.96$ ft/s (-8.83 m/s), $V_{1t} = 7.83$ ft/s (2.39 m/s), $V_{2n} = -28.96$ ft/s (-8.83 m/s), and $V_{2t} = 28.91$ ft/s (8.81 m/s). Because angular momentum is taken into account in this solution, final angular velocities are calculated: $\Omega_1 = -131.44°/s$ and $\Omega_2 = -111.41°/s$; the negative signs indicate a clockwise final yaw velocity for both vehicles. Finally, the initial kinetic energy of the two vehicles combined is 215,719 ft-lb (292 kJ) and the final kinetic energy is 141,928 ft-lb (192 kJ), so the energy loss is $T_L = 34.2\%$.

It is apparent that there are similarities and differences between the two solutions. The final velocity components in the east–west direction are identical for both solutions. Due to the inclusion of rotational inertia, the vehicles have final angular velocities from the planar solution, which are not included in the point-mass solution. The freedom to rotate and the fact that the contact area is not at the centers of gravity not only cause final angular velocities but also cause the final tangential velocity components to differ from the point-mass solution. Because of rotational effects, less momentum in the tangential

Figure 6.7
Results of a planar impact analysis.

		Vehicle 1		Vehicle 2	Initial speeds, mph			
		Vehicle 1		**Vehicle 2**	**Initial speeds, mph**			
5280/3600	1.467	146.70	mass, m	76.15	**Vehicle 1**		**Vehicle 2**	
g	32.2	3655.60	inertia, I	1317.50	30.0		30.0	
		7.30	distance, d	2.23				
e	0.00	0.00	angle, ϕ	-90.00	**Final speeds, mph**			
μ (% μ_0)	100.0	0.00	angle, θ	90.00	**Vehicle 1**		**Vehicle 2**	
μ	0.521				20.5		27.9	
μ_0	0.521		**initial**					
Γ	0.0	**Vehicle 1**	**velocity**	**Vehicle 2**		ΔV, ft/sec		
mbar	50.129	-44.00	v_x	0.00	**Vehicle 1**		**Vehicle 2**	
k_1^2	24.919	0.00	v_y	44.00	17.0		32.7	
k_2^2	17.301	0.00	ω	0.00				
q	1.000	44.00	v	44.00	**System Kinetic Energy**			
v_m	44.000	-44.00	v_n	0.00	Initial	215719		
v_{tn}	44.000	0.00	v_t	44.00	Final	141920		
r	1.000	-44.00	v_{cn}	0.00	Loss	73798	**34.2%**	
η_1	0.000	0.00	v_{ct}	44.00				
η_2	90.000				Range of Normal (Crush) Energy Loss:			
d_a	0.000		**final**		48525	22.5%	48525	22.5%
d_b	2.230	**Vehicle 1**	**velocity**	**Vehicle 2**	Range of Tangential Energy Loss:			
d_c	0.000	-28.96	V_x	-28.96	25274	11.7%	25274	11.7%
d_d	7.300	7.83	V_y	28.91	Total System Energy Loss			
d_e	-3.802	-131.44	Ω	-111.41	73798	34.2%	73798	34.2%
d_f	-1.161	30.00	V	40.93				
A	1.000	-28.96	V_n	-28.96		**Impulses**		
B	0.000	7.83	V_t	28.91	P_x	P_y	P	
C	0.920	-28.96	V_{cn}	-28.96	2205.7	1148.8	2486.9	
D	1.920	24.58	V_{ct}	24.58	P_n	P_t	P	
					2205.7	1148.8	2486.9	
					PDOF, deg			
					Vehicle 1		**Vehicle 2**	
					-27.5		62.5	

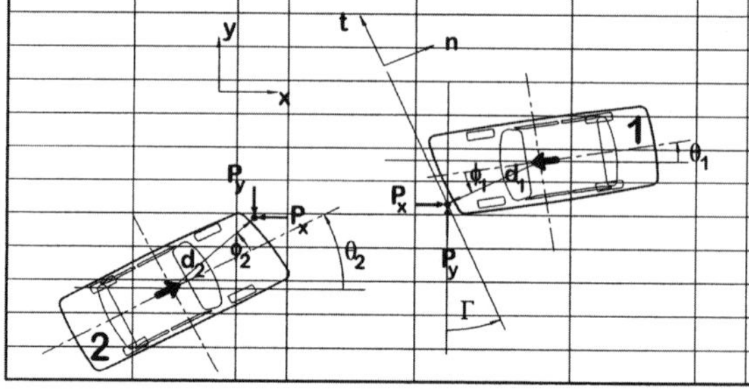

direction is transferred to Vehicle 1 from the impact, and so V_{1t} = 7.83 ft/s (2.39 m/s) instead of V_{1t} = 15.04 ft/s (4.59 m/s) from the point-mass solution. Momentum in the t direction is conserved; less momentum is consequently lost by Vehicle 2 and so V_{2t} = 28.91 ft/s (8.81 m/s) instead of the point-mass V_{2t} = 15.04 ft/s (4.58 m/s). ◇

6.5.2 Application Issues: Coefficients, Dimensions, and Angles

6.5.2.1 Coefficient of Restitution and Impulse Ratio

It was seen that for point-mass collisions (Newton's, or the kinematic) coefficient of restitution, e, was bounded such that $0 \le e \le 1$. Unfortunately, this is not the case for planar, rigid-body collisions;[7,8] based on energy conservation, the upper bound can sometimes exceed unity and can sometimes be limited by a number less than 1. Fortunately for applications to vehicle collisions, e never approaches values greater than about 0.4 in practice, so the upper bound on e should not cause a problem. If the planar impact solution equations are ever used for applications other than vehicle collisions, the user should ensure that the total energy loss never becomes negative for any combination of e and $\mu \leq |\mu_0|$. This will guarantee a realistic solution.[9]

Determination of an appropriate value of the coefficient of restitution for a specific collision is a problem faced frequently in accident reconstruction. Some insights are gained from examination of experimental vehicle collisions, as is done in Section 6.6 below. A study by Monson and Germane[10] contains useful information and data from controlled frontal and side barrier collisions as well as vehicle-to-vehicle collisions. Ishikawa[11] has developed an impact model similar to the planar impact model presented above. Ishikawa[12,13] also presents values of the coefficient of restitution normal to the crush surface from experiments conducted in Japan for two categories of collisions. Thirty-two values are computed from experimental side collisions and 13 from frontal collisions. The values from the frontal collisions ranged from 0.00 to 0.15 and had an average value of 0.07. The values from the side collisions ranged from −0.32 to 0.51 and had an average value of 0.10. According to Ishikawa (p. 10),[13] "a negative normal restitution coefficient implies that the vehicles continue to penetrate each other following the end of the collision at the impact center" (a "virtual" impact with the vehicles passing through each other). Such a collision for real vehicles is clearly impossible, so the utility of Ishikawa's experimental values of e is open to question.

As for the point-mass impact problem, a bounding, or limiting, value of the impulse ratio also exists for the planar impact mechanics problem. When the final relative tangential velocity component of the two vehicles is zero (sliding over the contact surface ends), the impulse ratio, μ, takes on a special, or critical, value, μ_0. This value is given by Eq. 6.60. For the planar impact mechanics solution for a two-vehicle collision, common velocity conditions become $e = 0$ and $\mu = \mu_0$. For a *sideswipe* collision, $\mu < \mu_0$. Values of $\mu > \mu_0$ should not be used for vehicle collisions because under some conditions these values can cause an unrealistic energy loss for the collision. Recall that μ is not a friction coefficient but represents the retardation impulse that controls sliding along the tangential plane representing the crush surface designated by the angle Γ in Fig. 6.5. For a given collision, the critical impulse ratio, μ_0, depends on the vehicle masses, their moments of inertia, the impact configuration, the coefficient of restitution and the initial conditions. It can vary drastically from collision to collision. Consequently, an arbitrary value of an intervehicular frictional drag coefficient, f, must never be used for the proper analysis and reconstruction of a collision satisfying the common velocity conditions.

Although impact analysis and reconstruction programs and software may recommend typical values of f, μ_0 should always be used as one of the common velocity conditions. This is true even when a value of the coefficient of restitution other than $e = 0$ is appropriate. A value of $\mu = f < \mu_0$ should be used only when sliding of the vehicles over the contact surface continues throughout the contact duration and exists at separation.

A convenient way of handling the selection of a value of μ is to express it as a percentage of μ_0 that ranges between 0% and 100%. This not only keeps $\mu \leq \mu_0$, but also ensures that it has the proper sign.

6.5.2.2   Distances, Angles, and Point C

A basic assumption of planar impact mechanics is that the position and configuration of the bodies do not change during contact and that all of the body dimensions remain constant. The deformation of vehicles from high-speed collisions is never elastic and rarely small. In fact, most vehicle structures are designed to have a controlled crush for the purposes of occupant protection. Figures 6.8 and 6.9 show some typical crush surfaces. A residual crush surface of a vehicle is reached in a short time, but still represents a change from the

Figure 6.8 (*left*) Example of residual crush of a vehicle struck from behind in an offset front-to-rear collision.

Figure 6.9 (*right*) Example of residual crush to a vehicle struck on the side in an intersection collision.

undeformed shape as a function of time and space. That is, it is a three-dimensional, dynamic event. To apply planar impact mechanics, it is necessary to make assumptions. One is that a single, intervehicular crush surface can be represented by one that lies in a vertical plane and that a common point, C, exists that represents the point of application of the intervehicular impulse, P. Point C is easy to define mathematically; it is the point that represents the location of the resultant vector impulse $\boldsymbol{P} = P_n\boldsymbol{n} + P_t\boldsymbol{t}$ (bold characters represent vectors). It represents an average of the distance from the center of gravity to the crushing region over space and time. Unfortunately, the location of point C never is exactly known and must be estimated. One approach is to lay out a plan view of the residual crush and use the centroid of the crushed area. Another is to use a point on the residual crush surface, because some springback of the body occurs. Another is to use the maximum crush surface.[13] Whatever method is used, judgment of the analyst is necessary. Consequently, the selection of point C, d_1, d_2, φ_1, φ_2, and Γ all require measurements and some judgment.

Another aspect of this topic is that vehicle dimensions, the moments of inertia I_1 and I_2, and their counterparts, the radii of gyration k_1 and k_2, are assumed to remain constant over the impact. In reality, they change with time as the vehicles deform. There seems never to have been a study of the significance of the changes in these inertial variables. Methods exist[1] to treat such changes in the context of planar mechanics, but they have rarely been applied in the reconstruction of accidents.

6.5.3   Work of Impulses and Energy Loss

A very useful feature of planar impact theory has to do with the work of impulses and energy loss. Many years ago, Thompson (Lord Kelvin) and Tait[14] determined that, in general, the work, W_P, done by an impulse, P, acting at a point is

$$W_P = \frac{1}{2}P(v+V), \tag{6.64}$$

where v is the initial velocity at the point and V is the final velocity at the point in the direction of P. In words, this states that the work of an impulse, P, is equal to the product of the impulse with the average velocity along the line of action of the impulse. When applying this to the contact impulse, P, whose components are P_n and P_t, the respective *relative* velocity components at point C must be used; that is,

$$W_P = \frac{1}{2}P_n[(v_{1Cn} - v_{2Cn}) + (V_{1Cn} - V_{2Cn})] + \frac{1}{2}P_t[(v_{1Ct} - v_{2Ct}) + (V_{1Ct} - V_{2Ct})] \tag{6.65a}$$

or

$$W_P = \frac{1}{2}P_n[(v_{1n} + d_c\omega_1) - (v_{2n} - d_a\omega_2) + (V_{1n} + d_c\Omega_1) - (V_{2n} - d_a\Omega_2)]$$
$$+ \frac{1}{2}P_t[(v_{1t} - d_d\omega_1) - (v_{2t} + d_b\omega_2) + (V_{1t} - d_d\Omega_1) - (V_{2t} + d_b\Omega_2)]. \tag{6.65b}$$

Because P_n and P_t are the only impulse components acting on the colliding bodies, their combined work, W_P, must equal the energy loss, T_L, of the collision. Actually, the work of the impulse is negative and energy loss is positive, so $W_P = -T_L$.

Various methods such as CRASH3[15] have been formulated to estimate by measurements and calculation the impact energy loss of a vehicle associated with residual crush *normal* to a damaged surface. Then the CRASH3 method uses a correction factor to determine the energy loss associated with *tangential* effects. Energy and energy loss is not a vector and cannot be split into normal and tangential components. As an approximation, however, the first term of Eq. 6.65 can be associated with the normal impulse and the second term with the tangential impulse. In this way, energy loss can be apportioned to "normal effects" and to "tangential effects" and used to compare with independent energy calculations. So the work of P_n can be compared directly to the crush energy calculated by the CRASH3 algorithm and the work of P_t to the tangential correction factor. Such an approach is covered in the next chapter.

Example 6.5 Using the same conditions as in Example 6.4, calculate the kinetic energy loss by subtracting the final from the initial energy of the vehicles. Using the values from Fig. 6.7, show that Eq. 6.65 gives the same results.

Solution The energy loss can be calculated as

$$T_L = \frac{1}{2}m_1(v_{1n}^2 + v_{1t}^2) + \frac{1}{2}m_2(v_{2n}^2 + v_{2t}^2) - \frac{1}{2}m_1(V_{1n}^2 + V_{1t}^2) - \frac{1}{2}m_2(V_{2n}^2 + V_{2t}^2)$$

$$= 215{,}719 - 141{,}928 = 73{,}791 \text{ ft-lb } (100 \text{ kJ}).$$

The impulse components, moment arms, and velocities can be obtained from Fig. 6.7. In particular, $v_{1n} = -44.00$ ft/s, $v_{1t} = 0.00$, $\omega_1 = 0.00$, $v_{2n} = 0.00$ ft/s, $v_{2t} = 44.00$, $\omega_2 = 0.00$, $V_{1n} = -28.96$ ft/s, $V_{1t} = 7.83$, $\Omega_1 = -131.44°/s$, $V_{2n} = -28.96$ ft/s, $V_{2t} = 28.91$, $\Omega_2 = -111.41°/s$, $d_a = 0.00$ ft, $d_b = 2.23$ ft, $d_c = 0.00$ ft, $d_d = 7.30$ ft, $P_n = 2205.7$ lb-s, and $P_t = 1148.8$ lb-s. Substituting these values into Eq. 6.59 gives

$$T_L = 48{,}524 + 25{,}267 = 73{,}791 \text{ ft-lb } (100 \text{ kJ}).$$

The first work term is 48,525 ft-lb and can be considered to be the energy of both vehicles lost due to crush normal to the common crush surface. The second term, 25,274 ft-lb, is the energy lost associated with the tangential resistance generated over the crush surface leading to a common relative tangential velocity. Note that the common-velocity conditions lead to a normal component of velocity of $V_{Cn} = -28.96$ ft/s and a tangential component velocity of $V_{Ct} = 24.58$ ft/s for both vehicles. ◯

6.6 RICSAC Collisions

In the 1970s, a group of staged two-vehicle collisions was conducted for the National Highway Traffic Safety Administration and was reported[16] for the purpose of collecting data for collision analysis. The name of the project was Research Input for Computer Simulation of Automobile Collisions and is more familiarly known by the acronym RICSAC. Data from 11 of the collisions was analyzed by Brach,[17,18] Brach and Smith,[19] McHenry and McHenry,[20] and Woolley.[21] In a 1987 paper, Brach presented values of experimentally measured velocities different from the original RICSAC publication, in that velocity components were corrected to include the effects of accelerometer locations remote from the vehicle centers of gravity.[18] This issue also was addressed in the paper by McHenry and McHenry.[20] A problem stems from the use of a vehicle-based coordinate system. Such a coordinate system is necessary in the data reduction stage because accelerometers are fixed to the vehicles and the accelerations and velocities must be transformed to a fixed, earth-based system. A listing of the experimentally measured initial and final velocities from the RICSAC collisions is included in Table 6.2, as well as information concerning the kinetic energy and energy loss values. Various aspects of the RICSAC data will be used and discussed in many examples to follow. Values of coefficients of restitution and impulse ratio coefficients were established from each collision by using a

Table 6.2
RICSAC staged
collision analysis.

Collision number	1	6	7	8	9	10
Collision geometry	60° front to side	60° front to side	60° front to side	90° front to side	90° front to side	90° front to side
Initial system energy[a]	100,900	106,300	178,580	132,820	107,410	260,340
Collision energy loss[a]	64,877	58,949	98,756	71,189	41,352	100,750
CE, crush energy[b]	48,392	45,365	71,995	34,805	26,732	32,190
Corrected CE[b]	92,013	123,053	137,651	55,833	35,920	45,629
Ratio, corrected/CE[b]	1.9	2.7	1.9	1.6	1.3	1.4
Restitution coefficient, e[c]	0.000	0.000	0.000	0.079	0.400	0.419
Impulse ratio, μ[c]	0.966	0.824	0.772	0.413	0.486	0.590
μ/μ_0[c]	1.0	1.0	1.0	1.0	1.0	1.0
Impact energy loss, %[c]	51.9	48.3	48.8	36.1	28.8	31.0
Impact energy loss[c]	52,367	51,343	87,147	47,948	30,934	80,705
Normal energy loss[c]	19,575	21,047	37,323	33,072	16,863	40,092
Tangential energy loss[c]	32,793	30,296	49,824	14,876	14,071	40,613
Ratio, impact to normal[c]	2.7	2.4	2.3	1.4	1.8	2.0

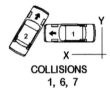

COLLISIONS
1, 6, 7

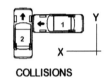

COLLISIONS
8, 9, 10

Collision number	11	12	3	4	5
Collision geometry	10° front to front	10° front to front	10° front to rear	10° front to rear	10° front to rear
Initial system energy[a]	109,700	253,300	74,292	249,170	2,424,400
Collision energy loss[a]	103,231	229,765	25,482	128,819	102,793
CE, crush energy[b]	78,127	122,700	17,634	118,855	117,020
Corrected CE[b]	78,908	124,818	17,646	120,349	117,035
Ratio, corrected/CE[b]	1.0	1.0	1.0	1.0	1.0
Restitution coefficient, e[c]	0.000	0.100	0.217	0.045	0.053
Impulse ratio, μ[c]	0.038	0.031	−0.065	−0.050	−0.090
μ/μ_0[c]	1.0	1.0	1.0	1.0	1.0
Impact energy loss, %[c]	90.9	91.9	34.2	36.3	32.0
Impact energy loss[c]	99,717	232,801	25,408	90,449	77,581
Normal energy loss[c]	100,046	233,561	25,779	91,196	78,793
Tangential energy loss[c]	−329	−760	−371	−747	−1212
Ratio, impact to normal[c]	1.0	1.0	1.0	1.0	1.0

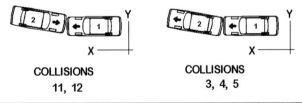

COLLISIONS
11, 12

COLLISIONS
3, 4, 5

Source: Data from Brach.[18]
Notes: All energy values expressed in ft-lb. Negative tangential energy losses are physically unrealistic, result from approximations, and are small (near zero).
[a] Values are from RICSAC tests.
[b] Values are calculated from CRASH3 algorithm with actual PDOF and crush stiffness coefficients.
[c] Values are based on data from tests and fit to the planar impact model by the method of least squares.

method of least squares to fit experimental data to the planar impact solution equations. This was done by finding the coefficient values that gave the best fit of the overall data to the equations of planar impact mechanics (Eqs. 6.48 through 6.53). Part of the fitting procedure was that constraints were used on the coefficient of restitution such that $e^2 \leq 1$. No constraints were placed on the impulse ratio. Table 6.2 shows that the values of e had some consistency within collision categories. The most consistent was for the 60° front-to-side collisions where all three coefficients were zero. Two of the coefficient values of the three 90° front-to-side collisions were considerably higher at 0.400 and 0.419, while the third was 0.079. It is quite possible that an impact to a "structurally hard" wheel area led to the two higher values. With the exception of one value at 0.217, the coefficients for the front-to-rear and front-to-front all ranged from 0.000 to 0.100.

The impulse ratio coefficients, μ, were very consistent. Although their actual values ranged from small negative values (collisions 3, 4, and 5) to near 1 (collisions 1, 6, and 7), they all are equal to their critical value, μ_0. This indicates that for all RICSAC collisions, relative tangential sliding ended at or before separation.

Reconstruction Applications, Impulse–Momentum Theory

7.1 Introduction

Although Chapter 6 includes examples, it covers considerable theory. This chapter develops additional applications and examples. Point-mass theory applications are covered first, followed by applications of planar impact mechanics where rotations of the impacting vehicles are taken into account. The point-mass equations are solved using spreadsheet technology. Point-mass solutions are useful when vehicle rotations are inconsequential or when used for a preliminary analysis. Planar impact analysis, including the effect of rotations and rotational inertia, are easily the most important set of equations for the analysis and reconstruction of vehicle collisions. The solution of the impact equations is an algebraic problem and is easily carried out using spreadsheet technology. The coverage here includes such use with some of the advanced features of spreadsheets. Low-speed, front-to-rear impacts are covered and require additional terms in the impulse–momentum equations.

The planar impact equations presented in the previous chapter are in the form directly applicable to the *analysis* of vehicle collisions. That is, given the vehicle properties, the collision configuration, and the initial conditions, the final velocities, ΔV values, impulses, and energy loss can be found. This is in distinction to the *reconstruction* of vehicle collisions where, more often than not, the final velocity components are known and the initial velocities are sought. This means that the impact equations have to be used in a trial-and-error fashion. Although not ideal, this approach is not overly difficult and even has some advantages; examination of the multiple solutions often provides an understanding of the sensitivity as variables are changed when searching for a solution. On the other hand, modern spreadsheet technology presents tools that can be used to directly provide input quantities for desirable, or target, values of selected output. Examples of these tools are provided in examples in this chapter.

7.2   Point-Mass Collision Applications, Collisions Followed by Skid to Rest

In some reconstructions, point-mass impact theory can provide useful information. One such instance occurs when the postimpact rotational velocities of vehicles are relatively small. Another occurs when carrying out preliminary calculations prior to a full planar impact analysis. Point-mass impact theory can sometimes be used for carrying out comparative, "what if" analyses of the feasibility of different collision scenarios.

Figure 7.1 shows two vehicles with preimpact velocities, v_1 and v_2, and postimpact velocities, V_1 and V_2. These velocities have angles θ_1, θ_2, φ_1, and φ_2, respectively. Frequently, the initial directions of travel, θ_1 and θ_2, of two vehicles are known. Following the collision, each vehicle travels to rest over a known,

Figure 7.1
Coordinates and variables for point-mass collision analysis.

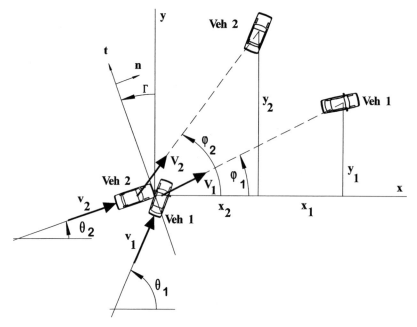

approximately straight-line, path. The distances traveled by the centers of gravity during the skid to rest are x_1, y_1, x_2, and y_2, and the path angles are φ_1 and φ_2. In addition, postimpact motion is over a relatively flat surface with uniform drag coefficients, f_1 and f_2. These coefficients can be actual or equivalent values. Under these conditions, the postimpact speeds, V_1 and V_2, can be computed using the stopping distance formula, Eq. 3.6. If, during the contact duration, the effect of forces other than the intervehicular contact force can be neglected (forces such as the friction between the wheels and the ground), conservation of momentum can be applied. This usually means that the collision should be at a relatively high speed and involve considerable damage. If this is the case, then conservation of momentum in the x direction is

$$m_1 v_1 \cos \theta_1 + m_2 v_2 \cos \theta_2 = m_1 V_1 \cos \varphi_1 + m_2 V_2 \cos \varphi_2. \quad (7.1)$$

Likewise, in the y direction,

$$m_1 v_1 \sin \theta_1 + m_2 v_2 \sin \theta_2 = m_1 V_1 \sin \varphi_1 + m_2 V_2 \sin \varphi_2. \quad (7.2)$$

Figure 7.1 also shows the angle, Γ, used to define a common intervehicular crush plane or surface. This also defines the normal and tangential axes, (n,t), as used in Chapter 6.

An important point to recognize about this approach is that after the postimpact speeds are calculated using the skid-to-rest equation for each vehicle, only two unknowns remain. Because the initial directions of motion are assumed known, only the initial speeds of Vehicle 1 and Vehicle 2 are unknown. This means that only two equations are needed; these are Eqs. 7.1 and 7.2. But it also means that Eqs. 6.11 and 6.12 for the coefficients e and μ are not supplied as input. This can be used to advantage. If the values of e and μ corresponding to the reconstructed velocities, v_1 and v_2, are unrealistic, this can be a warning that the reconstruction may also be unrealistic. A spreadsheet can be set to automatically calculate values of e and μ and give a warning if e is not between 0 and 0.3 and if μ is not between 0 and μ_0. It is possible that realistic values of the coefficient of restitution can be greater than 0.3, but such values are not usual. On the other hand, physically realistic values of μ must have a value between 0 and $|\mu_0|$ (keeping in mind that μ can take on negative values).

Example 7.1

Figure 7.2 shows an accident scene in which two vehicles collide in an intersection where traffic drives on the left side of the road. The postimpact distances (shown with dashed lines) are measured at the scene to be $x_1, y_1 = 60.0, 37.4$ ft (18.3, 11.4 m) and $x_2, y_2 = 71.2, 36.7$ ft (21.7, 11.2 m). It is assumed that the vehicles collided as they entered the intersection and while traveling in their respective lanes and directions of travel; therefore, $(\theta_1, \theta_2) = (0°, 90°)$. The vehicle weights are $W_1 = 3738.3$ lb (16.63 kN) and $W_2 = 3524.4$ lb (15.68 kN). The road surface is dry asphalt. The coefficient of friction was not measured at the site, so values of $f_1 = f_2 = 0.7$ are used as representative values. The crash surface is selected to be parallel to the left side of Vehicle 2, so $\Gamma = 0°$. Determine the initial speeds of the vehicles.

Solution This problem is solved using a spreadsheet solution of the point-mass impact equations. The results are shown in Fig. 7.3 and show initial speeds of Vehicle 1 and Vehicle 2 to be 67 mph (108 km/h) and 40 mph (65 km/h), respectively. The energy loss, in percent, is $T_L = 49\%$. This means that 49% of the combined preimpact kinetic energy of the vehicles was dissipated in the collision, whereas the remainder was dissipated during the slide to rest of each vehicle. It is important to note that for $\Gamma = 0$, the values of e and μ are $e = 0.06$

Figure 7.2
Intersection collision
(left-hand motorway)
showing impact and
rest positions.

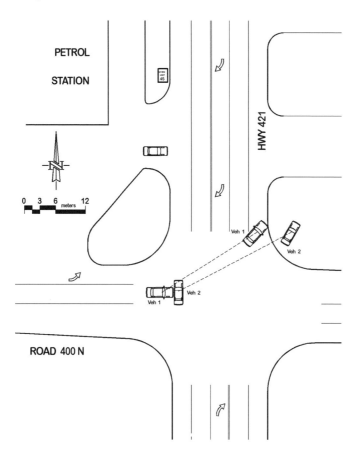

and $\mu = -0.59$, where $\mu_c = -0.60$. That these coefficients are so close to the common-velocity conditions imparts a sense of confidence that the reconstruction is realistic. If either e is not near 0 (or near the expected value) or μ does not have a value near μ_0 (except for a sideswipe collision), then the solution should be examined to find the cause of unrealistic values. ⬡

Example 7.2   Consider an example of a collision in an intersection with a 30° relative angle as shown in Fig. 7.4. Vehicle 1 is a sedan weighing 2800 lb (12.46 kN) and Vehicle 2 is a pickup truck with a weight of 3800 lb (16.90 kN). An x–y coordinate system is chosen with y to the north and x to the east. Postimpact center-of-gravity travel distances, (x, y), are measured as -38.3, 2.1 ft (-11.7, 0.6 m) for Vehicle 1 and -42.30, -10.8 ft (-12.9, -3.3 m) for Vehicle 2. The original headings of travel are assumed to be parallel to the respective roads and are $\theta_1 = 90°$ and $\theta_2 = 210°$. Vehicle 2 skids to rest entirely on a pavement with friction coefficient $f = 0.7$. Vehicle 1 skids into thick, heavy bushes that are likely to have significantly slowed it by an unknown amount. An equivalent value of $f = 0.7$ is used for both vehicles to initiate a reconstruction. The crush surface angle, Γ, is aligned with the side of Vehicle 1, so $\Gamma = 0°$. Estimate the initial speeds of both vehicles based on point-mass collisions.

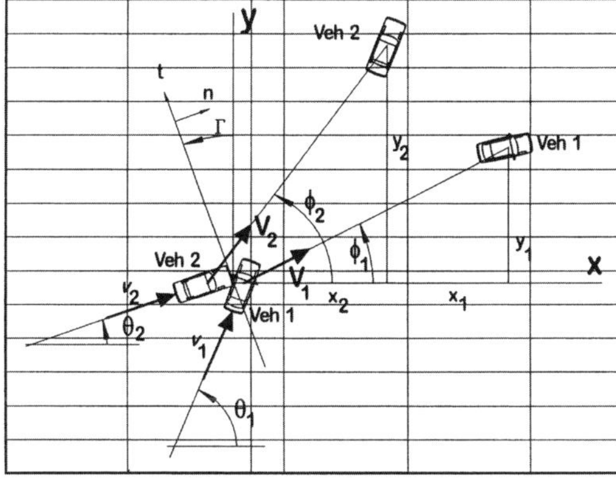

Figure 7.3
Results of point-mass collision analysis.

			SKID-TO-REST COLLISION RECONSTRUCTION					
		>						
frictional		ID:						
drag factors		>						
f_1:	0.70	>						
f_2:	0.70							
			postimpact skid distances, ft			postimpact skid distances, ft		
vehicle weights, lb			d_1:	70.70	x_1	60.0	y_1	37.4
W_1	3738.3		d_2:	80.10	x_2	71.2	y_2	36.7
W_2	3524.4							
mass, lb-s^2/ft			postimpact speeds, ft/s & mph			postimpact angles, deg & rad		
m_1	116.10		V_1:	56.46	38.49	ϕ_1	31.9	0.557
m_2	109.45		V_2:	60.09	40.97	ϕ_2	27.3	0.476
			V_{1x}	47.91	V_{1y}	29.86		
			V_{2x}	53.41	V_{2y}	27.53		
g	32.20							
conv	1.47							
			preimpact speeds, ft/s & mph			preimpact angles, deg & rad		
det	1.27E+04		v_1:	98.27	67	θ_1	0.0	0.000
R1	1.14E+04		v_2:	59.21	40	θ_2	90.0	1.571
R2	6.48E+03		v_{1x}	98.27	v_{1y}	0.00		
			v_{2x}	0.00	v_{2y}	59.21		
ΔV_1, ft/s:	58.55							
$\Delta V2$, ft/s:	62.10							
coeff, e	0.06		System Energy			Γ	0.0	
coeff, μ	-0.59		Initial, ft-lb	752392		$\sin\Gamma$	0.000	$\cos\Gamma$ 1.000
coeff, μ_c	-0.60		Final, ft-lb	382631		v_{1n}	98.27	v_{1t} 0.00
			Loss	369760		v_{2n}	0.00	v_{2t} 59.21
			%	49.1		V_{1n}	47.91	V_{1t} 29.86
						V_{2n}	53.41	V_{2t} 27.53

Solution Figure 7.5 shows the results of using the calculation sheet with $f_1 = f_2 = 0.7$. This shows that the initial speeds were 31 mph (49 km/h) for Vehicle 1 and 58 mph (93 km/h) for Vehicle 2. The calculation further shows that the coefficient of restitution $e = -0.02$, the impulse ratio $\mu = 1.03$, and the critical impulse ratio $\mu_0 = 1.19$. Although near zero, a negative coefficient of restitution is physically impossible, so some examination of the reconstruction is warranted. Remember that the drag of the bushes on Vehicle 1 is an

Figure 7.4
Intersection collision
showing impact position
on the roadway and
rest positions.

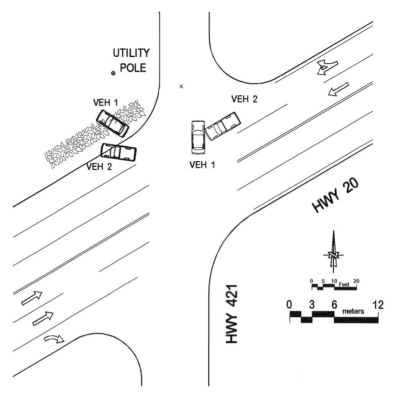

unknown factor. An approach that sometimes can provide useful results in a situation such as this is to use the search feature of the spreadsheet. This allows the user to specify a goal of $e = 0$ and find the value of f_1 that gives this value. In this case, the results in Fig. 7.6 show a corresponding value of $f_1 = 0.75$. From this, it can be interpreted that retardation by the bushes caused an effective average drag of $f_1 = 0.75$ for Vehicle 1. The impulse ratio value, 1.01, is not equal to its critical value, 1.19, but is a close enough approximation.

Although the point-mass solution is not as accurate as the solution of the planar impact problem, it often is adequate when the circumstances of the accident satisfy the assumptions. A point mass solution can be used to provide an initial or starting point for a planar impact mechanics problem.   ⬡

7.3   Rigid Body, Planar Impact Mechanics Applications; Vehicle Collisions with Rotation

The equations of planar impact mechanics were derived and solved in Chapter 6. The solution equations have a form where the vehicle dimensions, collision damage, initial velocity components, and coefficients are considered as known quantities, and the final velocities, impulses, energy loss, ΔV values, and other information are calculated. A spreadsheet that permits numerical solutions of

SKID-TO-REST COLLISION RECONSTRUCTION

			>	ID:					
frictional			>						
drag factors			>						
f_1:	0.70		>						
f_2:	0.70								
			postimpact skid distances, ft			postimpact skid distances, ft			
vehicle weights, lb			d_1:	38.36	x_1	-38.3	y_1	2.1	
W_1	2800.0		d_2:	43.66	x_2	-42.3	y_2	-10.8	
W_2	3800.0								
mass, lb-s^2/ft			postimpact speeds, ft/s & mph			postimpact angles, deg & rad			
m_1	86.96		V_1:	41.58	28.35	ϕ_1	176.9	3.087	
m_2	118.01		V_2:	44.36	30.25	ϕ_2	194.3	3.392	
			V_{1x}	-41.52	V_{1y}	2.28			
g	32.20		V_{2x}	-42.98	V_{2y}	-10.97			
conv	1.47								
			preimpact speeds, ft/s & mph			preimpact angles, deg & rad			
det	8.89E+03								
R1	-8.68E+03		v_1:	45.03	31	θ_1	90.0	1.571	
R2	-1.10E+03		v_2:	84.96	58	θ_2	210.0	3.665	
			v_{1x}	0.00	v_{1y}	45.03			
ΔV_1, ft/s:	59.60		v_{2x}	-73.58	v_{2y}	-42.48			
$\Delta V2$, ft/s:	43.92								
coeff, e	-0.02		**System Energy**			Γ	0.0		
coeff, μ	1.03		Initial, ft-lb	514104		$\sin\Gamma$	0.000	$\cos\Gamma$	1.000
coeff, μ_c	1.19		Final, ft-lb	191308		v_{1n}	0.00	v_{1t}	45.03
			Loss	322796		v_{2n}	-73.58	v_{2t}	-42.48
			%	62.8		V_{1n}	-41.52	V_{1t}	2.28
						V_{2n}	-42.98	V_{2t}	-10.97

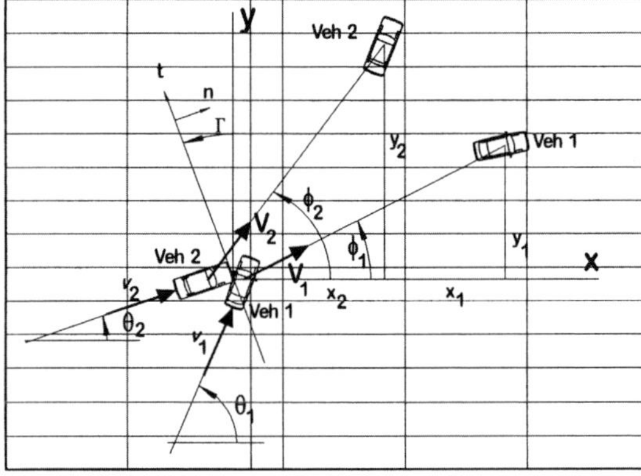

Figure 7.5
Results of point-mass collision analysis.

the planar impact equations is relatively simple to set up. For accident reconstructions, a postimpact trajectory analysis often is done first and provides the final velocities of the impact. In such cases, it is desirable to carry out an impact solution where the final velocities are known and the initial velocities are unknown. The system equations are linear and algebraic and theoretically can be solved in an inverse fashion; that is, it is possible to arrange the equations algebraically to determine the initial velocities for a given set of final velocities. Unfortunately, the solution is invalid when the coefficient of restitution is

Figure 7.6
Results of point-mass collision analysis using spreadsheet *Goal Seek* feature.

SKID-TO-REST COLLISION RECONSTRUCTION

		>				
frictional		ID:				
drag factors		>				
f_1:	0.75	>				
f_2:	0.70					
		postimpact skid distances, ft			**postimpact skid distances, ft**	
vehicle weights, lb		d_1:	38.36	x_1	-38.3	y_1	2.1
W_1	2800.0	d_2:	43.66	x_2	-42.3	y_2	-10.8
W_2	3800.0					
mass, lb-s^2/ft		**postimpact speeds, ft/s & mph**			**postimpact angles, deg & rad**	
m_1	86.96	V_1:	43.04	29.35	ϕ_1	176.9	3.087
m_2	118.01	V_2:	44.36	30.25	ϕ_2	194.3	3.392
		V_{1x}	-42.98	V_{1y}	2.36	
g	32.20	V_{2x}	-42.98	V_{2y}	-10.97	
conv	1.47					
		preimpact speeds, ft/s & mph			**preimpact angles, deg & rad**	
det	8.89E+03					
R1	-8.81E+03	v_1:	45.96	31	θ_1	90.0	1.571
R2	-1.09E+03	v_2:	86.20	59	θ_2	210.0	3.665
		v_{1x}	0.00	v_{1y}	45.96	
ΔV_1, ft/s:	61.22	v_{2x}	-74.65	v_{2y}	-43.10	
$\Delta V2$, ft/s:	45.11					
coeff, e	0.00	**System Energy**			Γ	0.0	
coeff, μ	1.01	Initial, ft-lb	530271		$\sin\Gamma$	0.000	$\cos\Gamma$	1.000
coeff, μ_c	1.19	Final, ft-lb	196678		v_{1n}	0.00	v_{1t}	45.96
		Loss	333593		v_{2n}	-74.65	v_{2t}	-43.10
		%	62.9		V_{1n}	-42.98	V_{1t}	2.36
					V_{2n}	-42.98	V_{2t}	-10.97

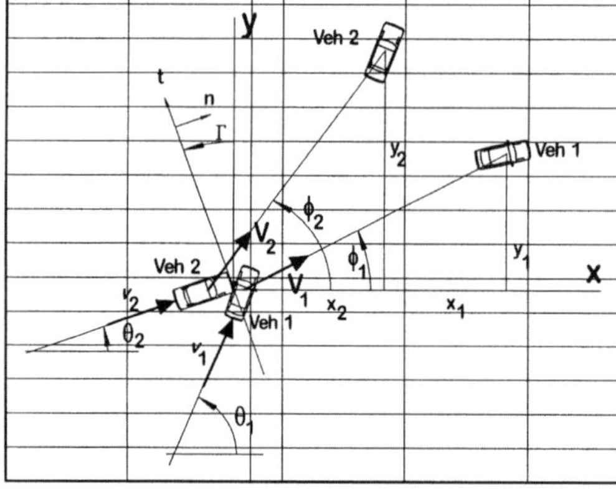

zero or near zero, one of the two common velocity conditions used for accident reconstruction. So other approaches are necessary. An effective way to reconstruct a collision is to use a forward approach in which the equations are solved for the desired final velocities in an iterative fashion. Later it will be seen that excellent reconstruction results can often be reached following an inverse search technique in which the final velocities are matched using a minimum least-squares approach called LESCOR, an acronym for least square collision reconstruction.

Although variations exist, a common procedure for using the planar impact equations in a forward mode to reconstruct a two-vehicle collision is summarized here (and discussed shortly in more detail):

1. Determine the impact configuration (positions and orientations of the vehicles during the contact duration).
2. Determine the vehicle dimensions and physical properties.
3. Examine and/or measure the crash damage of both vehicles to determine a common, average planar crush surface and the distances and angles from the centers of gravity to the common point on or near the crush surface.
4. Determine which, if any, velocities may be known (particularly initial angular velocities that are frequently zero) and which are unknown; and determine what other quantities may be known, such as crush energy, initial heading directions, etc.
5. Choose the appropriate impact coefficients, for example, the use of the common velocity conditions, $e = 0$ and $\mu = \mu_0$
6. Use the collision information to solve the impact equations.
7. Change the unknown initial conditions until they produce the knowns of the reconstruction.

Variations of the above procedure can also be followed. As mentioned earlier, a good starting solution sometimes can be found using a point mass solution. After establishing a reconstruction, it always is a good practice to examine the results to be sure they match all important conditions and are physically realistic. It also is good practice to estimate uncertainty and sensitivity.

7.4   Collision Analysis Using a Solution of the Planar Impact Equations

A numerical solution of Eqs. 6.48 through 6.55 along with other results following from the solution can be used to model a planar impact of two vehicles. The usual procedure is to solve for the final velocity components given the physical information for the vehicles, the impact configuration variables, the coefficients, and the initial velocity components. Input information consists of the masses m_1 and m_2, moments of inertia I_1 and I_2, distances d_1 and d_2, angles φ_1 and φ_2, angles θ_1 and θ_2, the common surface angle, Γ, coefficients e and μ, and the six initial velocity conditions for Vehicles 1 and 2. All other quantities such as energy loss are calculated from the input. All input quantities with dimensions are expressed in units of pounds, feet, seconds, and degrees except where otherwise indicated. SI units can also be used. It is a good idea to construct and place a diagram on the solution sheet to illustrate the main features of the planar impact model. The coordinates and vehicle orientations are arranged so that a head-on collision (nose to nose) has orientation angles $\theta_1 = \theta_2 = 0$ and all angles and angular velocities are positive in a counterclockwise sense (see Fig. 6.5).

Example 7.3   As a first example of the solution of the planar impact equations, consider a frontal offset impact of a 4340 lb (19.31 kN) pickup truck with a rigid barrier at a speed of 30 mph (44 ft/s, 13.41 m/s) as shown in Fig. 7.7. The objective

Figure 7.7
Offset frontal impact with
a fixed rigid barrier.

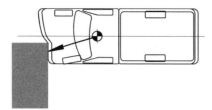

here is to determine the final velocity components, ΔV, impulse, and energy loss from such a collision. The physical information for the vehicle and collision is listed in Table 7.1. This information corresponds to the general collision depicted in Fig. 6.5. In this example, the impact is with a rigid barrier and not

Table 7.1
Input information,
Example 7.3.

mass, m_1	135 lb-s²/ft	1968 kg
Moment of inertia, I_1	3265 ft-lb-s²	4425 kg-m²
Orientation, θ_1	0°	0°
distance, d_1	4.66 ft	1.42 m
Angle, φ_1	21°	21°
Crush surface angle, Γ	0°	0°

another vehicle. To represent a rigid barrier, Vehicle 2 in the impact equations can be given an "infinite" mass, m_2, and moment of inertia, I_2. In practice, any large value that results in negligible final velocities of m_2 will do the job. Values of 1.0×10^7 will be used for m_2 and I_2. Initial velocity components must be established according to the (x,y) coordinate system in Fig. 7.5. This gives $v_{1x} = -44$ ft/s, $v_{1y} = \omega_1 = v_{2x} = v_{2y} = \omega_2 = 0$. Because the barrier is rigid, the (common) crush surface has an orientation such that $\Gamma = 0°$ where the (x,y) and (n,t) coordinate systems are aligned. It is typical for rigid barrier collisions that there will be some small rebound of the vehicle from the barrier. So a value of $e = 0.1$ is used. The critical value of $\mu = \mu_0$ is used. (Because $v_{1y} = 0$, this is a normal collision and only a relatively small tangential impulse can be developed.)

Solution   The results are shown in the form of a spreadsheet, Fig. 7.8. The final angular velocity of the pickup is 91.71°/s and is positive (counterclockwise). The final, normal contact velocity is $V_{cn} = -e\, v_{cn} = -2.68$ ft/s. Because $e \neq 0$, $\Delta V = 41.9$ ft/s; keep in mind that this is ΔV of the mass center (not at the point of contact). If the ΔV of some other point in the vehicle is needed, it must be calculated separately. The energy loss is 93.9% of the original kinetic energy. A large percentage of the residual kinetic energy, $\frac{1}{2}m_1 v_1^2 + \frac{1}{2}I_1\Omega^2$, is associated with the final rotational velocity, where $\Omega = 91.71°$/s. The normal impulse is equal to 5578.4 lb-s and the tangential impulse is 940.0 lb-s. Since the initial tangential contact velocity (v_{ct}) is zero and the final value (V_{ct}) also

		ANALYSIS OF A PLANAR VEHICLE COLLISION							
			(units: lb, ft, sec, deg)						
		Vehicle 1		Vehicle 2		Initial speeds, mph			
5280/3600	1.467	135.00	mass, m	1.0E+06		Vehicle 1		Vehicle 2	
g	32.2	3265.00	inertia, I	1.0E+06		30.0		0.0	
		4.66	distance, d	0.00					
e	0.00	21.00	angle, φ	0.00		Final speeds, mph			
μ (% μ₀)	100.0	0.00	angle, θ	0.00		Vehicle 1		Vehicle 2	
μ	0.169					5.1		0.0	
μ₀	0.169								
Γ	0.0	Vehicle 1	initial velocity	Vehicle 2		ΔV, ft/sec			
mbar	134.982	-44.00	vₓ	0.00		Vehicle 1		Vehicle 2	
k₁²	24.185	0.00	v_y	0.00		41.9		0.0	
k₂²	1.000	0.00	ω	0.00					
q	0.939	44.00	v	0.00		System Kinetic Energy			
vₘ	44.000	-44.00	vₙ	0.00		Initial	130680		
v_tn	0.000	0.00	v_t	0.00		Final	7956		
r	0.000	-44.00	v_cn	0.00		Loss	122724	93.9%	
η₁	0.000	0.00	v_ct	0.00					
η₂	0.000					Range of Normal (Crush) Energy Loss:			
dₐ	0.000		final			122724	93.9%	122724	93.9%
d_b	0.000	Vehicle 1	velocity	Vehicle 2		Range of Tangential Energy Loss:			
d_c	1.670	-2.68	Vₓ	-0.01		0	0.0%	0	0.0%
d_d	4.350	6.96	V_y	0.00		Total System Energy Loss			
d_e	0.937	91.71	Ω	0.00		122724	93.9%	122724	93.9%
d_f	0.000	7.46	V	0.01					
A	1.115	-2.68	Vₙ	-0.01		Impulses			
B	0.300	6.96	V_t	0.00		Pₓ	P_y	P	
C	0.782	-0.01	V_cn	-0.01		5578.4	940.0	5657.0	
D	1.782	0.00	V_ct	0.00		Pₙ	P_t	P	
						5578.4	940.0	5657.0	
						PDOF, deg			
						Vehicle 1		Vehicle 2	
						-9.6		-9.6	

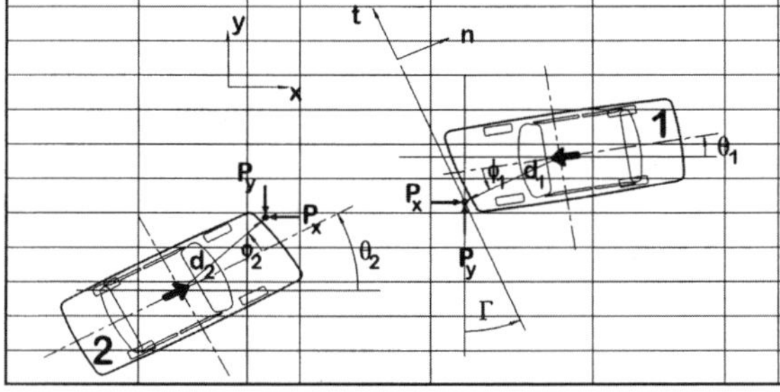

Figure 7.8
Results of a planar impact mechanics analysis of a frontal impact.

is zero, no work is done by the tangential impulse and all of the energy loss is associated with damage (normal residual crush). ◇

7.5 Reconstructions Using a Spreadsheet Solution of the Planar Impact Equations

The above examples are not strictly reconstructions because the final velocities are calculated from initial conditions. A reconstruction works in reverse to find initial velocities from final ones. An example of a reconstruction is now presented.

An example collision reconstruction is presented that is based on RICSAC staged collision 9 (see Section 6.6). All vehicle dimensions and characteristics

Example 7.4

have been published,[1] and all initial and final velocities have been measured. This collision reconstruction takes the perspective that the final impact velocities are known and the initial impact velocities are to be reconstructed. RICSAC 9 was a controlled 90° front-to-side crash between a 1975 Honda Civic (Vehicle 1) and a four-door 1974 Ford Torino (Vehicle 2). A photograph of the impact configuration is shown in Fig. 7.9. A scale diagram of the impact configuration in Fig. 7.10 shows the distances from the centers of gravity and the impact center. Figures 7.11 and 7.12 show photographs of the vehicles with residual damage. Examination of the impact configuration and frontal crush indicates that the area of primary impact between the vehicles was between the front center of the Honda and the right-front wheel of the Ford. The center of the impact shown in Fig. 7.10 is chosen to reflect this. Pertinent vehicle

Figure 7.9 (*left*)
Positions and orientations of vehicles at initiation of contact, RICSAC 9.

Figure 7.10 (*right*)
Diagram of positions and orientations of vehicles, RICSAC 9.

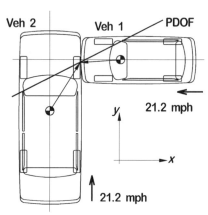

dimensions and physical properties, taken from published test conditions, are listed in Table 7.2. The distances d_1 and d_2 and the angles θ_1, θ_2, φ_1, and φ_2 in Table 7.2 reflect the dimensions of the vehicles and the coordinates and dimensions defined and illustrated in Fig. 6.5. For this collision, it is known that $v_{1y} = \omega_1 = v_{2x} = \omega_2 = 0$. Measured values of the final velocity components and the ΔVs also are listed in Table 7.2. The reconstruction for this example is based on an assumption that common-velocity conditions are appropriate for this

Figure 7.11
Photograph of Vehicle 1 showing damage, RICSAC 9.

Figure 7.12
Photograph of Vehicle 2 showing damage, RICSAC 9.

collision, so values of $e = 0$ and $\mu = 100\%\ \mu_0$ are used. This may or may not always be a good assumption and is reexamined later in another example.

A gallant, but not too successful, effort was made to find by iteration the initial velocity components, v_{1x} and v_{2y}, that give the final velocity components approximately equal to the measured values in Table 7.2. Results in the form

	Veh 1 (Honda)	Veh 2 (Ford)		Veh 1 (Honda)	Veh 2 (Ford)	
m_1, m_2	70.1	152.2	lb-s²/ft	1029	2221	kg
I_1, I_2	976	3953	ft-lb-s²	1323	5359	kg-m²
d_1, d_2	4.8	5.6	ft	1.5	1.6	m
θ_1, θ_2	0	90	°	0	90	°
φ_1, φ_2	6	−29.7	°	6	−29.7	°
v_x	−31.09	0	ft/s	−9.48	0	m/s
v_y	0	31.09	ft/s	0	9.48	m/s
ω	0	0	°/s	0	0	°/s
V_x	−5.1	−7.3	ft/s	−1.6	−2.2	m/s
V_y	17.6	20.2	ft/s	5.4	6.2	m/s
Ω	−180	45	°/s	−180	45	°/s
ΔV	28.6	12.6	ft/s	8.72	3.84	m/s

Table 7.2
Test conditions, RICSAC 9.

of a spreadsheet are given in Fig. 7.13. The velocity V_{1x} should be near −5.1 ft/s (1.6 m/s) but is −7.2 ft/s (−2.2 m/s); V_{1y} should be near 17.6 ft/s (5.36 m/s) but is 10.4 ft/s (3.2 m/s), and so on. The initial velocities reached by trial and error are $v_{1x} = -19.9$ ft/s (−6.1 m/s) and $v_{2y} = 27.9$ ft/s (8.5 m/s). These compare to the measured values from the RICSAC tests of $v_{1x} = -v_{2y} = -31.1$ ft/s (9.5 m/s). This is not a very good match. In addition, the ΔV values for Vehicle 1 and Vehicle 2 should have been 28.6 and 12.6 ft/s (8.72 and 3.84 m/s) but were found to be 16.3 and 7.5 ft/s (4.97 and 2.29 m/s), respectively. After the collision, Vehicle 1 had a negative angular velocity, $\Omega_1 = -174.9$°/s, and Vehicle 2 had a positive angular velocity, $\Omega_2 = 33.9$°/s. These compare to measured values of $\Omega_1 = -180$°/s and $\Omega_2 = 45$°/s. Note that the velocity components, V_{cn}, at the common point and normal to the crush surface for Vehicle 1 and Vehicle 2 are equal. This is a consequence of the use of the common-velocity conditions. The coefficient of restitution, e, is equal to zero, so the vehicles do not rebound

Figure 7.13
Results of a planar impact
mechanics analysis of
RICSAC 9, common
velocity conditions.

ANALYSIS OF A PLANAR VEHICLE COLLISION							
					(units: lb, ft, sec, deg)		
		Vehicle 1		**Vehicle 2**	**Initial speeds, mph**		
5280/3600	1.467	70.10	mass, m	152.20	**Vehicle 1**		**Vehicle 2**
g	32.2	976.00	inertia, I	3953.30	**13.6**		**19.0**
		4.80	distance, d	5.60			
e	0.00	6.00	angle, ϕ	-29.70	**Final speeds, mph**		
μ (% μ_0)	100.0	0.00	angle, θ	90.00	**Vehicle 1**		**Vehicle 2**
μ	0.806				**8.5**		**16.3**
μ_0	0.806		**initial**				
Γ	0.0	**Vehicle 1**	**velocity**	**Vehicle 2**		**ΔV, ft/sec**	
mbar	47.995	-19.91	v_x	0.00	**Vehicle 1**		**Vehicle 2**
k_1^2	13.923	0.00	v_y	27.88	16.3		7.5
k_2^2	25.974	0.00	ω	0.00			
q	0.932	19.91	v	27.88	**System Kinetic Energy**		
v_m	19.910	-19.91	v_n	0.00	Initial	73046	
v_{tn}	27.880	0.00	v_t	27.88	Final	54174	
r	1.400	-19.91	v_{cn}	0.00	Loss	18872	**25.8%**
η_1	0.000	0.00	v_{ct}	27.88			
η_2	90.000				Range of Normal (Crush) Energy Loss:		
d_a	4.864		**final**		8868	12.1%	9725	13.3%
d_b	2.775	**Vehicle 1**	**velocity**	**Vehicle 2**	Range of Tangential Energy Loss:		
d_c	0.502	-7.20	V_x	-5.85	10004	13.7%	9147	12.5%
d_d	4.774	10.24	V_y	23.16	Total System Energy Loss		
d_e	-3.344	-174.88	Ω	33.94	18872	25.8%	18872	25.8%
d_f	2.629	12.52	V	23.89			
A	1.300	-7.20	V_n	-5.85	**Impulses**		
B	0.282	10.24	V_t	23.16	P_x	P_y	P
C	1.214	-8.73	V_{cn}	-8.73	890.8	717.7	1143.9
D	2.214	24.81	V_{ct}	24.81	P_n	P_t	P
					890.8	717.7	1143.9
					PDOF, deg		
					Vehicle 1		**Vehicle 2**
					-38.9		51.1

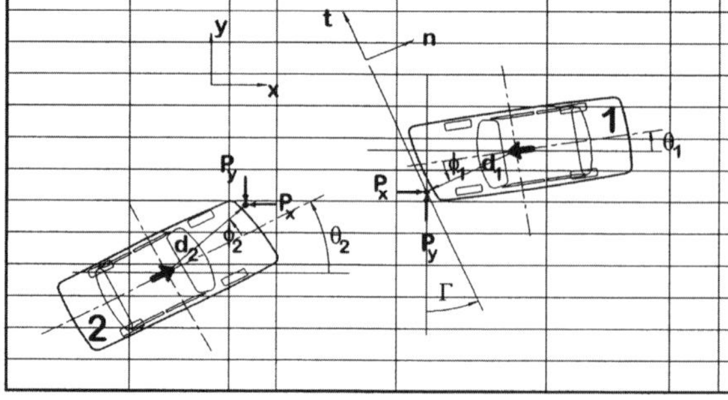

at the contact point. The velocity components, V_{ct}, tangent to the crush surface are equal because relative tangential sliding ended before separation. Note that the normal and tangential velocities at the contact point (point of action of the impulse) are not zero because they are the velocities of the vehicle in the n and t directions relative to a fixed reference.　　　◯

It is a good idea to set up an accounting of the energy loss. As discussed earlier, the work done by the normal impulse, P_n, can be used to estimate the residual crush energy and the work of the tangential impulse component, P_t, to estimate the energy loss due to relative tangential motion over the intervehicular surface. Since the breakdown of work done by each component depends on when (during the contact duration) sliding stops, a range of values of μ can be estimated. The range can be determined by using the case of relatively high frictional impulse to simulate an early end to sliding and $f = \mu_0$ for an end to sliding at the moment of separation. Based on these values of μ, comparisons of crush energy and ΔV values from the CRASH3 algorithm (see Chapter 8) can be made. For example, the results in Table 7.3 are from Brach and Smith,[2]

	Vehicle	Spreadsheet solution	CRASH3 algorithm
No tangential effects	1	16.2	16.6
	2	7.4	7.6
Including tangential effects	1	28.8	18.5[a]
	2	13.3	8.5[a]
Measured test values	1	31.4	
	2	13.1	

Table 7.3
ΔV values for RICSAC 9 (ft/s).

Source: Brach and Smith.[2]
[a] Corrected according to the CRASH3 algorithm.

and show that if ΔV is calculated from (normal) crush energy alone, it can be significantly low because the energy loss due to tangential effects is ignored. On the other hand, if the work of the tangential impulse is included, the results are more accurate. The CRASH3 algorithm offers a correction but it is arbitrary and requires a process that depends on visual estimation of the principal direction of force (PDOF). The planar impact mechanics solution determines the energy loss and ΔV values properly based on the choice of the coefficients e and μ.

Note that the impulse components are found from the planar impact mechanics solution equations. The line of action of the total impulse is what is referred to as the PDOF. The line of impulse for RICSAC 9 is shown in Fig. 7.10. In contrast to the CRASH3 method, the PDOF is not estimated but is determined by the damage surface (through the angle Γ) and the collision conditions.

Finally, the results of the reconstruction of RICSAC 9 in Fig. 7.13 show initial velocities considerably different from the measured values, $(v_{1x}, v_{2y}) = (-19.9 \text{ ft/s}, 27.9 \text{ ft/s})$, calculated, compared to $(v_{1x}, v_{2y}) = (-31.1 \text{ ft/s}, 31.1 \text{ ft/s})$ measured. Many reasons exist for the differences. One is that this collision borders on a low-speed collision; both vehicles initially had speeds of approximately 21 mph (34 km/h), and tire–roadway friction impulses may have been significant. But, as will be seen shortly, common velocity conditions, particularly $e = 0$, may not be a good condition for this impact.

In this example, the previous analysis of RICSAC 9 is continued. An approach using features of some spreadsheet tools is used to get a much better match between the planar impact analysis and the experimental results. A question arises as to whether a different value of e can provide a better match of the computed and measured ΔV values. Again, the initial conditions are $v_{1y} = \omega_1 = v_{2x} = \omega_2 = 0$.

Example 7.5

Solution In an analysis of the RICSAC collisions using optimal search techniques, Brach[3] fit the planar impact equations to the measured data from

11 collisions. A result of doing this was to recover the values of the impact coefficients e and μ that best fit the experiments. Results for all collisions are summarized in Table 6.2. One of the main conclusions was that *all* of the collisions were best fit by the common velocity condition that $\mu = \mu_0$. This was not true, however, for the other condition—that is, that $e = 0$. In fact, a value of $e = 0.4$ was found to be appropriate for RICSAC 9. A calculation can be set up in a spreadsheet to calculate the sum of squares of differences, Q, where

$$Q = \sum_{i=1}^{2} [(V_{ix} - V_{ixm})^2 + (V_{iy} - V_{iym})^2]. \tag{7.3}$$

In the computation of Q, V_{ix}, and V_{iy} are the final velocity components of the planar impact mechanics solution equations, and V_{ixm} and V_{iym} are the corresponding experimentally measured values. Initial velocity components are given their experimental values. The quantity, Q, is minimized by using a spreadsheet tool (not covered here) in which, for this example, the minimization procedure determines the coefficient of restitution value e that minimizes Q, and where the coefficient is constrained such that $0 \le e^2 \le 1$. (This approach is similar but not identical to that of Brach[3] and the results in Table 6.2.)

Figure 7.14 shows the output of a solution for a minimum Q. The coefficient of restitution is $e = 0.355$. This gives values of $\Delta V_1 = 19.1$ mph (30.7 km/h) and $\Delta V_2 = 8.8$ mph (14.2 km/h) compared to measured values of $\Delta V_1 = 19.5$ mph (31.4 km/h) and $\Delta V_2 = 8.8$ mph (14.2 km/h). This example points out that although the coefficient of restitution typically is zero for high-speed collisions, exceptions can occur. Such exceptions can occur when the collision surface includes "hard" structural parts. In RICSAC 9, the front of the Honda struck the right-front wheel assembly of the Ford. In addition, as noted before, the initial speeds of this collision are relatively low.

Another example follows using the solution of the planar impact equations in which, in addition to the usual information gathered at an accident site, one of the vehicles had an event data recorder (EDR). Such information can be used to improved the accuracy of an accident speed reconstruction.

Example 7.6   Suppose a collision occurs similar to that of RICSAC 7, but in this case collision information from one vehicle is available from an EDR record. The EDR record illustrated here is for Vehicle 1. It is fictitious but includes actual data from RICSAC 7, a 60° front-to-side collision. Some of the collision conditions are illustrated in Fig. 7.15. The EDR information is shown in Fig. 7.16 and consists of time traces of the acceleration and corresponding ΔV curves taken from the longitudinal axis of Vehicle 1.[1]

The heading axis of Vehicle 1 is oriented in the negative x direction of Fig. 7.15. Except for a change in angular position during the contact duration (neglected here), the acceleration and ΔV correspond to the x-components of the impact motion of Vehicle 1; that is, from Fig. 7.16, $\Delta V_{1x} = 21.96$ ft/s (6.69 m/s).

ANALYSIS OF A PLANAR VEHICLE COLLISION

(units: lb, ft, sec, deg)

		Vehicle 1		Vehicle 2	Initial speeds, mph			
5280/3600	1.467	70.10	mass, m	152.20	Vehicle 1		Vehicle 2	
g	32.2	976.00	inertia, I	3953.30	21.2		21.2	
		4.80	distance, d	5.60				
e	0.355	6.00	angle, φ	-29.70	Final speeds, mph			
μ (% μ₀)	100.0	0.00	angle, θ	90.00	Vehicle 1		Vehicle 2	
μ	0.512				9.7		18.9	
μ₀	0.512		initial					
Γ	0.0	Vehicle 1	velocity	Vehicle 2	ΔV, ft/sec			
mbar	47.995	-31.09	v_x	0.00	Vehicle 1		Vehicle 2	
k_1^2	13.923	0.00	v_y	31.09	28.0		12.9	
k_2^2	25.974	0.00	ω	0.00				
q	0.866	31.09	v	31.09	System Kinetic Energy			
v_m	31.090	-31.09	v_n	0.00	Initial	107436		
v_{tn}	31.090	0.00	v_t	31.09	Final	75953		
r	1.000	-31.09	v_{cn}	0.00	Loss	31483	29.3%	
η₁	0.000	0.00	v_{ct}	31.09				
η₂	90.000				Range of Normal (Crush) Energy Loss:			
d_a	4.864		final		17546	16.3%	19522	18.2%
d_b	2.775	Vehicle 1	velocity	Vehicle 2	Range of Tangential Energy Loss:			
d_c	0.502	-6.13	V_x	-11.50	13937	13.0%	11961	11.1%
d_d	4.774	12.79	V_y	25.20	Total System Energy Loss			
d_e	-1.944	-199.70	Ω	87.32	31483	29.3%	31483	29.3%
d_f	3.443	14.18	V	27.70				
A	1.300	-6.13	V_n	-11.50	Impulses			
B	0.282	12.79	V_t	25.20	P_x	P_y	P	
C	1.214	-7.87	V_{cn}	-18.91	1750.0	896.5	1966.3	
D	2.214	29.43	V_{ct}	29.43	P_n	P_t	P	
					1750.0	896.5	1966.3	
					PDOF, deg			
					Vehicle 1		Vehicle 2	
					-27.1		62.9	

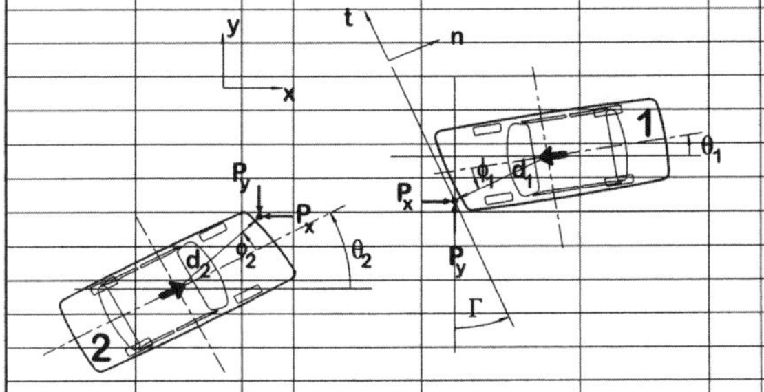

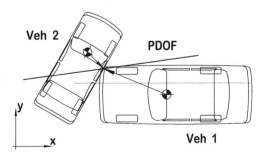

Figure 7.14
Results of a planar impact mechanics analysis of RICSAC 9, least-square fit to solution equations.

Figure 7.15
Impact orientation of vehicles.

Figure 7.16
Event data recorder
record of Vehicle I
showing the measured
acceleration in the *x*
direction, the integral of
the acceleration (Δ*V*,
mph), initial engine speed
(rpm), initial forward
speed (mph), and brake
and transmission status at
beginning of record.

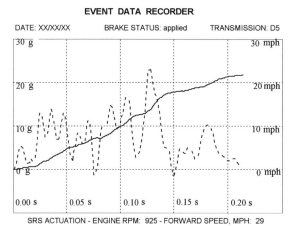

EVENT DATA RECORDER

DATE: XX/XX/XX   BRAKE STATUS: applied   TRANSMISSION: D5

SRS ACTUATION - ENGINE RPM: 925 - FORWARD SPEED, MPH: 29

For this example, it is assumed that the postimpact motion of the vehicles was not observed or recorded, but residual crush measurements of the vehicles were made and analyzed. Assume that a crush-energy analysis (see Chapter 8) indicates that the total crush energy dissipated in the collision was E_c = 37,260 ft-lb (50,518 J). The objective is to determine the initial speeds of both vehicles using these values of ΔV_{1x} and E_c. Other assumptions and/or conditions used are that the initial vehicle headings are known, the initial angular velocities are zero, both common velocity conditions apply, and the contact surface is chosen tangent to the passenger's side of Vehicle 2. Values of other physical and dimensional properties such as mass values, moments of inertia, etc., are shown in Fig. 7.17.

Solution   A spreadsheet is used in this example along with the spreadsheet's search tool. A sum of squares, Q, is set up to minimize the difference between the value of ΔV_{1x} computed by the planar impact equations and the target value of 21.96 mph (32.21 ft/s, 9.82 m/s), with a constraint applied such that the crush energy, E_c, is held at a constant value of 37,260 ft-lb (50,606 J). The initial speeds, V_1 and V_2, of the vehicles are the unknowns. The spreadsheet's search tool is directed to determine unknowns by minimizing Q and simultaneously satisfying the energy constraint. Initial guesses of 20 ft/s (6.1 m/s) are used for the values of V_1 and V_2. The results are shown in Fig. 7.17. The spreadsheet minimized Q, furnishing a final value of ΔV_{1x} = 22.2 ft/s (6.77 m/s), practically identical to the target value. The resulting initial speeds are v_1 = 42.66 ft/s (29.1 mph, 13.0 m/s) and v_2 = 42.66 ft/s (29.1 mph, 13.0 m/s).

The measured initial speeds from RICSAC 7 were v_1 = 42.68 ft/s (13.01 m/s) and v_2 = 42.68 ft/s (13.01 m/s). Because initial speeds have been found that satisfy the stated conditions (and that are known to accurately reflect the measured values from RICSAC 7), it could be concluded that the reconstruction is complete. In cases in which the "true" values are not known, it is prudent to examine the solution and investigate the uncertainty associated with the solution. This is done in the next example.   ◯

		ANALYSIS OF A PLANAR VEHICLE COLLISION						
		(units: lb, ft, sec, deg)						
		Vehicle 1		Vehicle 2		Initial speeds, mph		
5280/3600	1.467	115.00	mass, m	81.10		Vehicle 1		Vehicle 2
g	32.2	2985.20	inertia, I	1081.90		29.1		29.1
		8.41	distance, d	2.00				
e	0.00	-17.90	angle, ϕ	-90.00		Final speeds, mph		
μ (% μ_0)	100.0	0.00	angle, θ	60.00		Vehicle 1		Vehicle 2
μ	0.772					14.3		23.3
μ_0	0.772		initial					
Γ	-30.0	Vehicle 1	velocity	Vehicle 2		ΔV, ft/sec		
mbar	47.560	-42.66	v_x	21.33		Vehicle 1		Vehicle 2
k_1^2	25.958	0.00	v_y	36.95		22.2		31.4
k_2^2	13.340	0.00	ω	0.00				
q	1.148	42.66	v	42.66		System Kinetic Energy		
v_m	36.942	-36.94	v_n	0.00		Initial	178455	
v_{tn}	63.995	-21.33	v_t	42.66		Final	91365	
r	1.732	-36.94	v_{cn}	0.00		Loss	87090	48.8%
η_1	30.000	-21.33	v_{ct}	42.66				
η_2	90.000					Range of Normal (Crush) Energy Loss:		
d_a	0.000		final			37253	20.9%	40795 22.9%
d_b	2.000	Vehicle 1	velocity	Vehicle 2		Range of Tangential Energy Loss:		
d_c	1.763	-20.70	V_x	-9.81		49837	27.9%	46294 25.9%
d_d	8.223	2.96	V_y	32.75		Total System Energy Loss		
d_e	-4.588	-177.58	Ω	-164.97		87090	48.8%	87090 48.8%
d_f	-1.545	20.91	V	34.19				
A	1.050	-19.41	V_n	-24.87		Impulses		
B	0.231	-7.79	V_t	23.46		P_x	P_y	P
C	1.253	-24.87	V_{cn}	-24.87		2525.4	340.5	2548.2
D	2.253	17.70	V_{ct}	17.70		P_n	P_t	P
						2016.8	1557.5	2548.2
						PDOF, deg		
						Vehicle 1		Vehicle 2
						-7.7		52.3

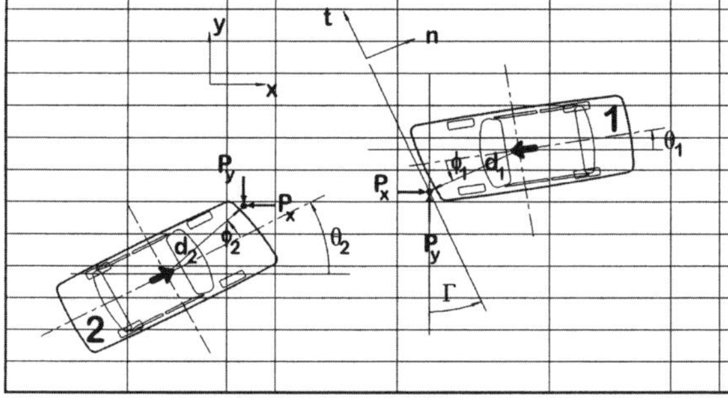

Figure 7.17
Results of a planar impact mechanics analysis of vehicle collision.

Example 7.7

In this example, the uncertainty and sensitivity of the results of the reconstruction in the previous example are examined by making changes in the input variables and observing the changes in the reconstructed initial velocity values. In accident reconstructions, input information rarely is known exactly. Sometimes variations in input do not result in large uncertainty, but in cases with high sensitivity, small changes can render a reconstruction useless. A residual crush energy constraint was used in the previous example such that E_c = 37,260 ft-lb (50,606 J). Suppose that E_c is known only to within $\pm 10\%$, that is, $33,534 \leq E_c \leq 40,986$ ft-lb ($45,465 \leq E_c \leq 55,569$ J). How does this affect the reconstruction? As a second part of this example, reconstruct the initial speeds for a $\pm 5\%$ variation in the value of ΔV_{1x} from the EDR.

Solution   Repeating the previous solution for changed values of E_c produces some surprises. Table 7.4 shows the resulting initial speeds from the previous example and those found for the higher and lower values of E_c. For a

Table 7.4
Values of V_1 and V_2 for
±5% changes ΔV.

Crush	V_1	V_2
Energy, ft-lb[a]	ft/s	ft/s
33534	39.93	50.77
37260	*42.66*	*42.67*
40986	45.27	34.93
ΔV_{1x}, ft/s[a]		
20.86	43.20	32.59
21.96	*42.66*	*42.67*
23.06	42.13	52.72

[a] Nominal values in italics.

±10% change in E_c, the corresponding changes in v_1 are −6.4% and +6.1%, and in v_2 are +19.0% and −18.1%, respectively. Now suppose that there could be a ±5% variation in the value of ΔV_{1x} from the EDR, that is, $20.86 \le \Delta V_{1x} \le 23.06$ ft/s. Table 7.4 shows that from repeating the reconstruction for a ±5% change in ΔV_{1x}, there is a corresponding change of about ±1.2% in v_1 and about ±23.5% in v_2. To find out what happens when there are simultaneous changes in ΔV_{1x} and E_c, a more complete uncertainty analysis (such as using Monte Carlo techniques) would have to be used. Based on the above individual variations for E_c and ΔV_{1x}, it can be concluded that the initial speeds can be reconstructed with uncertainty of v_2 in the range of ±23.5%.   ◯

The above examples show that some features of modern spreadsheet programs are useful to carry out collision reconstructions. The use of spreadsheet search tools raises questions, however, including:

- How many unknown quantities can be found, and how much information must be provided to find them?
- Is minimization of a sum of squares always the best procedure?
- Are there any cases in which a direct inverse solution of the planar impact equations can be used?
- How is it known if there is a unique answer?
- If there is a unique answer, how is it identified?
- What is the sensitivity to input quantities, and what is the uncertainty of the solution?

Although answering these questions is beyond the scope of this book, the user of spreadsheet tools should consider such questions.

7.6   Low Speed In-Line (Central) Collisions

While most planar collisions can be analyzed using the planar impact equations, a different approach sometimes is necessary for collisions at low speed.

At least two special characteristics of low-speed collisions require attention: the need to take into account values of the restitution coefficient significantly greater than zero, and the potential significance of tire forces and their impulses due to brake slip during the duration of contact. The collisions considered here typically occur when the vehicles are in line—when they have the same heading and have little or no lateral offset. Such collisions can be front-to-front and front-to-rear; however, at times, front-to-side collisions can fit this category as well. These collisions have little or no rotation during contact. Often there is little or no visible or residual damage to the vehicles. Despite the fact that these collisions appear to be relatively minor, there is a considerably large number of claims of significant injury, often referred to as "whiplash."

The usual categories of information and data to be considered in analyzing such collisions are the vehicles, the people, and the environment. Typical vehicle parameters are design and condition of the bumper systems; physical characteristics of the vehicles such as weight, seat, and headrest designs and conditions; restraint systems, etc. Examples of human parameters include age; gender; physical characteristics such as size, weight, etc.; neck–head–spinal physiology (length, strength, etc.); stature; muscularity; physical condition; awareness, anticipation, and response; seating position and posture of head and torso; arm actions (reaching, supported by steering wheel, etc.); injury tolerance; pain tolerance, etc. Environmental parameters include transient bumper heights (vehicle loading, braking, etc.); brake application; brake application effort; pavement conditions; vehicle angular alignment at contact; target vehicle stopped or moving, closing speed, etc.

Discussion of types of injury and the relationship between vehicle motion and level of injury is beyond the scope of this book. Given the proper physical information, the methods covered here will allow estimation of the vehicles' velocity changes and, to some extent, the corresponding peak accelerations.

Figure 7.18 represents two vehicles during contact in a front-to-rear collision of Vehicle 2 into Vehicle 1. The collision generates an intervehicular impulse,

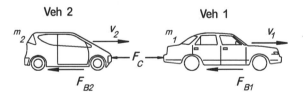

Figure 7.18
Free body diagram for front-to-rear collision of Vehicle 2 into Vehicle 1.

P, of the force, F_c, over the contact duration, $\Delta\tau$. In addition to P, each vehicle can receive an externally applied impulse, P_1 and P_2, due to the impulses of the forces from braking with wheel slip or locked wheels. In the following, these external impulses are assumed to be known quantities. The laws of impulse and momentum can be applied. For Vehicle 1,

$$m_1(V_1 - v_1) = P - P_1. \tag{7.4}$$

For Vehicle 2,

$$m_2(V_2 - v_2) = -P - P_2. \tag{7.5}$$

From the definition of the coefficient of restitution,

$$V_2 - V_1 = -e(v_2 - v_1). \tag{7.6}$$

Equations 7.4, 7.5, and 7.6 form a set of three equations with three unknowns, V_1, V_2, and P. The solution for the final velocities is

$$V_1 = v_1 + m_2(1 + e)(v_2 - v_1) / m_T - P_T / m_T, \tag{7.7}$$

$$V_2 = v_2 - m_1(1 + e)(v_2 - v_1) / m_T - P_T / m_T, \tag{7.8}$$

and

$$P = \overline{m} (1 + e)(v_2 - v_1) + (m_2 P_1 - M_1 P_2) / m_T, \tag{7.9}$$

where

$$\overline{m} = m_1 m_2 / (m_1 + m_2), \tag{7.10}$$

$$m_T = m_1 + m_2, \tag{7.11}$$

and

$$P_T = P_1 + P_2. \tag{7.12}$$

Expressions for velocity changes, ΔV_1 and ΔV_2, can be obtained from Eqs. 7.7 and 7.8, respectively. Equations 7.7 and 7.8 are extensions of Eqs. 6.13 and 6.14 that include effects of the impulses from externally applied forces. Applications of Eqs. 7.7, 7.8, and 7.9 are not difficult. However, care must be taken to ensure that results are meaningful and realistic.

For example, suppose that Vehicle 2 collides, as shown in Fig. 7.18, into the rear of Vehicle 1. Suppose further that the brakes of Vehicle 2 are not applied, and that the brakes of Vehicle 1 are locked. In such a case, $P_2 = 0$ because there is no impulse applied to Vehicle 2 other than P. An impulse from the skidding wheels of Vehicle 1 over the duration of contact does exist. It would be expected that it would have a magnitude equal to the product of the frictional force and time; that is, $P_1 = f_1 W_1 \Delta\tau$. However, if the initial speed of Vehicle 2 is low or the frictional drag coefficient for Vehicle 1 is high, or both, and the collision doesn't cause Vehicle 1 to begin to slide, then $V_1 = 0$ and $P_1 = m_2(1 + e)(v_2 - v_1) < f_1 W_1 \Delta\tau$. Consequently, it is necessary to take care in the application of these equations.

Example 7.8   Suppose that Vehicle 2 has a weight of 2400 lb (10.7 kN), is moving initially at a speed of $v_1 = 5$ mph (2.2 m/s), and strikes a stationary Vehicle 1. The brakes of the struck vehicle are applied lightly providing a frictional drag coefficient of $f = 0.2$. The weight of Vehicle 1 is 3350 lb (14.9 kN). Suppose it is known that the contact duration for this collision is $\Delta\tau = 0.125$ s and that the coefficient of restitution ranges between $e = 0.3$ and $e = 0.5$. Determine the ΔV of each vehicle and estimate the peak acceleration of the vehicles.

Solution   Figure 7.19 contains a spreadsheet solution of Eqs. 7.4 through 7.12. For the conditions given, ΔV_1 is in the range of 5.22 mph to 6.07 mph (2.3 m/s

		LOW SPEED FRONT-TO-REAR IMPACT OF VEHICLES						
		(including tire friction effects)						
	weight	lb	kN		friction coefficients			
struck	wt, W_A:	2,400	10.68		f_A	0.20		
striking	wt, W_B:	3,350	10.68		f_B	0.00		
	mass	lb-s²/ft	kg		contact duration, sec			
	m_A:	74.62	1,089		Δt	0.125		
	m_B:	104.15	1,520					
	mbar:	43.47	634					
	initial speeds, mph		km/hr		coefficient of restitution			
struck	Veh A	0.00	0.0		low e	0.30		
striking	Veh B	5.00	8.0		high e	0.50		
	range: **velocity changes**, ft/s			**mph**		**km/h**		
struck	ΔV_A	5.22	6.07	3.6	4.1	5.7	6.7	
striking	ΔV_B	-4.31	-4.93	-2.9	-3.4	-4.7	-5.4	
	average acceleration, g's			**peak** accel, g's, (2 to 3 x a_{avg})				
	a_A, avg:	1.30	1.51	a_A, peak:	2.6	4.5		
	a_B, avg:	-1.07	-1.23	a_B, peak:	-2.1	-3.7		
	energy equivalent barrier speed, ft/s			mph		km/h		
struck	$EEBS_A$	5.22	6.07	3.6	4.1	5.7	6.7	
striking	$EEBS_B$	6.68	6.93	4.6	4.7	7.3	7.6	
						tire friction impulses, lb-sec		
	B	striking		A	struck		P_A	-60.0
							P_B	0.0

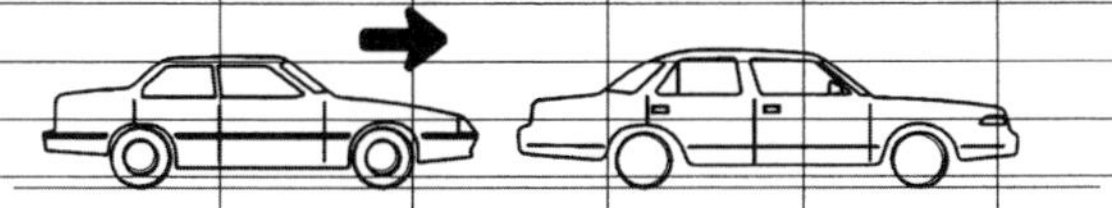

Figure 7.19
Solution of low-speed, front-to-rear impact equations.

to 2.7 m/s) and ΔV_2 is in the range of -4.31 mph to -4.93 mph (-1.9 m/s to -2.2 m/s). If the peak acceleration is between two and three times the average acceleration (see, for example, Fig. 6.4), then $a_{1peak} = 2.6$ to 4.5 g and $a_{2peak} = -2.1$ to -3.7 g. ⬡

When braking is present, Eqs. 7.7 through 7.12 can be used, but they must be applied with caution. There are several reasons for using caution:

1. The coefficient of restitution, e, is defined for a collision of the specific vehicles.[5] Barrier collision restitution coefficients differ from vehicle-to-vehicle collision coefficients. Conversion of barrier coefficients to vehicle-to-vehicle coefficients was discussed in Chapter 6 through the stiffness or mass equivalent coefficients.

2. The coefficient of restitution for a vehicle-to-vehicle collision without braking can change significantly when braking is present because the collision conditions change.[6]
3. The contact duration of a collision can change when braking exists.[6]
4. The frictional impulse used in a reconstruction is not arbitrary. That is, it is possible to choose a frictional drag coefficient and impulse duration that are physically impossible to attain for conditions of a given collision.

Consider items 2 and 3 above. For the same closing velocity as a collision without braking, as brakes of the struck vehicle are applied more strongly, the frictional drag increases. This causes the vehicles to stay in contact longer. The frictional drag removes energy from the system, the final velocities of both vehicles approach each other, and the coefficient of restitution decreases. Eventually, if the frictional drag becomes high enough, the struck vehicle begins to act more as a barrier (not a rigid barrier, however, because the "barrier"—that is, the struck vehicle—has an absorbing bumper), the contact duration then begins to drop, and the restitution begins to rise. In other words, e and $\Delta\tau$ depend on f in a relatively complex manner. This is discussed further in Chapter 11.

Crush Energy
and ΔV

8.1 Introduction

Early studies[1] of data from frontal, fixed rigid-barrier tests (at speeds above about 20 mph, 32 km/h) noted a nearly linear relationship between test speed and the amount of residual crush. An example of the linear data trend is shown in Fig. 8.1.[2] At speeds higher than about 30 mph (48 km/h), there is little restitution, and the energy lost in a barrier collision is close to the entire kinetic energy of approach. Because kinetic energy is proportional to the square of speed, this trend implies that the square root of the kinetic energy is approximately linearly proportional to the residual crush. The crush energy, E_C, per unit width, w, of a crushed chassis can then be expressed as a linear function of crush, C,[3] as

$$\sqrt{\frac{2E_C}{w}} = d_0 + d_1 C, \tag{8.1}$$

where the residual crush, C, is measured normal (perpendicular) to and from the nominal undeformed surface. The constants, d_0 and d_1, are called the crush stiffness coefficients and are determined experimentally. They differ from vehicle to vehicle and between the front, side, and rear of each vehicle. They can differ for different regions along a vehicle, although this is usually not taken into account, primarily because most existing methods do not accommodate such variations.

A 1972 Buick LeSabre has a curb weight of 4500 lb (20.0 kN) and a width of 79 in. (6.6 ft, 2.0 m). A direct frontal collision into a flat rigid concrete abutment produces a fairly uniform side-to-side residual crush of 42 in. (3.5 ft, 1.07 m). The rebound is negligible.

Example 8.1

Figure 8.1
Variation of residual crush
with impact speed, full
frontal rigid barrier tests,
1971–1972 full-sized
GM vehicles (reprinted
with permission from
Cheng et al.[2]).

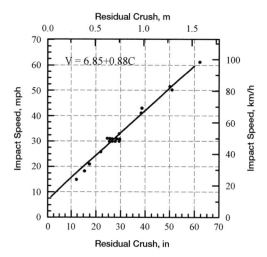

Figure 8.1 Variation of residual crush with impact speed, full frontal rigid barrier tests, 1971–1972 full-sized GM vehicles (reprinted with permission from Cheng et al.[2]).

A. Use the straight line equation from Fig. 8.1 to estimate the impact speed.

B. Use the answer to A and the equation from Fig. 8.1 to determine the coefficients d_0 and d_1 in Eq. 8.1.

Solution A   For a uniform residual crush of 42 in., the equation from Fig. 8.1 gives

$$V = 6.85 + (0.88)(42) = 43.8 \text{ ft/s (30 mph, 48 km/h)}.$$

Solution B   From the equation in Fig. 8.1, $C = 0$ occurs at a speed of $V = 6.85$ ft/s (4.7 mph, 7.5 km/s), when the kinetic energy is 3281.8 ft-lb (4449.5 J). Using Eq. 8.1 with $C = 0$ gives

$$d_0 = \sqrt{\frac{2(3281.8)}{6.58}} = 31.58 \text{ lb}^{1/2} \text{ (66.6 N}^{1/2}\text{)}.$$

From *Solution A*, at 43.8 ft/s the kinetic energy loss is 134,177 ft-lb (181,920 J). Solving Eq. 8.1 for d_1 gives

$$d_1 = \frac{1}{C}\left(\sqrt{\frac{2E_C}{w}} - d_0\right) = \frac{1}{3.5}\left(\sqrt{\frac{2(134,177)}{6.58}} - 31.58\right)$$

$$= 48.68 \text{ lb}^{1/2}\text{/ft (3.13 N}^{1/2}\text{/cm)}. \qquad \bigcirc$$

    Vehicles do not always collide head-on into flat rigid barriers, so the above relationship between energy (and speed) and residual crush is not generally applicable for accident reconstruction unless it can be adapted to nonuniform crush profiles and vehicle-to-vehicle collisions. This relationship was exploited and a method was developed for the National Highway Traffic Safety Administration[4] called CRASH3 (Calspan Reconstruction of Accident Speeds on the Highway, version 3). CRASH3 was developed for collisions of light vehicles only. The measurement process of residual crush is intended to follow a specific measurement protocol.[5] The protocol typically uses a series of six crush measurements equally spaced over a deformed surface. Measurements are made perpendicular to the undeformed surface of a damaged vehicle at a uniform height from the ground at a level corresponding to where vehicles are designed to resist and develop controlled crush forces. This is usually at front and rear bumper heights. In the theoretical development, crush is usually assumed to be uniform from top to bottom of the vehicle surface, but it rarely is in practice, particularly for side damage. For side damage, measurements are made at the vehicle structure near floor sill height, but if the damage is significantly greater above the sill, averaging of the maximum crush above the sill is often done to improve correlation with crash tests.[6] Residual crush measurements are made over the full lateral extent (beginning to end) of damage. This includes direct contact damage and induced damage. Induced damage is residual deformation that occurs not due to direct vehicle-to-vehicle contact but because of contact forces at adjacent areas. If the profile of the initial undeformed body shape is curved (such as looking at a bumper from above), it is important to measure each crush value from the corresponding curved, original, undeformed surface.

CRASH3 specifically is not applicable to under-ride situations where contact is not at or near bumper height. CRASH3 is not typically applicable to collisions with narrow objects, although it has been successfully applied if certain corrections are made.[7-10] If a damage profile is reasonably uniform, CRASH3 was originally set up to be used with four, or even two, measurements. The development in this book is for six measurements at equal lateral intervals, however. Figure 8.2 illustrates a series of six crush measurements made along damage of extent L of the front and the side of a vehicle where C_1 through C_6 are the measured distances from the undeformed, as manufactured, surface of the vehicle to the point of the crushed surface.

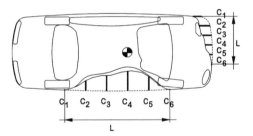

Figure 8.2
Example side and front (or rear) six-point crush measurement protocol.

Prasad[3,11,12] shows that if the crush profile is approximated by linear segments of crush between the six equally spaced points and if Eq. 8.1 is at least approximately true, then the crush energy can be computed from

$$E_C = d_0^2 K_1 + d_0 d_1 K_2 + d_1^2 K_3, \tag{8.2}$$

where

$$K_1 = L / 2, \tag{8.3}$$

$$K_2 = L[C_1 + 2(C_2 + C_3 + C_4 + C_5) + C_6] / 10, \tag{8.4}$$

and

$$K_3 = L[C_1^2 + 2(C_2^2 + C_3^2 + C_4^2 + C_5^2) + C_6^2 + \\ C_1C_2 + C_2C_3 + C_3C_4 + C_4C_5 + C_5C_6] / 30. \qquad (8.5)$$

Equations 8.2 through 8.5 form the CRASH3 crush energy algorithm.

Figure 8.3 shows a collision between two cars where the collinear arrows represent the equal and opposite impulses of the forces acting over the common

Figure 8.3
Collision orientation with arrows representing the equal and opposite impulse (PDOF) and distances h_1 and h_2.

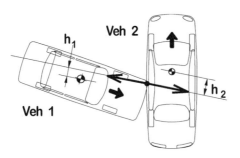

intervehicular crush surface during the collision. This line of the impulse is generally referred to as the *principal direction of force* (PDOF). Although it actually is the direction or line of impulse, it has a long history of being called a direction of force. The figure also shows distances h_1 and h_2, each measured perpendicularly from a center of gravity to the PDOF.

In the original version of CRASH3,[4] a model somewhat different from Eq. 8.1 was used in which the intervehicular crush force per unit width is assumed to have the form

$$F_C / w = A + BC, \qquad (8.6)$$

where the crush, $C = C(x)$, was taken to vary piece-wise linearly with the position, x, along the crush surface. The total crush energy is computed by integrating the energy per unit width over the entire crush width, L, to find the work of F_C. The result is

$$E_C / w = AC + BC^2 / 2 + A^2 / 2B. \qquad (8.7)$$

This produces a model in which A and B are the crush stiffness coefficients, and, by using a set of equations different from Eqs. 8.2 through 8.5, the crush energy can be calculated from residual crush measurements. Prasad[12] showed that the A and B model (Eq. 8.6) and the d_0 and d_1 model (Eq. 8.1) are equivalent (compare coefficients of Eq. 8.1 and Eq. 8.7) where

$$d_1 = \sqrt{B} \qquad (8.8)$$

and

$$d_0 = A / \sqrt{B}. \qquad (8.9)$$

Equations 8.6 and 8.7 are given for information but not used here.

To complete the CRASH3 model, crush energy is related to the velocity change, ΔV_i, of each vehicle using basic impact mechanics (see Chapters 6 and 7). Four assumptions are usually made to simplify the results:

1. The crush energy, E_C, is equal to the impact energy loss, T_L.
2. The collision is perfectly inelastic, that is, there is no rebound or restitution of the vehicles at and perpendicular to the crush surface.
3. Relative sliding velocity of the vehicles along (tangent to) the crush surface ends (becomes zero) before or at the time the vehicles separate.
4. Forces external to the colliding vehicles (including tire–ground forces) are negligibly small compared to the level of the force acting on the intervehicular crush surface.

Assumptions 2 and 3 are often referred to as the *common-velocity conditions* and often are valid assumptions except in low-speed collisions (where significant restitution can be present) and/or sideswipe collisions (where relative sliding continues through separation). Assumption 4 ensures that momentum is conserved. Assumptions 2 and 3 are not always exactly true, even for high-speed collisions. Consequently, the equation for ΔV_i is not as general as is needed in many crash reconstructions. This is discussed in more detail below.

According to the original CRASH3 formulation[4] and for the four conditions above, momentum is conserved, so

$$m_i \Delta V_i = \sqrt{2 m_e E_C}, \quad i = 1, 2, \tag{8.10}$$

where, in this equation, E_C is the total crush energy of both vehicles. The quantity $i = 1$ represents Vehicle 1 and $i = 2$ represents Vehicle 2; also,

$$m_e = \frac{\gamma_1 m_1 \gamma_2 m_2}{\gamma_1 m_1 + \gamma_2 m_2}, \tag{8.11}$$

where

$$\gamma_i = \frac{k_i^2}{k_i^2 + h_i^2}. \tag{8.12}$$

The quantity k_i is the yaw radius of gyration of vehicle i, and h_i is the perpendicular distance illustrated in Fig. 8.3 for Vehicles 1 and 2. Note that radius of gyration is the square root of the mass moment of inertia divided by mass

$$k_i = \sqrt{\frac{J_i}{m_i}}, \tag{8.13}$$

where J_i is the mass moment of inertia about the yaw axis of vehicle i, and m_i is the mass of vehicle i.

Equation 8.10 calculates ΔV from the residual crush energy. This method is based on the residual crush measured perpendicular to the undeformed surfaces and is based on the common-velocity conditions. It does not take into account the energy loss associated with the change in relative tangential velocities. That is, the energy dissipated due to sliding of one vehicle over the other and due to tangential deformation and entanglement over the crush surfaces is not included in the above equations for the energy loss, E_C. In some collisions, energy loss associated with tangential motion over the contact surface can be significant and must not be ignored. The original CRASH3 method suggests the use of a correction factor. As it is defined, however, the correction is not theoretically sound and its application is subjective, so its accuracy is questionable. A more accurate and rigorous assessment of the energy associated with tangential impulses is covered in Chapters 6 and 7 through the use of the impulse ratio and its critical value. There it is shown that impulse and momentum techniques can be used to estimate independently the energy dissipated by the normal crush (the same energy as determined above) and the additional energy dissipated by tangential effects under the common velocity conditions. Another advantage of using the methods of Chapters 6 and 7 for calculating ΔV from crush energy is that in the above approach, the PDOF must be visually estimated from the damaged surfaces (to determine h_1 and h_2). Without a great deal of experience and a knowledge of impulse mechanics, this can be difficult. On the other hand, the PDOF (direction of impulse) is automatically calculated using methods covered in Chapters 6 and 7 and need not be estimated in advance.

Therefore, when crush methods are used, it is recommended that the energy associated with the normal crush be calculated using Eq. 8.2, but the ΔV of each vehicle should not be computed by Eq. 8.8. It is recommended rather to calculate the (normal) crush energy followed by the methods of Chapters 6 and 7 to complete a reconstruction (for example, using planar impact mechanics). There is another reason for this approach. The CRASH3 method is based on the common-velocity conditions. These conditions only come into play in computation of the ΔV (Eq. 8.2), and not in the computation of E_C. It is quite possible that the coefficient of restitution is not zero (one of the two common-velocity conditions) for some collisions (see Tables 6.1 and 6.2). By using planar impact mechanics, nonzero restitution can easily be taken into account. In addition, the tangential common velocity condition assumption does not apply to sideswipe collisions. When there is measurable crush while the vehicles continue to slide through separation ($\mu < \mu_0$), planar impact mechanics can be used.

The calculations carried out in the original CRASH method and in commercial versions of CRASH3* are much more extensive than those above because they also include a postimpact spinout model. That is, the energy loss due to the motion of the vehicles from impact to rest is estimated using accident data when available. It is strongly recommended that vehicle dynamics simulation methods (see Chapter 11) be used to reconstruct postimpact motion.

---

* Commercially available versions of CRASH3 include EDCRASH, Engineering Dynamics Corporation, 8625 SW Cascade Blvd., Suite 200, Beaverton, OR 97008-7100, USA, 503 644 4500, http://www.edccorp.com; CRASHEX, Fonda Engineering Associates, 649 S Henderson Rd., Suite C307, King of Prussia, PA 19406, USA, 610 337 3311, http://www.crashex.com; and M-CRASH, McHenry Software, PO Box 5694 Cary, NC 27512, USA 919 468 9266, http://www.mchenrysoftware.com.

They are much more accurate, especially under special conditions such as a single locked wheel, changes in frictional drag, and so on.

All of the equations for calculating energy loss and ΔV of each vehicle (uncorrected for tangential effects) are algebraic and can be calculated conveniently using a spreadsheet.

Assume a collision of two vehicles with a configuration as shown in Fig. 8.4. Vehicle 1 has a weight at impact of W_1 = 3696 lb (16.4 kN) and Vehicle 2 has a

Example 8.2

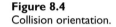
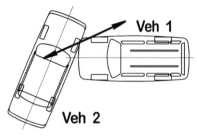

Figure 8.4
Collision orientation.

weight of W_2 = 3413 lb (15.18 kN). Crush measurements, crush widths, crush stiffness coefficients, and other data for these vehicles are given in Table 8.1. It is assumed for this example that the common-velocity conditions apply.

	Vehicle 1	Vehicle 2
Weight	3696 lb (16.44 kN)	3413 lb (15.18 kN)
Yaw moment of inertia	2437 ft-lb-s² (3304 kg-m²)	2165 ft-lb-s² (2935 kg-m²)
Wheelbase	8.9 ft (2.7 m)	8.6 ft (2.6 m)
h_1	1.3 ft (0.4 m)	5.6 ft (1.7 m)
C_1	21.3 in. (54.1 cm)	3.0 in. (7.6 cm)
C_2	20.3 in. (51.6 cm)	15.8 in. (40.1 cm)
C_3	13.8 in. (35.1 cm)	13.5 in. (34.3 cm)
C_4	11.3 in. (28.7 cm)	6.7 in. (17.0 cm)
C_5	5.3 in. (13.5 cm)	3.3 in. (8.4 cm)
C_6	4.8 in. (12.2 cm)	5.0 in. (12.7 cm)
Crush width	L = 65 in. (1.65 m)	L = 84 in. (2.13 m)
Crush stiffness coefficients		
d_0	35 lb¹ᐟ²	30 lb¹ᐟ²
d_1	115 lb¹ᐟ²/ft	77.5 lb¹ᐟ²/ft

Table 8.1
Input data for Example 8.2.

Solution The spreadsheet used to calculate the crush energy and ΔV values for these conditions and data is shown in Fig. 8.5. It shows that (without correction for the tangential impulse), the total crush energy of both vehicles is E_C = 103,864 ft-lb (140,821 J). It also gives a ΔV value for each vehicle. Tangential effects can be taken into account using planar impact mechanics covered in Chapters 6 and 7. For this collision, the impact parameters for Vehicle 1 are d_1 = 6.3 ft (1.9 m), θ_1 = 0°, and φ_1 = −22.4°; and for Vehicle 2, d_2 = 3.8 ft (1.2 m), θ_2 = 67°, and φ_2 = −39.0°. In addition, the impact surface was along the passenger side of Vehicle 2, so Γ = −23°. The common velocity conditions are applied by setting e = 0 and μ = μ_0. Additional information available from

Figure 8.5
Result of crush energy
calculation using
CRASH3 algorithm.

			ENERGY LOSS AND SPEED CHANGE FROM CRASH3							
			DELTA V VALUES (UNCORRECTED FOR TANGENTIAL IMPULSE)							
	g:	32.1740486	ft/s							
W_1:	3,696.00	lb		C1:	C2:	C3:	C4:	C5:	C6:	
W_2:	3,413.00	lb		21.30	20.30	13.80	11.30	5.30	4.80	inches
				1.78	1.69	1.15	0.94	0.44	0.40	feet
m_1:	114.88	lb-s^2/ft								
m_2:	106.08	lb-s^2/ft								
k_1:	4.61	ft								
k_2:	4.62	ft		crush width:	65.00	in				
h_1:	1.30	ft			5.42	ft				
h_2:	5.60	ft								
I_1:	2441.3	ft-lb-s^2		d0:	35.00	sqrt(lb)			A:	4025.00	lb/ft
I_2:	2167.2	ft-lb-s^2		d0:	35.00	sqrt(lb)			A:	335.42	lb/in
γ_1:	0.926									
γ_2:	0.394									
mbar:	30.04			d1:	115.00	sqrt(lb)/ft			B:	13225.00	lb/ft^2
				d1:	9.58	sqrt(lb)/in			B:	91.84	lb/in^2
									G:	612.50	lb
VEHICLE 1	Vehicle 1									
Velocity Change	21.74	ft/s		Energy loss due						
ΔV_1:	14.8	mph		to normal crush:	75352.87	ft-lb		VEHICLE 1	Vehicle 1	
					904234.39	in-lb				
VEHICLE 2	Vehicle 2			C1:	C2:	C3:	C4:	C5:	C6:	
Velocity Change	23.55	ft/s		3.00	15.80	13.50	6.70	3.30	5.00	inches
ΔV_2:	16.1	mph		0.25	1.32	1.13	0.56	0.28	0.42	feet
				crush width:	84.00	in				
Total Energy:	103864.5	ft-lb			7.00	ft				
	1.2464E+6	in-lb								
				d0:	30.00	sqrt(lb)			A:	2325.00	lb/ft
				d0:	30.00	sqrt(lb)			A:	193.75	lb/in
				d1:	77.50	sqrt(lb)/ft			B:	6006.25	lb/ft^2
				d1:	6.46	sqrt(lb)/in			B:	41.71	lb/in^2
									G:	450.00	lb
				Energy Loss Due						
				to Normal Crush:	28511.66	ft-lb		VEHICLE 2	Vehicle 2	
					342139.86	in-lb				

an investigation of this accident is that Vehicle 2 had stopped at a stop sign and accelerated to a speed of approximately 10 mph (16 km/h) in the direction of its heading. Thus, $v_{2x} = 5.73$ ft/s (1.75 m/s) and $v_{2y} = 13.50$ ft/s (4.12 m/s). Also, it is assumed that neither vehicle had a preimpact angular velocity, that is, $\omega_1 = \omega_2 = 0$. Finally, with these conditions, a spreadsheet solution can be used in an iterative fashion (or using the search tool of the spreadsheet) with the objective of reaching a value of normal (crush) energy loss $E_C = 103,864$ ft-lb (140,798 J) from Fig. 8.5. The results are given in Fig. 8.6 and show that for the initial speed of Vehicle 1 of 47.7 mph (76.7 km/h), the range of crush energy is from 100,484 ft-lb (136,216 J) to 103,864 ft-lb (140,798 J). In addition, it shows that the total energy loss is approximately $T_L = 130,331$ ft-lb (176,676 J). Finally, the velocity changes of the two vehicles in this collision are $\Delta V_1 = 20.4$ mph (32.8 km/h) and $\Delta V_2 = 22.1$ mph (35.6 km/h), significantly greater than the uncorrected ΔV values given directly from the crush energy equations in Fig. 8.5.

ANALYSIS OF A PLANAR VEHICLE COLLISION
(units: lb, ft, sec, deg)

			Vehicle 1		Vehicle 2	Initial speeds, mph		
5280/3600	1.467		114.89	mass, m	106.09	Vehicle 1		Vehicle 2
g	32.2		2437.00	inertia, I	2165.00	47.7		10.0
			6.30	distance, d	3.80			
e	0.00		-22.40	angle, φ	-39.00	Final speeds, mph		
μ (% μ0)	100.0		0.00	angle, θ	67.00	Vehicle 1		Vehicle 2
μ	0.455					27.3		20.1
μ0	0.455			initial				
Γ	-23.0	Vehicle 1	velocity	Vehicle 2		ΔV, ft/sec		
mbar	55.157	-69.89	v_x	5.73		Vehicle 1		Vehicle 2
k_1^2	21.212	0.00	v_y	13.50		29.9		32.4
k_2^2	20.407	0.00	ω	0.00				
q	0.880	69.89	v	14.67		System Kinetic Energy		
v_m	64.338	-64.34	v_n	0.00		Initial	292043	
v_{tn}	41.976	-27.31	v_t	14.67		Final	161712	
r	0.652	-64.34	v_{cn}	0.00		Loss	130331	44.6%
$η_1$	23.000	-27.31	v_{ct}	14.67				
$η_2$	90.000					Range of Normal (Crush) Energy Loss:		
d_a	2.953		final			100484 34.4% 103864 35.6%		
d_b	2.391	Vehicle 1	velocity	Vehicle 2		Range of Tangential Energy Loss:		
d_c	0.066	-40.03	V_x	-26.61		29847 10.2% 26467 9.1%		
d_d	6.300	0.77	V_y	12.67		Total System Energy Loss		
d_e	-2.802	-205.78	Ω	154.12		130331 44.6% 130331 44.6%		
d_f	1.864	40.04	V	29.47				
A	1.222	-37.15	V_n	-29.44		Impulses		
B	0.189	-14.93	V_t	1.26		P_x P_y P		
C	1.044	-37.39	V_{cn}	-37.39		3431.0 88.6 3432.1		
D	2.044	7.69	V_{ct}	7.69		P_n P_t P		
						3123.6 1422.1 3432.1		
						PDOF, deg		
						Vehicle 1		Vehicle 2
						-1.5		65.5

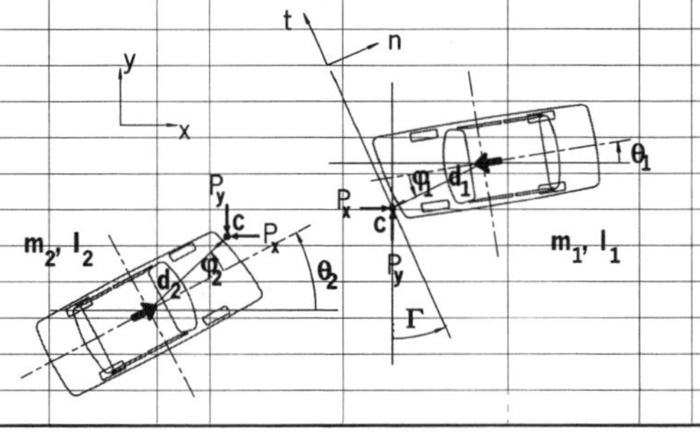

Figure 8.6
Results of planar impact mechanics calculation using Example 8.2 with the same normal crush energy as in Fig. 8.5.

8.2   Crush Stiffness Coefficients Based on Average Crush from Rigid Barrier Tests

One of the most common test methods used to determine frontal crush stiffness coefficients is from residual crush measurements made from a vehicle crashed into a fixed rigid barrier. This section shows how the crush stiffness coefficients can be determined from an average of six such crush measurements. Example 1 of this chapter lays a foundation for the method. The first task is to establish a threshold speed below which no measurable residual crush occurs, that is, a speed for which $C = 0$. Note that this does not necessarily mean no visible damage, but rather no significant residual crush. Often this speed is arbitrarily chosen to lie in the range of 5 to 7 mph (8.1 to 11.3 km/h).

Equation 8.1 is used to solve for d_0, then a weighted average of the six crush measurements is used to give C_{avg}, and Eq. 8.1 is used to give

$$d_1 = \frac{1}{C_{avg}}\left(\sqrt{\frac{2E_C}{w}} - d_0\right).$$ (8.14)

Because of the form of Eq. 8.4, it is more accurate if C_{avg} is computed using the weighted average:

$$C_{avg} = [C_1 + 2(C_2 + C_3 + C_4 + C_5) + C_6] / 10.$$ (8.15)

Example 8.3   A problem is posed[13] that gives frontal crush values of $C_1 = 17.8$ in., $C_2 = 18.7$ in., $C_3 = 21.1$ in., $C_4 = 20.6$ in., $C_5 = 18.2$ in., and $C_6 = 17.4$ in. for a 1997 Honda Accord with a test weight of 3293 lb and a test speed of 35.0 mph (56.3 km/h) into a rigid barrier. The corresponding energy loss is $E_C = 134,868$ ft-lb. The crush width is $w = 65.6$ in. Using Eq. 8.15 gives $C_{avg} = 19.2$ in. For $C = 0$ at 5 mph (6.8 km/h), Eq. 8.1 gives $d_0 = 31.7$ lb$^{1/2}$ (66.9 N$^{1/2}$). Equation 8.12 gives $d_1 = 119.0$ lb$^{1/2}$/ft (7.6 N$^{1/2}$/cm).

   To check the accuracy of these values of the crush stiffness coefficients, Eqs. 8.2 through 8.5 can be used to determine the energy loss for the measured crush values. (To represent a rigid barrier, the parameters of Vehicle 2 are given exaggerated values such as a crush width $w = 0$ and a weight of 999,999 lb.) Placing d_0, d_1, w, and C_1 through C_6 into Eqs. 8.2 though 8.5 gives an energy loss of 135,700 ft-lb (183,955 J). This is a difference of approximately 0.6% from $E_C = 134,868$ ft-lb (182,827 J) and validates the values of d_0 and d_1 as representative of a 1997 Honda Accord for a frontal crush analysis.   ⬡

   Rigid barrier tests of vehicles at high speed do not always have a coefficient of restitution exactly equal to zero. If a nonzero test value is known, the energy loss is reduced. This can be taken into account when calculating the stiffness coefficients. If, for the above example, it is known that during the Honda Accord barrier test the Honda rebounded with a value of $e = 0.1$, then less energy is lost and so the values of the coefficients would be $d_0 = 31.7$ lb$^{1/2}$ (66.9 N$^{1/2}$) and $d_1 = 111.9$ lb$^{1/2}$/ft (7.2 N$^{1/2}$/cm).

   Another point to keep in mind is that the accuracy of the crush stiffness coefficients d_0 and d_1 can be enhanced by using statistically averaged results of more than a single barrier test.

8.3   Crush Stiffness Coefficients from Vehicle-to-Vehicle Collisions

Sometimes the crush stiffness coefficients of a vehicle are obtained from a test in which a striking vehicle is crashed into a struck vehicle. Example collision geometries are shown in Fig. 8.7. This section covers a method for determining the crush stiffness coefficients from such a test. An important condition is that a reasonably accurate measurement of the impact energy loss can be made. Any energy dissipated by tire forces must not be included as crush energy. (If the striking vehicle is a moving rigid barrier, then its residual crush and its crush energy both are zero, and the methods of the previous section can be used.) Another condition is that the damage widths w_1 and w_2 must be equal.

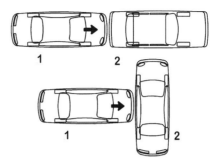

Figure 8.7
Two example orientations of controlled vehicle-to-vehicle crashes.

This rules out the use of oblique collisions and also means that any induced damage must be negligible.

A problem that arises with two-vehicle tests is that the total kinetic energy loss (of both vehicles) of the collision can be determined easily, but the crush energy for each vehicle is unknown. In fact, the struck vehicle ends up gaining kinetic energy as a result of the collision even though its crush contributes to the energy loss. Fortunately, this problem can be overcome. For a central collision, the total collision energy loss, T_L, is given by Eq. 6.22. If the collision energy loss, T_L, is entirely converted to crush energy, then $T_L = E_C$ and

$$E_C = \frac{1}{2}\,\overline{m}(1 - e^2)(v_2 - v_1)^2, \tag{8.16}$$

where $\overline{m}$ is given by Eq. 6.17. For each vehicle, Eq. 8.1 relates crush energy loss and the residual crush as

$$\sqrt{2E_1/w} = d_{01} + d_{11}C_{1\mathrm{avg}}, \tag{8.17}$$

$$\sqrt{2E_2/w} = d_{02} + d_{12}C_{2\mathrm{avg}}, \tag{8.18}$$

where the average values of crush are computed according to Eq. 8.15. Note that the speed at which negligible residual crush occurs can be used with each of Eq. 8.17 and Eq. 8.18 directly with an average crush of zero to calculate d_{01} and d_{02}. This means that they can be treated as knowns and d_{11} and d_{12} are the remaining unknowns.

Newton's third law says that the forces between two objects in contact must be equal in magnitude. Equating Eq. 8.6 for each vehicle and using Eq. 8.8 and Eq. 8.9 gives

$$d_{11}(d_{01} + d_{11}C_{1\mathrm{avg}}) = d_{12}(d_{02} + d_{12}C_{2\mathrm{avg}}). \tag{8.19}$$

Taking a ratio of the square of Eq. 8.1 for each vehicle gives an energy ratio, and using Eq. 8.19,

$$\frac{E_1}{E_2} = \left(\frac{d_{01} + d_{11}C_{1\mathrm{avg}}}{d_{02} + d_{12}C_{2\mathrm{avg}}}\right)^2 = \left(\frac{d_{12}}{d_{11}}\right)^2. \tag{8.20}$$

Because $E_C = E_1 + E_2$, Eq. 8.20 gives

$$E_1 = \frac{E_C}{1 + (d_{11}/d_{12})^2},$$
(8.21)

$$E_2 = \frac{E_C}{1 + (d_{12}/d_{11})^2}.$$
(8.22)

Equations 8.17, 8.19, 8.21, and 8.22 form a set of four nonlinear equations with the unknowns of E_1, E_2, d_{11}, and d_{12}. These can be solved conveniently using various methods, but not done here.

8.3.1 Damage to One Vehicle Unknown

Sometimes one of two vehicles involved in a crash is not available for crush measurements. Following certain assumptions, a method has been developed that can be used to estimate the ΔV values of the two vehicles without the residual crush values of one.[14] The reader is referred to that reference.

8.3.2 Side Crush Stiffness Coefficients, Two-Vehicle, Front-to-Side Crash Tests

Crush stiffness values can be obtained from test data for additional collision configurations. Sometimes the front of a vehicle (striking vehicle) with known crush stiffness coefficients can be crashed into the side of a vehicle (struck vehicle) with unknown crush stiffness coefficients. A method has been developed that allows determination of accident-specific crush stiffness coefficients for the target vehicle.[15] The reader is referred to that reference.

8.3.3 Nonlinear Models of Crush

Equation 8.1 is a linear relationship between the square root of energy and residual crush. Nonlinear models have been proposed but are not covered here. Two notable approaches are available. Woolley[7] extends the model covered here to nonlinear ranges. This allows more accurate application over a wider range of collision speeds. Of course, the coefficients of the nonlinear model must be determined experimentally for the vehicles being analyzed. Wood et al.[16] have derived a model, basically different from Eq. 8.1, which is nonlinear and follows a power law. They show the model's agreement with crash test data using European vehicles.

Frontal Vehicle–Pedestrian Collisions

9.1 Introduction

The reconstruction of collisions between vehicles and pedestrians requires a different approach than does the reconstruction of collisions between vehicles. Initial motion of pedestrians often is unimportant because their speeds at impact typically are much lower than the speed of the vehicle. Also, the large mass difference and the friction developed between the vehicle and pedestrian at impact will result in the pedestrian moving predominantly in the direction of the vehicle. The postimpact motion of a pedestrian frequently includes a trajectory through the air followed by an impact with the ground and a tumble or slide to rest. The speed and frontal geometry of the striking vehicle can significantly affect the nature of the postimpact motion of the pedestrian. Physical evidence such as the location and pattern of vehicle deformation, type and locations of injuries, vehicle and pedestrian impact and rest positions, ground and roadway markings, and so forth can be used to establish the nature and details of a vehicle–pedestrian collision and can lead to a successful and reasonably accurate reconstruction. When the motion and damage of a vehicle, and the motion and injuries to a pedestrian, a bicycle rider, or an animal fit those types of collisions discussed in this chapter, reliable and reasonably accurate reconstructions can be carried out.

Vehicle–pedestrian collisions often are categorized according to the type of vehicle–pedestrian contact interaction and the pedestrian postimpact motion.[1] These categories are neither mutually exclusive nor exhaustive but serve as descriptive guides. The most common categories are *forward projection, wrap, carry, roof vault*, and *fender vault*. In a *forward projection* collision, the frontal surface of the vehicle is relatively vertical and flat with respect to the pedestrian and extends above and below the pedestrian's center of gravity. Examples are frontal collisions of buses and cab-over trucks with adult pedestrians, as shown in Fig. 9.1, and pickup trucks and children. A forward projection collision drives the pedestrian straight forward relative to the vehicle. In *wrap* collisions,

Figure 9.1
Illustration of forward projection (*left*) and wrap (*right*) vehicle–pedestrian collision.

because of a low frontal contact surface of the vehicle relative to the pedestrian's center of gravity as well as the pedestrian's body flexibility and freedom to rotate, the pedestrian's body wraps back onto the hood following an initial contact, as shown in Fig. 9.1. If the speed of the vehicle is high enough, the pedestrian impacts the vehicle again at the windshield, a windshield pillar, or the roof. Following this secondary impact, the pedestrian often is thrown or projected forward at some angle relative to the ground in a trajectory through the air. If the pedestrian wraps back onto a hood and remains on the hood or fender for a period of time while the vehicle moves forward, this is the *carry* category. For a carry, if the pedestrian and/or clothing is not snagged on a part of the vehicle, the pedestrian eventually slides forward from the hood or fender as the vehicle decelerates. A *roof vault* begins as a wrap collision but, usually because of the high speed of the vehicle, the pedestrian continues up onto the roof. In such cases, the pedestrian continues rearward relative to the vehicle and may hit a rear surface such as a trunk lid before reaching the ground. A *fender vault* collision occurs when the pedestrian is struck by the front of a vehicle near one of its sides, wraps up onto the fender and sloughs off to the side of the moving vehicle without a significant secondary impact with a pillar or windshield.

Acceleration or deceleration of the vehicle after initial impact can play a role in a pedestrian collision. In a carry collision, the pedestrian remains on the hood of the vehicle for a period of time. If the vehicle continues to accelerate, this period will be increased; if the vehicle begins to decelerate, the pedestrian will tend to slide forward from the vehicle. Other factors, such as the slope of the hood, play a role. In a roof vault, an accelerating vehicle will tend to move out from underneath the pedestrian while a decelerating vehicle will tend to remain below the pedestrian. In a wrap collision, vehicle deceleration allows the pedestrian to move forward without sustained interactive contact with the vehicle.

Different approaches may be taken to reconstruct a vehicle–pedestrian accident. The approach, to a large extent, depends on the goals of the reconstruction and the available information. A distinction is made between *speed reconstruction* and reconstruction of *vehicle–pedestrian interaction dynamics*. The former is the determination of vehicle speed from the physical evidence from the accident. Examples of such evidence are throw distance and distance between vehicle and pedestrian rest positions. Throw distance is defined as the distance between the position of the initial pedestrian contact and the final uncontrolled rest position, that is, the distance the pedestrian moves between initial contact and rest. Vehicle–pedestrian interaction dynamics is aimed substantially at the determination of detailed pedestrian–vehicle interaction motion and forces in order to assess a specific injury or to assess effects of changes in vehicle geometry. This analysis typically is done using relatively sophisticated, multibody dynamics computer software; see, for example, van Wijk et al.[2] and Moser et al.[3] If such detailed information is not particularly important, a speed reconstruction can be done using relatively simple equations. Speed reconstruction is the topic covered in this chapter.

Several approaches are available for carrying out speed reconstructions. They are distinguished by the source of the equations. One approach is to use empirical equations, developed from vehicle–pedestrian experimental data. These empirical models are based on a wide range of tests, some involving reconstructed collisions, tests with dummies, tests with cadavers, etc. Another approach is to use equations derived from principles of mechanics that have been compared favorably to experiments. A third is a hybrid approach in which equations are based both on mechanics models and experiments. Empirical equations have proven to be a practical method of speed reconstruction because a strong relationship has been found to exist between throw distance, s_p, and the square of the vehicle speed, v_{c0}.[4–6]

Each of the speed reconstruction approaches has advantages and disadvantages. Empirical equations are simple and easy to apply. Although empirical models are usually presented with variations, these variations are due primarily to the differences in test conditions and represent experimental error. These variations do not represent reconstruction uncertainty. Theoretical models based on mechanics and that contain physical parameters have a distinct advantage. Variations in these models are based on changes in the physical parameters, so the physical models can be used not only for reconstruction, but to estimate uncertainty of a specific reconstruction. Hybrid models combine analytical and empirical equations and have advantages and disadvantages of both.

A hybrid approach[7] is first presented for wrap collisions followed by an experimental model[8] for forward projection collisions. Then, a mechanics model is developed, based on the work of Han and Brach, that can be used to analyze and reconstruct forward projection and wrap collisions.

9.2 General and Supplementary Information

A great deal of literature has developed over the years related to vehicle–pedestrian collisions. Well over 400 technical articles have been published on various aspects of the subject over the years. A summary of some pertinent papers is contained in Backaitis.[9]

The collision and postimpact motion of the vehicle and pedestrian are only two parts of a pedestrian accident. Events prior to impact often play an important role. In many cases, it is necessary to take into account factors such as visibility, driver inattention, the direction and speed of the pedestrian (or bicycle rider, or animal, etc.). These aspects of a reconstruction are not explicitly treated here. Various sources exist containing information and data on walking, jogging, and running speeds as well as acceleration capability of adults and children. Some of this information is contained in references such as Eubanks,[1] Fugger et al.,[10] Toor,[6] and Vaughan and Bain.[11,12]

9.3   Hybrid Wrap Model

A single-segment physical model of a pedestrian and its impact with a vehicle was developed by Wood.[13] It is a relatively sophisticated model of vehicle–pedestrian impact that takes into account possible multiple impacts between the pedestrian and vehicle, head contact position, head velocities, time of wrap, and time of head contact, among other considerations. In a later work, Wood and Simms[7] developed a hybrid model based on the single-segment physical model. This model is also based on a number of vehicle–pedestrian tests. The results comprise a simple algebraic relationship between the initial vehicle speed, v_{c0}, and the throw distance, s_p:

$$v_{c0} = c_W \sqrt{s_p} \, , \text{m/s}, \tag{9.1}$$

where three different values of c_W provide estimates of the mean and the experimental uncertainty. In this equation, velocity has units of m/s and pedestrian throw distance has units of meters. The three values of the constant are

$$c_W = 2.5, 3.6, 4.5, \tag{9.2}$$

where $c_W = 3.6$ is a mean value and the other values provide lower and upper bounds. Wood's hybrid model is intended primarily for wrap and forward projection collisions.

9.4   Forward Projection Model

Wood and Walsh[8] present a model specifically intended for forward projection vehicle–pedestrian collisions. Results are given as bounds with minimum and maximum speeds as functions of throw distance for children and adults. For a child,

$$v_{c0} = c_c \sqrt{s_p} \, , \text{m/s}, \tag{9.3}$$

where a minimum value of the initial speed is for $c_c = 2.03$ and the maximum value is for $c_c = 3.90$. For adults, the equation is written as

$$v_{c0} = c_a \sqrt{s_p} \, , \text{m/s}, \tag{9.4}$$

where $c_a = 1.95$ gives a minimum value or lower bound and $c_a = 3.77$ gives the maximum or upper bound.

9.5 Analysis Model

Figure 9.2 shows a sequence of images corresponding to vehicle–pedestrian collision events and indicates various variables that enter into the model. Initial

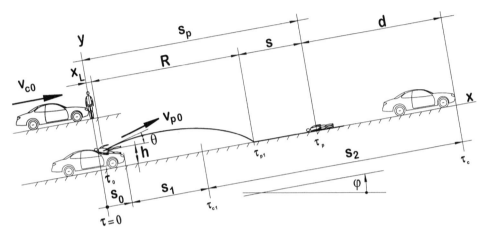

Figure 9.2
Diagram showing coordinates and variables associated with a vehicle–pedestrian collision model.

contact is at time $\tau = 0$ with a velocity of the vehicle of v_{c0}. The vehicle and pedestrian move forward at different speeds until time $\tau = \tau_0$, when a secondary impact occurs. Between $\tau = 0$ and $\tau = \tau_0$ the center of gravity of the pedestrian has moved forward a distance x_L; at $\tau = \tau_0$ it is at a height, h, above the ground. For a forward projection collision, x_L is zero and there is no secondary impact. As a result of the impact at height h, the pedestrian instantaneously rebounds and is launched in an airborne trajectory with a velocity of v_{p0} and at an angle θ. The trajectory has a range (distance parallel to the ground) of R and reaches the ground at time τ_{p1}. At that time the pedestrian impacts the ground with a velocity determined by the trajectory. From the point of ground impact to the point of rest, a distance of s, the pedestrian is assumed to be uniformly decelerated with a frictional drag coefficient, f_p. The motion over the distance s typically consists of rolling, sliding, and/or tumbling. The total distance from initial impact to rest is the pedestrian throw distance, s_p. It is assumed that from the time of the secondary impact, τ_0, to the time of rest, τ_p, the pedestrian motion is independent of the vehicle. To provide a degree of generality for reconstructions, the vehicle motion is given an arbitrary travel distance, s_1, from $\tau = 0$ to $\tau = \tau_{c1}$, over which the velocity remains constant. Following this, the vehicle decelerates to rest over a distance, s_2, with an acceleration of a_2. With this information, equations can be derived to develop the analysis model. See Table 9.1 for a list of variable notations and definitions.

a_2	Deceleration of vehicle over distance s_2
d	Distance between rest positions of vehicle and pedestrian
f_p	Drag resistance coefficient of pedestrian over distance s
g	Acceleration of gravity
h	Height of pedestrian center of gravity at launch, τ_0
m_c	Mass of vehicle, weight /g
m_p	Mass of pedestrian, weight /g
R	Range of pedestrian throw, launch to ground impact
s	Pedestrian ground contact distance, impact to rest
s_0	Distance of travel of vehicle with pedestrian contact
s_1	Distance of travel of vehicle at uniform speed
s_2	Distance of travel of vehicle with uniform deceleration, a_2
s_p	Pedestrian throw distance; total distance, initial contact to rest
τ_c	Vehicle travel time, initial contact to rest
τ_{c1}	Time of travel of vehicle at steady speed
τ_p	Total time of travel of pedestrian, initial contact to rest
τ_{p1}	Time from impact to pedestrian initial contact with ground
v'_{c0}	Velocity of vehicle after impact with pedestrian
v_{c0}	Initial speed of vehicle
v_{p0}	Initial speed of pedestrian
x_L	x-distance of pedestrian from initial contact to launch
α	Ratio of pedestrian speed to vehicle speed at time of launch
θ	Angle of launch of pedestrian relative to x axis
μ	Impulse ratio for pedestrian–ground impact
φ	Road grade angle

9.5.1 Pedestrian Motion

Based on the above and on Fig. 9.2, the throw distance is

$$s_p = x_L + R + s. \tag{9.5}$$

The mass of the pedestrian, m_p, is negligible in comparison to the mass of the vehicle, m_c. There are, however, some cases in which the momentum loss is important (such as an impact with a large animal), so allowance is made for a momentum loss of the vehicle due to the collision with the pedestrian. This gives

$$v'_{c0} = \frac{m_c}{m_c + m_p} v_{c0}. \tag{9.6}$$

Again for generality, a factor α is used to relate the pedestrian throw velocity to the vehicle velocity such that

$$v_{p0} = \alpha v'_{c0}. \tag{9.7}$$

It is assumed that air drag is negligible as the pedestrian undergoes the trajectory through the air. Under such a condition, the trajectory is parabolic with zero horizontal acceleration and uniform vertical acceleration due to gravity. This leads to the following equations for the range, R, and trajectory time, τ_R:

$$R = v_{p0} \cos \theta \, \tau_R - \frac{1}{2} g \sin \varphi \, \tau_R^2, \tag{9.8}$$

$$\tau_R = \frac{v_{p0} \sin \theta}{g \cos \varphi} = \frac{\sqrt{v_{p0}^2 \sin^2 \theta + 2gh \cos \varphi}}{g \cos \varphi}. \tag{9.9}$$

The trajectory velocity components at the instant before ground impact are

$$v_{pRx} = v_{p0} \cos \theta - g\tau_R \sin \varphi, \tag{9.10}$$

$$v_{pRy} = v_{p0} \sin \theta - g\tau_R \cos \varphi. \tag{9.11}$$

The normal component of the impact of the pedestrian with the ground is assumed to be perfectly inelastic. That is, there is a single impact with the ground with no vertical bounce or rebound. According to the planar impact theory developed in Chapter 6, this defines a vertical impulse, $P_n = -m_p v_{pRy}$. A corresponding tangential impulse, $P_t = \mu P_n$, develops. The pedestrian slides throughout the ground impact, so $\mu = -f_p$. This leads to a velocity at the beginning of the slide distance, s, of

$$v'_{pRx} = v_{pRx} + \mu v_{pRy}. \tag{9.12}$$

This allows determination of the distance, s, using Eqs. 3.6 and 3.9:

$$s = \frac{(v'_{pRx})^2}{2g(f_p \cos \varphi + \sin \varphi)}. \tag{9.13}$$

9.5.2 Vehicle Motion

Except for the momentum change of the vehicle due to impact with the pedestrian, the motion of the vehicle and pedestrian are assumed to be independent of each other for $\tau > \tau_0$. Any incidental contact during the early part of the trajectory is neglected. Over the distance, s_0, and time, τ_0, the speed of the vehicle is v_{c0}. Over the distance, s_1, and time interval, $\tau_{c1} - \tau_0$, the vehicle travels with speed v'_{c0}. Uniform acceleration of $-a_2$ occurs over the distance s_2. The difference, d, between the total travel distance of the vehicle and the pedestrian throw distance is

$$d = v_{c0}\tau_0 + v'_{c0}(\tau_{c1} - \tau_0) + \frac{a_2}{2}(\tau_c - \tau_{c1})^2 - s_p. \tag{9.14}$$

This distance can be important in a reconstruction because after a vehicle–pedestrian accident, the point of impact often is unknown, whereas the distance d is known. In such cases, it sometimes is possible to reconstruct the vehicle speed using d; this technique is illustrated in Example 9.2.

9.6 Values of Physical Variables

If all of the physical information is known or can be determined, the pedestrian throw distance and vehicle travel distance can be calculated from the above equations, called the analysis model. The model results can be compared to experimental data. This was done by Han and Brach[5] for more than 14 selected sets of data corresponding to wrap and forward projection collisions. Results showed excellent agreement with the analysis model and the data trends. The comparisons provide information about realistic range values of some of the physical variables. Information concerning some of the variables, such as α, θ, R, and s, could not be determined directly from experimental data because in many of the experiments these variables were not measured. Some information was inferred from the comparison process. Information about the pedestrian drag factor, f_p, has been determined from measurements and reports of others and is covered below.

By definition, the value for the launch angle for forward projection collisions must be $\theta = 0$ because the pedestrian is projected directly forward. This allows fitting of the analysis model equations and determination of values of the constant α. As defined in Eq. 9.7, α corresponds to a coefficient of restitution. If the pedestrian were to be caught or snagged on some part of the vehicle, there would be no rebound and $\alpha = 0$. Although of academic interest, there would be no trajectory, so this case has little practical application to reconstructions. On the other hand, a value of $\alpha > 1$ has the implication that the impact between the pedestrian and vehicle has an elastic component; that is, the pedestrian rebounds and is projected forward at a speed higher than the vehicle. Values of α as high as 1.2 and 1.3 were found by Han and Brach. They caution, however, that values this high need to be substantiated by additional tests, possibly in which α is measured directly. Generally, values of $\alpha = 1$ are expected for wrap collisions. For forward projection collisions, Wood and Walsh[13] also noted values of α greater than 1, though smaller than Brach and Han's values. Wood and Walsh also noted a speed dependence.

Existing pedestrian collision experiments appear never to have directly measured the launch angle, θ. From comparison to adult-reconstructed and adult-dummy wrap experimental collisions, typical values of θ from about 4° to 13° were found by Han and Brach. Some evidence of higher values, up to $\theta = 35°$, were found. Although physically possible, these occurred in only one or two groups of experiments and are believed not to represent common conditions. A range of $0 \leq \theta \leq 15°$ should be considered for reconstruction of typical wrap collisions.

9.6.1   Pedestrian–Ground Drag Coefficient

One of the most important variables in determination of throw distance is the pedestrian–ground frictional drag coefficient, f_p. Han and Brach[5] and Wood and Simms[14] analyzed the data from a group of measurements by Hill.[15] Hill's experiments were conducted using dummies dressed in various types of clothing that were dropped from a moving vehicle onto an asphalt type pavement (described as an old airfield tarmac). Wood and Simms determined average values of 0.70 and 0.73 from Hill's data. Han and Brach concluded that for application to the above vehicle–pedestrian analysis model, values in the range of $0.7 \leq f_p \leq 0.8$ are appropriate for dry pavements. Dummies in nylon clothing, however, produced a value near $f_p = 0.6$. This exception indicates that the clothing can affect f_p, but that there is not a high sensitivity to the clothing because none of the other four types of clothing made a significant difference. Roadway pavements such as rough concrete and ground conditions such as grass, ice, and so on are expected to require different values. Unfortunately, it appears that no comprehensive experiments have been conducted under such widely different conditions.

Based on experiments inclusive of Hill's, Wood and Simms[14] report a mean value of $f_p = 0.58$ with a standard deviation of $s_f = 0.1$, with upper and lower bounds at $\pm 3s_f$. This value may differ from that above because it was fit to a different analytical model.

A vehicle–pedestrian wrap collision occurs under the conditions listed in Table 9.2 representing a vehicle with a low frontal geometry traveling at 30 mph (48 km/h) and a pedestrian who has a secondary impact with the windshield. Calculate the throw distance, s_p. Determine the effect on the throw distance of varying the launch angle, θ, from $\theta = 0$ to $\theta = 10°$.

Example 9.1

Symbol	Value	Variable
a_2	0.90	Deceleration of vehicle over distance s_2
f_p	0.80	Drag resistance coefficient of pedestrian over distance s
h	4.00 ft	Height of pedestrian center of gravity at launch, τ_0
s_1	0.00 ft	Distance of travel of vehicle at uniform speed
v_{c0}	44.00 ft/s	Initial speed of vehicle
	30 mph	Initial speed of vehicle
x_L	2.00 ft	x-distance of pedestrian from initial contact to launch
α	1.00	Ratio of pedestrian speed to vehicle speed at time of launch
θ	5.00	Angle of launch of pedestrian relative to x axis
φ	0.00	Road grade angle
μ	0.80	Impulse ratio for pedestrian-ground impact
m_c	93.24 lb-s²/ft	Mass of vehicle, weight/g
m_p	5.44 lb-s²/ft	Mass of pedestrian, weight/g

Table 9.2
Vehicle–pedestrian wrap collision conditions.

Solution The pedestrian-throw equations can be set up for a solution in a spreadsheet. Such a solution, using the values from Table 9.2, produces the results shown in Fig. 9.3. There it is seen that the throw distance is 43.35 ft. Additional solutions for the launch angle values of $\theta = 0$ and $\theta = 10°$ show that the throw distance has corresponding values of $s_p = 38.78$ ft (11.82 m) to $s_p = 47.60$ ft (14.51 m), respectively. Note that in all cases the pedestrian travels farther than the vehicle and the vehicle comes to rest more quickly than the pedestrian, resulting in a negative value of d.   ◇

Consider the same collision as given by the data in Table 9.2 with the speed of the vehicle unknown. Consequently, both the throw distance and the vehicle speed are unknown. However, the distance traveled by the pedestrian was measured and found to exceed that of the vehicle by 20 ft (6.1 m). Determine the speed of the vehicle.

Example 9.2

Solution The spreadsheet can again be used here, but because one of the input values is unknown, the search feature of the spreadsheet can be exploited. Figure 9.4 shows that for a distance of $d = -20$ ft (6.10 m) stated as a goal, the initial speed of the vehicle is $v_{c0} = 66.62$ ft/s (20.31 m/s). This reconstruction indicates that point of impact is about 73 ft (22 m) back from the vehicle rest position.   ◇

Analysis of Pedestrian Throw Distance from Initial Conditions

NOTATION, COORDINATES, UNITS & VARIABLES:

x	-		coordinate parallel to ground
y	-		coordinate perpendicular to ground

INPUT INFORMATION (KNOWNS):

a_2	0.90		deceleration of vehicle over distance s_2
f_p	0.80		drag resistance coefficient of pedestrian over distance s
g	32.17	ft/s2	acceleration of gravity
h	4.00	ft	height of pedestrian center of gravity at launch, t_0
s_1	0.00	ft	distance of travel of vehicle at uniform speed
v_{c0}	44.00	ft/s	initial speed of vehicle
	30	mph	initial speed of vehicle
x_L	2.00	ft	x-distance of pedestrian from initial contact to launch
α	1.00		ratio of pedestrian speed to vehicle speed at time of launch
θ	5.00	deg	angle of launch of pedestrian relative to x axis
φ	0.00	deg	road grade angle
μ	0.80		impulse ratio for pedestrian-ground impact
m_c	93.24	lb-s2/ft	mass of vehicle, weight / g
m_p	5.44	lb-s2/ft	mass of pedestrian, weight / g

OUTPUT INFORMATION (UNKNOWNS):

v'_{c0}	41.57	ft/s	velocity of vehicle after impact with pedestrian
v_{p0}	41.57	ft/s	initial speed of pedestrian
R	25.84	ft	range of pedestrian throw, launch to ground impact
τ_{p1}	0.72	s	time from impact to pedestrian initial contact with ground
s	15.51	ft	pedestrian ground contact distance, impact to rest
s_p	43.35	ft	pedestrian throw distance; total distance, initial contact to rest
τ_p	1.82	s	total time of travel of pedestrian, initial contact to rest
τ_{c1}	0.10	s	time of travel of vehicle at steady speed
s_0	4.23	ft	distance of travel of vehicle with pedestrian contact
s_2	29.85	ft	distance of travel of vehicle with uniform deceleration, a_2
$s_0+s_1+s_2$	34.08	ft	total distance of travel of vehicle
τ_c	1.44	s	vehicle travel time, initial contact to rest
d	-9.27	ft	distance between rest positions of vehicle and pedestrian

Analysis of Pedestrian Throw Distance from Initial Conditions			
NOTATION, COORDINATES, UNITS & VARIABLES:			
x	-		coordinate parallel to ground
y	-		coordinate perpendicular to ground
INPUT INFORMATION (KNOWNS):			
a_2	0.90		deceleration of vehicle over distance s_2
f_p	0.80		drag resistance coefficient of pedestrian over distance s
g	32.17	ft/s2	acceleration of gravity
h	4.00	ft	height of pedestrian center of gravity at launch, t_0
s_1	0.00	ft	distance of travel of vehicle at uniform speed
v_{c0}	66.62	ft/s	initial speed of vehicle
	45	mph	initial speed of vehicle
x_L	2.00	ft	x-distance of pedestrian from initial contact to launch
α	1.00		ratio of pedestrian speed to vehicle speed at time of launch
θ	5.00	deg	angle of launch of pedestrian relative to x axis
φ	0.00	deg	road grade angle
μ	0.80		impulse ratio for pedestrian-ground impact
m_c	93.24	lb-s2/ft	mass of vehicle, weight / g
m_p	5.44	lb-s2/ft	mass of pedestrian, weight / g
OUTPUT INFORMATION (UNKNOWNS):			
v'_{c0}	62.94	ft/s	velocity of vehicle after impact with pedestrian
v_{p0}	62.94	ft/s	initial speed of pedestrian
R	43.74	ft	range of pedestrian throw, launch to ground impact
τ_{p1}	0.76	s	time from impact to pedestrian initial contact with ground
s	46.91	ft	pedestrian ground contact distance, impact to rest
s_p	92.64	ft	pedestrian throw distance; total distance, initial contact to rest
τ_p	2.67	s	total time of travel of pedestrian, initial contact to rest
τ_{c1}	0.06	s	time of travel of vehicle at steady speed
s_0	4.23	ft	distance of travel of vehicle with pedestrian contact
s_2	68.41	ft	distance of travel of vehicle with uniform deceleration, a_2
$s_0+s_1+s_2$	72.65	ft	total distance of travel of vehicle
τ_c	2.17	s	vehicle travel time, initial contact to rest
d	-20.00	ft	distance between rest positions of vehicle and pedestrian

Figure 9.4
Results of calculations of a wrap vehicle–pedestrian collision using pedestrian throw model with a spreadsheet search procedure.

9.7 Reconstruction Model

Although the analysis model above can be used for reconstruction purposes as seen in Example 9.2, sometimes it is better to calculate initial speed directly from throw distance. An important example of this is for estimation of the uncertainty of a reconstruction. If the area where the vehicle-pedestrian collision occurs is level, that is, grade angle $\varphi = 0$, then the pedestrian throw equations can be inverted, solving for v_{p0} in terms of s_p. This gives

$$v_{c0} = A \sqrt{s_p - B},$$ (9.15)

where

$$A = A_p \frac{m_c + m_p}{\alpha m_c},$$ (9.16)

$$A_p = \sqrt{\frac{2f_p g}{\sqrt{f_p^2 \sin^2 \theta + f_p \sin 2\theta + \cos^2 \theta}}}, \qquad (9.17)$$

and

$$B = x_L + f_p h. \qquad (9.18)$$

Example 9.3   Consider again the collision for which conditions are given in Table 9.2, except the throw distance is known from physical evidence to be 43.35 ft. The initial speed of the car is unknown and is to be reconstructed. In addition, suppose that in order to provide an estimate of the uncertainty of the reconstruction and to examine its sensitivity to different input values, the launch angle and pedestrian frictional drag coefficient are given uniform statistical distributions as

$$\theta = u(0, 10),$$

$$f_p = u(0.7, 0.8), \qquad (9.19)$$

where the notation is that $u(\min, \max)$ represents a uniform statistical distribution with min and max variable values. Estimate the reconstruction uncertainty as represented by the distribution of the initial speed obtained using Eq. 9.19.

Solution   Equation 9.15 is nonlinear. According to Eq. 1.20, the mean vehicle speed is approximately the value from Eq. 9.15 evaluated at the mean values of f_p and θ. These are $f_p = 0.75$ and $\theta = 5°$ and give $A = 6.93$, $B = 5.00$, and an initial vehicle speed of $v_{c0} = 42.9$ ft/s (13.08 m/s). The distributions given by Eq. 9.19 both are uniform, so the upper and lower limits of the vehicle speed can be obtained by solving Eq. 9.15 for all combinations of the minimum and

Figure 9.5
Statistical distribution of the vehicle speed from a Monte Carlo analysis of the reconstruction model equations.

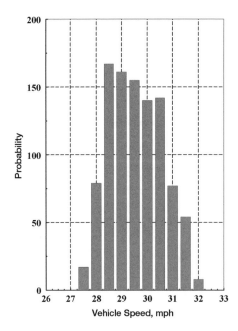

maximum values of the distributions. These solutions provide the range of initial vehicle speeds of $39.86 \leq v_{c0} \leq 46.90$ ft/s ($12.15 \leq v_{c0} \leq 14.3$ m/s) for the conditions given.

Although the vehicle speed has been bounded and the mean or average value determined according to the material in Chapter 1, the distribution is unknown. Other methods must be used. To determine the distribution, the Monte Carlo method is used. These calculations were performed using commercial software[16] and are not presented here. The distribution of the initial vehicle speed is shown in Fig. 9.5. Although the input distributions are uniform, the distribution of the vehicle speed is not. In fact, it is not too far from a normal distribution. This is not unusual, and the reader is encouraged to consult a statistics reference to explore this further.   ○

Wood's hybrid model as well as Han and Brach's analysis and reconstruction models have been presented in this chapter. The analysis and reconstruction models include the most important parameters and physical variables that play a role in planar vehicle–pedestrian collisions. In specific reconstructions, reasonably accurate values of these variables must be used. Variations of the variables should be used to estimate sensitivity and uncertainty of reconstructions.

Photogrammetry

10.1   Introduction

Photogrammetry is the process of obtaining quantitative dimensional information about physical objects through recording, interpreting, and measuring photographic images.[1] It has been used extensively with aerial photographs for the purposes of mapping ground terrain. Books have been written on this subject, including works by Hallert,[2] Moffitt and Mikhail,[3] and Slama.[1] These books describe the mathematical foundation of this topic and present many applications of the theory. In general, there are two types of photogrammetry: aerial photogrammetry, which involves two cameras with parallel view lines at a fixed, known distance apart, and close-range photogrammetry, which involves two or more camera positions with large differences in view angles and variable separation distance with the object being measured.

Close-range photogrammetry is the specific area of photogrammetry that is applicable in the field of automotive accident reconstruction. The title "close range photogrammetry" is appropriate in the application of these techniques to automotive accident investigation and reconstruction due to the fact that the camera-to-subject distance is short as compared to aerial photogrammetry. Moreover, the specific needs of accident reconstructionists have led to the use of two variations of the classical application of photogrammetry.

Some of the details and technical background of these variations are presented in various references. Baker and Fricke[4] consider photogrammetry for use in accident reconstruction and approach the topic as the use of photographs for constructing diagrams (scaled charts depicting local attributes and physical characteristics) of accident scenes and sites. Husher et al.[5] narrow the presentation to the uses of photogrammetry in accident reconstruction, discussing two techniques used to obtain accurate quantitative information from a single photograph. Another technique beginning to find more use employs multiple photographs of a single subject for acquiring dimensional information.

The first of the two single-photograph methods, reverse projection or camera reverse projection, is empirical, and it is quite useful for extracting information about the location of information from a single photograph. The second method, sometimes referred to as numerical rectification, four-point transformation, or planar photogrammetry,[6] is based on a mathematical transformation between the film plane and a physical geometric plane visible in the photograph. This transformation enables quantitative information to be determined from a single photograph. This method will be referred to as planar photogrammetry in this book. The third method presented here involves a more general application of the mathematical equations of photogrammetry. This method permits the general determination of coordinates in three-dimensional space from a series of photographs of a single object. Although the complete mathematical detail involved in the derivation of the equations is left to other authors,[2,3] this chapter presents an overview of the equations and considers the application of the method to measure vehicle crush.

10.2   Reverse Projection Photogrammetry

The reverse projection photogrammetric method is useful for extracting information about the location or size of an object that is no longer visible at the accident site but is contained on a single scene photograph. The photograph is usually taken with a camera whose properties are unknown to the analyst, and the information shown in the photograph—such as tire marks on a roadway that have worn away through time, a snow pile that has since melted, or markings or characteristics that have been lost due to road improvements or modifications—has often changed or been removed from the accident site. Frequently, this information pertains to the position of a vehicle, vehicle component, or mark made by a vehicle.

10.2.1   Overview and Requirements of the Reverse Projection Process

The reverse projection process is empirical in nature, and the application of the process is straightforward. In classical photogrammetry, with a photograph that contains three or more objects with known three-dimensional coordinates, known principal distance of the camera (focal length), and known principal point of the image (essentially the geometric center of the image), the location of the lens and the orientation of the camera can be determined relative to a coordinate system. This process is known as a spatial resection or simply as a resection. If the principal distance and principal point location are not known, five or more points with known spatial coordinates are required to perform the resection analytically. Reverse projection photogrammetry is the analog process of performing this resection.

Once the analog resection is completed, the method uses the camera to project information onto the site. The typical role of the camera—gathering light rays from the environment and focusing them onto the film plane—is reversed in this process: the image and camera are used to project information visually into the environment. This reversal in the role of the camera from capturing information to projecting information has prompted this method to become known as reverse projection. It has also been referred to as camera reverse projection.

Various techniques have been presented in the literature,[4] but the procedure described here employs digital technology for image handling and is based loosely on the technique presented previously in the literature.[7] Previous versions of this photogrammetric method used techniques considered more analog in nature.[4] Both techniques work adequately, but the newer, computer-based image-handling methods make the process much simpler to implement. The process described herein outlines the steps required for analysis of one photograph, but this process can be performed sequentially or simultaneously with more than one photograph of the same scene, yielding similar, related, or complementary information. This multi-image analysis is a means for refinement of the location or dimension of the attribute or characteristic of interest or to obtain additional information about the object or characteristic of interest. Example 10.2 shows the application of the reverse projection process using two photographs simultaneously.

The recognition of a good photograph depicting the desired (transient) information is the prerequisite for the application of the reverse projection project. The next step is to obtain a first-generation, full-frame print of the photograph of interest, if possible. A full-frame, high resolution, digital scan of the negative for the print(s) of interest is a superior alternative to obtaining a full-frame photograph. A full-frame photograph is one in which the entire exposed portion of the negative is visible. The best way to ensure that the full frame is available is to request that the shop printing the photograph or scanning the negative include the sprocket holes on the top and bottom and a portion of the unexposed negative on the sides of the image in the printing or scanning process. Typical prints from the local pharmacy, in addition to not including the sprocket holes, routinely crop the negative when printing. Negatives of accident photographs are not always obtainable, but some law enforcement officials preserve their negatives. If a digital camera was used to capture the image, the original, unmodified version of the image data should be requested. An unmodified version of the original electronic data file for a digital photograph is by definition full-frame for a digital camera.

Full-frame photographs are important for project accuracy in that the specific orientation of the camera is discernible because the "frame" of the full-frame photograph is determined by the limits of the light path dictated by the camera body and lens combination. This frame will assist in the positioning of the image in the camera in an attempt to place the principal point of the image at the location of the principal ray in the camera used in the method. If the principal distance (focal length) of the camera is not known, a zoom lens can be used to enable the determination of this parameter.

In addition to the characteristic or object of interest, a photograph useful for reverse projection must also include several immovable landmarks (street signs, road markings, light/utility poles, roadway cracks, lines, sewer grates, manhole covers, fence lines, etc.). These landmarks must still be present at the accident site. They will be used to complete the analog resection process. The importance of these landmarks should not be underestimated. They will be used in the positioning of the camera at the site to obtain a match between the information captured in the photograph and its counterpart at the site. Once the resection is completed, the camera is positioned in approximately the same location as the camera used to capture the original image at the time the photograph was taken. Moreover, a full-frame photograph includes the entire exposed portion of the negative and may contain additional landmarks not visible in a cropped print.

The absence of a full-frame photograph does not preclude the use of reverse projection photogrammetric analysis. Use of a cropped photograph may reduce the accuracy of the determination of the position of the camera at the scene at the time the original image was captured. For some analyses, however, this may not be significant. Use of a conventional cropped photograph for reverse projection photogrammetry will preserve the relative location of the characteristics and attributes depicted in an image and can therefore produce useful results. Convergence of the image with the actual site may be more difficult with an image that is less than full-frame.

If possible, the make and model of the camera and lens used to take the photographs at the accident scene should be determined. The focal length of the lens on the camera at the time the photograph was taken is of particular importance. Knowledge of the camera body permits the assessment of the percentage of the full image that the camera is capable of showing. While using the same model camera in the analysis as the one used to create the image may enhance credibility if the results are to be used in court, it is not required to successfully conduct a reverse projection photogrammetric reconstruction. As will be shown later, the attributes of certain single-lens reflex cameras simplify the process significantly.

10.2.2 Reverse Projection Procedure

The reverse projection process begins by digitally scanning the image in the (full-frame) photograph at a high resolution. Scanning the negative rather than the photograph produces better results but is not essential. Once the scanned image of the photograph has been obtained, the entire image of the photograph is imported into a computer-aided design (CAD) package. It is convenient, for reasons to be described later, to have the lower left corner of the photograph located at the origin of the coordinate system of the CAD drawing. The main features of the photograph are then outlined onto a separate layer of the drawing using the drawing capabilities of the CAD package. The outlines must include the information of interest that no longer exists at the site and the landmarks expected to be at the site when the camera positioning is done. In addition to all the major features, the four corners of the frame should be carefully marked. The layer with the outlines is printed onto transparent material at a size prescribed by the physical requirements of the camera to be used for the reverse projection. The details of each step are included in Example 10.1.

An analog approach to create the transparency can also be used. In this approach, a transparent film is placed over the print and affixed in place such that there is no movement between the transparency and the print. The main features of the photograph are then traced by hand with a thin indelible marker in a manner similar to the outlining that is done with the CAD program described above. The transparency is then placed on a flatbed scanner and scanned back into the computer. This image can be printed onto transparent film at the size appropriate for insertion into the camera to be used for the positioning exercise. Regardless of whether the analog or digital method is used to capture the necessary information from the photograph, a reduced-size transparency displaying the outlines of that information is created.

The transparency is then fit into the camera in such a manner that the image is centered about the visible portion of the viewfinder. This locates the principal point of the transparency such that the principal ray of the lens travels through it. The principal ray is the light ray not refracted by the lens. For practical purposes, the principal ray of the lens can be considered the ray that passes through the geometric center of the lens. Some careful trimming of the transparency may be necessary to complete this step in the process. Alignment braces located equidistant from the four corners and a border outline of the exposed region of the photograph, both shown in Fig. 10.5, are particularly useful for this purpose. These alignment braces give a visual assessment of the position of the image in the viewfinder. For obvious reasons, it is important that the transparency not move while positioned in the camera. Typically, the means of securing the focusing screen to the camera will hold the transparency in place. Careful evaluation of the transparency and the camera should be made prior to taking the camera with the transparency into the field where it will be subjected to forces due to handling.

The size of the image on the transparency and the trimming requirements will depend on the specific camera being used for the analysis. Some 35-mm single-lens reflex cameras, such as the Canon F-1 and the Nikon F-3, permit the complete and convenient removal of the focusing screen by removal of the prism or eyepiece (see Fig. 10.1). This capability greatly simplifies the process of installation and removal of the transparency. This may be of particular importance if the intentions of the photogrammetrist are to conduct more than one reverse projection analysis during a single inspection. (More than one camera could be outfitted with an overlay in the office and multiple cameras from different viewpoints could be used in the field. However, the typical situation would be a single camera and multiple transparencies, necessitating a transfer of the overlay in the field.) Removal and installation of an overlay in the field can be handled much more quickly with a camera equipped with a removable eyepiece and focusing screen.

After the overlay is correctly installed in the camera, the image on the

Figure 10.1
Removal of the focusing
screen of the Canon F-1.

overlay is continuously visible in the eyepiece of the camera. Because the overlay is positioned above the mirror, it will not appear in any photographs taken with the camera. A photograph taken with the camera in the final adjusted position can be useful for comparison with the original photo. Similarly, the authors have heard of but have not yet employed the use of a video camera "looking" through the viewfinder of the camera to capture the view of the camera with the overlay in place. Interested readers can experiment with this technique.

As mentioned previously, the traced image of the original photograph should be printed at a reduced size. This percent reduction is dictated by the characteristics of the viewing area versus the exposure area for the camera from which the image is to be viewed. For example, as with most 35-mm film-format cameras, the size of the exposed portion of a 35-mm negative is approximately 36 mm × 24 mm. The viewfinder has reduced coverage of the light that is passed to the negative when the shutter is released. For example, for the Nikon N90 35-mm camera, this reduction is 8%, or the image visible in the viewfinder is 92% of the exposed area of the negative when the photograph is taken. Therefore, in recreating the 36 mm × 24 mm image, the image visible in the viewfinder of the N90 does not necessarily represent what the original photographer saw in the viewfinder of the camera at the time the photo was taken, unless of course the original photograph was also taken with an N90. Because the task in reverse projection is to use the image as viewed through the viewfinder of the camera to recreate the position of the camera at the time the photograph was taken and thereby determine the position of the missing characteristics, this reduction in the visible portion of the image should be taken into account in setting up the reverse projection project.

To modify the image appropriately in the case of the use of the N90 for the reverse projection camera, the reduction in area is 8%. To account for this reduction, the dimensions of the smaller visible image must be computed. Figure 10.2 shows the size of the original image and the visible area depicted by the inside box. To determine the size of the viewable area, shown by the cross-hatched inside box, assume that the long side of the actual negative is length B

and its reduced counterpart is b, and the shorter side of the actual negative is length A and its reduced counterpart is a. Assuming that the areas have the same aspect ratio, that is, $A/B = a/b$, and that the camera specifications in this

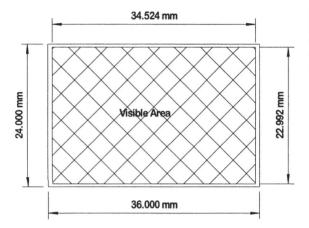

example are 8% reduction in visible area, $0.92AB = ab$, then the following calculations give the differences in the dimensions of the two regions:

$$0.92AB = ab,$$

$$0.92AB = \frac{A}{B}b^2,$$

$$0.92B^2 = b^2,$$

$$b = 0.959B. \tag{10.1}$$

Using this to determine the spacing between the sides, and maintaining the position of the center of the two areas, we get the following:

$$\frac{B-b}{2} = \frac{B - 0.959B}{2},$$

$$\frac{B-b}{2} = 0.021B,$$

$$\frac{B-b}{2} = 0.738 \text{ mm.} \tag{10.2}$$

Similarly,

$$\frac{A-a}{2} = 0.504 \text{ mm.} \tag{10.3}$$

Figure 10.2 shows the relationship between the two areas. The area visible through the viewfinder is indicated with the hatch.

After these calculations are completed, the size of the visible region of the camera to be used in the analysis can be included on the tracing prior to printing the overlay. This permits the accurate location of the reduced transparency to be set visually through the viewfinder of the camera. This is needed because objects near the perimeter of the exposed image will not be visible when the small transparency is located in the view of the camera. In fact, it has proven useful to put locating indicators at an even further reduced location for better locating of the image in the viewfinder. This allows for easier assessment of the symmetric positioning of the insert in the camera. As mentioned above, the location of these indicators on the image inside the CAD program is simpler to address numerically if the lower left corner of the image is located at a convenient coordinate such as the origin.

After the transparency has been placed into the camera, the next step in the process is establishing the location and orientation of the camera at the site. This is done by positioning the camera and adjusting its orientation to match the conditions at the time the original image was taken. A trial and error method is used, positioning the camera equipped with the overlay at the approximate location of where the photographer was standing when the original photograph was taken. Looking through the eyepiece, adjustments can be made to the various degrees of freedom until a match is obtained between the feature outlines on the overlay and the corresponding image visible through the camera lens. A list of the degrees of freedom of movement of the camera available to the analyst in this process is presented in Table 10.1.

Table 10.1
The seven degrees of freedom for the reverse projection method.

Translation parallel to the ground plane (two degrees of freedom)
Translation perpendicular to the ground plane (may not be needed if the height of the photographer is known with reasonable accuracy and the photographer was standing erect when the image was captured)
Rotation about the normal to the film plane
Rotation about one axis in the film plane
Rotation about the other axis in the film plane
Zoom lens should be used if the focal length of the original camera is not known

Systematic techniques can be used to change the camera position to obtain the location and orientation of the camera at the time the original photograph was taken. After an initial estimate has been made of the location of the camera, it is beneficial to try to locate objects in the background of the image that have been included on the transparency, such as distant utility poles, signs, tree lines, the horizon, and so forth. Once the background objects have been appropriately located, landmarks in the foreground that have been marked can be matched to the insert. A final fit can then be made using small adjustments of the location and orientation of the camera. Several additional techniques can simplify this adjustment process:

- Accurate information about the height of the photographer and his/her position at the time the image was captured eliminates one of the degrees of freedom in the camera positioning.

- Information about the focal length of the camera and lens that was used to capture the original image eliminates another degree of freedom. If the focal length of the original camera cannot be determined, a zoom lens can be used during the trial and error locating process to vary that degree of freedom, but this adds complexity to the operation.
- Use of a tripod is indispensable in this process. Locating and adjusting the camera is time-consuming and holding the camera steady and at a fixed location will become increasingly difficult. An adjustable pistol grip attachment on the head of the tripod, available at most full-service camera stores, simplifies the small adjustments that are needed for a good match between the landmarks at the site and the outlines on the overlay.

Once the process of adjusting the camera position and orientation to match the overlay with the site landmarks has been completed, the process of locating the features of interest in such a way that they can be measured by conventional means can be done. The marks can be preserved using means such as spray paint, staking, cones, and so forth.

10.2.3   Summary of the Reverse Projection Photogrammetry Process

1. Obtain a photograph (negative, print, or digital file) in which the characteristic of interest appears.
2. Using a CAD program, trace the outline of the landmarks and the required information that appear in the photograph.
3. Prepare an image of the traced information on a transparency and fit it into a camera such that the image is centered in the viewfinder.
4. At the site, visually compare the outlines in the viewfinder with the landmarks, making adjustments to the camera location and orientation until a match between the two is obtained.
5. Use the information visible in the camera viewfinder to place marks at the locations required by the analysis.

Example 10.1

This application of the reverse projection method determines the height and width of a pile of snow located on a median adjacent to a turn lane on a highway. The dimensions of the pile were needed to determine if the snow pile affected the ability of drivers in vehicles using the turn lane to assess oncoming traffic. In this reconstruction, good photographs were available from the investigating officer. However, the photographs were taken at night, making the process slightly more difficult. The main difficulty resulting from the darkness was the lack of sufficient visible fixed landmarks to set the position of the camera, particularly landmarks in the distance. Ultimately, enough signs, streetlights, and other landmarks were available to make the project tractable. In this case, the local law enforcement officials allowed high-resolution full-frame color scans of the negatives to be made. Two photographs were selected for the

Figure 10.3
Scanned image as obtained from local law enforcement officials.

Figure 10.4
Image with the major features traced onto a layer separate from the photograph. Both layers are shown.

Figure 10.5
Transparency created from the photograph shown in Fig. 10.3.

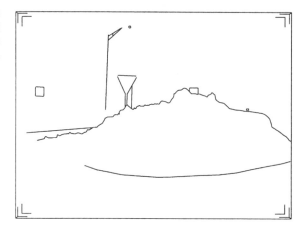

purposes of reverse projection photogrammetry. Digital scans were imported into a CAD program, and outlines of the landmarks were traced onto a separate layer of the drawing. Figures 10.3 and 10.4 show the original full-frame image as scanned and the image with the feature outlines displayed, respectively, for one of the photographs chosen for analysis. The original images were obtained in color but are shown here in black and white with no loss in generality.

Note that on the image with the outlines (Fig. 10.4), the exposed region of the negative has been blocked in along with two sets of corner braces. These braces will appear at the corners of the visible region of the viewfinder. The outer corner braces correspond to the reduction in visible area compared to the exposed area. The inside corner braces correspond to an arbitrary but consistent area-reduction location inward from the corners but located completely in the visible area of the viewfinder. This is done for purposes of visually locating the overlay symmetrically within the viewfinder. If the insert is located properly, these braces will appear equidistant from the corners of the limits of the viewfinder. Figure 10.5 depicts the tracing that appears on the overlay separate from the photograph.

The image shown in Fig. 10.5 was printed onto transparent material at a size determined by the characteristics of a Canon F-1. The transparency was trimmed and placed into the camera under the focusing screen. The camera was taken to the accident site for the resection. Using the landmark information on the transparency, the camera was positioned at approximately the same location and orientation as at the time the original image was captured. The information on the transparency associated with the pile of snow was then used by the analyst in directing a colleague to mark points on the roadway where the snow pile ended. The profile of the snow pile, including its height, was needed to assess its effect on the visibility of drivers approaching the intersection. The analysis determined that the photographer was standing in the turn lane used by traffic approaching the snow pile.

The height of the snow pile along a section line was determined by placing a telescoping measuring rod at intervals along the section line and noting the height of the intersection of the line on the transparency with the rod. The locations of the measuring rod along the section line were noted and surveyed along with the rest of the accident site using a theodolite. The heights of the snow pile at the various locations were incorporated into a CAD program and used to create the profile of the pile of snow that would have been seen by a driver approaching the intersection.   ⬡

10.2.4   Further Considerations

Many reverse projection projects present practical difficulties in following the theory directly. In the majority of projects, the negative of the photograph is not available and the photograph itself must be digitally scanned. The photograph is unlikely to be full-frame. Although these factors require the analyst to deviate from the ideal situation, acceptable results can be obtained from reverse projection projects under these circumstances. Useful information has been obtained using reverse projection photogrammetry under extreme circumstances. For example, the careful use of the reverse projection method with an image captured from a videotape has yielded useful data.

The use of the method under less-than-ideal circumstances leads to the question of the accuracy of the method. The empirical nature of this method makes evaluation of accuracy difficult, and only one reference was found in the literature that addresses the accuracy of the method.[7]

In addition to discussing accuracy of reverse projection photogrammetry, Wooley[7] presents a variation of the method that uses two cameras performing reverse projection simultaneously. In that application, both cameras use transparencies created from photographs of the same object taken from different positions to determine the crush profile of a vehicle. The second reverse projection example uses this same technique to determine the location of a tire mark on a roadway that has been resurfaced.

In a typical application of the reverse projection method, the analyst uses the camera as a means to project the information contained on the transparency out into the object space. Typically, an assistant is guided to mark a location in object space at the intersection of a light ray with some feature in the object space. This is usually done by locating the intersection of the light ray with a plane, often the surface of a roadway. In circumstances in which the object of interest does not lie on a plane or the plane is inaccessible, a plane in the object environment or some other means must be defined by the analyst to determine the location of interest on the ray projected from the camera. In the previous example with the upper profile of the snow pile, a plane was defined along a section line through the pile prior to conducting the analysis. The intersection of the projected ray with the plane was used to delineate the outline of the snow pile. When the definition of a plane in the object space by the analyst is not possible or when the location of the plane is physically inaccessible, two cameras can be used, and the intersection of the two light rays from the two cameras through the same point can be used to locate the point of interest on the rays. An application of this technique is presented in the following example.

Example 10.2 In this application, two police photographs were available in which several tire marks of interest appeared. Between the time of the accident and the time of the inspection, the road at the accident site had been stripped and resurfaced, thereby eliminating any possibility of examining the evidence. Moreover, the new road surface was higher than the old surface, making the plane on which the mark appeared in the scene photographs completely inaccessible. Under these circumstances, two cameras were required to conduct the reverse projection analysis. Figures 10.6 and 10.7 show the view of the site with the new roadway surface through the lens of the cameras used in the analysis at their respectively reconstructed camera locations. The markings from the transparency and their corresponding accident site counterparts are visible in the photographs.

Because the location of the intersection of the two light rays from the two cameras was below the surface of the new roadway, no physical means was available at the site to locate the point in three space. A diagram of this situation is shown in Fig. 10.8. Therefore, a theodolite was used to document the location and orientation of each camera and the location of the intersection point

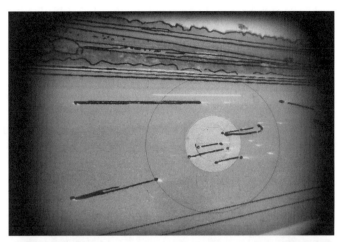

Figure 10.6
Photograph of site through the eyepiece of one camera.

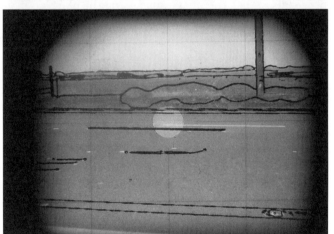

Figure 10.7
Photograph of site through the eyepiece of a second camera.

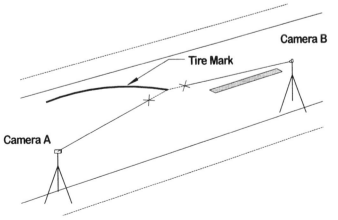

Figure 10.8
Diagram showing the use of two cameras, each implementing reverse projection for the same tire mark which is located below the new road surface. The dashed line indicates the portion of the ray below the surface of the new roadway.

of both light rays from each camera with the new road surface for a given feature. These latter two points are indicated in Fig. 10.8 by the cross-hairs. Using the location of the cameras and the intersection of their respective light rays with the new, higher road surface, two lines in three space were defined. These lines were subsequently extended in a CAD program to locate their intersection point. A series of points located using this technique were used to define the length of the tire mark.   ⬡

10.3 Planar Photogrammetry

There are times when it is appropriate to use a different tool to determine the location of a mark that has been captured on a photograph taken at an accident scene. When the mark lies on a surface that can be reasonably approximated by a geometric plane, usually the surface of a roadway, a one-to-one mathematical transformation between a coordinate system in the film plane and a planar coordinate system on the roadway can be established provided certain information about the road surface is available. A generalized development of the coordinate transformation between the planar coordinate system in the film plane (also called the image space) and the planar coordinate system on the roadway surface (also called the object space) can be found elsewhere.[2] The Appendix to this chapter presents the salient points of this derivation. The results of the derivation are two equations that relate points in the two coordinate systems:

$$x_m = \frac{c_1 + c_2 x_p + c_3 y_p}{c_4 x_p + c_5 y_p + 1},\qquad(10.4a)$$

$$y_m = \frac{c_6 + c_7 x_p + c_8 y_p}{c_4 x_p + c_5 x_p + 1}.\qquad(10.4b)$$

In Eqs. 10.4, the m subscript refers to the coordinate system corresponding to the roadway plane and has traditionally been referred to as the map coordinate system giving the m subscript. The p subscript refers to the coordinate system on the photograph, or the film plane. The c_i variables represent eight unique constants involved in the transformation. In these equations, eight constants appear and must be determined to yield a useful transformation between the two planar coordinate systems.

To determine the eight unknown constants, eight equations are required. Four points are needed in which the coordinate pairs in both film plane and roadway plane, the p coordinates and the m coordinates, respectively, are known. The eight resulting equations are linear in the constants c_1 through c_8, and any suitable means to solve linear equations can be used to determine c_1 through c_8. Once the eight coefficients are known, the same equations can then be used to determine the map coordinates of any other point visible in the photograph that lies on the roadway plane. Solution of linear equations can be treated in some spreadsheets, sometimes with the assistance of macro programming. This technique, used for the examples in this book, can be used to locate a single point on a roadway, or repetitive calculations can be used to create a piecewise linear approximation of characteristics or objects such as tire marks located on a roadway.

An assumption made in the development of this method is that both the captured image on film and the physical characteristics lie on a plane. In the case of the captured image, the film itself is contained securely in the "film plane" of the camera and inherently meets this requirement. The same is true of a digital camera that uses a CCD (charge coupled device) to capture the image. The CCD satisfies the assumption of being a plane. The assumption that the physical objects that appear in the image lie on a plane is usually just that, an assumption. In the case of accident investigation, the physical object is usually a roadway. Typically, roadways have a curvature, a crown, or both, and it may be difficult to assess the planar condition quantitatively. Any non-planarity of the physical object captured in the photograph introduces error in the results of the analysis. The first example presented in this section considers the magnitude of the error associated with a nonplanar condition and some of the factors that influence it.

A simple and practical way to obtain the coordinates from the photograph is to digitize the photo (or the negative if it is available) and import the image into a CAD program. A convenient point of the image should be designated as the origin of the film plane coordinate system. Using the lower left corner of the image as the origin gives all the points on the image positive coordinates. As with the technique described in the section on reverse projection, it may also be useful to draw lines, points, etc. on the photograph in the CAD program. The image in Fig. 10.9 was created this way. With the attributes marked on

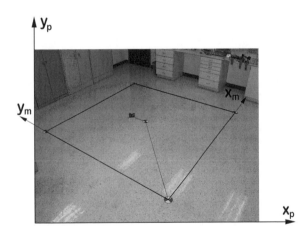

Figure 10.9
Photograph prepared for four-point transformation analysis.

the photo, the coordinate values associated with them can be obtained easily and directly from the CAD program.

The quality of the photograph can have a large influence on the accuracy of the results of this analysis. For this reason, it is important to obtain the best generation photograph possible at the start of the process. A high-resolution scan of the negative or use of a digital photograph can produce better results than a scan of a photograph from a flatbed scanner. Care should still be taken with digital photographs. The mere existence of a given digital file of a photograph does not necessarily preclude the existence of another digital file of higher resolution as images can be downsampled, that is, saved to a new file with a reduced number of pixels in the image.

Example 10.3   The image shown in Fig. 10.9 was acquired using a digital camera (3.1 megapixel), and the assumption is that the tile floor is a close approximation to a geometric plane. High-contrast markers placed on the floor were used to designate the four corners of a square that is 10 ft on a side. The corner of the square at the bottom of the photograph serves as the origin of the object-space coordinate system to be used in the analysis that follows. Additionally, the positions of the four corners are known in both the map and photograph coordinate systems and can be used to determine the eight coefficients. The coordinates of other points in the photograph that lie on the plane (whether within the square or outside it) can then be obtained from the transformation.

This example was staged to evaluate the accuracy of the planar photogrammetry process. It is not meant to be a demonstration of the technique as it applies to a real situation. An additional example will be presented that addresses a practical application of the method. Every reasonable attempt was made in this example to control the parameters involved. The center of the high-contrast corner markers was placed at the intersection lines of the tile floor; each tile is a square with each side having a length of one foot. The photograph was intentionally taken with a lens aperture yielding sufficient depth of field to ensure proper focus of both the foreground and background.

In the coordinate system on the floor plane, the corner closest to the camera is assigned as the origin (0,0) with the corner up and to the right in the photograph assigned (10,0). Figure 10.10 shows a drawing that depicts this

Figure 10.10
Coordinates assigned
to the floor plane
(plan view).

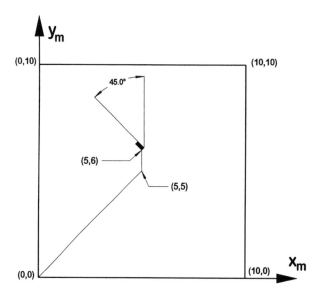

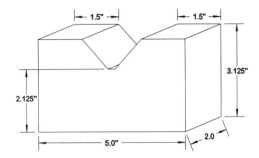

Figure 10.11
Detail of the V-block
used in the evaluation.

coordinate system in a plan view. A machined V-block with precise dimensions was also placed on the floor at a specific known location and will be used later to assess the error for an "out of plane" point. For reference, the dimensions of the V-block are given in Fig. 10.11. For example, in an actual setting, a non-planar condition can occur when a crown in a road is present.

Description	Computed (ft)		Actual (ft)	
	x	y	x	y
Center of the square	4.999	5.004	5.000	5.000
Corner of the V-block at (5,6) but 3.125 in. out of plane	5.341	6.313	5.000	6.000
Base of the V in the V-block, 2.125 in. above the floor plane	5.079	6.372	4.843	6.147

Table 10.2
Comparison of computed versus actual coordinate values.

The position of other points measured in the photograph coordinate system can be used for computation of their corresponding coordinates on the floor plane. Table 10.2 lists the points that were transformed and the corresponding actual coordinates. ⬡

Another source of error in the planar photogrammetry process comes from the accuracy of the coordinates associated with the four points used to determine the constants in the transformation. Using the photograph presented in Example 10.3 and shown in Fig. 10.9, and allowing for inaccuracies in the selection of the four base points on the photograph, the magnitude associated with base-point error can be investigated.

In this example, an error is introduced into the base point measurement by intentionally introducing a five-pixel error in the selection of the base point. Pixels were used to define the error, as opposed to photograph coordinate system units or absolute distances in the plane, as it is this resolution that will be the likely limitation in the process of selecting these points. The error of absolute distance per pixel is greater the further the point is from the camera that captured the image. In general, a higher resolution image can help mitigate this type of error.

The direction of the error from the actual point will have an effect on the magnitude of the error. Therefore the error was selected systematically as follows:

Example 10.4

- The errors of the points (10,0) and (10,10) were selected to be to the right in the image.
- The errors of the points (0,10) and (0,0) were selected to be to the left in the image.

The net effect of the errors is an enlarging and a slight skewing of the square. Using the dimensions associated with these new base point dimensions from the photograph, the analysis can be performed. A comparison can

Table 10.3
Comparison of computed and actual locations with the computed values determined from base-point locations with introduced error.

	Computed (ft)		Actual (ft)	
Description	x	y	x	y
Center of the square	4.995	5.023	5.000	5.000
Lower right corner of the V-block	4.985	6.025	5.000	6.000

be made between the center of the square (5,5) and the right lower corner of the V-block (5,6). Table 10.3 presents the results for comparison.   ◯

Note that in Examples 10.3 and 10.4, the plane used in the object space—the tile floor with the high-contrast markers—creates an almost ideal situation for the application of planar photogrammetry. Applications of this method in the field will certainly be done with photographs that do not have high-contrast markers at the base points, and the points of interest will not be as easily determined. Errors will increase with the less accurate information. The following example illustrates a practical application of planar photogrammetry.

Example 10.5   Having considered the development and accuracy of planar photogrammetry, a practical field situation is presented. A vehicle is traveling north along a two-lane rural road and makes a sudden move to the left across the oncoming lane. Figure 10.12 shows a plan view diagram of the accident site. Figure 10.13 shows

Figure 10.12
Plan view of the accident scene.

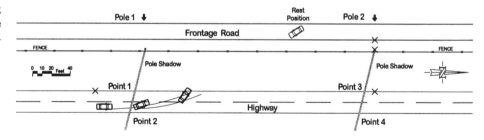

the photograph to be used with planar photogrammetry to determine the location of the tire marks. As a result of the sudden steer input to the left, the vehicle began to yaw in a counterclockwise direction. It crossed the southbound lane and left the roadway at an angle of about 50° counterclockwise from north. It came to rest on a parallel frontage road. During the yaw maneuver, the right side tires left visible tire marks on the roadway. It is desired to determine the speed of the vehicle on the roadway. The critical speed formula (see Chapter 4) can be used to estimate the speed of the vehicle if the radius of the tire marks can be determined. Planar photogrammetry is used to reconstruct the tire marks.

Although the details of the application have not yet been described, the tire marks have already been added to Fig. 10.12 for simplicity. The tire marks were not measured by the police and were no longer visible during a site inspection. The police took photographs of the accident scene and one of the photos, shown in Fig. 10.13, was chosen for analysis. The assumption that all of the points of interest lie in a plane is reasonable as the road is essentially flat over the region of interest. This can readily be assessed visually from the scene photograph.

Figure 10.13
Police photograph (looking north) showing the tire marks and the utility pole shadows.

In this instance, the known position of four physical landmarks required for implementation of the method and associated with the physical roadway could not be established in the scene photograph. An alternative was needed. The intersection of the utility pole shadows across the roadway with the east and west edges of the roadway presented a convenient solution to the dilemma. This is a somewhat unconventional approach to solve the problem, but it illustrates the flexibility that can be offered by this photogrammetric analysis technique.

The information required to locate the intersection points between the poles and the east and west edges of the highway is the positions of the poles relative to the highway, which had not changed, and the angles of the shadows relative to the highway. The distance between the poles and from the poles to the roadway were measured at the site. The time of day, day of the year, and geoposition of the site[8] was used to determine the angle between the pole shadow and the highway. At the time of the accident this angle was 14°. The location of the four intersection points of the pole shadows with the highway and the measured road width were used for the four known points needed to determine the eight constants in the transformation.

The planar photogrammetry equations were used to establish the location of three points along the mark left by the leading front tire. The radius of curvature of the mark can be determined from these three points and the critical speed formula can be used to reconstruct the speed of the vehicle. In this case, it was determined that the vehicle was exceeding the speed limit posted for this section of road.

In practical applications of planar photogrammetry, it is not always possible to estimate the error in the analysis. However, one or more additional points with known coordinates in both the film plane and object plane coordinate systems can be used to assess the accuracy of the analysis. After the transformation has been determined, the film plane coordinates of the additional point are used to calculate the coordinates of the point in the object space. These calculated coordinates are then compared to the measured coordinates to assess the accuracy of the analysis.

In this example, an additional point on the photograph with known object plane coordinates was available for the evaluation of the accuracy of the analysis. A third utility pole located north of Poles 1 and 2 (not shown in Fig. 10.12) and its corresponding shadow can be seen in the photograph (Fig. 10.13). Close inspection of a first-generation photograph indicated that the shadow crosses the edge line on the east side of the road just south of the northernmost northbound vehicle shown in the photograph. This point permits the comparison of the value calculated using the transformation to the value determined via the CAD drawing and the known position of the sun.

The location of Pole 3 was also measured during the site inspection. With the location of Pole 3 and the angle of the sun known, the location of the intersection of the shadow of the pole with the east edge of the northbound lane was determined from the site diagram. It was found to be 453.7 ft north of the intersection of the shadow from Pole 1 along the west edge of the roadway. The corresponding location of the same intersection point calculated using planar photogrammetry was found to be 436.4 ft. Assuming the location of the point calculated from the site diagram based on the location of the pole and sun is the true value, calculation yields an error of $(453.7 - 436.4)/453.7 \times 100 = 3.8\%$. This low error indicates that reasonable accuracy for the radius of the tire mark was achieved in this analysis. $\bigcirc$

10.4 Three-Dimensional Photogrammetry

The photogrammetric techniques presented in the previous two sections are commonly used in accident reconstruction. They address specific needs related to obtaining quantitative information of objects from a single photograph. These methods have been the subject of numerous technical papers over the last 30 or 40 years and have found acceptance in the accident reconstruction community. Other methods must be used in applications where three-dimensional measurements are required. A mathematical foundation has been developed for three-dimensional photogrammetry,[1] but its complexity has kept it beyond the reach of most potential users, including automotive accident reconstructionists. Developments in personal computer hardware and software over the last 8 to 10 years, however, have changed this situation dramatically. New hardware, software, and image capturing and handling methodologies have put the use of three-dimensional photogrammetry into the hands of accident reconstructionists as well as others.[9] This type of photogrammetry, in which the distance between the camera and the subject is small compared to aerial photogrammetry, is referred to as close-range photogrammetry.

This section presents the fundamentals of the mathematical basis for transforming coordinates on a photograph into three-dimensional coordinates. Readers interested in the method for program development, or a deeper understanding, are referred to books with more detail.[2,3] This chapter also includes some practical insights about the application of the technique to automotive accident reconstruction.

For a given set of inputs, the mathematics produce a one-to-one transformation between two coordinate systems. However, although some information has been puiblished about the accuracy of the method,[2] the accuracy of the process of three-dimensional photogrammetry is difficult to characterize. Software that performs close-range photogrammetry typically does not advertise the accuracy of the results, as accuracy in the practical application of three-dimensional photogrammetry depends heavily on factors related to the input to the software program. These factors include the quality of the photographs, the accuracy of the measurements used to control the scale of the photograph, as well as the number of points marked in the photographs used in the analysis and the quality with which they have been marked by the analyst. This inability to advertise accuracy is in contrast to the other instruments that the accident reconstructionist community uses, wherein accuracy is frequently a performance specification provided by the manufacturer—the accuracy of the instrument does not usually depend on how the instrument is used. This is true for instruments such as total stations, coordinate measuring machines, and so forth. In three-dimensional photogrammetry, *the accuracy of the output dimensions from the analysis cannot be more accurate than the input dimensions that control the scale of the analysis.* Hence care must be exercised when using this method.

Despite some of the concerns that exist, there are times when three-dimensional photogrammetry offers the only means for the extraction of useful dimensional information from an accident site. Accident reconstructionists routinely encounter a situation in which the accident site has changed prior to an inspection; information such as the height of an object no longer at the accident site or an unmeasured rest position of a vehicle shown in photographs is required for reconstruction purposes, and the reverse projection or planar photogrammetry methods cannot be applied.

One characteristic of photogrammetry is that it allows measurements to be made without necessarily contacting the measurement point. In certain situations this characteristic can be an advantage over other measurement methods. An example would be when the items to be measured are in a location where it is dangerous to make direct measurements, such as a roadway where traffic cannot be conveniently stopped to gain access for direct measurement. Other environmental conditions may render information needed from an accident site accessible only from a distance by taking photographs. An example of this is the height of a street light above the roadway for visibility assessment pertaining to a night accident. Often, photogrammetric analysis can be used to acquire the needed dimensional information. Moreover, under certain circumstances, the remote, nonintrusive nature of the method may be an advantage, as access to the site or specimen under study may be restricted to a noncontacting level.

The nature of a typical photogrammetry project consists of preparing for and taking the necessary photographs and using appropriate software to perform the analysis to obtain the desired dimensional information. Two options related to this process can make photogrammetry an alternative to other measurement methods, such as a total station or hand measurements (tapes and measuring wheels). The first is that the necessary photographs for a successful photogrammetric analysis can be taken during a site or vehicle inspection typically with little additional time investment. The time and expense associated with the photogrammetric analysis can be deferred until it is decided that the unknown site or vehicle dimensions are actually needed. If the dimensions are never needed, the money for the analysis is not spent. Another advantage is that after the analysis is performed and the required dimensional information is obtained, the same photographs can frequently be used at a later time to obtain additional dimensional information with minimal time and expense and no need to visit the accident site again. These options are illustrated using the example of the measuring of the residual crush profile of a vehicle using photogrammetry. For this task, the vehicle can be set up for the photographic session and the appropriate photographs taken. The analysis can be deferred until such time that the profile of the crush is explicitly needed. If, after an initial analysis is performed, additional profile or dimensional information is needed, such as the location of a displaced front axle, the same set of photographs can be used to determine this information with little effort. This analysis can be performed long after the vehicle has been disposed of.

10.4.1 Mathematical Basis of Three-Dimensional Photogrammetry

Three-dimensional photogrammetry and photogrammetry in general have a certain vocabulary associated with them. This section introduces the technical basis for the method and familiarizes the reader with some of the terminology. In addition, information is presented that provides the users of photogrammetric software with insight into the mathematical process that takes place when the analysis is carried out on the computer. An understanding of the mathematics assists in the proper taking of the photographs and the assessment of the suitability of photographs taken by another photographer for photogrammetric analysis. This will become clearer as the section progresses.

Photogrammetry in its most basic sense is a series of coordinate point transformations. Three coordinate systems are used in photogrammetry.[10,11] The coordinate systems are associated with the space in which they exist. *Object space* is the three-dimensional coordinate space that we operate in daily. *Image space* is the coordinate system associated with the camera at the moment that the image is captured. This coordinate system can be considered to be fixed to the camera and defined in location and orientation by the action of capturing the image. The third coordinate system resides in image space and is referred to as the coordinate system of the measuring instrument. It is a coordinate system that exists in the plane of the film or on the face of the CCD in the camera.

There are certain attributes of these coordinate systems that serve to relate them. The first is that a unique line exists along which the light that enters the camera through the lens glass along that line is not refracted. This line is called the *principal ray*. The point at which the principal ray intersects the image capturing device (film or CCD) is called the *principal point*. This point can be considered to be the geometric center of the image and is typically designated as the origin of the image space coordinate system. The x axis of this system is in the plane of the film in the camera, intersects the principal point, and is usually parallel to the base of the camera. The y-axis of the image space coordinate system lies in the plane of the film, passes through the principal point, and is perpendicular to the x axis. The z axis of the image space coordinate system is perpendicular to the x and y axes and runs along the principal ray.

The lens axis lies along the principal ray, and a certain location along this axis is designated as a single point, usually denoted O. This point is also frequently referred to as the *lens nodal point*. Although in reality, complex multi-lens arrangements don't follow this approximation strictly, particularly zoom lenses, this approximation will suffice here. The distance between the lens nodal point, O, and the principal point is the effective focal length of the camera–lens combination. For a fixed focal length lens, this value is provided with the lens, but for a zoom lens, this value can change. When this value is known, it can be provided as input to the analysis routine, and when it is unknown, it is calculated as part of the analysis.

Ultimately, as part of the analysis required for the determination of measurements from the photographs, points will be located on the photographic images. The location of these points will be defined in another coordinate system. This system is referred to as the measuring instrument coordinate system. In the analysis, these coordinates need to be transformed into the image-space and then to the object-space coordinates. Once these transformations exist, they can be performed in either direction. Typically we are looking for the three-dimensional object-space coordinates associated with known coordinates from the measuring instrument coordinate system.

10.4.2 Projection Equations

The coordinate transformation from object-space coordinates to image-space coordinates is composed of a coordinate translation and coordinate rotation. If the coordinates in the object-space are given as $\{X, Y, Z\}^{\mathrm{T}}$, then the translation to the camera position at the nodal point is

$$\begin{Bmatrix} X' \\ Y' \\ Z' \end{Bmatrix} = \begin{Bmatrix} X - X_O \\ Y - Y_O \\ Z - Z_O \end{Bmatrix}, \tag{10.5}$$

where the O subscript refers to the nodal point of the lens and $\{X_O,\ Y_O,\ Z_O\}^{\mathrm{T}}$ are the coordinates of the nodal point of the lens in the object-space coordinate system. At this point, the coordinate system has been translated to point O, but it needs to be rotated to the orientation of the camera/image-space system. A three-dimensional coordinate rotation needs to be performed. This takes the form

$$X'' = m_{11}(X - X_O) + m_{12}(Y - Y_O) + m_{13}(Z - Z_O),$$

$$Y'' = m_{21}(X - X_O) + m_{22}(Y - Y_O) + m_{23}(Z - Z_O),$$

$$Z'' = m_{31}(X - X_O) + m_{32}(Y - Y_O) + m_{33}(Z - Z_O), \tag{10.6}$$

where

$$\begin{bmatrix} m_{11} & m_{12} & m_{13} \\ m_{21} & m_{22} & m_{23} \\ m_{31} & m_{32} & m_{33} \end{bmatrix} \tag{10.7}$$

is called the rotation matrix. Note that the form of Eq. 10.6 incorporates both the coordinate rotation and coordinate transformation.

Another transformation relates the coordinate system as defined in Eq. 10.6, which is at the nodal point of the lens, to the plane of the film. In making this second and last transformation, it is instructional to first consider what is

Figure 10.14
Single axis projection.

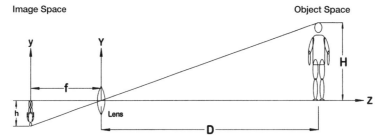

referred to as the thin lens approximation of a single axis projection. Referring to Fig. 10.14, the quantity, f, is the effective focal length of the camera–lens combination. For this geometry and the use of similar triangles,

$$\frac{f}{h} = \frac{D}{H}. \tag{10.8}$$

The equations for the projection of the coordinate system located at the lens nodal point to the plane of the film can be written using this relationship. Because this is a projection of the coordinate system onto a plane, there are only two equations. In keeping with the development by Townes and Williamson,[11] the resulting coordinates are assigned lowercase letters:

$$x = -f\frac{X''}{Z''}, \tag{10.9a}$$

$$y = -f\frac{Y''}{Z''}. \tag{10.9b}$$

Using the relationships in Eq. 10.6, a single transformation for each coordinate can be written between the object-space coordinates and the image-space film plane coordinate space:

$$x - x_p = -f\frac{m_{11}(X - X_O) + m_{12}(Y - Y_O) + m_{13}(Z - Z_O)}{m_{31}(X - X_O) + m_{32}(Y - Y_O) + m_{33}(Z - Z_O)}, \tag{10.10a}$$

$$y - y_p = -f\frac{m_{21}(X - X_O) + m_{22}(Y - Y_O) + m_{23}(Z - Z_O)}{m_{31}(X - X_O) + m_{32}(Y - Y_O) + m_{33}(Z - Z_O)}. \tag{10.10b}$$

In these equations, the values of x_p and y_p are the distances from the principal point to the origin of any arbitrary film-plane–based coordinate system and have been introduced for generality. For background on the m coefficients, interested readers can refer to many advanced mathematics or engineering texts, such as D'Souza and Garg.[12]

If all of the quantities on the right side of Eq. 10.10 are known, then the object-space coordinates (X, Y, Z) can be transformed to image-space coordinates (x,y).

10.4.3 Collinearity Equations

At the start of a typical photogrammetry session, the parameters described above that appear on the right side of Eq. 10.10 are not known. The m coefficients depend on knowing the orientation of the camera at the time the image was captured, and the coordinates (X_O, Y_O, Z_O) specify the lens nodal point location at the same time. These six parameters, three orientation angles and three location coordinates, along with the focal length, f, provide for seven parameters that need to be determined. The process used for determining these parameters is called a resection, and is accomplished by using Eq. 10.10 with four points, where both the image-space coordinates and the object-space coordinates are known. This creates a set of eight equations and seven unknowns. This is an overspecified system, and a solution is possible using iterative methods. A solution is still possible if more than four known points are available, but four equations are the minimum number.

10.4.4 Coplanarity Equations

After the parameters are determined, Eq. 10.10 can be used to transform two-dimensional coordinates in image space to three-dimensional coordinates in object space. In accident reconstruction, this is typically done for points in the photographs that are of particular interest, such as points along the residual crush of a vehicle, a vehicle location, or any object visible in the photograph for which location is desired.

10.4.5 Multiple Image Considerations

The description above is the photogrammetric process as it applies to a single image. Once the seven parameters for the transformation are computed and the image space coordinates for a point of interest are determined, the only unknowns are the three-object space coordinates for the point of interest. Because one photograph provides only two equations, those listed in Eq. 10.10, more than one photograph containing the point of interest must be available to determine all three unknown coordinates. If one of the three coordinates is available by some other means, then the solution for the other two coordinates can be obtained using one photograph. For the general case where all three coordinates need to be determined, another photograph taken from a location different than the first photograph must be used to provide for another set of two equations. The two photographs together yield four equations for three unknowns, an overspecified system. In practice, a single point whose object-space coordinates are needed can be located on more than two photographs. The solution process remains the same because the system under all situations is overspecified.

10.4.6   Considerations of the Use of Three-Dimensional Photogrammetry in Practice

The first and foremost consideration in the practice of photogrammetry, particularly as it applies to accident investigation and reconstruction, is that the process of three-dimensional photogrammetric analysis takes practice to develop proficiency. This fact is true independent of the software used to perform the analysis. It cannot be overstated that there is a ramp-up time associated with acquiring the tools and the eye for the process. It is recommended that prospective users who are serious about including photogrammetry in their repertoire of accident investigation measurement tools perform several practice projects before trying to apply the method in an actual reconstruction. In addition to the tutorials that typically accompany photogrammetric software, the user should set up several projects with relatively simple geometries to develop the skills associated with a successful project. Examples of simple photogrammetry projects appropriate for practice include

- One or two sides of a building with regular patterns associated with windows, bricks, roof line, and so forth.
- The front profile of an undamaged vehicle
- Part of the interior of a large room, such as a gymnasium, that has brick work, windows, and other regular patterns as part of the wall

Because the scale of the objects does not matter, it may be simpler to perform the practice analysis on a scale model vehicle. This can make the session easier to stage and can make it easier to introduce scaled items into the photographs. For instance, the scale model can be placed on a large sheet of graph paper, thereby establishing an object-space coordinate system while providing a simple means to select points in the foreground and background.

Three-dimensional photogrammetry will not likely replace any of the other measurement tools or techniques that are currently in use in the accident investigation community. It does, however, offer an alternative that, like other measurement techniques and tools, has advantages and disadvantages. Frequently these various measurement techniques need to be used together to produce the desired results.

The practice that is required to develop proficiency in this method should commence with the analyst taking a series of photographs specifically for photogrammetric analysis. In addition to traditional knowledge about photographic topics such as shutter speed, aperture, film speed, CCD resolution, and so forth, knowledge pertaining to the application of photography to 3-D photogrammetry can greatly simplify the process. The following section lists several guidelines about photography for three-dimensional photogrammetric purposes.

- Photographs should be taken with the largest possible depth of field (smallest physical aperture size, highest aperture number). A tripod should be used, as a smaller physical aperture will typically require slower shutter speeds for correct exposure. These slower shutter speeds are frequently at or beyond the limit of hand-held steadiness for a camera. The larger the depth of field, the better the opportunity to use points in the foreground and distant background of the photograph that are in focus. The use of these points enhances the accuracy of the process.

- High-contrast markers should be used and placed at the points of interest in the scene when possible. These markers include fluorescent color stickers or reflective markers. They are essential when using photogrammetry for crush measurements, as selecting the same point on a damaged vehicle from photographs taken from different camera angles can be difficult. Reflective roadway and driveway markers can be introduced into a site. These markers can be either free-standing or affixed to a stationary object such as a pole. These have a dual function, as they appear prominently in the photograph and most total stations will shoot the marker directly, thereby simplifying the use of this point as a control dimension.

- The introduction of high-contrast markers assists in creating common points between photographs. An example of this technique is to place small cones on the top of a crushed vehicle to serve as common control points in the photographs taken for the purpose of measuring crush profile. If composed properly, the top point of some or all of the cones will be visible in multiple photographs. This simple technique serves to relate photographs taken on one side of the vehicle to those taken on the other.

- The location of the same point in different photographs can be visualized as that point at the intersection of two light rays, each from a different photograph, that intersect the same point in object space. Photographs taken from the same location and "nearly" the same angle can create numerical problems for the solution routines of photogrammetry software. The same would be true for camera angles that are approximately 180° apart. Proper camera angle separation is important in the accuracy of the solution. In photogrammetry applied to automotive accident reconstruction, it is convenient to consider the possible camera positions for a photograph session of an object of interest described loosely as cameras positioned on a hemisphere. Typically, photographs from inspections related to accident investigation are captured by a camera position that encompasses an approximate circle approximately 5½ to 6 ft off the ground. This should be modified to include camera positions higher up (and lower) on the hemisphere, giving angular separation by vertical camera motion rather than horizontal camera separation only. The use of a stepladder, squatting, or using a monopod with the camera held in the air to take a picture facilitates camera angle separation.

Accuracy of the three-dimensional photogrammetry session is influenced by many aspects of the process. Several of these are:

- The analyst must adequately mark the points in the photographs used for control. This marking requires that the analyst compose the photographs ahead of time to determine whether adequate object-space features exist to provide sufficient control to the project.
- The measurements of the control points are critical to the accuracy of the process. The accuracy of the measurements made using the photogrammetric process can be no more accurate than the measurements of the control points. It should be pointed out that measurements of the control points made using pacing, visual estimates, and tape measures are not acceptable for the use of establishing control points for photogrammetric analysis. The preferred method is to use a laser measuring device to establish the three-dimensional points on immovable objects such as points on fire hydrants, guardrail components, markings on utility poles, features associated with structures (corners of windows, peaks of roofs, bridges, etc.), road markings, features of traffic signs, and others.
- The quality of the photographs can affect the overall quality of the photogrammetry process. When possible, the negatives or earliest generation of the required photographs should be used. This is true for digital photographs as well as film format. Digital photographs can be resampled for a reduction in resolution. Inferior photographs can be avoided when the analyst is also the photographer.
- Calibration of the camera and lens combination is typically required for the photogrammetric analysis. Therefore, as a practical matter, photographers should use the set of photographs as a means to document the process to avoid confusion during the analysis. For example, a documentation sheet should be photographed at the beginning of the photography session that lists the camera and lens combination used to take the photos. If the lens on the camera is a zoom lens, the sheet should indicate the focal length setting that was used for the photographs (typically the shortest). For practical purposes, the focal length of a zoom lens used for photogrammetric purposes should be set only at either extreme.

The software used to perform the calculations generally does not provide a direct means to assess the accuracy of the results of the process. However, there are certain relatively simple means to internally check the accuracy of a three-dimensional photogrammetric project. In the scope of this discussion, the accurate control points obtained from a survey of the object space are used to establish the transformation needed to calculate the desired coordinates of unknown features of interest. The process typically requires that there be four control points per photograph. An indication of the accuracy of the project can be easily assessed by obtaining more than the minimum required control points but leaving one or more of the control points as desired information to be calculated in the session. After the project is complete, the computed location of these "pseudo-control" points can be compared to the known measured location. With a number of these pseudo-control points located throughout the object space (foreground, background, and close to the object of interest), a quantitative assessment of the accuracy of the overall project can be obtained.

In a similar vein, if the analyst is also the photographer, various devices of known dimension can be introduced into various locations of the object space prior to the photographs being taken. In the analysis of the project, the location of points defining these dimensions can be calculated and compared to the known quantity. Several of these devices located throughout the object space can provide a quantitative assessment of the accuracy of the other dimensions calculated in the project for which measurements do not exist.

Example 10.6

This example demonstrates the use of three-dimensional photogrammetry for determining the residual crush (see Chapter 8) of a vehicle involved in an accident. The photographs used in the analysis were taken with a 35-mm film camera. The negatives of the photographs were scanned (3072 × 2048 pixels) to enable importation into the analysis software. The software used for the photogrammetric analysis was Photomodeler.[13] Six photographs, shown in Figs. 10.15 through 10.20, were used in the photogrammetric analysis. The fiducial marks shown on the left side of the photographs were created by a fiducial insert provided with the software. These fiducial marks are needed for film cameras and are not required for digital cameras.

Figure 10.15
Photo used in photogrammetric analysis.

Figure 10.16
Photo used in
photogrammetric analysis.

Figure 10.17
Photo used in
photogrammetric analysis.

Figure 10.18
Photo used in
photogrammetric analysis.

The residual crush was the result of a staged accident, for which the vehicle was marked in various locations with red and white high-contrast circular markers and checked tape. Some of these markers were used in the photogrammetric

Figure 10.19
Photo used in
photogrammetric analysis.

Figure 10.20
Photo used in
photogrammetric analysis.

analysis. Additional markers were added to the vehicle prior to taking the photographs as described later.

In this situation, the photographs were taken with the express purpose of determining the residual crush of the vehicle. Therefore, items visible in the photographs were included to facilitate the photogrammetric analysis. The unusual-looking chart situated on the floor in front of the vehicle (Fig. 10.15) was used to set the scale of the analysis. The distance between the dots at the center of the two lobes on either end of the device was measured and recorded at the start of the inspection. This distance is used later as an input during the analysis. The circular format of the chart was selected not only to enhance visibility, even at great distances, but also to take advantage of the automatic target marking utility in the software that locates the center of circular targets.

As with hand measurements of the residual crush of vehicles, the location of an undamaged part of the vehicle is required for a reference. The location of the rear axle is typically used when measuring frontal damage. In this situation, the damage to the vehicle was so severe that the rear axle may have moved due to the impact. Therefore, the rear face of the rear bumper was used as the reference. This requires that the photographs of the undamaged rear end of the vehicle be referenced directly with the photographs of the damaged front end of the vehicle. Direct referencing of the photographs of the rear of the vehicle with the photographs of the front of the vehicle is accomplished using several small cones placed on top of the vehicle. These cones appear in the photographs of the front and the rear of the vehicle. The blunt hemispherical tips of the cones were made sharper by piercing the tips from the underside with a large screw. This simplifies marking the very tip of the cone during the computer analysis. Several of the cones appear in most of the six photographs used in the analysis, thereby creating a set of common points in all of the photographs. Additional points marked on the sides of the vehicle link the photographs of the front of the vehicle with those of the rear of the vehicle through intermediate photographs. Direct referencing between photographs enhances the accuracy of the analysis, but use of both methods of referencing between points on opposite sides of the vehicle should be used.

Measurement of the deformation to the front end of the vehicle is the task to be performed. As such, the front end of the vehicle is marked using circular adhesive dots of various colors demarcating the deformation at different positions on the front end. Dots of different colors were used to mark the deformation along the upper radiator support, the middle of the radiator, and the center and bottom of the bumper. Additional dots were placed at several locations that were deemed to be of interest for possible later reference. These locations include the ends of the frame rails and a point at the base of the driver side of the windshield. Dots made of fluorescent colors or even dots made of retro-reflective material are typically easier to distinguish than dots of other colors, although both types can be used. Also note that a fill flash should be used in these situations to prevent a marker from being hidden in a shadow in one or more of the photographs. This is a common problem when photographing a damaged vehicle.

It is important to note that dimensional information about the residual crush of the vehicle is obtained only at the points marked in the analysis. In this example, the dots are these locations. If dimensional information of a particular feature or characteristic of the vehicle is needed, a marker of some sort attached to the feature is recommended. It is possible that the feature may be prominent enough that a marker is not needed. An example of this would be the head of a dark bolt located on a light background.

Once the photographs are available digitally, the analysis is basically a three-step process:

1. Calibrate the camera to be used. This calibration can be done before or after the photographs of the subject are taken (as long as the fiducial insert is used for a film format camera). The camera calibration requires that the camera and lens combination be used to take a series of nine photographs of a calibration chart provided (electronically) with the software and that a separate calibration program be run using the nine photographs.

2. Load the photographs into the software. This requires the photos to be available digitally either through the use of a digital camera or through a scanning process. Higher-resolution photographs make the accurate marking of the individual points a simpler task. A six-megapixel image for the type of analysis performed in this example is usually sufficient, provided the photographs are taken with adequate lighting and depth of field.

3. Mark the points of interest and reference the same points between photographs. These points include those associated with the deformation on the front of the vehicle, the points along the undeformed rear of the vehicle, the intermediate points for referencing, and the points for the scaling of the photograph. The markings placed on the image in the marking process in Photomodeler are shown in Fig. 10.21. The markings on the other five photographs look similar.

Figure 10.21
Photograph showing the markings associated with point designations in Photomodeler.

Once all the points are marked and referenced between photographs, the photogrammetric analysis can be performed. The process of marking the photographs and referencing the points between the photographs requires practice to acquire proficiency. Most software packages provide tools to assist in this process.

After a successful analysis, the dimensional information of the residual crush can be obtained in a number of ways. The simplest means for the users of Photomodeler to access the dimensional data is to export it to drawing interchange file (DXF) format and read it into a CAD program. The data can then be oriented to a plan view and compared to a scale drawing of an undeformed vehicle to obtain the dimensions required for use in the speed reconstruction. Figure 10.22 shows the data from this example analysis located on a plan view of an undeformed vehicle.

Figure 10.22
Diagram showing the plan view of the damaged vehicle profile and the undamaged vehicle profile.

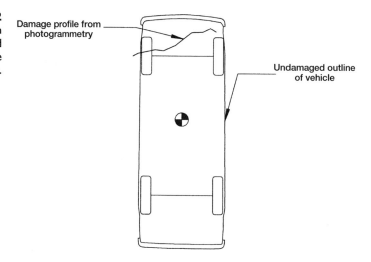

The traditional application of three-dimensional photogrammetry presented above is flexible enough to permit special uses. As an example, the method described can be augmented with additional techniques to determine the three-dimensional coordinates associated with a point in the engine compartment that is not visible to the camera. In the photographs of the front of the vehicle, a straight, slender, white rod is protruding from the engine compartment. The end of the rod that is not visible is resting on a component whose location is desired. This rod is of known length and the visible end has been sharpened to a point and marked with a black marker. A black stripe has been made on the rod one foot below the tip. The coordinates of these two points on the rod can be located through the photogrammetric analysis just presented. These two points define a line in three-dimensional space, and the location of the other end of the rod can be determined using geometry or through the use of the CAD package. In this way, the location of individual points not visible in the photogrammetric analysis can be determined.

10.5   Appendix: Projective Relation for Planar Photogrammetry

The following development of the equations for the four-point photogrammetric transformation follows the presentation in Hallert.[2] In Fig. 10A.1, the image-space and object-space planes are parallel. The origins of the coordinate systems in the two planes are located at N′ and N, respectively. The following relationships can be written for the coordinates between the points P and P′:

$$x = \frac{x'h}{f}, \tag{10A.1}$$

$$y = \frac{y'h}{f}. \tag{10A.2}$$

For an image that was captured when the camera was at the same location as shown in Fig. 10A.1 but that has been rotated about the x_r, y_r, and z_r axes by

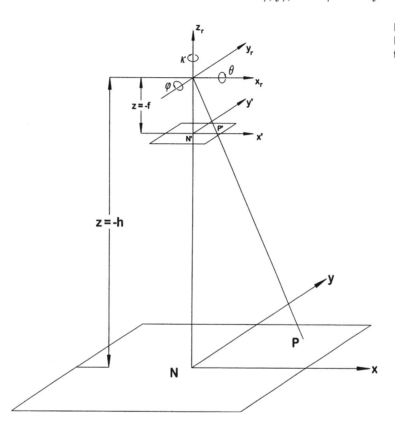

Figure 10A.1
Image and object planes for projective relation.

angles θ, φ, κ, respectively, as shown, and using the transformation for a general rotation about three axes, Eqs. 10A.1 and 10A.2 can be rewritten as

$$x =$$
$$\frac{h\{x'(\cos\varphi\cos\kappa - \sin\varphi\sin\theta\sin\kappa) + y'(\cos\varphi\sin\kappa + \sin\varphi\sin\theta\cos\kappa) + f\sin\varphi\cos\theta\}}{-x'(\sin\varphi\cos\kappa + \cos\varphi\sin\theta\sin\kappa) + y'(\cos\varphi\sin\theta\cos\kappa - \sin\varphi\sin\kappa) + f\sin\varphi\cos\theta}$$
$$\tag{10A.3}$$

$$y =$$
$$\frac{h(-x'\cos\theta\sin\kappa + y'\cos\theta\cos\kappa - f\sin\theta)}{-x'(\sin\varphi\cos\kappa + \cos\varphi\sin\theta\sin\kappa) + y'(\cos\varphi\sin\theta\cos\kappa + \sin\varphi\sin\kappa) + f\sin\varphi\cos\theta}$$
$$\tag{10A.4}$$

These equations express the relationship between the image coordinates x', y', and $z = -f$ on a plane that has been rotated through the angles θ, φ, and κ, and the object coordinates x, y, and $z = -h$. Note that these equations can be rewritten in the form presented in Eq. 10.4 with some algebraic manipulation and letting $x' = x_p$, $y' = y_p$, $x_m = x$, and $y_m = y$.

$$x_m = \frac{c_1 + c_2 x_p + c_3 y_p}{c_4 x_p + c_5 y_p + 1} \qquad (10\text{A}.5)$$

$$y_m = \frac{c_6 + c_7 x_p + c_8 y_p}{c_4 x_p + c_5 y_p + 1} \qquad (10\text{A}.6)$$

CHAPTER

11

Vehicle Dynamics Simulation

11.1 Introduction

In engineering, a *simulation* is a mathematical model that relates the variables and parameters of some physical process or system in a way that the model mimics the behavior of the process or system. Typically, the model is formed using differential equations and is solved using a computer. The results produce the system behavior as a function of time for given conditions of the system. In this chapter, a simulation is presented. It is a simulation of the dynamic motion of a vehicle, with or without a semitrailer, as it is braked or accelerated and steered over a roadway. This is referred to as a *vehicle dynamics simulation*. In the context of accident reconstruction, a simulation can be used to examine preimpact and postimpact motion of a single vehicle, either by itself or when pulling a semitrailer. Vehicle motion under various conditions can be simulated, such as during a lane change maneuver, sudden avoidance maneuver, braking over dual coefficient roadway surfaces, etc. Not only is the motion produced, but tire forces are modeled and calculated as well.

11.2 Planar Vehicle Dynamics

When carrying out an accident reconstruction, it is often useful to predict the motion of a vehicle under various conditions and combinations of acceleration, braking, and steering. For example, it may be desirable to determine what steering input at the front wheels of an automobile is necessary to complete a lane change maneuver in 4 s at 97 km/h (60 mph), and to find out what frictional forces are developed between the tires and pavement during the maneuver. Such information can be obtained experimentally by carrying out the maneuver with an instrumented vehicle. The information can also be obtained using a vehicle dynamic simulation. Simulation software exists with a wide range of capabilities. Some are three-dimensional, such as Highway Vehicle Obstacle Simulation Model (HVOSM)[1,2] and Engineering Dynamics Vehicle Simulation Model (EDVSM)[3] for vehicles and vehicle–barrier interactions. Some, such as Simulation Model for Automobile Collisions (SMAC),[4,5] not only simulate vehicle motion but model collision deformation as well. Some vehicle simulations, such as Vehicle Dynamics Analysis Nonlinear (VDANL) and Vehicle Dynamics Models for Roadway Analysis and Design (VDM RoAD, University of Michigan Transportation Research Institute),[6] include a vehicle suspension system model. Others, such as vdynXL[7] and EDSVS,[8] use a rigid suspension; these include a semitrailer model. Driving simulators need an underlying vehicle dynamics simulation.[9,10] More sophisticated models that include simulation of crash deformation continue to be developed.[11]

One of the most important parts of accurately predicting vehicle motion over a road is the tire model. In the large majority of applications, the most important forces that control vehicle motion come from the tires. In some cases, aerodynamic forces can be significant, but these are not included here. Tire forces used in the simulation are covered in Chapter 2 and are discussed only briefly here. There are two important aspects to tire models. The first is each of the individual characteristics of the tire's traction (longitudinal) force and the transverse (cornering) force. Second is the way in which these characteristics are combined for simultaneous braking and steering. One effective tire model for traction and cornering forces is attributed to Fiala.[8] Another, used for both on-road and off-road applications, is presented by Allen et al.[12] The model used here is a combination of the BNP tire characteristics[13] and the Modified Nicolas-Comstock model,[14] both discussed in Chapter 2.

Compared to other vehicle dynamic simulations, the simulation developed in this chapter is relatively versatile yet not overly complicated. In accident reconstruction, it is rare to have access to accurate values of vehicle physical parameters for the specific vehicle condition and at the specific time of an accident. This includes parameters such as nonlinear suspension system stiffness, damping and limiting coefficients, tire condition and inflation pressure, transient braking or acceleration information, and so forth. For that reason, a reasonably versatile model called vdynXL is presented here that requires a minimal number of vehicle and road parameters. VdynXL is developed for the following conditions (see Fig. 11.1):

1. A flat, level road surface
2. A two-axle, four-wheeled rigid-body vehicle, C (car or cab), with mass m_C and moment of inertia, J_C
3. An optional rigid-body semitrailer, T, with mass m_T and moment of inertia, J_T, pinned to m_C at pin P, and with a single axle
4. A rigid suspension system (no roll or pitch motion of either vehicle)

Simulations such as this are based on differential equations. Obtaining results from such a simulation requires a numerical solution of the differential equations. Such a solution is not easily done using a spreadsheet directly; however, some spreadsheets allow coupling the spreadsheet to a macro. The macro can be used with a computer language to solve the equations and transmit the results back to a spreadsheet. Examples that follow use this process.

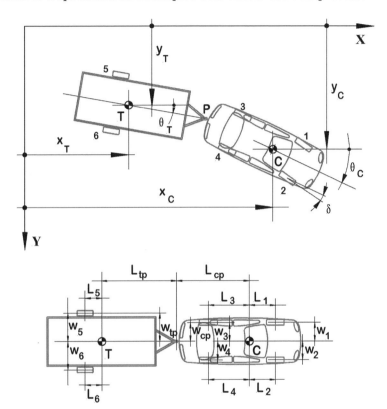

Figure 11.1
Diagram showing coordinates and variables associated with the vehicle dynamics simulation for a tow vehicle pulling a semitrailer.

The model is derived by applying Newton's second law for planar motion of each body and by applying the constraint equations of the pinned connection. For planar motion, the variables are the position coordinates of the center of gravity of each body, x_C, y_C, and θ_C of the car (or cab) and x_T, y_T, and θ_T of the semitrailer. There are three equations of motion for each body and two constraint equations at the pin, leaving four second-order differential equations which can be integrated numerically. The equations and their integration are referred to as a time-forward simulation because an integration process determines the positions and velocities of the vehicles as functions of time. Specifically, integration of the four differential equations produces the values of x_C, y_C, θ_C, and θ_T and their velocities as functions of time starting with a set of initial conditions. Positions x_T, y_T can be found from the kinematical equations after integration. The actual equations are presented in the Appendix to this chapter. The planar equations of motion are solved using Runge-Kutta-Gill numerical integration[15] in a macro coupled to a spreadsheet.

A simulation based on the equations presented here can be set up with various features, including:

1. The vehicle moves over a flat, level surface with tire–roadway frictional drag coefficients, f_R, for a roadway bounded by $0 \le Y \le R_W$, and with a coefficient f_B to represent a berm, or shoulder, outside this region ($Y < 0$ and $Y > R_W$)
2. Three modes of steering can be considered:
   A. KM = 1, preprogrammed, sinusoidal-steer, lane-change maneuver over a given time duration
   B. KM = 0, braking with all wheels locked
   C. KM = −1, an arbitrary, tabular front-wheel steer input, $\delta(\tau)$, where τ is time
3. Arbitrary braking wheel-slip values, s_i, for each wheel, or arbitrary acceleration with traction coefficients at each wheel for the lane-change and tabular-steer modes
4. Arbitrary initial conditions for the displacements x_C, y_C, θ_C, and θ_T and their velocities
5. Calculation of individual wheel normal forces based on quasi-static vehicle lateral accelerations for center of gravity heights h_C and h_T of the car/cab and semitrailer, respectively
6. Selectable integration time interval and print intervals

The most common way of choosing the integration interval is to start very small and increase it until the results begin to change significantly. Then go back and use the last interval before the significant change occurred. An interval of 0.005 s should be satisfactory for most cases.

The dimensions of the vehicles (track widths, wheelbase lengths, etc.) used as input to the software are illustrated in Fig. 11.1. This figure also is reproduced as the first page of a spreadsheet solution (Fig. 11.2). Particular note should be taken of the lateral pin locations on the tow vehicle and trailer, which are referenced to wheel 3 of the car/cab and wheel 5 of the semitrailer. When the pin location is behind the rear axle of the tow vehicle car (cab) a weight-equilibrating hitch is automatically used that causes the static weight distribution of the tow vehicle to remain the same, as if no trailer existed. Otherwise, the hitch is treated as a simple pin joint.

Because of the large number of input combinations and versatility of vehicle dynamic simulations, it is impractical to present an exhaustive number of examples. The following four examples should provide a good start for the user. For convenience, all examples use the same vehicles. The input parameters are given in Table 11.1.

Example 11.1 Consider a single, four-wheeled vehicle with no trailer and with conditions listed in Table 11.1. Determine the rear-wheel brake slip values, s_3 and s_4, that cause a drag on the rear wheels to equal about 15% of the normal force at the rear wheels.

VEHICLE DYNAMICAL SIMULATION

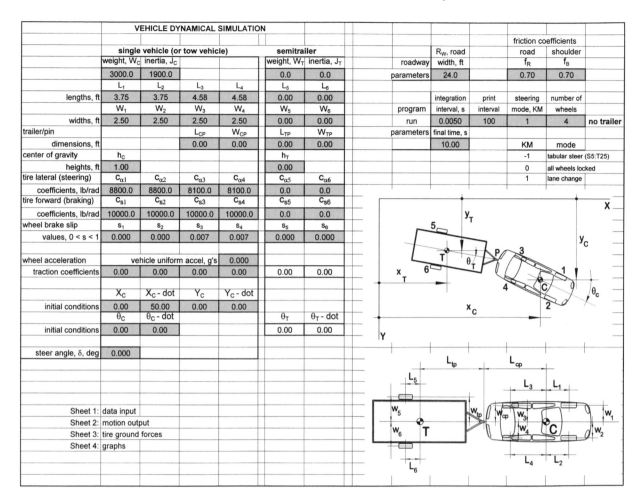

	single vehicle (or tow vehicle)			semitrailer				R_W, road		friction coefficients	
	weight, W_C	inertia, J_C		weight, W_T	inertia, J_T		roadway	width, ft		road f_R	shoulder f_B
	3000.0	1900.0		0.0	0.0		parameters	24.0		0.70	0.70
	L_1	L_2	L_3	L_4	L_5	L_6		integration	print	steering	number of
lengths, ft	3.75	3.75	4.58	4.58	0.00	0.00	program	interval, s	interval	mode, KM	wheels
	W_1	W_2	W_3	W_4	W_5	W_6	run	0.0050	100	1	4	no trailer
widths, ft	2.50	2.50	2.50	2.50	0.00	0.00	parameters	final time, s			
trailer/pin			L_{CP}	W_{CP}	L_{TP}	W_{TP}		10.00		KM	mode
dimensions, ft			0.00	0.00	0.00	0.00				-1	tabular steer (S5:T25)
center of gravity	h_C				h_T					0	all wheels locked
heights, ft	1.00				0.00					1	lane change
tire lateral (steering)	$C_{\alpha 1}$	$C_{\alpha 2}$	$C_{\alpha 3}$	$C_{\alpha 4}$	$C_{\alpha 5}$	$C_{\alpha 6}$					
coefficients, lb/rad	8800.0	8800.0	8100.0	8100.0	0.0	0.0					
tire forward (braking)	C_{s1}	C_{s2}	C_{s3}	C_{s4}	C_{s5}	C_{s6}					
coefficients, lb/rad	10000.0	10000.0	10000.0	10000.0	0.0	0.0					
wheel brake slip	s_1	s_2	s_3	s_4	s_5	s_6					
values, 0 < s < 1	0.000	0.000	0.007	0.007	0.000	0.000					
wheel acceleration	vehicle uniform accel, g's			0.000							
traction coefficients	0.00	0.00	0.00	0.00	0.00	0.00					
	X_C	X_C - dot	Y_C	Y_C - dot							
initial conditions	0.00	50.00	0.00	0.00							
	θ_C	θ_C - dot			θ_T	θ_T - dot					
initial conditions	0.00	0.00			0.00	0.00					
steer angle, δ, deg	0.000										

Sheet 1: data input
Sheet 2: motion output
Sheet 3: tire ground forces
Sheet 4: graphs

Figure 11.2
Spreadsheet 1 showing input data.

Weight, W_C, 3,000 lb (13.34 kN)
Moment of inertia, J_C, 1900 ft-lb-s² (2.58 m-kN-s²)
Lengths, $L_1 = L_2 = 3.75$ ft (1.14 m), $L_3 = L_4 = 4.58$ ft (1.40 m)
Widths, $W_1 = W_2 = W_3 = W_4 = 2.50$ ft (0.76 m)
Height of cg, $h_C = 1.0$ ft (0.3 m)
Tire lateral steer coefficients,
    $C\alpha_1 = C\alpha_2 = 8800$ lb/rad (39.14 kN/rad),
    $C\alpha_3 = C\alpha_4 = 8100$ lb/rad (26.03 kN/rad)
Tire braking (forward) coefficients, $C_{s1} = C_{s2} = C_{s3} = C_{s4} = 10,000$ lb (44.48 kN)
Friction coefficients, $f_R = f_B = 0.7$
Integration interval, 0.005 s
Final time, 10 s
Road width, 24 ft

Table 11.1
Common vehicle parameters for spreadsheet, Examples 11.1 through 11.4.

Chapter 11

Figure 11.3
Spreadsheet 3 showing tire forces.

Front Wheel Steer Solution, KM = 1									program		use only
Static Normal Forces, lb											
Fz(1), LF	Fz(2), RF	Fz(3), LR	Fz(4), RR	Fz(5), TL	Fz(6), TR			f (ROAD)	0.70		
824.7	824.7	675.3	675.3	0.0	0.0			f (OFF ROAD)	0.70		

	LF		RF		LR		RR		TL		TR	
	wheel 1	friction	wheel 2	friction	wheel 3	friction	wheel 4	friction	wheel 5	friction	wheel 6	friction
time, s	total force	limit, lb	total force	limit, lb	total force	limit, lb	total force	limit, lb	total force	limit, lb	total force	limit, lb
0.000	0.0%	577.3	0.0%	577.3	0.0%	472.7	0.0%	472.7				
0.500	0.0%	583.1	0.0%	583.1	14.9%	466.9	14.9%	466.9				
1.000	0.0%	583.1	0.0%	583.1	14.9%	466.9	14.9%	466.9				
1.500	0.0%	583.1	0.0%	583.1	14.9%	466.9	14.9%	466.9				
2.000	0.0%	583.1	0.0%	583.1	14.9%	466.9	14.9%	466.9				
2.500	0.0%	583.1	0.0%	583.1	14.9%	466.9	14.9%	466.9				
3.000	0.0%	583.1	0.0%	583.1	14.9%	466.9	14.9%	466.9				
3.500	0.0%	583.1	0.0%	583.1	14.9%	466.9	14.9%	466.9				
4.000	0.0%	583.1	0.0%	583.1	14.9%	466.9	14.9%	466.9				
4.500	0.0%	583.1	0.0%	583.1	14.9%	466.9	14.9%	466.9				
5.000	0.0%	583.1	0.0%	583.1	14.9%	466.9	14.9%	466.9				
5.500	0.0%	583.1	0.0%	583.1	14.9%	466.9	14.9%	466.9				
6.000	0.0%	583.1	0.0%	583.1	14.9%	466.9	14.9%	466.9				
6.500	0.0%	583.1	0.0%	583.1	14.9%	466.9	14.9%	466.9				
7.000	0.0%	583.1	0.0%	583.1	14.9%	466.9	14.9%	466.9				
7.500	0.0%	583.1	0.0%	583.1	14.9%	466.9	14.9%	466.9				
8.000	0.0%	583.1	0.0%	583.1	14.9%	466.9	14.9%	466.9				
8.500	0.0%	583.1	0.0%	583.1	14.9%	466.9	14.9%	466.9				
9.000	0.0%	583.1	0.0%	583.1	14.9%	466.9	14.9%	466.9				
9.500	0.0%	583.1	0.0%	583.1	14.9%	466.9	14.9%	466.9				
10.000	0.0%	583.1	0.0%	583.1	14.9%	466.9	14.9%	466.9				

Solution The information from Table 11.1 is entered into a simulation. All of the acceleration traction coefficients are set to zero. Choose the steer mode for a lane change maneuver (KM = 1) and steer angle amplitude $\delta = 0°$. The rear brake wheel slip values s_3 and s_4 are found by iteration in the following fashion. Start with any forward speed, say 50 ft/s (15.25 m/s), and any common value for s_3 and s_4 between 0 and 1 (see Chapter 2). Carry out the simulation and examine the tire forces on spreadsheet 3 (Fig. 11.3) as a percentage of the normal forces. It will be found that a value of $s_3 = s_4 = 0.007$ causes the wheel drag to be 14.9% of the normal force, 466.9 lb (2.08 kN), developed at the rear wheels. This means that if the rear brakes are actuated to develop a wheel slip of $s_3 = s_4 = 0.007$, a braking drag force is developed equal to about 15% of the rear wheel normal forces. These same values can be retained to emulate a condition of 15% powertrain drag at the rear wheels for other simulation conditions. ⬡

Example 11.2 Consider again the vehicle with the properties listed in Table 11.1, with an initial speed of 60 mph (96.6 km/h) that makes an 8-s lane change maneuver. Determine the necessary (maximum) steer angle that will cause the vehicle to move laterally 12 ft (3.66 m) in that time. Estimate the maximum tire force that occurs during such a maneuver.

Solution VdynXL has a built-in lane change maneuver feature accessed by setting mode KM = 1. It uses a steer angle shape composed of sine and cosine segments as illustrated in Fig. 11.4 beginning at time $\tau = 1$ s and ending 1 s before the final time chosen for the simulation. For an 8-s lane change, the final time should be specified as 10 s. For the specified input values, the simulation can be run in an iterative fashion, changing δ each time and observing

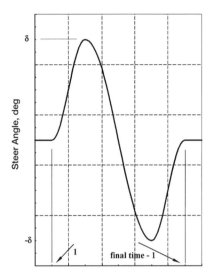

Figure 11.4
Steer angle, $\delta(\tau)$, for simulation of a lane change maneuver.

Front Wheel Steer Solution, KM = 1									
time, t	X_C	X_C - Vel	Y_C	Y_C - Vel	θ_C	θ_C - Vel	θ_T	θ_T - Vel	δ
sec	ft	ft/s	ft	ft/s	deg	deg/s	deg	deg/s	deg
0.00	0.00	88.00	0.00	0.00	0.00	0.00			0.000
0.50	44.00	88.00	0.00	0.00	0.00	0.00			0.000
1.00	88.00	88.00	0.00	0.00	0.00	0.00			0.000
1.50	132.00	88.00	0.00	0.01	0.01	0.05			0.019
2.00	176.00	88.00	0.02	0.08	0.09	0.30			0.065
2.50	220.00	88.00	0.11	0.32	0.33	0.65			0.110
3.00	264.00	87.99	0.38	0.78	0.72	0.90			0.129
3.50	307.99	87.98	0.92	1.41	1.18	0.92			0.119
4.00	351.98	87.97	1.79	2.07	1.61	0.77			0.091
4.50	395.96	87.95	2.97	2.64	1.93	0.50			0.049
5.00	439.93	87.93	4.40	3.02	2.10	0.16			0.000
5.50	483.89	87.93	5.95	3.16	2.09	-0.20			-0.049
6.00	527.86	87.93	7.51	3.04	1.90	-0.54			-0.091
6.50	571.83	87.94	8.95	2.67	1.56	-0.79			-0.119
7.00	615.80	87.96	10.15	2.11	1.13	-0.92			-0.129
7.50	659.79	87.97	11.04	1.45	0.67	-0.89			-0.110
8.00	703.77	87.97	11.60	0.82	0.28	-0.63			-0.064
8.50	747.75	87.97	11.88	0.34	0.05	-0.28			-0.019
9.00	791.73	87.97	11.98	0.09	-0.01	-0.03			0.000
9.50	835.71	87.97	12.00	0.01	-0.01	0.02			0.000
10.00	879.70	87.97	12.00	0.00	0.00	0.01			0.000

Figure 11.5
Spreadsheet 2 showing positions as functions of time.

Figure 11.6
Spreadsheet 3
showing tire forces.

Front Wheel Steer Solution, KM = 1										program		use only
Static Normal Forces, lb												
Fz(1), LF	Fz(2), RF	Fz(3), LR	Fz(4), RR	Fz(5), TL	Fz(6), TR			f (ROAD)	0.70			
824.7	824.7	675.3	675.3	0.0	0.0			f (OFF ROAD)	0.70			
	LF		RF		LR		RR		TL		TR	
	wheel 1	friction	wheel 2	friction	wheel 3	friction	wheel 4	friction	wheel 5	friction	wheel 6	friction
time, s	total force	limit, lb	total force	limit, lb	total force	limit, lb	total force	limit, lb	total force	limit, lb	total force	limit, lb
0.000	0.0%	577.3	0.0%	577.3	0.0%	472.7	0.0%	472.7				
0.500	0.0%	577.3	0.0%	577.3	0.0%	472.7	0.0%	472.7				
1.000	0.0%	577.3	0.0%	577.3	0.0%	472.7	0.0%	472.7				
1.500	0.3%	577.6	0.3%	577.0	0.1%	473.0	0.1%	472.4				
2.000	1.5%	579.1	1.5%	575.5	1.0%	474.5	1.0%	470.9				
2.500	3.3%	581.9	3.4%	572.7	2.8%	477.3	2.9%	468.1				
3.000	5.0%	584.6	5.1%	570.0	4.8%	480.0	5.0%	465.4				
3.500	5.8%	586.0	5.9%	568.6	5.9%	481.4	6.1%	464.0				
4.000	5.4%	585.6	5.5%	569.1	5.7%	480.9	5.9%	464.4				
4.500	4.1%	583.7	4.2%	570.9	4.6%	479.1	4.7%	466.3				
5.000	2.1%	580.9	2.2%	573.8	2.7%	476.2	2.7%	469.1				
5.500	0.2%	577.4	0.2%	577.2	0.4%	472.8	0.4%	472.6				
6.000	2.5%	574.0	2.4%	580.6	2.0%	469.4	2.0%	476.0				
6.500	4.4%	571.1	4.3%	583.5	4.1%	466.5	4.0%	478.9				
7.000	5.7%	569.1	5.5%	585.5	5.6%	464.5	5.4%	480.9				
7.500	5.9%	568.6	5.8%	586.1	6.2%	463.9	6.0%	481.4				
8.000	4.9%	569.8	4.8%	584.8	5.5%	465.2	5.3%	480.2				
8.500	3.0%	572.6	3.0%	582.1	3.5%	467.9	3.5%	477.4				
9.000	1.2%	575.3	1.2%	579.3	1.5%	470.7	1.4%	474.7				
9.500	0.3%	576.9	0.3%	577.8	0.3%	472.2	0.3%	473.1				
10.000	0.0%	577.3	0.0%	577.3	0.0%	472.7	0.0%	472.7				

the lateral displacement, y_c, on spreadsheet 2. When this reaches 12 ft (3.66 m), as shown in Fig. 11.5, the steer angle should be $\delta = 0.129°$. Examination of spreadsheet 3 (Fig. 11.6) shows that the maximum tire force occurs for wheel 2 (right front) is 5.9% of 568.6 lb (2.53 kN), or 33.6 lb (0.149 kN), at about 3.5 s. This occurs again at $\tau = 7.5$ s for wheel 1. Such low tire forces indicate a relatively casual lane change maneuver for that vehicle speed.   ◯

The same results can be obtained by using the tabular steer mode. This can be done by copying the steer angle values of the previous example into the tabular front wheel steer angle, δ, and setting KM = −1. Rerunning the simulation produces the same results.

Example 11.3   Consider the vehicle described by the parameters listed in Table 11.1, but now it is pulling a semitrailer. Table 11.2 lists the additional information required to describe and specify the semitrailer. In addition, suppose that while traveling at 60 mph (96.6 km/h), the semitrailer has been hit from the side by another vehicle and given an initial angular velocity of 50°/s. What motion will take place if the tow vehicle and semitrailer both have fully locked brakes following the impact?

Table 11.2
Semitrailer
parameters.

Trailer weight, W_T, 1200 lb (5.34 kN)
Trailer moment of inertia, J_T, 650 ft-lb-s² (0.88 m-kN-s²)
Lengths, $L_5 = L_6 = 2.0$ ft (0.61 m); $L_{CP} = 6.0$ ft (1.8 m)
Widths, $W_5 = W_6 = 3.7$ ft (1.13 m); $W_{CP} = 6.0$ ft (0.8 m)
Height of cg, $h_T = 0.5$ ft (0.15 m)
Tire lateral steer coefficients, $C\alpha_5 = C\alpha_6 = 9200$ lb/rad (40.92 kN/rad)
Tire braking (forward) coefficients,
    $C_{s5} = C_{s6} = 10,000$ lb (44.48 kN)

VEHICLE DYNAMICAL SIMULATION

											friction coefficients	
	single vehicle (or tow vehicle)				semitrailer			R_W, road			road	shoulder
	weight, W_C	inertia, J_C			weight, W_T	inertia, J_T	roadway	width, ft			f_R	f_B
	3000.0	1900.0			1200.0	650.0	parameters	24.0			0.70	0.70
	L_1	L_2	L_3	L_4	L_5	L_6						
lengths, ft	3.75	3.75	4.58	4.58	2.00	2.00		integration	print	steering	number of	
	W_1	W_2	W_3	W_4	W_5	W_6	program	interval, s	interval	mode, KM	wheels	
widths, ft	2.50	2.50	2.50	2.50	3.70	3.70	run	0.0050	50	0	6	trailer
trailer/pin			L_{CP}	W_{CP}	L_{TP}	W_{TP}	parameters	final time, s				
dimensions, ft			6.00	2.50	6.50	3.70		10.00		KM	mode	
center of gravity	h_C				h_T					-1	tabular steer (S5:T25)	
heights, ft	1.00				0.50					0	all wheels locked	
tire lateral (steering)	$C_{\alpha 1}$	$C_{\alpha 2}$	$C_{\alpha 3}$	$C_{\alpha 4}$	$C_{\alpha 5}$	$C_{\alpha 6}$				1	lane change	
coefficients, lb/rad	8800.0	8800.0	8100.0	8100.0	9200.0	9200.0						
tire forward (braking)	C_{s1}	C_{s2}	C_{s3}	C_{s4}	C_{s5}	C_{s6}						
coefficients, lb/rad	10000.0	10000.0	10000.0	10000.0	10000.0	10000.0						
wheel brake slip	s_1	s_2	s_3	s_4	s_5	s_6						
values, 0 < s < 1	0.000	0.000	0.000	0.000	0.000	0.000						
wheel acceleration	vehicle uniform accel, g's			0.000								
traction coefficients	0.00	0.00	0.00	0.00	0.00	0.00						
	X_C	X_C - dot	Y_C	Y_C - dot								
initial conditions	0.00	88.00	0.00	0.00								
	θ_C	θ_C - dot			θ_T	θ_T - dot						
initial conditions	0.00	0.00			0.00	50.00						
steer angle, δ, deg	0.000											

Sheet 1: data input
Sheet 2: motion output
Sheet 3: tire ground forces
Sheet 4: graphs

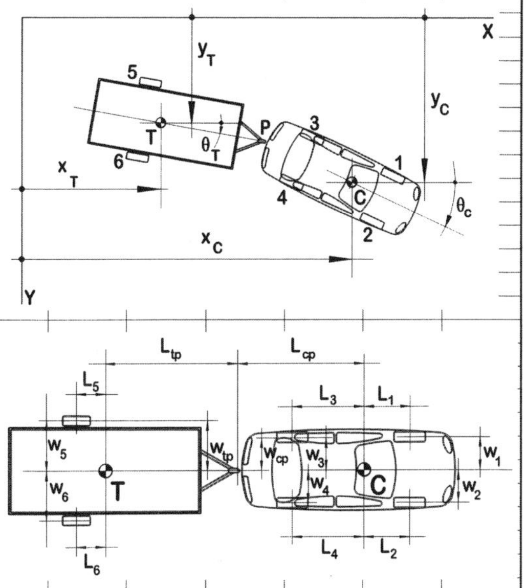

Figure 11.7
Spreadsheet 1 showing input data.

Note that the initial conditions of this example may not realistically represent the final velocities of an impact of an articulated vehicle (see Brach[16]) because an initial transverse velocity for the semitrailer would also be developed from a side impact as well as initial transverse and rotational velocity components for the tow vehicle. Also note that because this simulation is for a locked-wheel skid, the lateral and longitudinal tire coefficients do not enter into the solution.

Solution For this example, Fig. 11.7 shows page 1 of the simulation, containing primarily the data input. Note that KM = 0 is specified to simulate a locked-wheel skid, and the number of wheels must be set to 6 to include the semitrailer dynamics. Figures 11.8, 11.9, and 11.10 show output spreadsheets 2, 3, and 4, respectively. The results show that the center of gravity of the tow vehicle skids about 171 ft (52 m) as it rotates about 29° before coming to rest in somewhat over 3.75 s. The semitrailer rotates about 40°. Figure 11.9 shows that the tire forces all are 100% of the frictional value throughout the motion. Figure 11.10 shows plots of the main motion variables. ⬡

Figure 11.8
Spreadsheet 2
showing positions as
functions of time.

Locked Wheel Skid Solution, KM = 0										
time, t	X_C	X_C - Vel	Y_C	Y_C - Vel	θ_C	θ_C - Vel	θ_T	θ_T - Vel	δ	
sec	ft	ft/s	ft	ft/s	deg	deg/s	deg	deg/s	deg	
0.00	0.00	88.00	0.00	0.00	0.00	0.00	0.00	50.00	0.000	
0.25	21.26	82.06	0.00	-0.04	0.06	0.70	12.02	45.86	0.000	
0.50	41.04	76.24	-0.02	-0.13	0.43	2.37	22.82	40.45	0.000	
0.75	59.38	70.52	-0.07	-0.23	1.26	4.27	32.21	34.57	0.000	
1.00	76.31	64.89	-0.14	-0.31	2.55	5.98	40.11	28.62	0.000	
1.25	91.83	59.31	-0.22	-0.38	4.22	7.34	46.52	22.74	0.000	
1.50	105.97	53.78	-0.32	-0.42	6.19	8.34	51.48	16.96	0.000	
1.75	118.73	48.27	-0.43	-0.44	8.37	9.04	55.01	11.30	0.000	
2.00	130.11	42.77	-0.54	-0.44	10.69	9.54	57.14	5.77	0.000	
2.25	140.11	37.27	-0.65	-0.43	13.13	9.93	57.91	0.40	0.000	
2.50	148.74	31.77	-0.75	-0.42	15.65	10.28	57.36	-4.75	0.000	
2.75	156.00	26.25	-0.86	-0.41	18.27	10.63	55.56	-9.57	0.000	
3.00	161.87	20.71	-0.96	-0.41	20.97	10.93	52.62	-13.82	0.000	
3.25	166.35	15.13	-1.06	-0.42	23.72	11.00	48.74	-17.03	0.000	
3.50	169.43	9.50	-1.17	-0.41	26.41	10.38	44.28	-18.20	0.000	
3.75	171.09	3.84	-1.26	-0.35	28.77	8.05	39.99	-15.02	0.000	

Locked Wheel Skid Solution, KM = 0													program		use only
	Static Normal Forces, lb														
Fz(1), LF	Fz(2), RF	Fz(3), LR	Fz(4), RR	Fz(5), TL	Fz(6), TR				f (ROAD)	0.70					
824.7	824.7	765.3	765.3	510.0	510.0				f (OFF ROAD)	0.70					
	LF		RF		LR		RR		TL		TR				
	wheel 1	friction	wheel 2	friction	wheel 3	friction	wheel 4	friction	wheel 5	friction	wheel 6	friction			
time, s	total force	limit, lb	total force	limit, lb	total force	limit, lb	total force	limit, lb	total force	limit, lb	total force	limit, lb			
0.000	100.0%	577.3	100.0%	577.3	100.0%	535.7	100.0%	535.7	100.0%	357.0	100.0%	357.0			
0.250	100.0%	665.4	100.0%	668.7	100.0%	458.9	100.0%	462.2	100.0%	353.5	100.0%	331.3			
0.500	100.0%	663.8	100.0%	666.8	100.0%	460.4	100.0%	463.3	100.0%	361.2	100.0%	324.4			
0.750	100.0%	664.7	100.0%	663.2	100.0%	463.1	100.0%	461.7	100.0%	368.0	100.0%	319.3			
1.000	100.0%	667.4	100.0%	658.4	100.0%	466.9	100.0%	457.9	100.0%	373.5	100.0%	315.9			
1.250	100.0%	671.5	100.0%	652.9	100.0%	471.4	100.0%	452.7	100.0%	377.8	100.0%	313.7			
1.500	100.0%	676.4	100.0%	646.8	100.0%	476.5	100.0%	446.9	100.0%	381.0	100.0%	312.4			
1.750	100.0%	681.7	100.0%	640.3	100.0%	482.2	100.0%	440.9	100.0%	383.2	100.0%	311.7			
2.000	100.0%	687.1	100.0%	633.6	100.0%	488.5	100.0%	435.0	100.0%	384.4	100.0%	311.4			
2.250	100.0%	692.6	100.0%	626.8	100.0%	495.1	100.0%	429.4	100.0%	384.8	100.0%	311.3			
2.500	100.0%	697.9	100.0%	619.8	100.0%	502.2	100.0%	424.1	100.0%	384.3	100.0%	311.6			
2.750	100.0%	703.3	100.0%	612.6	100.0%	509.8	100.0%	419.1	100.0%	383.1	100.0%	312.2			
3.000	100.0%	708.8	100.0%	605.2	100.0%	517.8	100.0%	414.1	100.0%	380.9	100.0%	313.1			
3.250	100.0%	714.6	100.0%	597.2	100.0%	526.6	100.0%	409.2	100.0%	377.8	100.0%	314.7			
3.500	100.0%	720.5	100.0%	588.4	100.0%	536.2	100.0%	404.1	100.0%	373.8	100.0%	317.0			
3.750	100.0%	726.5	100.0%	577.6	100.0%	547.8	100.0%	398.8	100.0%	368.2	100.0%	321.0			

Figure 11.9
Spreadsheet 3
showing tire forces.

Note that in the solution to Example 11.3, above, the final velocities were not exactly zero when the simulation terminated. If closer approximations to the final distances and angles are needed, the print interval should be reduced to a small number. In this way, the final printed values will be closer to the rest values. Smaller print intervals will also give smoother plots of the dynamic motion on spreadsheet 4.

Example 11.4   Example 11.3 simulated a tow vehicle and semitrailer with the properties listed in Tables 11.1 and 11.2. Consider here the problem of determining the motion of the same vehicles starting with the same initial conditions, but the brakes on the semitrailer are not applied at all and the tow vehicle's brakes are fully locked.

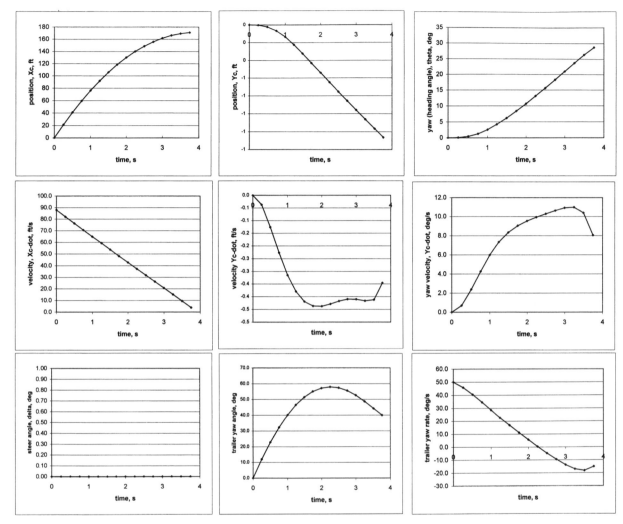

Figure 11.10
Spreadsheet 4 showing plots of motion variables.

Solution   The conditions in this example are not those of a locked-wheel skid, because the semitrailer brakes are not applied. The spreadsheet solution must be set up in a different way to simulate the desired motion. The lane change option (KM = 1) can be used to simulate this motion by setting the steer angle amplitude, δ = 0°, by setting the brakes of the tow vehicle to a locked condition using brake slip values of $s_1 = s_2 = s_3 = s_3 = 1$ and leaving the trailer brake slip values set to $s_5 = s_6 = 0$. Figures 11.11 through 11.14 show pages 1 through 4 from a simulation corresponding to this example.

Note that the lack of semitrailer braking makes significant and remarkable changes. The total distance traveled by the tow vehicle center of gravity increases to 221 ft (67.3 m) and it takes about 5 s to come to rest. With the semitrailer brakes locked, the tow vehicle has an angle at rest of +29°; it now is −230°. The rotation of the semitrailer was +40° and now is −34°.

VEHICLE DYNAMICAL SIMULATION

								friction coefficients	
single vehicle (or tow vehicle)				semitrailer			R_W, road	road	shoulder
weight, W_C	inertia, J_C			weight, W_T	inertia, J_T	roadway	width, ft	f_R	f_B
3000.0	1900.0			1200.0	650.0	parameters	24.0	0.70	0.70

	L_1	L_2	L_3	L_4	L_5	L_6				
lengths, ft	3.75	3.75	4.58	4.58	2.00	2.00		integration	print	steering	number of
	W_1	W_2	W_3	W_4	W_5	W_6	program	interval, s	interval	mode, KM	wheels
widths, ft	2.50	2.50	2.50	2.50	3.70	3.70	run	0.0050	50	1	6	trailer
trailer/pin			L_{CP}	W_{CP}	L_{TP}	W_{TP}	program	final time, s			
dimensions, ft			6.00	2.50	6.50	3.70	parameters	10.00		KM	mode
center of gravity	h_C				h_T					-1	tabular steer (S5:T25)
heights, ft	1.00				0.50					0	all wheels locked
tire lateral (steering)	$C_{\alpha1}$	$C_{\alpha2}$	$C_{\alpha3}$	$C_{\alpha4}$	$C_{\alpha5}$	$C_{\alpha6}$				1	lane change
coefficients, lb/rad	8800.0	8800.0	8100.0	8100.0	9200.0	9200.0					
tire forward (braking)	C_{s1}	C_{s2}	C_{s3}	C_{s4}	C_{s5}	C_{s6}					
coefficients, lb/rad	10000.0	10000.0	10000.0	10000.0	10000.0	10000.0					
wheel brake slip	s_1	s_2	s_3	s_4	s_5	s_6					
values, 0 < s < 1	1.000	1.000	1.000	1.000	0.000	0.000					

wheel acceleration	vehicle uniform accel, g's		0.000			
traction coefficients	0.00	0.00	0.00	0.00	0.00	0.00

	X_C	X_C - dot	Y_C	Y_C - dot
initial conditions	0.00	88.00	0.00	0.00
	θ_C	θ_C - dot	θ_T	θ_T - dot
initial conditions	0.00	0.00	0.00	50.00
steer angle, δ, deg	0.000			

Sheet 1: data input
Sheet 2: motion output
Sheet 3: tire ground forces
Sheet 4: graphs

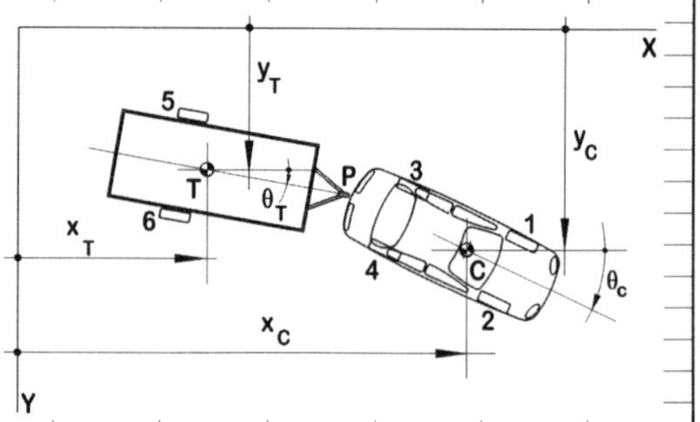

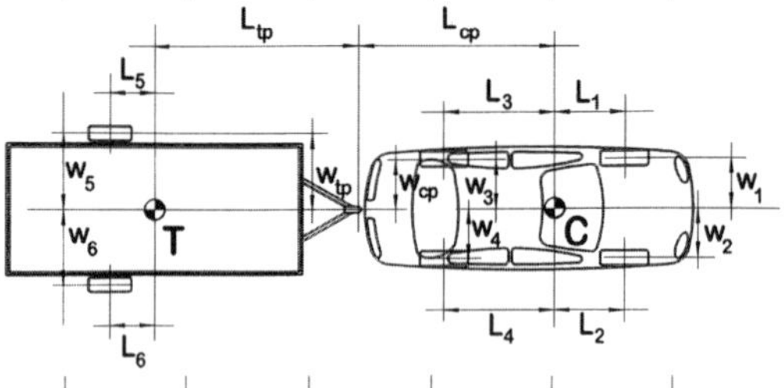

Figure 11.11 Spreadsheet 1 showing input data.

Front Wheel Steer Solution, KM = 1									
time, t	X_C	X_C - Vel	Y_C	Y_C - Vel	θ_C	θ_C - Vel	θ_T	θ_T - Vel	δ
s	ft	ft/s	ft	ft/s	deg	deg/s	deg	deg/s	deg
0.00	0.00	88.00	0.00	0.00	0.00	0.00	0.00	50.00	0.000
0.25	21.43	83.51	0.02	0.16	-0.32	-2.97	8.74	20.40	0.000
0.50	41.77	79.14	0.08	0.38	-1.62	-7.57	10.45	-6.50	0.000
0.75	61.00	74.74	0.20	0.55	-4.07	-11.70	5.73	-28.75	0.000
1.00	79.14	70.35	0.34	0.50	-7.16	-12.68	-0.02	-12.38	0.000
1.25	96.18	66.03	0.45	0.38	-10.42	-13.61	-0.33	7.53	0.000
1.50	112.15	61.68	0.53	0.34	-14.19	-17.03	1.85	7.13	0.000
1.75	127.02	57.30	0.62	0.35	-19.08	-22.24	2.90	1.89	0.000
2.00	140.79	52.86	0.71	0.35	-25.40	-28.48	3.25	1.67	0.000
2.25	153.45	48.34	0.80	0.37	-33.43	-36.00	3.85	2.98	0.000
2.50	164.95	43.71	0.90	0.44	-43.53	-45.05	4.63	2.95	0.000
2.75	175.29	38.98	1.02	0.60	-56.08	-55.60	5.20	1.32	0.000
3.00	184.44	34.16	1.21	0.89	-71.44	-67.57	5.13	-2.20	0.000
3.25	192.38	29.40	1.48	1.34	-89.95	-80.55	3.88	-8.32	0.000
3.50	199.16	24.97	1.88	1.83	-111.68	-92.95	0.74	-17.20	0.000
3.75	204.92	21.17	2.37	1.99	-136.05	-100.77	-4.81	-26.97	0.000
4.00	209.80	17.99	2.82	1.47	-161.25	-99.12	-12.37	-32.23	0.000
4.25	213.92	14.87	3.07	0.55	-184.81	-88.03	-20.14	-28.50	0.000
4.50	217.20	11.34	3.10	-0.26	-204.77	-70.97	-26.26	-20.59	0.000
4.75	219.55	7.37	2.99	-0.59	-220.03	-50.70	-30.62	-14.54	0.000
5.00	220.87	3.19	2.86	-0.34	-229.88	-27.36	-33.58	-8.89	0.000

Figure 11.12 Spreadsheet 2 showing simulation output as function of time.

	Front Wheel Steer Solution, KM = 1									program		use only	
	Static Normal Forces, lb												
	Fz(1), LF	Fz(2), RF	Fz(3), LR	Fz(4), RR	Fz(5), TL	Fz(6), TR			f (ROAD)	0.70			
	824.7	824.7	765.3	765.3	510.0	510.0			f (OFF ROAD)	0.70			
		LF		RF		LR		RR		TL		TR	
		wheel 1	friction	wheel 2	friction	wheel 3	friction	wheel 4	friction	wheel 5	friction	wheel 6	friction
	time, s	total force	limit, lb	total force	limit, lb	total force	limit, lb	total force	limit, lb	total force	limit, lb	total force	limit, lb
	0.000	0.0%	577.3	0.0%	577.3	0.0%	535.7	0.0%	535.7	0.0%	357.0	0.0%	357.0
	0.250	99.2%	649.0	99.2%	639.3	99.4%	486.1	99.4%	476.4	94.8%	376.2	96.5%	313.0
	0.500	99.2%	646.3	99.2%	641.2	99.4%	484.5	99.4%	479.4	93.3%	375.9	95.1%	312.8
	0.750	99.3%	638.3	99.2%	651.1	99.5%	473.8	99.5%	486.6	31.0%	356.7	31.5%	333.3
	1.000	99.3%	625.0	99.3%	659.4	99.5%	466.4	99.4%	500.8	69.9%	323.8	64.5%	364.6
	1.250	99.3%	618.9	99.3%	664.2	99.5%	461.6	99.5%	506.9	26.4%	336.3	25.6%	352.1
	1.500	99.4%	613.5	99.3%	669.5	99.5%	456.1	99.5%	512.0	25.5%	353.5	27.2%	335.5
	1.750	99.4%	603.1	99.3%	678.1	99.6%	447.1	99.5%	522.1	18.8%	352.0	19.6%	337.7
	2.000	99.5%	588.7	99.3%	688.7	99.6%	436.0	99.5%	536.0	8.7%	349.2	8.9%	341.4
	2.250	99.5%	570.7	99.4%	700.4	99.7%	423.6	99.5%	553.3	10.5%	350.2	10.8%	341.9
	2.500	99.6%	547.8	99.4%	712.1	99.8%	411.0	99.6%	575.2	13.2%	351.0	13.7%	342.9
	2.750	99.8%	519.9	99.6%	720.9	99.9%	401.4	99.7%	602.4	12.4%	349.6	12.6%	345.8
	3.000	99.9%	489.1	99.8%	721.4	100.0%	400.8	99.8%	633.1	8.1%	345.1	7.9%	350.5
	3.250	100.0%	461.9	100.0%	705.1	100.0%	418.3	100.0%	661.5	0.9%	337.0	0.9%	356.2
	3.500	99.7%	451.9	99.8%	662.0	99.8%	464.6	99.9%	674.7	18.9%	325.8	16.0%	361.0
	3.750	99.6%	474.7	99.5%	593.0	99.6%	537.8	99.7%	656.1	48.7%	316.5	39.5%	361.9
	4.000	99.5%	519.2	99.5%	530.0	99.4%	602.9	99.5%	613.8	74.2%	315.4	62.5%	358.7
	4.250	99.5%	555.6	99.6%	492.4	99.3%	639.6	99.4%	576.4	78.6%	321.5	67.2%	354.5
	4.500	99.5%	580.7	99.8%	469.2	99.1%	659.9	99.4%	548.4	62.9%	333.0	51.1%	348.6
	4.750	99.6%	596.6	99.8%	455.7	99.1%	670.3	99.4%	529.4	50.0%	341.6	37.8%	346.5
	5.000	99.6%	600.7	99.9%	453.9	99.1%	669.2	99.4%	522.3	49.0%	347.5	30.0%	346.4

Changing the tire forces applied to the semitrailer (which are at a large distance from the center of gravity of the tow vehicle) has a very large effect on its motion. ◇

Figure 11.13
Spreadsheet 3 showing tire forces.

It should be noted that although the simulation model is based on a single rear axle for the car/cab and a single rear axle for the semitrailer, a simulation can represent multiple axles and dual wheels such as are associated with tractors and semitrailers[7] with reasonable accuracy. This is done by using midaxle dimensions and using combined tire properties (lateral steering coefficients) of tandem and multiple wheel sets.

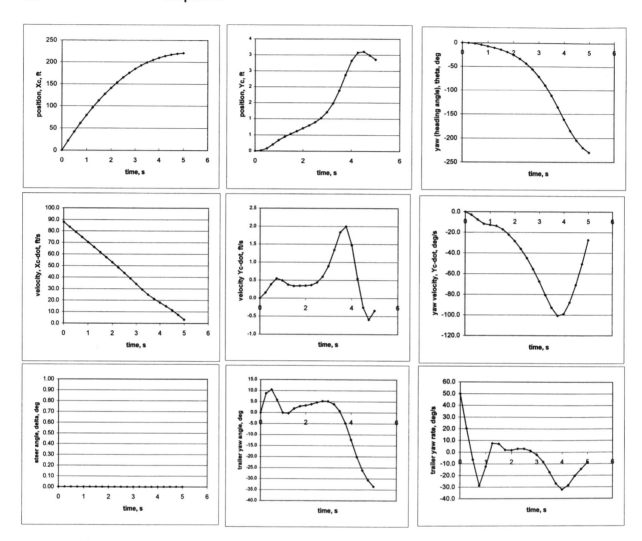

Figure 11.14
Spreadsheet 4
showing plots of
motion variables.

11.3   Appendix: Differential Equations of Planar Motion

The four differential equations of motion for the simulation of a tow vehicle pulling a semitrailer are listed in this Appendix. Equations defining intermediate variables are presented along with a list of symbols. All of the variables are illustrated in Fig. 11.1. The equations here already have the pin impulse eliminated and are in the form of four equations and four unknowns. The unknowns are $\ddot{X}_C$, $\ddot{Y}_C$, $\ddot{\theta}_C$, $\ddot{\theta}_T$.

$$(m_C + m_T)\,\ddot{X}_C = -\,m_T(R_{CP}\,\ddot{\theta}_{CP}\cos\theta_{CP} + R_{CP}\dot{\theta}_{CP}^2\sin\theta_{CP} + R_{TP}\ddot{\theta}_T\cos\theta_{TP}$$

$$+\, R_{TP}\dot{\theta}_T^2\sin\theta_{TP}) + \sum_{i=1}^{6} f_{iX} + F_{CX} + F_{TX} \tag{11A.1}$$

$$(m_C + m_T)\,\ddot{Y}_C = -\,m_T(-R_{CP}\ddot{\theta}_C\sin\theta_{CP} + R_{CP}\dot{\theta}_C^2\cos\theta_{CP} - R_{TP}\ddot{\theta}_T\sin\theta_{TP}$$

$$+\, R_{TP}\dot{\theta}_T^2\cos\theta_{TP}) + \sum_{i=1}^{6} f_{iY} + F_{CY} + F_{TY} \tag{11A.2}$$

$$[J_C + \overline{m}R_{CP}(r_{PCX}\cos\theta_{CP} - r_{CPY}\sin\theta_{CP})]\,\ddot{\theta}_C =$$

$$\sum_{i=1}^{4}(r_{iX}f_{iX} + r_{iY}f_{iY}) + r_{CPX}\left(\frac{\overline{m}}{m_T}\sum_{i=1}^{6}f_{iX} - \sum_{i=1}^{4}f_{iX}\right) + r_{CPY}\left(\frac{\overline{m}}{m_T}\sum_{i=1}^{6}f_{iY} - \sum_{i=1}^{4}f_{iY}\right)$$

$$-\, r_{CPY}\overline{m}(R_{CP}\dot{\theta}_C^2\cos\theta_{CP} - R_{TP}\ddot{\theta}_T\sin\theta_{TP} - R_{TP}\dot{\theta}_T^2\cos\theta_{TP})$$

$$-\, r_{CPX}\overline{m}(R_{Cp}\dot{\theta}_T^2\sin\theta_{CP} + R_{TP}\ddot{\theta}_T\cos\theta_{TP} + R_{TP}\dot{\theta}_T^2\sin\theta_{TP}) \tag{11A.3}$$

$$[J_T + \overline{m}R_{TP}(r_{TPY}\sin\theta_{TP} - r_{TPXY}\cos\theta_{TP})]\ddot{\theta}_T =$$

$$\sum_{i=5}^{6}(r_{iX}f_{iX} + r_{iY}f_{iY}) + r_{TPX}\left(\sum_{i=1}^{4}f_{iX} - \frac{\overline{m}}{m_T}\sum_{i=1}^{6}f_{iX}\right) + r_{TPY}\left(\sum_{i=1}^{4}f_{iY} - \frac{\overline{m}}{m_T}\sum_{i=1}^{6}f_{iY}\right)$$

$$+\, r_{TPY}\overline{m}(-R_{CP}\ddot{\theta}_C\sin\theta_{CP} + R_{CP}\dot{\theta}_C^2\cos\theta_{TP} + R_{TP}\dot{\theta}_T^2\cos\theta_{TP})$$

$$+\, r_{TPX}\overline{m}(R_{CP}\ddot{\theta}_C\cos\theta_{CP} + R_{CP}\dot{\theta}_C^2\sin\theta_{CP} + R_{TP}\dot{\theta}_T^2\sin\theta_{TP}) \tag{11A.4}$$

Variables

$$R_{CP} = [L_{CP}^2 + (W_3 - W_{CP})^2]^{1/2} \tag{11A.5}$$

$$R_{TP} = [L_{TP}^2 + (W_{TP} - W_5)^2]^{1/2} \tag{11A.6}$$

$$\theta_{CP} = \frac{\pi}{2} - \theta_C - \tan^{-1}[(W_3 - W_{CP})/L_{CP}] \tag{11A.7}$$

$$\theta_{TP} = \frac{\pi}{2} - \theta_T - \tan^{-1}[(W_{TP} - W_5)/L_{TP}] \tag{11A.8}$$

$$r_{TPX} = -L_{TP}\sin\theta_T - (W_{TP} - W_5)\cos\theta_T \tag{11A.9}$$

$$r_{TPY} = L_{TP} \cos \theta_T - (W_{TP} - W_5) \sin \theta_T \qquad (11A.10)$$

$$r_{CPX} = L_{CP} \sin \theta_C + (W_3 - W_{CP}) \cos \theta_C \qquad (11A.11)$$

$$r_{TPX} = -L_{TP} \sin \theta_T - (W_{TP} - W_5) \cos \theta_T \qquad (11A.12)$$

$$r_{CPY} = -L_{CP} \cos \theta_C + (W_3 - W_{CP}) \cos \theta_C \qquad (11A.13)$$

$$\overline{m} = \frac{m_C m_T}{m_C + m_T} \qquad (11A.14)$$

Notation

F_{CX}, F_{CY}	External force components on car (tow vehicle)
F_{TX}, F_{TY}	External force components on semitrailer
F_Z	Normal force between a wheel and the roadway
f_{iX}, f_{iY}	Components of the tangential force between the ith tire and the roadway surface
h_C, h_T	Vertical heights of car (tow vehicle) and semitrailer centers of gravity, respectively
J_C, J_T	Mass moments of yaw inertia of car (tow vehicle) and semitrailer, respectively, about their centroidal axis
L_{CP}, L_{TP}	Longitudinal distance from vehicle centroidal axis to the hitch pin in each the car (tow vehicle) and semitrailer, respectively
L_i	Distance parallel to heading axis from the centroidal axis to the ith wheel
m_C, m_T	Mass of car (tow vehicle) and semitrailer, respectively
r_{CPX}, r_{CPY}	Moment arms from car (tow vehicle) centroidal axis to force components, f_{CPX} and f_{CPY}, respectively
r_{TPX}, r_{TPY}	Moment arms from semitrailer centroidal axis to force components, f_{TPX} and f_{TPY}, respectively
r_{iX}, r_{iY}	Moment arms from car (tow vehicle) centroidal axis to tire–roadway force components, f_{iX} and f_{iY}, respectively
W_{CP}, W_{TP}	Transverse distance from wheel 3 and wheel 5 in car (tow vehicle) and semitrailer to the pin, respectively
X, Y	Ground fixed inertial coordinates
δ	Front wheel steer angle
C	Subscript, car or cab (tow vehicle)
T	Subscript, semitrailer

Units and Numbers

A.1   Use of SI (Metric Units of Measure in SAE Technical Papers)

The long-term goal for SAE is international communication with minimal effort and confusion. Therefore, the use of SI units in all technical publications and presentations is preferred. The SAE will strive toward universal usage of SI units and will encourage their use whenever appropriate.

However, the SAE also recognizes that sectors of the mobility market do not yet use SI units because of tradition, regulatory language, or other reasons. Mandating the use of SI units in these cases will impede rather than facilitate technical communication. Therefore, it is the policy to allow non-SI units and dual dimensioning where communication will be enhanced. This shall not be viewed as an avenue to circumvent the long-term goal of 100 percent SI usage.

Instructions on SAE-approved techniques for conversion of units are contained in "SAE Recommended Practices, Rules for SAE Use of SI (METRIC) Units – TSB003." Copies of TSB003 can be obtained from SAE Headquarters.

Although what follows in Table A.1 represents a change to the current policy, it is not a change to the SAE Board of Directors' Policy, because it falls within the scope of the words, "where a conflicting industry practice exists." Dual (metric/U.S. customary) units for the vehicle characteristics in Table A.1 may be considered where communication will be enhanced.

Vehicle characteristic	Metric units	U.S. customary units
Volume, engine displacement	liters, L, or cubic cm, cm^3	cubic inches, $in.^3$
Liquid volume	liters, L	pints/quarts/gallons
Engine power	kilowatts, kW	brake horse power, bhp
Engine torque	Newton-meters, $N\text{-}m$	foot-pounds, $lb\text{-}ft$
Mass	kilograms, kg	slugs, $lb\text{-}s^2/ft$
Pressure, stress	kiloPascals, kPa	pounds per square inch, psi
Temperature	degrees Celsius, $°C$	degrees Fahrenheit, $°F$
Area	square cm, cm^2	square inches, $in.^2$
Linear dimensions	millimeters, mm, meters, m or kilometers, km	inches, $in.$, feet, ft, miles, mi
Spring rates	Newtons per mm, N/mm	pounds per inch, $lb/in.$
Speed	kilometers per hour, km/h or kph	miles per hour, mph
Fuel economy	kilometers per liter, km/L or $kmpL$	miles per gallon, mpg
Force	Newtons, N	pounds, lb
Acceleration	kilometers per second per second, km/s^2, g's	feet per second per second, ft/s^2, g

Table A.1
Metric and
U.S. customary units.

A.2   Numbers, Significant Figures, Rounding, and Unit Conversions

A.2.1   Significant Figures

In all branches of science and technology, numbers are used to express values, i.e., levels or amounts of physical quantities. It is important to state numbers appropriately so that they properly convey the intended information. The number of significant figures contained in a stated number reflects the precision to which that quantity is known. For example, suppose the speed of a vehicle is reported as 21 m/s (69 ft/s). Is 21 m/s different from 21.0 m/s? According to the rules of significant figures, yes, but in practice, it may or may not. Could the number 21 m/s imply 20.9 m/s or less or could it imply 21.1 m/s or greater? It could, but such implications or interpretations must be determined from context, not the number 21 itself. Answers to some of these questions are related to the topic of uncertainty (covered in Chapter 1). To properly quantify and communicate a physical measurement or property, it should be stated as a reference value plus and minus an uncertainty. For example, a speed stated as $v = 21.0 \pm 0.6$ m/s clearly is meant to be between 20.4 and 21.6 m/s. This is one of the ways of estimating and revealing the uncertainty of results. But the basic rules of using significant figures and rounding must be understood before uncertainty can be expressed. Some of the rules for handling and interpreting the significance of numbers are covered in this Appendix. Note that the terms *significant figures* and *significant digits* are used synonymously.

The number of significant figures in a number is defined in the following way (see, for example, Bevington and Robinson[1] and IEEE/ASTM-SI-10[2]):

1. The leftmost nonzero digit of a number is the most significant digit.
2. If there is no decimal point, the rightmost nonzero digit is the least significant digit.

3. If there is a decimal point, the rightmost digit is the least significant digit, even if it is a zero.
4. All digits, from the least to the most significant, are counted as significant.

For example, 2.610 and 2498 have four significant digits each, whereas 0.125 and 728,000 have three significant digits. The following numbers each has five significant digits: 1000.0, 1206.5, 12,065,000 and 0.00012065. Unless it is stated to be exact, the speed of 21 m/s has two significant figures. If it is *exact*, then 21 is equivalent to 21.0000 . . . , with an unlimited number of zeros. Each of the speeds 20.4 and 21.6 has three significant figures.

When numbers are very large or very small it is convenient to express them in *scientific notation*. To use scientific notation, a decimal point is placed immediately after the leftmost significant digit and the number is given a suffix of 10 raised to a power n. The value of n is positive or negative. If the magnitude (disregarding the sign) of the stated number is less than 1, then $n < 0$. If the stated number is greater than 10, $n > 0$. If the stated number is between 1 and 10, $n = 0$. The value of n is the power of 10 that returns the number in scientific notation to its original value. For example, 0.0000687 becomes 6.87×10^{-5} and 12,360,000 becomes 1.236×10^7. Note that the number of significant digits does not change when converting to or from scientific notation.

A.2.2 Rounding of Numbers

After completing calculations or when listing the results of measurements, it usually is necessary to round numbers to a lesser number of significant figures by discarding digits. Three possibilities can arise:

1. *The leftmost discarded digit is less than 5.* When rounding such numbers, the last digit retained should remain unchanged. For example, if 3.46325 is to be rounded to four digits, the digits 2 and 5 would be discarded and 3.463 remains,
2. *The leftmost discarded digit is greater than 5 or it is a 5 followed by at least one digit other than 0.* In such cases, the last figure retained should be increased by one. For example, if rounded to four digits, 8.37652 would become 8.377; if rounded to three digits, it would be 8.38.
3. *The leftmost discarded digit is a 5, followed only by zeros or no other numbers.* Here, the last digit retained should be rounded up if it is an odd number, but no adjustment made if it is an even number. For example, 21.165, when rounded to four significant digits, becomes 21.16. The number 21.155 would likewise round to the same value, 21.16.

A reason for this last rule is to avoid systematic errors that otherwise would be introduced into the average of a group of such numbers. Not all computer software* follows this rule, however, and when rounding for purposes of reporting results of measurments and/or calculations, the even-odd rule is not critical.

---

*The reader may wish to try such an example in their favorite software.

A.2.3 Consistency of Significant Figures When Adding and Subtracting

When adding and subtracting numbers, proper determination of the number of significant figures is stated as a rule (IEEE/ASTM SI-10[2]). The rule is, *the answer shall contain no significant digits farther to the right than occurs in the number with the least significant digits.* The simplest way of following this rule is first to add or subtract the numbers using all of the stated significant figures* followed by rounding of the final answer. For example, consider the addition of the three numbers, 964,532 and 317,880 and 563,000. These have six, five, and three significant figures, respectively. The sum by direct addition is 1,845,412. The answer then is adjusted, or rounded, to conform to the number with the least significant figures (563,000 with three), giving the final result, 1,845,000. This number has no more zero digits to the right of the comma than does 563,000. Now consider the sum of the three numbers 964,532, −317,880, and −563,000; the direct result is 83,652. As above, this must be made to conform with the significant figures of 563,000 by using rounding rule and is 84,000.

In the last example, the concept being conveyed is that the number 563,000 is "indefinite" to the right of the "3" digit. It is not known if 563,000 could really mean 562,684 or 563,121 or other values since 563,000, itself, may have been obtained by rounding. If it had been stated as 563,000.0, then everything would be different (since 563,000.0 would have seven significant figures and 317,880 would then have the least significant digits of the three numbers to be added in the above example).

A.2.4 Consistency of Significant Figures When Multiplying and Dividing

ASTM SI-10 states a rule for multiplying and dividing as *the product or quotient shall contain no more significant digits than are contained in the number with the fewest significant digits.* For example, consider the product, $125.64 \times 829.4 \times 1.25$, of the three numbers with five, four, and three significant digits, respectively. The answer from straight-forward multiplication is 130,257.27. After rounding to three significant figures the proper end result of the multiplication is 130,000. Note that the answer, 130,000, by itself appears to have only two significant figures. This illustrates that ambiguities sometimes can arise when determining significant figures and that the amount of significant figures of a number may need to be found from context. A way of resolving such ambiguities is to express results of rounding in scientific notation. In this case the result would be 1.30×10^5.

A.2.5 Other Forms of Number Manipulation

Not all calculations are done with addition, subtraction, multiplication, and division. There are the taking of roots, logarithms, trigonometric functions,

---

* ASTM SI-10 suggests first rounding each individual number to one significant figure greater than the least *before* adding or subtracting and then rounding the final answer. Though this may be better, it is not the way most computer software operates. Rounding after summing typically gives the same result.

etc. In addition, sometimes strict adherence of rounding rules can produce paradoxical or impractical results (see the following example). So more general rules are needed. In summary, two very general, but some *practical* rules are recommended:

1. In rounding of numbers and conversion of units, retain a number of significant digits such that accuracy and precision are neither sacrificed nor exaggerated.
2. When making and reporting calculations, continually carry all of the significant figures of a calculating device without rounding intermediate values and round only the final answer.
3. Unit conversion should precede rounding.
4. Whenever possible, explicitly state the uncertainty of the results of measurements and calculations.

Suppose a vehicle skids to a stop over a distance of $d = 33.9$ m from an initial   **Example A**
speed, v, on a pavement with a uniform frictional drag coefficient of $f = 0.7 \pm 0.1$. Use the minimum and maximum values of f and Eq. 1.1 to calculate bounds on the initial speed. Convert the results to U.S. customary units of ft/s.

Solution   The lower value of speed for $f = 0.6$ is

$$v = \sqrt{2fgd} = \sqrt{2 \times 0.6 \times 9.806650 \times 33.9} = 19.973345\ldots, \text{m/s}.$$

Similarly, the initial speed for $f = 0.8$ is

$$v = \sqrt{2 \times 0.8 \times 9.806650 \times 33.9} = 23.063233\ldots, \text{m/s}.$$

The frictional drag coefficient and its uncertainty have the fewest number of significant figures of the input values. According to the rules the final results should be rounded to one significant figure. Rounding $19.973345\ldots$ to a single significant digit gives a speed of $v = 20$ m/s. Rounding $23.063235\ldots$ to a single significant digit also gives a speed of $v = 20$ m/s. Both upper and lower bounds result with the same speed, $v = 20$ m/s. Clearly the result is an exaggeration of precision. Consider now another approach.

The variation of $f = \pm 0.1$ is another way of saying that because of uncertainty, f can take on any value between 0.6 to 0.8.* From the above discussion of significant figures and rounding, a point of view can be taken that the lower value, 0.6, for example, could be the result of rounding to one significant figure of any number from 0.55^+ to 0.65^- (such as 0.551, 0.642, etc.). Similarly, the upper value, 0.8, could be viewed as the result of rounding of any number from 0.75^+ to 0.85^- (such as 0.751, 0.842, etc.). So the full range of values of the frictional drag coefficient corresponding to the stated uncertainty and from the concepts of significant figures is $0.55 \leq f \leq 0.85$. At this point the calculations are performed *as if* all numbers are exact giving a speed range of $19.123022\ldots \leq v \leq 23.773036\ldots$ m/s. Since rounding to one significant figure here produces an

---

* Note that there is no implication of the likelihood of any of the values within this range.

exaggeration of precision (as above), rounding is done to an additional significant figure. Consequently, the final result is stated as: $19 \leq v \leq 24$ m/s, or $v = 21.5 \pm 2.5$ m/s. Precision no longer is exaggerated. An initial $\pm14\%$ variation (0.7 ± 0.1) becomes a 12% variation of v (21.5 ± 2.5) through the use of Eq 1.1.

Finally, the speed is to be converted to the U.S. customary units of ft/s. The proper conversion factor is 1 ft = 0.3048 m (this is an *exact* conversion; see the following unit conversion table). Unit conversions should be done before rounding, so $19.123022 \ldots \leq v \leq 23.773036 \ldots$ m/s becomes $62.739573 \ldots \leq v \leq 77.995525 \ldots$ ft/s. Rounding again to one significant figure gives the same result, 70 ft, so another significant figure is acceptable, giving $63 \leq v \leq 78$ ft/s, or $v = 70.5 \pm 7.5$ ft/s. ⬡

Another consideration that must be kept in mind when rounding is the use or purpose of the results. For example, if the speed calculated in the last example is to be compared to a speed limit, say 25 m/s. Rounding to a number of significant digits to the right of the decimal point is superfluous. The result $19 \leq v \leq 24$ m/s is satisfactory to conclude that the calculated speed is less than the speed limit. Instead, suppose that the calculated speed is a measure of vehicle braking performance and is to be compared to a governmental regulation stated to 3 significant figures. Rounding to an additional significant figure leads to an exaggeration of accuracy. To compare the speed to such a regulation requires a more accurate value of friction, stated at least to two significant figures.

A.3 Unit Conversions for Common Units[3]

Factors in **boldface** are exact. When options exist, units in the first column printed in *italics* are preferred by the National Institute for Science and Technology.

To convert from	To	Multiply by	
acre (based on U.S. survey foot)	square meter (m²)	4.046 873	E+03
acre foot (based on U.S. survey foot)	cubic meter (m³)	1.233 489	E+03
ampere hour (A·h)	coulomb (C)	**3.6**	**E+03**
atmosphere, standard (atm)	pascal (Pa)	**1.013 25**	**E+05**
atmosphere, standard (atm)	kilopascal (kPa)	**1.013 25**	**E+02**
atmosphere, technical (at)	pascal (Pa)	**9.806 65**	**E+04**
atmosphere, technical (at)	kilopascal (kPa)	**9.806 65**	**E+01**
bar (bar)	pascal (Pa)	**1.0**	**E+05**
bar (bar)	kilopascal (kPa)	**1.0**	**E+02**
barn (b)	square meter (m²)	**1.0**	**E-28**
barrel [for petroleum, 42 gallons (U.S.)] (bbl)	cubic meter (m³)	1.589 873	E−01
barrel [for petroleum, 42 gallons (U.S.)] (bbl)	liter (L)	1.589 873	E+02
British thermal unit (mean) (Btu)	joule (J)	1.055 87	E+03
bushel (U.S.) (bu)	cubic meter (m³)	3.523 907	E−02
bushel (U.S.) (bu)	liter (L)	3.523 907	E+01
calorie (cal) (mean)	joule (J)	4.190 02	E+00

To convert from	To	Multiply by	
candela per square inch (cd/in²)	candela per square meter (cd/m²)	1.550 003	E+03
carat, metric	kilogram (kg)	**2.0**	**E−04**
carat, metric	gram (g)	**2.0**	**E−01**
centimeter of mercury (0°C)	pascal (Pa)	1.333 22	E+03
centimeter of water (4°C)	pascal (Pa)	9.806 38	E+01
centimeter of water, conventional (cm H₂O)	pascal (Pa)	**9.806 65**	**E+01**
centipoise (cP)	pascal second (Pa·s)	**1.0**	**E−03**
centistokes (cSt)	meter squared per second (m²/s)	**1.0**	**E−06**
chain (based on U.S. survey foot) (ch)	meter (m)	2.011 684	E+01
circular mil	square meter (m²)	5.067 075	E−10
cord (128 ft³)	cubic meter (m³)	3.624 556	E+00
cubic foot (ft³)	cubic meter (m³)	2.831 685	E−02
cubic inch (in³)	cubic meter (m³)	1.638 706	E−05
cubic mile (mi³)	cubic meter (m³)	4.168 182	E+09
cubic yard (yd³)	cubic meter (m³)	7.645 549	E−01
cup (U.S.)	cubic meter (m³)	2.365 882	E−04
cup (U.S.)	liter (L)	2.365 882	E−01
day (d)	second (s)	**8.64**	**E+04**
day (sidereal)	second (s)	8.616 409	E+04
degree (angle) (°)	radian (rad)	1.745 329	E−02
degree Celsius (temperature) (°C)	kelvin (K)	K = °C + **273.15**	
degree Celsius (temperature interval) (°C)	kelvin (K)	**1.0**	**E+00**
degree centigrade (temperature) 16	degree Celsius (°C)	°C = deg. cent.	
degree centigrade (temperature interval) 16	degree Celsius (°C)	1.0	E+00
degree Fahrenheit (temperature) (°F)	degree Celsius (°C)	°C= (°F − **32)/1.8**	
degree Fahrenheit (temperature) (°F)	kelvin (K)	K = (°F + **459.67)/1.8**	
degree Fahrenheit (temperature interval) (°F)	degree Celsius (°C)	5.555 556	E−01
degree Fahrenheit (temperature interval) (°F)	kelvin (K)	5.555 556	E−01
degree Rankine (°R)	kelvin (K)	K = (°R)/**1.8**	
degree Rankine (temperature interval) (°R)	kelvin (K)	5.555 556	E−01
denier	kilogram per meter (kg/m)	1.111 111	E−07
dyne (dyn)	newton (N)	**1.0**	**E−05**
dyne centimeter (dyn·cm)	newton meter (N·m)	**1.0**	**E−07**
dyne per square centimeter (dyn/cm²)	pascal (Pa)	**1.0**	**E−01**
erg (erg)	joule (J)	**1.0**	**E−07**
erg per second (erg/s)	watt (W)	**1.0**	**E−07**
fathom (based on U.S. survey foot)	meter (m)	1.828 804	E+00
fluid ounce (U.S.) (fl oz)	cubic meter (m³)	2.957 353	E−05
fluid ounce (U.S.) (fl oz)	milliliter (mL)	2.957 353	E+01
foot (ft)	meter (m)	**3.048**	**E−01**
foot (U.S. survey) (ft)	meter (m)	3.048 006	E−01
footcandle	lux (lx)	1.076 391	E+01
footlambert	candela per square meter (cd/m²)	3.426 259	E+00
foot of water, conventional (ftH₂O)	pascal (Pa)	2.989 067	E+03
foot of water, conventional (ftH₂O)	kilopascal (kPa)	2.989 067	E+00
foot per hour (ft/h)	meter per second (m/s)	8.466 667	E−05
foot per minute (ft/min)	meter per second (m/s)	**5.08**	**E−03**
foot per second (ft/s)	meter per second (m/s)	**3.048**	**E−01**

To convert from	To	Multiply by	
foot per second squared (ft/s²)	meter per second squared (m/s²)*	**3.048**	**E−01**
foot poundal	joule (J)	4.214 011	E−02
foot pound-force (ft·lbf)	joule (J)	1.355 818	E+00
foot pound-force per hour (ft·lbf/h)	watt (W)	3.766 161	E−04
foot pound-force per minute (ft·lbf/min)	watt (W)	2.259 697	E−02
foot pound-force per second (ft·lbf/s)	watt (W)	1.355 818	E+00
gal (Gal)	meter per second squared (m/s²)	**1.0**	**E−02**
gallon [Canadian and U.K. (Imperial)] (gal)	cubic meter (m³)	**4.546 09**	**E−03**
gallon [Canadian and U.K. (Imperial)] (gal)	liter (L)	**4.546 09**	**E+00**
gallon (U.S.) (gal)	cubic meter (m³)	3.785 412	E−03
gallon (U.S.) (gal)	liter (L)	3.785 412	E+00
gallon (U.S.) per day (gal/d)	cubic meter per second (m³/s)	4.381 264	E−08
gallon (U.S.) per day (gal/d)	liter per second (L/s)	4.381 264	E−05
gallon (U.S.) per horsepower hour [gal/(hp·h)]	cubic meter per joule (m³/J)	1.410 089	E−09
gallon (U.S.) per horsepower hour [gal/(hp·h)]	liter per joule (L/J)	1.410 089	E−06
gallon (U.S.) per minute (gpm) (gal/min)	cubic meter per second (m³/s)	6.309 020	E−05
gallon (U.S.) per minute (gpm) (gal/min)	liter per second (L/s)	6.309 020	E−02
grain (gr)	kilogram (kg)	**6.479 891**	**E−05**
grain (gr)	milligram (mg)	**6.479 891**	**E+01**
grain per gallon (U.S.) (gr/gal)	kilogram per cubic meter (kg/m³)	1.711 806	E−02
grain per gallon (U.S.) (gr/gal)	milligram per liter (mg/L)	1.711 806	E+01
gram-force per square centimeter (gf/cm²)	pascal (Pa)	**9.806 65**	**E+01**
gram per cubic centimeter (g/cm³)	kilogram per cubic meter (kg/m³)	**1.0**	**E+03**
hectare (ha)	square meter (m²)	**1.0**	**E+04**
horsepower (550 ft·lbf/s) (hp)	watt (W)	7.456 999	E+02
horsepower (boiler)	watt (W)	9.809 50	E+03
horsepower (electric)	watt (W)	**7.46**	**E+02**
horsepower (metric)	watt (W)	7.354 988	E+02
horsepower (U.K.)	watt (W)	7.4570	E+02
horsepower (water)	watt (W)	7.460 43	E+02
hour (h)	second (s)	**3.6**	**E+03**
hour (sidereal)	second (s)	3.590 170	E+03
hundredweight (long, 112 lb)	kilogram (kg)	5.080 235	E+01
hundredweight (short, 100 lb)	kilogram (kg)	4.535 924	E+01
inch (in)	meter (m)	**2.54**	**E−02**
inch (in)	centimeter (cm)	**2.54**	**E+00**
inch of mercury, conventional (in. Hg)	pascal (Pa)	3.386 389	E+03
inch of mercury, conventional (in. Hg)	kilopascal (kPa)	3.386 389	E+00
inch of water, conventional (inH₂O)	pascal (Pa)	2.490 889	E+02
kelvin (K)	degree Celsius (°C)	$t/°C = T/K -$ **273.15**	
kilocalorie (mean) (kcal)	joule (J)	4.190 02	E+03
kilogram-force (kgf)	newton (N)	**9.806 65**	**E+00**
kilogram-force meter (kgf·m)	newton meter (N·m)	**9.806 65**	**E+00**
kilogram-force per square centimeter (kgf/cm²)	kilopascal (kPa)	**9.806 65**	**E+01**

*Standard value of free-fall acceleration is g = 9.80665 m/s².

To convert from	To	Multiply by	
kilogram-force per square meter (kgf/m²)	pascal (Pa)	**9.806 65**	**E+00**
kilometer per hour (km/h)	meter per second (m/s)	2.777 778	E−01
kilopond (kilogram-force) (kp)	newton (N)	**9.806 65**	**E+00**
kilowatt hour (kW·h)	joule (J)	**3.6**	**E+06**
kilowatt hour (kW·h)	megajoule (MJ)	**3.6**	**E+00**
kip (1 kip= 1000 lbf)	newton (N)	4.448 222	E+03
kip (1 kip= 1000 lbf)	kilonewton (kN)	4.448 222	E+00
kip per square inch (ksi) (kip/in²)	pascal (Pa)	6.894 757	E+06
kip per square inch (ksi) (kip/in²)	kilopascal (kPa)	6.894 757	E+03
knot (nautical mile per hour)	meter per second (m/s)	5.144 444	E−01
lambert	candela per square meter (cd/m²)	3.183 099	E+03
light year (l.y.)	meter (m)	9.460 73	E+15
liter (L)	cubic meter (m³)	**1.0**	**E−03**
lumen per square foot (lm/ft²)	lux (lx)	1.076 391	E+01
microinch	meter (m)	**2.54**	**E−08**
microinch	micrometer (μm)	**2.54**	**E−02**
micron (μ)	meter (m)	**1.0**	**E−06**
micron (μ)	micrometer (μm)	**1.0**	**E+00**
mil (0.001 in)	meter (m)	**2.54**	**E−05**
mil (0.001 in)	millimeter (mm)	**2.54**	**E−02**
mil (angle)	radian (rad)	9.817 477	E−04
mil (angle)	degree (°)	**5.625**	**E−02**
mile (mi)	meter (m)	**1.609 344**	**E+03**
mile (mi)	kilometer (km)	**1.609 344**	**E+00**
mile (based on U.S. survey foot) (mi)	meter (m)	1.609 347	E+03
mile (based on U.S. survey foot) (mi)	kilometer (km)	1.609 347	E+00
mile, nautical	meter (m)	**1.852**	**E+03**
mile per gallon (U.S.) (mpg) (mi/gal)	meter per cubic meter m/m³)	4.251 437	E+05
mile per gallon (U.S.) (mpg) (mi/gal)	kilometer per liter (km/L)	4.251 437	E−01
mile per gallon (U.S.) (mpg) (mi/gal)	liter per 100 kilometer (L/100km)	divide 235.215 by number of miles per gallon	
mile per hour (mi/h)	meter per second (m/s)	**4.4704**	**E−01**
mile per hour (mi/h)	kilometer per hour (km/h)	**1.609 344**	**E+00**
mile per minute (mi/min)	meter per second (m/s)	**2.682 24**	**E+01**
mile per second (mi/s)	meter per second (m/s)	**1.609 344**	**E+03**
millibar (mbar)	pascal (Pa)	**1.0**	**E+02**
millibar (mbar)	kilopascal (kPa)	**1.0**	**E−01**
millimeter of mercury, conventional (mmHg)	pascal (Pa)	1.333 224	E+02
millimeter of water, conventional (mm H₂O)	pascal (Pa)	**9.806 65**	**E+00**
minute (angle) (N)	radian (rad)	2.908 882	E−04
minute (min)	second (s)	**6.0**	**E+01**
minute (sidereal)	second (s)	5.983 617	E+01
ounce (avoirdupois) (oz)	kilogram (kg)	2.834 952	E−02
ounce (avoirdupois) (oz)	gram (g)	2.834 952	E+01
ounce (troy or apothecary) (oz)	kilogram (kg)	3.110 348	E−02
ounce (troy or apothecary) (oz)	gram (g)	3.110 348	E+01
ounce [Canadian and U.K. fluid (Imperial)] (fl oz)	cubic meter (m³)	2.841 306	E−05
ounce [Canadian and U.K. fluid (Imperial)] (fl oz)	milliliter (mL)	2.841 306	E+01
ounce (U.S. fluid) (fl oz)	cubic meter (m³)	2.957 353	E−05
ounce (U.S. fluid) (fl oz)	milliliter (mL)	2.957 353	E+01
ounce (avoirdupois)-force (ozf)	newton (N)	2.780 139	E−01
ounce (avoirdupois)-force inch (ozf·in)	newton meter (N·m)	7.061 552	E−03
ounce (avoirdupois)-force inch (ozf·in)	millinewton meter (mN·m)	7.061 552	E+00

To convert from	To	Multiply by	
ounce (avoirdupois) per cubic inch (oz/in³)	kilogram per cubic meter (kg/m³)	1.729 994	E+03
peck (U.S.) (pk)	cubic meter (m³)	8.809 768	E−03
peck (U.S.) (pk)	liter (L)	8.809 768	E+00
pennyweight (dwt)	kilogram (kg)	1.555 174	E−03
pennyweight (dwt)	gram (g)	1.555 174	E+00
pica (computer) (1/6 in)	meter (m)	4.233 333	E−03
pica (computer) (1/6 in)	millimeter (mm)	4.233 333	E+00
pica (printer's)	meter (m)	4.217 518	E−03
pica (printer's)	millimeter (mm)	4.217 518	E+00
pint (U.S. dry) (dry pt)	cubic meter (m³)	5.506 105	E−04
pint (U.S. dry) (dry pt)	liter (L)	5.506 105	E−01
pint (U.S. liquid) (liq pt)	cubic meter (m³)	4.731 765	E−04
pint (U.S. liquid) (liq pt)	liter (L)	4.731 765	E−01
point (computer) (1/72 in)	meter (m)	3.527 778	E−04
point (computer) (1/72 in)	millimeter (mm)	3.527 778	E−01
point (printer's)	meter (m)	3.514 598	E−04
point (printer's)	millimeter (mm)	3.514 598	E−01
poise (P)	pascal second (Pa·s)	**1.0**	**E−01**
pound (avoirdupois) (lb)	kilogram (kg)	4.535 924	E−01
pound (troy or apothecary) (lb)	kilogram (kg)	3.732 417	E−01
poundal	newton (N)	1.382 550	E−01
poundal per square foot	pascal (Pa)	1.488 164	E+00
poundal second per square foot	pascal second (Pa·s)	1.488 164	E+00
pound foot squared (lb·ft²)	kilogram meter squared (kg·m²)	4.214 011	E−02
pound-force (lbf)	newton (N)*	4.448 222	E+00
pound-force foot (lbf·ft)	newton meter (N·m)	1.355 818	E+00
pound-force foot per inch (lbf·ft/in)	newton meter per meter (N·m/m)	5.337 866	E+01
pound-force inch (lbf·in)	newton meter (N·m)	1.129 848	E−01
pound-force inch per inch (lbf·in/in)	newton meter per meter (N·m/m)	4.448 222	E+00
pound-force per foot (lbf/ft)	newton per meter (N/m)	1.459 390	E+01
pound-force per inch (lbf/in)	newton per meter (N/m)	1.751 268	E+02
pound-force per pound (lbf/lb) (thrust to mass ratio)	newton per kilogram (N/kg)	**9.806 65**	**E+00**
pound-force per square foot (lbf/ft²)	pascal (Pa)	4.788 026	E+01
pound-force per square inch (psi) (lbf/in²)	pascal (Pa)	6.894 757	E+03
pound-force per square inch (psi) (lbf/in²)	kilopascal (kPa)	6.894 757	E+00
pound-force second per square foot (lbf·s/ft²)	pascal second (Pa·s)	4.788 026	E+01
pound-force second per square inch (lbf·s/in²)	pascal second (Pa·s)	6.894 757	E+03
pound inch squared (lb·in²)	kilogram meter squared (kg·m²)	2.926 397	E−04
pound per cubic foot (lb/ft³)	kilogram per cubic meter (kg/m³)	1.601 846	E+01
pound per cubic inch (lb/in³)	kilogram per cubic meter (kg/m³)	2.767 990	E+04
pound per cubic yard (lb/yd³)	kilogram per cubic meter (kg/m³)	5.932 764	E−01

* If the local value of the acceleration of free fall is taken as the standard value g = 9.90665 m/s², then the exact conversion factor is 4.448 221 615 260 5 E+00.

To convert from	To	Multiply by	
pound per foot (lb/ft)	kilogram per meter (kg/m)	1.488 164	E+00
pound per foot hour [lb/(ft·h)]	pascal second (Pa·s)	4.133 789	E−04
pound per foot second [lb/(ft·s)]	pascal second (Pa·s)	1.488 164	E+00
pound per gallon [Canadian and U.K. (Imperial)] (lb/gal)	kilogram per cubic meter (kg/m³)	9.977 637	E+01
pound per gallon [Canadian and U.K. (Imperial)] (lb/gal)	kilogram per liter (kg/L)	9.977 637	E−02
pound per gallon (U.S.) (lb/gal)	kilogram per cubic meter (kg/m³)	1.198 264	E+02
pound per gallon (U.S.) (lb/gal)	kilogram per liter (kg/L)	1.198 264	E−01
pound per horsepower hour [lb/(hp·h)]	kilogram per joule (kg/J)	1.689 659	E−07
psi (pound-force per square inch) (lbf/in²)	pascal (Pa)	6.894 757	E+03
psi (pound-force per square inch) (lbf/in²)	kilopascal (kPa)	6.894 757	E+00
quad (10^{15} Btu$_{IT}$)	joule (J)	1.055 056	E+18
quart (U.S. dry) (dry qt)	cubic meter (m³)	1.101 221	E−03
quart (U.S. dry) (dry qt)	liter (L)	1.101 221	E+00
quart (U.S. liquid) (liq qt)	cubic meter (m³)	9.463 529	E−04
quart (U.S. liquid) (liq qt)	liter (L)	9.463 529	E−01
rad (absorbed dose) (rad)	gray (Gy)	**1.0**	**E−02**
revolution (r)	radian (rad)	6.283 185	E+00
revolution per minute (rpm) (r/min)	radian per second (rad/s)	1.047 198	E−01
rod (based on U.S. survey foot) (rd)	meter (m)	5.029 210	E+00
rpm (revolution per minute) (r/min)	radian per second (rad/s)	1.047 198	E−01
second (angle) (O)	radian (rad)	4.848 137	E−06
second (sidereal)	second (s)	9.972 696	E−01
shake	second (s)	**1.0**	**E−08**
shake	nanosecond (ns)	**1.0**	**E+01**
slug (slug)	kilogram (kg)	1.459 390	E+01
slug per cubic foot (slug/ft³)	kilogram per cubic meter (kg/m³)	5.153 788	E+02
slug per foot second [slug/(ft·s)]	pascal second (Pa·s)	4.788 026	E+01
square foot (ft²)	square meter (m²)	**9.290 304**	**E−02**
square foot per hour (ft²/h)	square meter per second (m²/s)	**2.580 64**	**E−05**
square foot per second (ft²/s)	square meter per second (m²/s)	**9.290 304**	**E−02**
square inch (in²)	square meter (m²)	**6.4516**	**E−04**
square inch (in²)	square centimeter (cm²)	**6.4516**	**E+00**
square mile (mi²)	square meter (m²)	2.589 988	E+06
square mile (mi²)	square kilometer (km²)	2.589 988	E+00
square mile (based on U.S. survey foot) (mi²)	square meter (m²)	2.589 998	E+06
square mile (based on U.S. survey foot) (mi²)	square kilometer (km²)	2.589 998	E+00
square yard (yd²)	square meter (m²)	8.361 274	E−01
stokes (St)	meter squared per second (m²/s)	**1.0**	**E−04**
tablespoon	cubic meter (m³)	1.478 676	E−05
tablespoon	milliliter (mL)	1.478 676	E+01
teaspoon	cubic meter (m³)	4.928 922	E−06
teaspoon	milliliter (mL)	4.928 922	E+00
therm (EC)	joule (J)	**1.055 06**	**E+08**
therm (U.S.)	joule (J)	**1.054 804**	**E+08**
ton, assay (AT)	kilogram (kg)	2.916 667	E−02
ton, assay (AT)	gram (g)	2.916 667	E+01
ton-force (2000 lbf)	newton (N)	8.896 443	E+03
ton-force (2000 lbf)	kilonewton (kN)	8.896 443	E+00
ton, long (2240 lb)	kilogram (kg)	1.016 047	E+03
ton, long, per cubic yard	kilogram per cubic meter (kg/m³)	1.328 939	E+03

To convert from	To	Multiply by	
ton, metric (t)	kilogram (kg)	**1.0**	**E+03**
tonne (called "metric ton" in U.S.) (t)	kilogram (kg)	**1.0**	**E+03**
ton of refrigeration (12 000 Btu$_{\mathrm{IT}}$/h)	watt (W)	3.516 853	E+03
ton of TNT (energy equivalent)	joule (J)	**4.184**	**E+09**
ton, register	cubic meter (m^3)	2.831 685	E+00
ton, short (2000 lb)	kilogram (kg)	9.071 847	E+02
ton, short, per cubic yard	kilogram per cubic meter (kg/m^3)	1.186 553	E+03
ton, short, per hour	kilogram per second (kg/s)	2.519 958	E−01
torr (Torr)	pascal (Pa)	1.333 224	E+02
watt hour (W·h)	joule (J)	**3.6**	**E+03**
yard (yd)	meter (m)	**9.144**	**E−01**
year (365 days)	second (s)	**3.1536**	**E+07**
year (sidereal)	second (s)	3.155 815	E+07
year (tropical)	second (s)	3.155 693	E+07

Glossary

Common Terms and Acronyms in Accident Reconstruction

The terms defined here are for the convenience of the readers, both those learning accident reconstruction as well as those already familiar with the field. Not all terms included in the list are used in this book.

18-wheeler: A tractor, semitrailer with a total of 18 wheels. *See* tractor, semitrailer.

A, B, C, D, pillars and posts: The vertical pillars and posts of a light vehicle forming the major vertical structural members of the body; see Fig. B.1. Pillars typically are at window height; posts are below window height. From front to rear, the A post/pillar is the most forward member, the B post/pillar is the second most forward vertical member, etc.

AADT: Average annual daily traffic.

AASHTO: American Association of State Highway and Transportation Officials.

acceleration: Time rate of change of linear or angular velocity or speed with respect to time.

accelerometer: An instrument used to measure acceleration, usually linear acceleration.

accident, vehicle: An event in which one or more vehicles undergo unexpected action(s), usually involving contact with another vehicle or other object, producing injury, death, and/or property damage; an accident is an unstable situation which includes at least one harmful event. *See* crash.

accident investigation: The process of observation, acquisition, and documentation of physical evidence and other information regarding an accident or crash.

accident reconstruction: A procedure carried out with the specific purpose of estimating in both a qualitative and quantitative manner how an accident occurred using engineering, scientific, and mathematical principles and based on evidence obtained through accident investigation.

accident scene: A place where a traffic accident occurs, both during and immediately following the accident, and before vehicles and participants have departed. *See* accident site.

Figure B.1

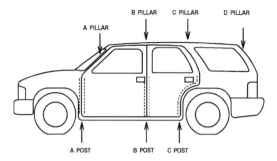

accident site: A place where a traffic accident occurred, after vehicles and participants have departed the scene. *See* accident scene.

AFV: Alternative fuel vehicle.

aggressivity: The properties and characteristics of a vehicle, such as mass and structural stiffness, that cause a vehicle to provide more protection for occupants than another vehicle in a crash.

agricultural commodity trailer: Trailer designed to transport bulk commodities from harvest sites to process or storage sites.

air bag: A device in the interior of a vehicle that inflates and acts between an occupant and an interior vehicle surface to prevent injury in a crash. *See* supplemental restraint system.

angular acceleration: The time rate of change of angular velocity.

angular velocity: The time rate of change of rotational displacement.

animation: The process by which the movement of objects is illustrated.

ANSI: American National Standards Institute.

approach speed: Speed of a vehicle just prior to the first significant event such as contact in an accident. *See* closing speed.

aquaplaning: *See* hydroplaning.

area of impact: Area encompassed by the interface between colliding objects projected onto the road. *See* impact center.

asphalt: *See* bituminous pavement.

BAC: Blood alcohol concentration.

backlite: The rear or back window which spans from the driver's to passenger's side of the vehicle.[1]

backlite header: The structural body member which connects the upper portions of the rearmost driver and passenger pillars and forms the top edge of the backlite (back window).[1]

barrier equivalent velocity (BEV): The forward speed and corresponding kinetic energy with which a vehicle contacts a flat fixed rigid barrier at 90° with no rebound. *See* also equivalent energy speed (EES).

bicycle model: A two-wheeled vehicle used conceptually in vehicle dynamical studies to represent a four-wheeled vehicle where the side-to-side extent of the vehicle is neglected for simplicity.

bituminous pavement: A pavement comprising an upper layer or layers of aggregate with a bituminous binder (asphalt, coal tars, natural tars, etc.) and surface treatments such as chip seals, slurry seals, sand seals, and cape seals.

black box: *See* event data recorder.

blacktop: *See* bituminous pavement.

bobtail: A term used to refer to a truck tractor being driven without a semitrailer.

brake slip: *See* wheel slip.

braking distance: The distance to bring a vehicle to rest during brake application in straight forward motion. *See* stopping distance.

braking force: The force over the contact surface between a tire and a road in the direction of heading of the braked wheel that develops as a result of brake application.

braking force, peak: The largest force that can be developed during brake application as wheel slip is varied over the range of free rolling slip to locked wheel slip.

BTS: Bureau of Transportation Statistics.

Btu: British thermal unit.

bus: A vehicle designed to transport more than 15 passengers including the driver.

CAA: Clean Air Act.

CAFE: Corporate average fuel economy.

center of gravity (cg): That point of a body through which the resultant force of gravity (weight) acts irrespective of the orientation of the body.

center of impact: *See* impact center.

center of mass: *See* center of gravity.

central impact: An impact in which the contact impulse passes through the center of gravity. *See* oblique impact.

CFR: Code of Federal Regulations.

change in momentum: The difference of the momentum (product of mass and velocity) of a mass from one time to another; the difference of the momentum of a mass between the beginning and end of contact with another mass; the difference in the momentum of a system of bodies. *See also* conservation of momentum.

change of velocity: The difference between velocity vectors at two points in time. *See also* delta-v (ΔV).

chop: A broad shallow gouge in a road surface, beginning with an even, regular, deeper side and terminating in scratches and striations on the opposite shallower side; a depression in pavement made by strong, sharp metal edge moving under heavy pressure,[2] more commonly occurring at an impact event as opposed to postimpact trajectory.

clearance lamp: Light used on the front or rear of a motor vehicle to indicate overall width or height.

closing speed: The magnitude of the relative velocity between two vehicles at a given point in time as they approach each other; the magnitude of relative velocity between two vehicles as they approach each other at the beginning of an accident; normal component of the closing velocity. *See* approach speed.

closing velocity: The magnitude of the relative velocity between two vehicles at a given point in time as they approach each other; the magnitude of the relative velocity between two vehicles at the beginning of a crash; the vector difference between the velocity of the vehicle and the vehicle/object struck immediately before impact.

CO: Carbon monoxide.

CO_2: Carbon dioxide.

coefficient of friction: A number representing the resistance to sliding of two flat surfaces in contact; defined as the ratio of the resistance force to the normal force between the surfaces. *See* frictional drag factor.

coefficient of restitution: The ratio of the relative normal velocity at the time of separation to the relative normal velocity at the time of initial contact between the
impact center of two colliding bodies.

coefficient of rolling resistance: The ratio of the force of resistance to rolling with
zero slip to the vertical load of a wheel or vehicle. *See* rolling resistance.

collision: Sudden contact of a vehicle with an object or another vehicle, usually resulting in visible damage. *See* crash; impact.

collision deformation classification (CDC): A classification of the extent of deformation to an automobile, utility vehicle, pickup, or van from a crash.[3]

common contact point: *See* impact center.

common velocity conditions: Two independent conditions applicable to a collision
where at the time of separation the relative normal velocity component is zero (no
restitution) and the relative tangential component of velocity is zero (sliding has
ended).

concrete pavement: A solidified pavement with an upper layer of aggregate (such as
sand and stone) mixed with Portland cement paste binder.

conservation of momentum: The principle of physics for vehicles in dynamic contact
stating that in the absence of external forces, the sum of the preimpact momentum
is equal to the sum of the postimpact momentum of the vehicles.

contact damage: Deformation sustained in a vehicle from physical engagement with
another vehicle or object. *See* dynamic crush; induced damage; residual crush.

contact patch: The area or region of mutual contact between a tire and the surface
over which it rests or moves.

contact point: The point of intersection of the resultant contact impulse with the
intervehicular contact surface of each of two colliding vehicles. *See* impact center.

contact surface: *See* intervehicular contact surface.

coordinate system, vehicle: *See* three-axis vehicle coordinate system.

cornering coefficient: *See* sideslip coefficient.

crash: An event in which one or more vehicles make unintended contact with another
vehicle or other object producing injury, death, and/or property damage. *See* accident, vehicle; collision; impact.

CRASH3: an acronym for Calspan Reconstruction of Speeds on the Highway, Version
3; a method of reconstruction that uses the calculation of the crush energy of a collision and an approximate postimpact trajectory spinout simulation.

crash reconstruction: *See* accident reconstruction.

crashworthiness: The characteristics of a motor vehicle which represent occupant
protection of that vehicle in a specific collision.

critical speed: The maximum speed at which a vehicle can traverse a path with a specific radius of curvature without loss of directional control; the speed of a vehicle
undergoing a sudden turn maneuver at which the tires leave visible sideslip marks.

critical speed formula: A formula, $v_{cr} = \sqrt{fgR}$ that calculates the speed of a vehicle
from its radius of curvature, R, frictional drag coefficient, f, and acceleration of
gravity, g.

crumple zone: That portion of the front or rear of a vehicle designed to absorb energy
of a collision for the protection of the occupants.

crush area: Area defined by the original vehicle exterior and a crush profile.

crush equivalent speed: *See* energy equivalent speed (EES).

crush profile: The geometric shape in a specified plane (e.g., vertical, horizontal) that describes the vehicle damage resulting from an impact.

crush stiffness: *See* crush stiffness coefficient.

crush stiffness coefficient: An empirical quantity used in the calculation of the energy dissipated in a collision and associated with each vehicle's velocity change, ΔV. *See* CRASH3.

curb weight: The weight of a motor vehicle with standard equipment and maximum fuel capacity.

delta-t (Δt): A time interval associated with an event such as vehicle-to-vehicle contact; the time duration of impulse.

delta-v (ΔV): The difference or change of a velocity vector over a time interval; the difference in the velocity vector of the center of gravity of a vehicle between separation and first contact in a crash.

departure velocity: *See* separation velocity.

DGPS: Differential global positioning system.

direction of principal force (DOPF): *See* principal direction of force (PDOF).

divot: A piece of turf or sod torn up by dynamic contact.

DOE: U.S. Department of Energy.

DoT, DOT: United States Department of Transportation. *See* NHTSA.

drag factor, *f*: *See* frictional drag coefficient.

drag sled: A weighted device (whose bottom surface is covered with a portion of tire tread) which is pulled along a roadway surface and provides a sliding friction coefficient of that device and roadway surface by computing the ratio of the pull force to its weight.

dwt: Deadweight tons.

dynamic crush: The deformation formed by the external surface of a vehicle at any time during an impact, usually measured relative to the corresponding as-manufactured undeformed surface. *See* crush area; crush profile; residual crush.

eccentric impact: *See* oblique impact.

elastic deformation: Deformation which is fully recovered after an applied force is removed.

elastic impact: An idealized impact where the kinetic energy at separation equals the kinetic energy at the initiation of contact; a fully elastic impact is an impact where the coefficient of restitution is equal to one.

electronic control module (ECM): *See* electronic control unit (ECU).

electronic control unit (ECU): The computer in a vehicle that controls vehicle system operation, including functions such as engine operation, on board diagnostics (OBD), stability control, safety system operation, etc.

electronic data recorder (EDR): *See* event data recorder (EDR).

energy equivalent speed (EES): The speed and corresponding kinetic energy with which a vehicle must contact a fixed rigid object with no rebound for equivalence to conditions of another collision; for example, the energy may be equal to a specified level of residual crush; EES is the preferred term, broader than barrier equivalent velocity (BEV), equivalent barrier speed (EBS), and equivalent test speed (ETS).

energy equivalent velocity: *See* energy equivalent speed (EES); equivalent barrier speed (EBS).

EPA: U.S. Environmental Protection Agency.

equivalent barrier speed (EBS): The forward speed and corresponding kinetic energy with which a vehicle must contact a flat fixed rigid barrier at 90° with no rebound for equivalence to conditions of another collision; for example, the energy may be equal to a specified level of residual crush. *See also* equivalent energy speed (EES).

equivalent test deformation: *See* equivalent energy speed (EES).

equivalent test speed (ETS): ISO term, and is a nonpreferred term. *See* equivalent barrier speed (EBS); equivalent energy speed (EES).

ETC: Electronic toll collection.

ETMS: Enhanced Traffic Management System.

event data recorder (EDR): An onboard device capable of monitoring, recording, and displaying precrash, crash, and postcrash data and information from a vehicle, event, and driver.

FAA: Federal Aviation Administration.

FAF: Freight Analysis Framework.

farm tractor: A powered farm vehicle, designed to pull farm implements, such as a plow, farm trailer, manure spreader, etc.

FARS: Fatality Analysis Reporting System.

FARs: Federal Aviation Regulations.

FHWA: Federal Highway Administration.

first contact position: The position or location at an accident scene (measured relative to a coordinate system fixed to the earth) of a vehicle, pedestrian, or other object at the time it first has contact with another body in a collision.

first contact velocity: The velocity of the center of gravity of a vehicle, pedestrian, or other object at its first contact position.

fixed object: A stationary object such as a guardrail, bridge railing or abutment, construction barricade, impact attenuator, tree, embedded rock, utility pole, ditch side, steep earth or rock slope, culvert, fence, or building.[4]

flip: Movement of a vehicle from a place where the forward velocity of a part of the vehicle suddenly is stopped by an object below its center of gravity such as a curb, rail, or furrow, with the result that the ensuing rotation lifts the vehicle from the ground.

FMCSA: Federal Motor Carrier Safety Administration.

FMCSR: Federal Motor Carrier Safety Regulations.

FMVSS: Federal Motor Vehicle Safety Standard. *See* NHTSA.

forward projection pedestrian collision: A frontal collision of vehicle and pedestrian or cyclist in which the initial contact area is at or above the height of the center of gravity of the pedestrian or cyclist and in which a single impact with the frontal geometry of the vehicle causes the pedestrian or cyclist to be projected forward relative to the vehicle.

four point transformation: A photogrammetric technique whereby points positioned on a surface reasonably approximated by a plane with unknown locations can be located through the use of four additional points whose locations are known. *See* photogrammetry.

FRA: Federal Railroad Administration.

friction coefficient: *See* coefficient of friction.

frictional drag coefficient: An average, uniform (constant) value of a friction coefficient applied to a specific sliding event such as when an object slides from an initial speed to a stop over a distance, d, or during a speed change, ΔV.

frictional drag factor: *See* frictional drag coefficient.

frontal impact: An impact or collision involving the front of a vehicle.

FTA: Federal Transit Administration.

full trailer: A towed vehicle with a fixed rear axle and a front axle that pivots and is made to be pulled by a powered tow vehicle (an example is a farm trailer).

furrow: A channel in a loose or soft material, such as snow or soil, made by a vehicle tire or some other part of a moving vehicle.

GA: General aviation.

GAW: Gross axle weight is the total weight carried by an individual axle (front or rear) including the vehicle weight and cargo.

GAWR: Gross axle weight rating is the maximum allowable weight that can be carried by a single axle (front or rear).

GCW: Gross combined weight is the weight of a loaded vehicle plus the weight of a fully loaded semitrailer.

GCWR: Gross combined weight rating is the maximum allowable weight of a vehicle and loaded semitrailer.

GHG: Greenhouse gas.

GIS: Geographic information systems.

gouge, gouge mark: Pavement or ground scar deep enough to be easily felt with the fingers; see Fig. B.2. *See also* chop; groove.

GPS: Global positioning system.

groove: A long, narrow, pavement gouge or a channel in a pavement.

gross vehicle weight: The combined weight of a vehicle and its cargo.

Figure B.2

gross vehicle weight rating (GVWR): The upper limit of combined weight and cargo for a vehicle established by design, regulation, or both.

HAPs: Hazardous air pollutants.

heading angle: The angle between a reference axis fixed in the vehicle and a reference axis fixed in the roadway, giving a measure of vehicle yaw rotation or directional orientation relative to the roadway.[5]

head-on impact: Frontal impact where the PDOF is at or near zero degrees.

HELP: Heavy Vehicle Electronic License Plate.

HMIS: Hazardous Materials Information System.

HPMS: Highway Performance Monitoring System.

HSR: High-speed rail.

HTF: Highway Trust Fund.

hydroplaning: A phenomenon in which a layer of fluid (usually water) on a roadway separates the load-bearing surface of one or more tires of a moving vehicle from the road surface and causes a full loss of traction (longitudinal) and steering (transverse) force components.

IBET: Intermodal Bottleneck Evaluation Tool.

impact: The striking of one body against another; short-duration, high-force contact of two objects; a collision of a vehicle with another vehicle, a pedestrian, or some other object. *See* collision; crash.

impact center: The point of intersection of the contact impulse and the intervehicular contact surface for an impact. *See* contact point.

impact force (lever arm) moment arm: *See* impulse moment arm.

impact velocity: The velocity of an object's center of gravity relative to a coordinate system fixed in the earth during an impact. *See* preimpact velocity, postimpact velocity.

impulse: A combination of force, F, and time, τ, defined as a mathematical integral, $\int F d\tau$, of the force over a specific time duration.

impulse moment arm: The perpendicular distance from an object's center of gravity to the line of action of an impulse; see Fig. B.3.

Figure B.3

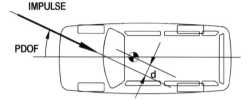

impulse ratio: The ratio of the tangential and normal impulse components in planar impact mechanics. *See* impulse.

induced damage: Residual deformation caused without direct contact by virtue of being adjacent to deformation caused by direct contact. *See* residual crush.

inertia: A physical property of a body that represents its resistance to translation.

initial contact: The point in time and space when two objects begin to touch or interact with no significant force. The beginning of an impact.

intervehicular contact surface: A single, planar surface that represents the average (over time and space) deformed contact surface between two vehicles or a vehicle and barrier.

intervehicular crush plane: *See* intervehicular contact surface.

intrusion: Reduction of the precrash space within the passenger space compartment.[6]

ISO: International Organization for Standardization, Geneva, Switzerland.

ISTEA: Intermodal Surface Transportation Efficiency Act.

ITS: Intelligent transportation system.

kph: Kilometers per hour, km/h.

leading edge: The foremost part of a vehicle with respect to the vehicle's motion and attitude.

light vehicle: An automobile, passenger van, pickup truck, or sport utility vehicle.

LNG: Liquefied natural gas.

LPG: Liquefied petroleum gas.

LTV: Light trucks and vans.

maximum crush depth: Deepest part of a crush profile. *See* dynamic crush; residual crush.

maximum engagement: The point in time when the maximum dynamic crush occurs.

moment of inertia: A physical property of a body that represents its resistance to rotational acceleration.

mpg: Miles per gallon.

mph: Miles per hour.

MUTCD: Manual on Uniform Traffic Control Devices.

NASS: National Automotive Sampling System.

NCAP: New Car Assessment Program (DoT, NHTSA).

neutral steer: When a vehicle, traveling on a circular path at constant speed and a constant front wheel steer angle, is accelerated, it will remain on a path with the same radius, tend to increase its radius or tend to decrease its radius, these are defined as neutral steer, understeer, and oversteer, respectively. *See* oversteer; understeer.

NHTSA: National Highway Traffic Safety Administration. *See* DoT.

NO₂: Nitrogen dioxide.

NOx: Nitrogen oxides.

NPTS: Nationwide Personal Transportation Survey.

NTL: National Transportation Library.

NTSB: National Transportation Safety Board.

OBD: Onboard diagnostics.

oblique impact: An impact in which the contact impulse does not pass through the center of gravity. *See* central impact.

occupant compartment: That portion of a vehicle's interior designed for the accomodation of passengers.

offset: The distance between the longitudinal heading axes of two vehicles in frontal contact; see Fig. B.4. *See also* overlap.

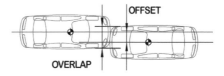

Figure B.4

OPEC: Organization of Petroleum Exporting Countries.

overhang, front rear: The longitudinal dimension of a vehicle from the center of the front/rear wheels to the foremost/rearmost point on the vehicle including bumper, bump guards, tow hooks, and/or rub strips if standard equipment.

overlap: The length of mutual contact damage; see Fig. B.4. *See also* offset.

override: A condition in a collision where the main structural members, such as a bumper, of the striking vehicle are above the main structural members, such as frame rails, of the struck vehicle; see Fig. B.5. *See also* underride.

Figure B.5

oversteer: When a vehicle, traveling on a circular path at constant speed and a constant front wheel steer angle, is accelerated, it will remain on a path with the same radius, tend to increase its radius, or tend to decrease its radius; these are defined as neutral steer, understeer, and oversteer, respectively. *See* neutral steer; understeer.

PDR time: *See* perception-decision-reaction time.

perception-decision-reaction time: The time required by a person to complete a response to an event or stimulus.

photogrammetry: The process of determining the quantitative dimensional information of objects in two or three dimensions through the process of recording, interpreting, and transforming measurements from flat photographic images.

pitch, roll, yaw: Terms that distinguish rotations of a vehicle about three perpendicular axes with origin at the vehicle's center of gravity; pitch is rotation about the horizontal side-to-side axis, roll is rotation about a horizontal front-to-rear axis, and yaw is rotation about the vertical axis; see Fig. B.6. *See also* yaw angle.

Figure B.6

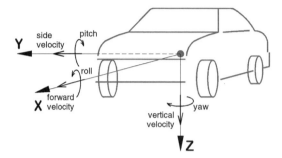

planar impact: An impact in which all forces, moments, and motion take place in a plane.

plastic impact: An impact with little or no rebound at the end of impact; a perfectly plastic impact is where the coefficient of restitution is equal to zero.

pmt: Passenger-miles of travel.

point mass: An idealized concept from mechanics in which an object is considered to have mass but no extent, no finite dimensions, and, as a consequence, its rotation is irrelevant. *See* rigid body.

point of contact: The point of intersection of the contact impulse and the intervehicular contact surface during an impact. *See also* direction of principal force (DOPF); first contact position; impact center; principal direction of force (PDOF).

point of impact: Location on road or other surface where objects such as vehicles collided.

postcollision trajectory: *See* postimpact trajectory.

postcrash damage: Damage existing to a vehicle after it comes to rest, including damage that may result during rescue, towing, and salvage operations.

postimpact speed: The magnitude of the velocity of an object in a collision at the time of separation or end of contact. *See* postimpact velocity; separation speed.

postimpact trajectory: The path of the center of gravity of a vehicle from impact to rest.

postimpact velocity: The velocity of an object in a collision at the time of separation or end of contact. *See* postimpact speed; separation speed.

preimpact velocity: The velocity of a vehicle in a collision at the instant of its initial contact.

principle direction of force (PDOF): The direction of the line of action of the contact impulse in a planar collision expressed in degrees, measured positive clockwise from the longitudinal axis of a vehicle; see Fig. B.3.

PUV: Personal-use vehicle.

radius of gyration: The square root of the quotient of the moment of inertia and the mass of a rigid body. *See* moment of inertia.

reaction time: *See* perception-decision-reaction time.

residual crush: The permanent deformation formed by the nominal external surface of a vehicle caused by an impact, usually measured relative to the corresponding as-manufactured undeformed surface. *See* crush area; crush profile.

rest position: The location of the center of gravity of a vehicle following an accident measured relative to a coordinate system fixed in the earth.

reverse projection photogrammetry: The photogrammetric procedure of inserting a transparency that contains outlines of transient and fixed objects of a scene into a camera for the purpose of determining the position and orientation of the camera at the time the original photograph was taken and to facilitate the relocation of the transient information.

RFG: Reformulated gasoline.

rigid body: A concept from mechanics in which an object is considered to have mass and dimensions (such as length, width, radius, etc.) that remain constant and which provide resistance to rotation. *See* moment of inertia; point mass.

roll: *See* pitch, roll, yaw; yaw angle.

roll out: Part or all of a postimpact trajectory in which little or no sideslip of a vehicle's wheels occurs. *See* spinout.

rolling resistance: The retarding force of a freely rolling wheel due to interaction with a contact surface, parallel to the heading axis of a wheel of a moving vehicle; also:

- A force opposite to the direction of travel resulting from deformation of a rolling tire;[7,8]
- Several resistances to motion that may be classified as due to friction in the wheel bearings, friction in the tire walls and tread as they flex when rolling along the road surface, deformation of road surface, impact resistance due to irregularities of road surface, and churning of air by wheels.

rollover: Vehicle motion in which its wheels leave the road surface and at least one side or top of the vehicle contacts the ground. *See* flip; vault.

ROR: Run-off-the-road.

SAE coordinate system: *See* three-axis vehicle coordinate system.

scrape: A mark on a surface that is wider than it is deep and that can usually be felt with fingers.

scratch: A light and usually irregular scar made on a hard surface, such as paving, by a sliding metal part without great pressure.[2] Scratches are visible but not normally distinguishable to the touch.

SCTG: Standard Classification of Transported Goods.

scuff marks: Relatively short marks made by a moving tire on a road or other surface in an erratic fashion with no specific, consistent features; for example, acceleration scuff, impact scuff, flat tire mark; see Fig. B.2. *See also* skid mark; yaw mark.

SDM: Sensing and diagnostic module. *See* event data recorder (EDR).

second impact: An impact between an occupant and an interior surface of a vehicle caused by and following an impact between the vehicle and another object.

secondary impact: A second or subsequent impact between the same two vehicles during a crash.

semi: *See* farm tractor; semitrailer; truck tractor.

semitrailer: A semitrailer is a towed vehicle equipped with one or more axles to the rear of its laden center of gravity and whose front end forms part of a pivot joint attached to a truck tractor or other powered tow vehicle (examples are cargo, recreational, boat, and livestock trailers).

separation speed: The speed at the time of loss of contact of two vehicles in a collision; it can refer to the speed of the centers of gravity or of the contact point.

separation velocity: The vector velocity at the time of loss of contact of two vehicles in a collision; it can refer to the speed of the centers of gravity or at the contact point.

service brake system: The primary brake system used for slowing and stopping a vehicle.

SI system of units: Metric system (Système International d'Unités).

side rail: The outermost edge on the side of a vehicle's roof connecting the upper ends of the A, B, C, and D pillars.

sideslip: Lateral/transverse translation of a vehicle perpendicular to its heading; see Fig. B.7. *See also* wheel slip.

Figure B.7

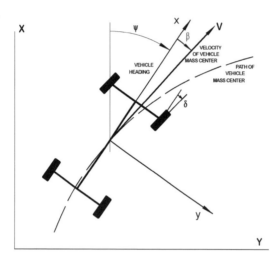

sideslip angle, tire: *See* wheel sideslip angle.

sideslip angle, vehicle: The angle between the vehicle's heading and its velocity vector (β in Fig. B.7). *See* sideslip.

sideslip coefficient: The slope of the initial linear portion of the sideforce-sideslip curve of a tire.

sideslip stiffness: *See* sideslip coefficient.

sideswipe collision: A collision of a vehicle where sliding (relative tangential motion) over the intervehicular contact surface does not end at or before separation. *See* common velocity conditions.

simulation: The use of mathematics and mechanics, usually done using a computer, to represent, reproduce, or model a physical process.

skid number: A number representing tire-pavement frictional drag determined by measurements made according to standard equipment, conditions, and procedures and usually stated as 100 times a friction coefficient.

skid mark: A friction mark on a pavement made by a tire that is sliding without rotation and, if along the heading axis of the tire, that displays a tread pattern.

sliding friction coefficient: *See* coefficient of friction.

slip: *See* sideslip; wheel slip.

slip angle, tire: *See* wheel sideslip angle.

slip stiffness: *See* wheel slip coefficient.

SO_2: Sulfur dioxide.

speed: The rate of change of vehicle displacement with respect to time; the magnitude of velocity.

spinout: A descriptive term for postimpact vehicle motion including significant yaw rotation. *See* postimpact trajectory.

static crush: *See* residual crush.

static stability factor: A dimensionless number meant to indicate the resistance of a vehicle to roll over. The number is calculated using the formula $SSF = T/2h$, where T is the vehicle track width and h is the height of the center of gravity of the vehicle.

stiffness coefficient: *See* crush stiffness coefficient.

stopping distance: The distance taken by a driver to bring a vehicle to rest in straight forward motion by braking, including the distance traveled during perception-decision-reaction time prior to brake application. *See* braking distance.

STRAHNET: Strategic Highway Network.

striations: Periodic stripes that appear transverse to the tire marks from a yawing vehicle.

superelevation: A side-to-side slope of a road measured in degrees or percent.

supplemental restraint system: An interior vehicle device that inflates when actuated by accelerometers and/or crash sensors and acts between an occupant and an interior vehicle surface to prevent injury due to sudden contact. *See* air bag.

SUV: Sport utility vehicle.

TEA-21: Transportation Equity Act for the 21st Century.

theodolite: A surveying instrument with a rotating telescope for measuring horizontal and vertical angles.

three-axis vehicle coordinate system: Fig. B.6 shows the standard, three-dimensional vehicle coordinate system.

throw distance: The distance a pedestrian is propelled (in the direction of vehicle motion at impact) between the location of the pedestrian at first contact and pedestrian's rest position.

tire marks: General term for marks on a surface generated by tires; can be scuffs, skids, yaw marks, prints, etc.

tire sideslip angle: *See* wheel sideslip angle.

total station: An electronic device that measures the angle of inclination, angle of rotation, and distance to point in space.

tractor: *See* farm tractor; truck tractor.

tractor, semitrailer: A truck tractor (cab) with two or more axles pulling a semitrailer.

tractor trailer: A truck tractor (cab) with two or more axles pulling a trailer.

trailer: A trailer is a towed vehicle equipped with two axles, the front axle is attached to the tow vehicle and pivoted for turning whereas the rear axle is fixed.

trailing edge: The term used to describe that portion of a vehicle component (such as door, window, fender, quarter, etc.) which is closest to the rear of the vehicle; the rearmost part of a vehicle with respect to a vehicle's motion and attitude.

trajectory: The path of the center of gravity of a body as it moves through space; usually associated with coordinates of the center of gravity as a function of time; see Fig. B.7.

trip point: That location along a ground surface at which the motion of a vehicle component is suddenly halted followed by a flip, rollover, or vault.

truck deformation classification (TDC): A classification system used to appropriately describe a collision-damaged truck. It consists of seven alphanumeric characters arranged in specific order to form a descriptive composite of the vehicle damage.[6]

truck tractor: A motor vehicle designed for pulling semitrailers. Basic types are cab-over-engine and conventional.

underride: A condition in a collision in which the main structural components of one vehicle are below the main structural components of the other vehicle; see Fig. B.8. *See also* override.

Figure B.8

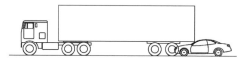

understeer: When a vehicle, traveling along a circular path on a flat level surface with a constant speed and a constant front wheel steer angle, is accelerated, it will remain on a path with the same radius, tend to increase its radius, or tend to decrease its radius; these are defined as neutral steer, understeer, and oversteer, respectively. *See* neutral steer; oversteer.

USGS: U.S. Geological Survey.

vault: A roll or pitch motion of a vehicle made following loss of ground contact.

vehicle coordinate system: See Figs. B.6 and B.7. *See also* three-axis vehicle coordinate system.

vehicle length: The maximum dimension measured longitudinally between the foremost point and the rearmost point in the vehicle, including bumper, bumper guards, tow hooks, and/or rub strips, if standard equipment.[1] Also known as overall length (OAL).

vehicle width: The maximum dimension measured between the widest point on the vehicle, excluding exterior mirrors, flexible mud flaps, and marker lamps, but including bumpers, moldings, sheet metal protrusions, or dual wheels if standard equipment.[1] Also known as overall width (OAW).

velocity: The rate of change of displacement with both a magnitude and direction; the magnitude of velocity is referred to as speed.

velocity-time curve (v-т or v-t curve): A graphical depiction of velocity of the center of gravity of a vehicle as it changes over time.

vmt: Vehicle-miles of travel.

VOC: Volatile organic compounds.

wheel base: The perpendicular distance between axes through front and rear wheel centerlines of a vehicle. In case of dual axles, the distance is to the midpoint of the centerlines of the dual axles.

wheel sideslip angle: The angle between a wheel's heading axis (x-axis) and direction of the velocity vector of the center of the wheel.

wheel slip: The ratio of the forward velocity of a tire at the road contact patch to the forward velocity at the center of the wheel (for braking) or the ratio of the forward velocity of a tire at the center of the wheel to the forward velocity at the road contact patch (for traction or acceleration).

wheel slip coefficient: The slope of the initial linear portion of the forward force-wheel slip curve of a tire.

windshield header: The structural body member which connects the upper portions of the left and right A-pillars and is above the top edge of the windshield.

wrap pedestrian collision: A frontal collision of vehicle and pedestrian or cyclist in which initial contact occurs at a point below the center of gravity of the pedestrian or cyclist and where the frontal geometry of the vehicle allows the pedestrian to move rearward relative to the vehicle and strike another portion of the vehicle such as a windshield. The latter impact causes the pedestrian or cyclist to develop an airborne trajectory followed by an impact with the ground.

yaw: *See* pitch, roll, yaw; yaw angle.

yaw angle: The angle between the heading of a vehicle and a fixed reference; see Fig. B.7.

yaw mark: A tire mark caused by a sideslipping tire often showing a striped pattern called striations.

yaw moment of inertia: The moment of inertia about a vertical axis of a vehicle. *See* moment of inertia; radius of gyration

yaw rate: Angular velocity about the z-axis; see Fig. B.6.

References

CHAPTER I

1. Fricke, L.B., "Traffic Accident Reconstruction," *Traffic Accident Investigation Manual*, vol. 2, Northwestern University Traffic Institute, Evanston, IL, 1990.
2. Goudie, D.W., J.J. Bowler, C.A. Brown, B.E. Heinrichs, C.A. Brown, and G.P. Siegmund, "Tire Friction During Locked Wheel Braking," Paper No. 2000-01-1314, SAE International, Warrendale, PA, 2000.
3. Taylor, J.R., *An Introduction to Error Analysis*, University Science Books, Mill Valley, CA, 1982.
4. Beers, Y., *Introduction to the Theory of Error*, Addison-Wesley, Reading, MA, 1957.
5. Taylor, B.N., and C.E. Kuyatt, "Guidelines for Evaluating and Expressing the Uncertainty of NIST Measurement Results," NIST Technical Note 1297, National Institute of Standards and Technology, U.S. Department of Commerce, Gaithersburg, MD, 1994.
6. Mandel, J., *The Statistical Analysis of Experimental Data*, Dover Publications, New York, NY, 1964.
7. Rizenbergs, R.L., J.L. Burchett, and L.A. Warren, "Relation of Accidents and Pavement Friction on Rural, Two-Lane Roads," Transportation Research Record 633, Pavement Surface Properties and Performance, National Academy of Science, Washington, DC, 1977.
8. Guttman, I., S.S. Wilks, and J.S. Hunter, *Introductory Engineering Statistics*, John Wiley, New York, NY, 1982.
9. Montgomery, D.C., and G.C. Runger, *Applied Statistics and Probability for Engineers*, John Wiley, New York, 1999.
10. Brach, R.M., and P.F. Dunn, *Uncertainty Analysis for Forensic Science*, Lawyers and Judges Publishing Co., Tucson, AZ, 2004.

CHAPTER 2

1. "Vehicle Dynamics Terminology, SAE Recommended Practice," SAE Standard J670e, SAE International, Warrendale, PA, 1976.

2. Milliken, W.F., and D.L. Milliken, *Race Car Vehicle Dynamics*, SAE International, Warrendale, PA, 1995.

3. Gim, G., and P.E. Nikravesh, "An Analytical Model of Pneumatic Tyres for Vehicle Dynamic Simulations. Part 1: Pure Slips," *International Journal of Vehicle Design*, vol. 11, no. 6, Inderscience, Geneva, Switzerland, 1990.

4. Gim, G., and P.E. Nikravesh, "An Analytical Model of Pneumatic Tyres for Vehicle Dynamic Simulations. Part 2: Comprehensive Slips," *International Journal of Vehicle Design*, vol. 12, no. 1, Inderscience, Geneva, Switzerland, 1991.

5. Gim, G., and P.E. Nikravesh, "An Analytical Model of Pneumatic Tyres for Vehicle Dynamic Simulations. Part 3: Validation Against Experimental Data," *International Journal of Vehicle Design*, vol. 12, no. 2, Inderscience, Geneva, Switzerland, 1991.

6. Clark, S.K. [ed.], "Mechanics of Pneumatic Tires," DOT HS 805 952, U.S. Department of Transportation, National Highway Traffic Safety Administration, Washington, DC, 1981.

7. Wong, J.Y., *Theory of Ground Vehicles*, John Wiley and Sons, Inc., New York, NY, 1993.

8. Nielsen, L., and T. Sandberg, "A New Model For Rolling Resistance of Pneumatic Tires," Paper 2002-01-1200, SAE International, Warrendale, PA, 2002.

9. Adler, Ulrich [ed.], *Automotive Handbook*, 3rd edition, Robert Bosch, Stuttgart, Germany, 1993.

10. Warner, C Y., G.C. Smith, M.B. James, and G.J. Germane, "Friction Applications in Accident Reconstruction," Paper 830612, SAE International, Warrendale, PA, 1983.

11. "Statement of Work, Truck Tire Characterization Phase 1 Part 2," Cooperative Research, Funding by NHTSA (National Highway Traffic Safety Administration) Contract No. DTNH22-92-C-17189, SAE International, Warrendale, PA, 1995.

12. Nguyen, P.K., and E.R. Case, "Tire Friction Models and Their Effect on Simulated Vehicle Dynamics," Proceedings of a Symposium on Commercial Vehicle Braking and Handling, UM-HSRI-PF-75-6, Ann Arbor, MI, 1975.

13. Schuring, D.J., W. Pelz, and M.G. Pottinger, "A Model for Combined Tire Cornering and Braking Forces," Paper 960180, SAE International, Warrendale, PA, 1996.

14. Brach, R. Matthew, and Raymond M. Brach, "Modeling Combined Braking and Steering Forces," Paper 2000-01-0357, SAE International, Warrendale, PA, 2000.

15. Fiala, E., "Seitenkräfte am rollenden Luftreifen" (Lateral Forces at the Rolling Pneumatic Tire), no. 96, VDI-Zeitschrift, 1954, p. 973.

16. Nicolas, V.T., and T.R. Comstock, "Predicting Directional Behavior of Tractor Semi-trailers When Wheel Anti-Skid Brake Systems Are Used," Paper No. 72—WA/Aut-16, Winter Annual Meeting, November 26–30, ASME, New York, NY, 1972.

17. Bakker, E., L. Nyborg, and H.B. Pacejka, "Tyre Modeling for Use in Vehicle Dynamic Studies," Paper 870421, SAE International, Warrendale, PA, 1987.

18. Schuring, D.J., W. Pelz, and M.G. Pottinger, "The BNPS Model·—An Automated Implementation of the 'Magic Formula' Concept," Paper 931909, SAE International, Warrendale, PA, 1993.

19. d'Entremont, K.L., "The Behavior of Tire-Force Model Parameters Under Extreme Operating Conditions," Paper 970558, SAE International, Warrendale, PA, 1997.

20. Blythe, W., and T.D. Day, "Single Vehicle Wet Road Loss of Control; Effects of Tire Tread Depth and Placement," Paper 2002-01-0553, SAE International, Warrendale, PA, 2002.

21. Browne, A.L. "Mathematical Analysis for Pneumatic Tire Hydroplaning," ASTM STP 583, American Society for Testing Materials, West Conshohocken, PA, 1975, pp. 75–94.

CHAPTER 3

1. Gillespie, T., *Fundamentals of Vehicle Dynamics*, SAE International, Warrendale, PA, 1992.
2. Wong, J.Y., *Theory of Ground Vehicles*, John Wiley, New York, NY, 2001.
3. Olson, P.L., *Forensic Aspects of Driver Perception and Response*, Lawyers and Judges Publishing, Tucson, AZ, 1996.
4. Dewar, R.E., and P.L. Olson, *Human Factors in Traffic Safety*, Lawyers and Judges Publishing, Tucson, AZ, 2002.
5. Muttart, J.W., "Development and Evaluation of Driver Response Time Predictors Based Upon Meta Analysis," Paper 2003-01-0885, SAE International, Warrendale, PA, 2003.
6. Tustin, B.H., H. Richards, H. McGee, and R. Peterson, *Railroad-Highway Grade Crossing Handbook*, 2nd ed., FHWA TS-86-215, Federal Highway Administration, McLean, VA, 1986.
7. Reed, W.S., and A.T. Keskin, "A Comparison of Emergency Braking Characteristics of Passenger Cars," Paper 880231, SAE International, Warrendale, PA, 1988.

CHAPTER 4

1. Brach, R.M., "An Analytical Assessment of the Critical Speed Formula," Paper 970857, SAE International, Warrendale, PA, 1997.
2. Fittano, D.A., and J. Puig-Suari, "Using a Genetic Algorithm to Optimize Vehicle Simulation Trajectories: Determining Initial Velocity of a Vehicle in Yaw," Paper 2000-01-1616, SAE International, Warrendale, PA, 2000.
3. Sledge, N.H., and K.M. Marshek, "Formulas for Estimating Vehicle Critical Speed from Yaw Marks—A Review," Paper 971147, SAE International, Warrendale, PA, 1997.
4. Semon, M., "Determination of Speed from Yaw Marks," Chapter 4 in *Forensic Accident Investigation: Motor Vehicles*, Bohan and Damask [ed.], Michie Butterworth, Charlottesville, VA, 1995.
5. Dickerson, C.P., M.W. Arndt, S.M. Arndt, and G.A. Mowry, "Evaluation of Vehicle Velocity Predictions Using the Critical Speed Formula," Paper 950137, SAE International, Warrendale, PA, 1995.
6. Lambourn, R.F., "The Calculation of Motor Car Speeds from Curved Tire Marks," *Journal of the Forensic Science Society* (U.K.), 29, 1989, pp. 371–386.
7. Fricke, L.B., *Traffic Accident Reconstruction, Traffic Accident Investigation Manual*, vol. 2, Northwestern University Traffic Institute, Evanston, IL, 1990.
8. Garber, N.J., and L.A. Hoel, *Traffic and Highway Engineering*, PWS Publishing Co., Boston, 1997.
9. Baxter, A.T., and J.R. Mentzer, "Critical Speed Field Testing of a Passenger Vehicle," Annual Meeting of the National Association of Traffic Accident Reconstructionists and Investigators, Atlantic City, NJ, 1991.
10. Milliken, W.F., and D.L. Milliken, *Race Car Vehicle Dynamics*, SAE International, Warrendale, PA, 1995.
11. Wong, J.Y., *Theory of Ground Vehicles*, John Wiley & Sons, Inc., New York, NY, 1993.
12. Sledge, N.H., and K.M. Marshek, "Vehicle Critical Speed Formula—Values for the Coefficient of Friction—A Review," Paper 971148, SAE International, Warrendale, PA, 1997.
13. Shelton, Sgt. Thomas, "Validation of the Estimation of Speed from Critical Speed Scuffmarks," *Accident Reconstruction Journal,* Waldorf, MD, January/February 1995.

14. Heusser, R., J. Hunter, and D. Martin, "Critical Speed Evaluation with Acceleration/Deceleration," Newsletter of WATAI (Washington Association of Traffic Accident Investigators), Bellevue, WA, 1994.

15. Martinez, L., "Estimating Speed from Yawmarks—An Empirical Study," *Accident Reconstruction Journal*, Waldorf, MD, May/June 1993.

CHAPTER 5

1. Winkler, C.B., D. Blower, R.D. Ervin, and R.M. Chalasani, "Rollover of Heavy Commercial Vehicles," RR-004, SAE International, Warrendale, PA, 2000.

2. Orlowski, K.F., R.T. Bundorf, and E.A. Moffatt, "Rollover Crash Tests—The Influence of Roof Strength on Injury Mechanics," Paper 851734, SAE International, Warrendale, PA, 1985.

3. Bahling, G.S., R.T. Bundorf, G.S. Kaspzyk, E.A. Moffatt, K.F. Orlowski, and J.E. Stocke, "Rollover and Drop Tests—The Influence of Roof Strength on Injury Mechanics Using Belted Dummies," Paper 902314, SAE International, Warrendale, PA, 1990.

4. Moffatt, E.A., and J. Padmanaban, "The Relationship Between Vehicle Roof Strength and Occupant Injury in Rollover Crash Data," 39th Annual Proceedings, Association for the Advancement of Automotive Medicine, Chicago, IL, October 1995.

5. Rains, G.C., and J.N. Kanianthra, "Determination of the Significance of Roof Crush on Head and Neck Injury to Passenger Vehicle Occupants in Rollover Crashes," Paper 950655, SAE International, Warrendale, PA, 1995.

6. "Occupant Crash Protection," 10-01-2002, Code of Federal Regulations, Title 49, Chapter 5, Part 571.208.

7. Larson, R.E., J.W. Smith, S.M. Werner, and G.F. Fowler, "Vehicle Rollover Testing in Recreating Rollover Collisions," Paper 2000-01-1641, SAE International, Warrendale, PA, 2000.

8. Ponticel, P., "Dynamic Rollover Testing On the Way," Automotive Engineering International, SAE International, Warrendale, PA, November 2003, pp. 26–28.

9. Cooperrider, N.K., T.M. Thomas, and S.A. Hammoud, "Testing and Analysis of Vehicle Rollover Behavior," Paper 900366, SAE International, Warrendale, PA, 1990.

10. Cooperrider, N.K., S.A. Hammoud, and J. Colwell, "Characteristics of Soil-Tripped Rollovers," Paper 980022, SAE International, Warrendale, PA, 1998.

11. D'Entremont, K.L., "The Effects of Light-Vehicle Design Parameters in Tripped-Rollover Maneuvers—A Statistical Approach Using an Experimentally Validated Computer Model," Paper 950315, SAE International, Warrendale, PA, 1995.

12. Dickerson, C.P., S.M. Arndt, G.A. Mowry, and M.W. Arndt, "Effects of Outrigger Design on Vehicle Dynamics," Paper 940226, SAE International, Warrendale, PA, 1994.

13. Carter, J.W., J.L. Habberstad, and J. Croteau, "A Comparison of the Controlled Rollover Impact System (CRIS) with the J2114 Rollover Dolly," Paper 2002-01-0694, SAE International, Warrendale, PA, 2002.

14. Orlowski, K.R., E.A. Moffatt, R.T. Bundorf, and M.P. Holcomb, "Reconstruction of Rollover Collisions," Paper 890857, SAE International, Warrendale, PA, 1989.

15. Martinez, J.E., and R.J. Schlueter, "A Primer on the Reconstruction and Presentation of Rollover Accidents," Paper 960647, SAE International, Warrendale, PA, 1996.

16. Baker, J.S., and L.B. Fricke, *The Traffic Accident Investigation Manual*, Northwestern University Traffic Institute, Evanston, IL, 1986.

17. Fay, R.J., and J.D. Scott, "New Dimensions in Rollover Analysis," Paper 1999-01-0448, SAE International, Warrendale, PA, 1999.

18. Jones, I.S., and L.A. Wilson, "Techniques for the Reconstruction of Rollover Accidents Involving Sport Utility Vehicles, Light Trucks and Minivans," Paper 2000-01-0851, SAE International, Warrendale, PA, 2000.

19. Cliff, W.E., J.M. Lawrence, B.E. Heinrichs, and T.R. Fricker, "Yaw Testing of an Instrumented Vehicle with and without Braking," Paper 2004-01-1187, SAE International, Warrendale, PA, 2004.

20. Clark, S.K. [ed.], *Mechanics of Pneumatic Tires*, DOT HS 805 952, Washington, DC, August 1981.

21. Pacejka, H.B., *Tire and Vehicle Dynamics*, Butterworth-Heinemann, Woburn, MA, 2002.

22. Bernard, J., J. Shannon, and M. Vanderploeg, "Vehicle Rollover on Smooth Surfaces," Paper 891991, SAE International, Warrendale, PA, 1989.

23. Gillespie, T., *Fundamentals of Vehicle Dynamics*, SAE International, Warrendale, PA, 1992.

24. Hac, A., "Rollover Stability Index Including Effects of Suspension Design," Paper 2002-01-0965, SAE International, Warrendale, PA, 2002.

25. Erdogan, L., D. Guenther, and G. Heydinger, "Suspension Parameter Measurement Using Side-Pull Test to Enhance Modeling of Vehicle Roll," Paper 1999-01-1323, SAE International, Warrendale, PA, 1999.

26. Heydinger, G., N.J. Durisek, D.A. Coovert, D.A. Guenther, and S.J. Novak, "The Design of a Vehicle Inertia Measurement Facility," Paper 950309, SAE International, Warrendale, PA, 1995.

27. Lund, Y.I., and J.E. Bernard, "Analysis of Simple Rollover Metrics," Paper 950306, SAE International, Warrendale, PA, 1995.

28. Marine, M.C., J.L. Wirth, and T.M. Thomas, "Characteristics of On-Road Rollovers," Paper 1999-01-0122, SAE International, Warrendale, PA, 1999.

29. Rosenthal, T.J., H.T. Szostak, and R.W. Allen, "User's Guide and Program Description For Tripped Roll Over Vehicle Simulation," DOT HS 807 140 Final Report, Washington, DC, 1987.

30. Day, T.D., and J.T. Garvey, "Applications and Limitations of 3-Dimensional Vehicle Rollover Simulation," Paper 2000-01-0852, SAE International, Warrendale, PA, 2000.

31. Tamny, S., "Friction Induced Rollover from Lift-Off to Launch," Paper 2000-01-1649, SAE International, Warrendale, PA, 2000.

32. Chace, M.A., and T.J. Wielenga, "A Test and Simulation Process to Improve Rollover Resistance," Paper 1999-01-0125, SAE International, Warrendale, PA, 1999.

33. Meyer, S.E., M. Davis, S. Forrest, D.Chng, and B. Herbst, "Accident Reconstruction of Rollovers—A Methodology," Paper 2000-01-0853, SAE International, Warrendale, PA, 2000.

34. Kaplan, M., D. Bilek, S. Kaplan, D. Vellos, and M.G. Gilbert, "An Examination of Rim Gouging and Its Relation to On-Road Vehicle Rollover," *SOARce*, Society of Accident Reconstructionists, Wheat Ridge, CO, Spring 2004.

35. Bready, J.E., A.A. May, and D. Allsop, "Physical Evidence Analysis and Roll Velocity Effects in Rollover Accident Reconstruction," Paper 2001-01-1284, SAE International, Warrendale, PA, 2001.

36. Stevens, D.C., "Passenger Vehicle Rollover Reconstruction: Investigation, Analysis and Presentation of Results," Passenger Vehicle Rollover TOPTEC: Causes, Prevention and Injury Prevalence, April 22–23, Scottsdale, AZ, SAE International, Warrendale, PA, 2002.

37. Chen, H.F., and D. Guenther, "Modeling of Rollover Sequences," Paper 931976, SAE International, Warrendale, PA, 1993.

CHAPTER 6

1. Brach, R.M., *Mechanical Impact Dynamics*, John Wiley & Sons, New York, NY, 1991.

2. Varat, M.S., and S.E. Husher, "Vehicle Impact Response Analysis through the Use of Accelerometer Data," Paper 2000-01-0850, SAE International, Warrendale, PA, 2000.

3. Prasad, A.K., "Coefficient of Restitution of Vehicle Structures and its Use in Estimating the Total ΔV in Automobile Collisions," AMD Vol 126/BED Vol 19, Crashworthiness and Occupant Protection in Transportation Systems, ASME, New York, NY, 1991.

4. McHenry, B.G., and R.R. McHenry, "SMAC-97—Refinement of the Collision Algorithm," Paper 970947, SAE International, Warrendale, PA, 1997.

5. McHenry, B.G., and R.R. McHenry, "CRASH-97—Refinement of the Trajectory Solution Procedure," Paper 970949, SAE International, Warrendale, PA, 1997.

6. McHenry, B.G., and R.R. McHenry, "Effects of Restitution in the Application of Crush Coefficients," Paper 970960, SAE International, Warrendale, PA, 1997.

7. Brach, R.M., "Restitution in Point Collisions," in *Computational Aspects of Impact and Penetration*, R.F. Kulak and L. Schwer [ed.], Elmepress International, Lausanne Switzerland, 1991.

8. Stronge, W.J., *Impact Mechanics*, Cambridge University Press, Cambridge, U.K., 2000.

9. Brogliato, B., *Nonsmooth Impact Mechanics: Models, Dynamics and Control*, Springer, London, NY, 1996.

10. Monson, K.L., and G. J. Germane, "Determination and Mechanisms of Motor Vehicle Structural Restitution from Crash Test Data," Paper 1999-01-0097, SAE International, Warrendale, PA, 1999.

11. Ishikawa, H., "Computer Simulation of Automobile Collision—Reconstruction of Accidents," Paper 851729, SAE International, Warrendale, PA, 1985.

12. Ishikawa, H., "Impact Model for Accident Reconstruction—Normal and Tangential Restitution Coefficients," Paper 930654, SAE International, Warrendale, PA, 1993.

13. Ishikawa, H., "Impact Center and Restitution Coefficients for Accident Reconstruction," Paper 940564, SP1030, SAE International, Warrendale, PA, 1994.

14. Lord Kelvin and P.G. Tait, *Treatise on Natural Philosophy*, Cambridge University Press, Cambridge, U.K., 1903.

15. "CRASH3 User's Guide and Technical Manual," DOT Report DOT HS 805 732, Washington, DC, February 1981.

16. Jones, I.S., and A.S. Baum, "Research Input for Computer Simulation of Automobile Collisions (RICSAC)," vol. IV: "Staged Collision Reconstructions," DOT HS-805 040, Washington, DC, December 1978.

17. Brach, R.M., "Impact Analysis of Two-Vehicle Collisions," Paper 830468, SAE International, Warrendale, PA, 1987.

18. Brach, R.M., "Energy Loss in Vehicle Collisions," Paper 871993, SAE International, Warrendale, PA, 1987.

19. Brach, R.M., and R.A. Smith, "Re-Analysis of the RICSAC Car Crash Accelerometer Data," Paper 2002-01-1305, SAE International, Warrendale, PA, 2002.

20. McHenry, B.G., and R.R. McHenry, "RICSAC-97—A Re-evaluation of the Reference Set of Full Scale Crash Tests," Paper 970961, SAE International, Warrendale, PA, 1997.

21. Woolley, R.L., "The 'IMPAC' Program for Collision Analysis," Paper 8700476, SAE International, Warrendale, PA, 1987.

CHAPTER 7

1. Jones, I.S., and A.S. Baum, "Research Input for Computer Simulation of Automobile Collisions (RICSAC)," vol. IV: "Staged Collision Reconstructions," DOT HS-805 040, Washington, DC, 1978.
2. Brach, R.M., and R.A. Smith, "Re-Analysis of the RICSAC Car Crash Accelerometer Data," Paper 2002-01-1305, SAE International, Warrendale, PA, 2002.
3. Brach, R.M., "Energy Loss in Vehicle Collisions," Paper 871993, SAE International, Warrendale, PA, 1987.
4. Brach, Raymond M., and R. Matthew Brach, "Crush Energy and Planar Impact Mechanics for Accident Reconstruction," Paper 980025, SAE International, Warrendale, PA, 1998.
5. Brach, R.M., *Mechanical Impact Dynamics*, John Wiley & Sons, New York, NY, 1991.
6. Brach, R.M., "Modeling of Low-Speed, Front-to-Rear Vehicle Impacts," Paper 2003-01-0491, SAE International, Warrendale, PA, 2003.

CHAPTER 8

1. Campbell, K., "Energy as a Basis for Accident Severity," Paper 74056, SAE International, Warrendale, PA, 1974.
2. Cheng, P.H., M.J. Sens, J.F. Weichel, and D.A. Guenther, "An Overview of the Evolution of Computer Assisted Motor Vehicle Accident Reconstruction," SAE Paper 871991, in *Reconstruction of Motor Vehicle Accidents: A Technical Compendium*, PT-34, SAE International, Warrendale, PA, 1987.
3. Prasad, A.K., "CRASH3 Damage Algorithm Reformulation for Front and Rear Collisions," Paper 900098, SAE International, Warrendale, PA, 1990.
4. "CRASH3 User's Guide and Technical Manual," DOT Report HS 805 732, NHTSA, Washington, DC, 1981.
5. Tumbas, N.S., and R.A. Smith, "Measurement Protocol for Quantifying Vehicle Damage From an Energy Basis Point of View," Paper 880072, SAE International, Warrendale, PA, 1988.
6. Willke, D.T., and M.W. Monk, "CRASH III Model Improvements: Derivation of New Side Stiffness Parameters from Crash Tests," *Accident Reconstruction Journal*, Waldorf, MD, Spring 1995.
7. Woolley, R.L., "Nonlinear Damage Analysis in Accident Reconstruction," Paper 2001-01-0504, SAE International, Warrendale, PA, 2001.
8. Asay, A.F., D.B. Jewkes, and R.L. Woolley, "Narrow Object Impact Analysis and Comparison with Flat Barrier Impacts," Paper 2002-01-0552, SAE International, Warrendale, PA, 2002.
9. Welsh, K.J., and D.E. Struble, "Crush Energy & Structural Characterization," Paper 1999-01-0099, SAE International, Warrendale, PA, 1999.
10. Varat, M.S., and S.E. Husher, "Vehicle Crash Severity Assessment in Lateral Pole Impacts," Paper 1999-01-0100, SAE International, Warrendale, PA, 1999.
11. Prasad, A.K., "Energy Absorbed by Vehicle Structures in Side Impacts," Paper 910599, SAE International, Warrendale, PA, 1991.
12. Prasad, A.K., "Energy Absorbing Properties of Vehicle Structures and Their Use in Estimating Impact Severity in Automobile Collisions," Paper 925209, SAE International, Warrendale, PA, 1992.
13. *Accident Reconstruction Journal*, Sample Problems, Waldorf, MD, November/December, 1998.

14. Prasad, A.K., "Missing Vehicle Algorithm (OLDMISS) Reformulation," Paper 910121, SAE International, Warrendale, PA, 1992.

15. Neptune, J.A., and J.E. Flynn, "A Method for Determining Accident Specific Crush Stiffness Coefficients," Paper 940913, SAE International, Warrendale, PA, 1994.

16. Wood, D.P., A. Ydenius, and D. Adamson, "Velocity Changes, Mean Accelerations and Displacements of Some Car Types in Frontal Collisions," *International Journal of Crashworthiness*, vol. 8, no. 6., Woodhead Publishing, Ltd., Cambridge, U.K., 2003, pp. 591–603.

CHAPTER 9

1. Eubanks, J.J., *Pedestrian Accident Reconstruction*, Lawyers & Judges Publishing Company, Tucson, AZ, 1994.

2. van Wijk, J., J. Wismans, J. Maltha, and L. Wittebrood, "MADYMO Pedestrian Simulations," International Congress and Exposition, Paper 830060, SAE International, Warrendale, PA, 1983.

3. Moser, A., H. Steffan, H. Hoschopf, and G. Kasanicky, "Validation of the PC-Crash Pedestrian Model," Paper 2000-01-0847, SAE International, Warrendale, PA, 2000.

4. Happer, A., M. Araszewski, A. Toor, R. Overgaard, and R. Johal, "Comprehensive Analysis Method for Vehicle/Pedestrian Collision," Paper 2000-10-0846, SAE International, Warrendale, PA, 2000.

5. Han, I., and R.M. Brach, "Throw Model for Frontal Pedestrian Collisions," Paper 2001-01-0898, SAE International, Warrendale, PA, 2001.

6. Toor, A., "Theoretical Versus Empirical Solutions for Vehicle/Pedestrian Collisions," Paper 2003-01-0883, SAE International, Warrendale, PA, 2003.

7. Wood, D., and C.K. Simms, "A Hybrid Model for Pedestrian Impact and Projection," *International Journal of Crashworthiness*, vol. 5, no. 4, Woodhead Publishing, Ltd., Cambridge, U.K., 2000, pp. 393–403.

8. Wood, D.P., and D.G. Walsh, "Pedestrian Forward Projection Impact," *International Journal of Crashworthiness*, vol. 7, no. 3, Woodhead Publishing, Ltd., Cambridge, U.K., 2002.

9. Backaitis, Stanley H., *Accident Reconstruction Technologies—Pedestrians and Motorcycles in Automotive Collisions*, PT-35, SAE International, Warrendale, PA, 1990.

10. Fugger, T.F., B.C. Randles, J.L. Wobrock, A.C. Stein, and W.C. Whiting, "Pedestrian Behavior at Signal-Controlled Crosswalks," Paper 2001-01-0896, SAE International, Warrendale, PA, 2001.

11. Vaughan, R., and J. Bain, "Acceleration and Speeds of Young Pedestrians Phase II," Paper 2000-01-0845, SAE International, Warrendale, PA, 2000.

12. Vaughan, R., and J. Bain, "Acceleration and Speeds of Young Pedestrians," Paper 1999-01-0440, SAE International, Warrendale, PA, 1999.

13. Wood, D.P., "Impact and Movement of Pedestrians in Frontal Collisions with Vehicles," *Proceedings of the Institution of Mechanical Engineers*, vol. 202, no. D2, London, U.K., 1988, pp. 101–110.

14. Wood, D., and C.K. Simms, "Coefficient of Friction in Pedestrian Throw," *Impact*, vol. 9, no. 1, Institute of Traffic Accident Investigators, Shrewsbury, U.K., 2000, pp. 12–15.

15. Hill, G.S., "Calculations of Vehicle Speed from Pedestrian Throw," *Impact,* Institute of Traffic Accident Investigators, Shrewsbury, U.K., 1994, pp. 18–20.

16. @RISK, Palisade Corporation, Newfield, NY, 1998.

CHAPTER 10

1. Slama, Chester C., *Manual of Photogrammetry*, 4th ed., American Society of Photogrammetry, Falls Church, VA, 1980.

2. Hallert, Bertil, *Photogrammetry, Basic Principles and General Survey*, McGraw-Hill Book Company, New York, NY, 1960.

3. Moffitt, Francis H., and Edward M. Mikhail, *Photogrammetry*, 3rd ed., Harper and Row, New York, NY, 1980.

4. Baker, J. Standard, and Lynn B. Fricke, *The Traffic Accident Investigation Manual*, 9th ed., Northwestern University Traffic Institute, Evanston, IL, 1986.

5. Husher, Stein E., Michael S. Varat, and John F. Kerkhoff, *Survey of Photogrammetric Methodologies for Accident Reconstruction*, Proceedings of the Canadian Multidisciplinary Road Safety Conference VII, Vancouver, BC, Canada, June 1991.

6. Bleyl, Robert L., "Using Photographs to Map Traffic Accident Scenes: A Mathematical Approach," *Journal of Safety Research*, vol. 8, no. 2, National Safety Council, Chicago, IL, June 1976.

7. Woolley, R., et al. "Determination of Vehicle Crush from Two Photographs and the Use of 3D Displacement Vectors in Accident Reconstruction," Paper 910118, SAE International, Warrendale, PA, 1991.

8. Sunbear Associates, http://home.pacbell.net/vondaa, 2003.

9. Pappa, Richard S., et al., "Photogrammetry Methodology for Gossamer Spacecraft Structures," *Sound and Vibration*, Bay Village, OH, August 2002.

10. Townes, Harry, "Photogrammetry in Accident Reconstruction," SAE Professional Development Seminar, July 1998.

11. Townes, Harry W., and James R. Williamson, "Close Range Photogrammetry in Accident Reconstruction," Chapter 9 in *Forensic Accident Investigation: Motor Vehicle—2*, Thomas L. Bohan [ed.], Lexis Law Publishing, Charlottesville, VA, 1997.

12. D'Souza, Frank A., and Vijay K. Garg, *Advanced Dynamics, Modeling and Analysis*, Prentice-Hall, Englewood Cliffs, NJ, 1984.

13. Photomodeler Pro 4.0, Eos Systems, Inc., Vancouver, BC, Canada, 2002.

CHAPTER 11

1. McHenry, B.G., and R.R. McHenry, "HVOSM-87," Paper 880228, SAE International, Warrendale, PA, 1988.

2. Leatherwood, M.D., and D.D. Gunter, "Vehicle Dynamics of a Heavy Truck/Trailer Combination using Simulation," Paper 1999-01-0119, SAE International, Warrendale, PA, 1999.

3. Day, T.D., "Validation of the EDVSM 3-Dimensional Vehicle Simulator," Paper 970958, SAE International, Warrendale, PA, 1997.

4. McHenry, B.G., and R.R. McHenry, "SMAC-97: Refinement of the Collision Algorithm," Paper 970947, SAE International, Warrendale, PA, 1997.

5. Day, T.D., "Further Validation of EDSMAC using the RICSAC Staged Collisions," Paper 900102, SAE International, Warrendale, PA, 1990.

6. Chrstos, J.P., and G.J. Heydinger, "Evaluation of VDANL and VDM RoAD for Predicting the Vehicle Dynamics of a 1994 Ford Taurus," Paper 970566, SAE International, Warrendale, PA, 1997.

7. Brach, R.M., "Vehicle Dynamics Model for Simulation on a Microcomputer," *International Journal of Vehicle Design*, vol. 12, no. 4, Inderscience, Geneva, Switzerland, 1991.

8. Day, T.D., and D.E. Siddall, "Validation of Several Reconstruction and Simulation Models in the HVE Scientific Visualization Environment," Paper 960891, SAE International, Warrendale, PA, 1996.

9. Salaani, M.K., D.A. Guenther, and G.J. Heydinger, "Vehicle Dynamics Modeling for the National Advanced Driving Simulator of a 1997 Jeep Cherokee," Paper 1999-01-0121, SAE International, Warrendale, PA, 1999.

10. Lozia, Z., "Vehicle Dynamics and Motion Simulation versus Experiment," Paper 980220, SAE International, Warrendale, PA, 1998.

11. Day, T.D., S.G. Roberts, and A.R. York, "SIMON: A New Vehicle Simulation Model for Vehicle Design and Safety Research," Paper 2001-01-0503, SAE International, Warrendale, PA, 2001.

12. Allen, R.W., T.J. Rosenthal, and J.P. Chrstos, "A Vehicle Dynamics Tire Model for both Pavement and Off-Road Conditions," Paper 970559, SAE International, Warrendale, PA, 1999.

13. Bakker, E., L. Nyborg, and H.B. Pacejka, "Tyre Modeling for Use in Vehicle Dynamic Studies," Paper 870421, SAE International, Warrendale, PA, 1987.

14. Brach, R. Matthew, and Raymond M. Brach, "Tire Forces: Modeling the Combined Braking and Steering Forces," Paper 2000-01-0357, SAE International, Warrendale, PA, 2000.

15. Todd, J. [ed.], *Survey of Numerical Analysis*, McGraw-Hill, New York, NY, 1962.

16. Brach, R.M., "Impact of Articulated Vehicles," Paper 860015, SAE International, Warrendale, PA, 1987.

APPENDIX A

1. Bevington, P.R., and D.K. Robinson, *Data Reduction and Error Analysis for the Physical Sciences*, 2nd ed., McGraw-Hill, New York, NY, 1992.

2. IEEE/ASTM-SI-10 Standard for Use of the International System of Units (SI): The Modern Metric System, ASTM International, West Conshohocken, PA.

3. National Institute for Science and Technology, "Guide for the Use of the International System of Units (SI)," Special Publication 811, abridged, Gaithersburg, MD, 1995.

APPENDIX B

1. "Motor Vehicle Dimensions," SAE Standard J1100, SAE International, Warrendale, PA, July 2002.

2. Baker, J. Stannard, Glossary, *Traffic Accident Investigation Manual*, Northwestern University Traffic Institute, Evanston, IL, 1975, pp. 313–321.

3. "Collision Deformation Classification," SAE Standard J224, SAE International, Warrendale, PA, March 1980.

4. "Manual on Classification of Motor Vehicle Traffic Accidents," 6th ed., ANSI D16.1, National Safety Council, Chicago, IL, 1996.

5. *Handbook of Motor Vehicle Safety and Environmental Terminology*, SAE HS-215, SAE International, Warrendale, PA, December 1995.

6. "Truck Deformation Classification," SAE Standard J1301, SAE International, Warrendale, PA, August 2003.

7. "Vehicle Dynamics Terminology," SAE Standard J670, SAE International, Warrendale, PA, July 1976.

8. "A Dictionary of Terms for the Dynamics and Handling of Single Track Vehicles (Motorcycles, Mopeds and Bicycles)," SAE Standard J1451, SAE International, Warrendale, PA, January 2000.

Index

Locators followed by *f* indicate figures; those followed by *t* indicate tables.

About the Authors

Raymond M. Brach, PhD, PE, is a consultant in the field of accident reconstruction and a professor emeritus of the Department of Aerospace and Mechanical Engineering, University of Notre Dame. He is a fellow member of the Society of Automotive Engineers (SAE). Other professional memberships include the American Society of Mechanical Engineers (ASME), The Acoustical Society of America (ASA), The Institution of Noise Control Engineers (INCE), and the National Association of Professional Accident Reconstruction Specialists (NAPARS). He was granted a PhD in Engineering Mechanics from the University of Wisconsin, Madison, and a BS and MS in Mechanical Engineering from Illinois Institute of Technology, Chicago. His specialized areas of teaching and research include mechanical design, mechanics, vibrations, acoustics, applications of statistics and quality control, vehicle dynamics, accident reconstruction, and microparticle dynamics. He is a licensed professional engineer in the state of Indiana. In addition to more than 100 research papers and numerous invited lectures, he has authored *Mechanical Impact Dynamics* published by Wiley Interscience in 1991 and is a coauthor of *Uncertainty Analysis for Forensic Science*, Lawyers and Judges Publishing Company, 2004.

RAYMOND M. BRACH

R. Matthew Brach, PhD, PE, is an engineering consultant with the firm Brach Engineering, LLC. His principal areas of professional activities include vehicle impact analysis, vehicle dynamics, and automotive accident reconstruction. He has a PhD in Mechanical Engineering from Michigan State University, East Lansing (1995), an MS in Mechanical Engineering from the University of Illinois at Chicago (1986), and a BS in Electrical Engineering from the University of Notre Dame (1982). He served as an adjunct professor in the Mechanical Engineering Department at Lawrence Technological University, Southfield, Michigan from 1994 to 2000. He is a member of the Society of Automotive Engineers (SAE), the American Society of Mechanical Engineers (ASME), the Institute of Electrical and Electronics Engineers (IEEE), the International Association of Arson Investigators (IAAI), and the National Association of Professional Accident Reconstruction Specialists (NAPARS). He is a licensed professional engineer in the states of Indiana and Michigan. He is the author of technical papers covering a range of topics that includes nonlinear vibrations, automotive engine mount design, vehicular accident analysis methodologies, and tire forces.

R. MATTHEW BRACH

VCRware – Vehicle Crash Reconstruction Soft*ware*

VCRware™, software in the form of Microsoft Excel™ spreadsheets similar to those used to solve examples throughout this book, is available for purchase. The VCRware™ suite of programs includes the following:

> Critical Speed Formula
> Collision Analysis for Two Point Masses
> Planar Impact Mechanics Analysis
> Low Speed Vehicle Impact Analysis
> Crush Stiffness Coefficients from Vehicle to Barrier Test
> Energy Loss and Speed Change from CRASH3
> Vehicle to Pedestrian Collision Analysis
> Planar Photogrammetric Analysis
> Vehicle and Trailer Dynamics Program
> Stopping Distance of a Vehicle

Additional information about each program, a fully functional trial version of the program and ordering information are available at www.brachengineering.com.